4

SHOPPING

ARCHITECTURE NOW!

1

IMPRINT

PROJECT MANAGEMENT
Florian Kobler, Cologne

COLLABORATION
Harriet Graham, Turin

PRODUCTION
Ute Wachendorf, Cologne

DESIGN
Sense/Net, Andy Disl
and Birgit Eichwede,
Cologne

GERMAN TRANSLATION
Kristina Brigitta Köper, Berlin

FRENCH TRANSLATION
Jacques Bosser, Paris

© VG BILD-KUNST
Bonn 2010, for the works of
Ben van Berkel

PRINTED IN ITALY
ISBN 978–3–8365–1738–6

© 2010 TASCHEN GMBH
Hohenzollernring 53
D–50672 Cologne
www.taschen.com

SHOPPING

ARCHITECTURE NOW!

SHOPPING-*Architektur heute!*
L'architecture COMMERCIALE *d'aujourd'hui!*

Philip Jodidio

1

TASCHEN

CONTENTS

INTRODUCTION

SHOPPING IS GOOD FOR YOU!

Shopping is defined as the the activity of visiting shops and stores to look at and buy things. The word "retail" has a French origin, from the old word *retailler* (to "cut" or, more precisely, to "re-cut" or "re-tailor"). As it is understood in English, retail means the sale of goods to ultimate consumers, usually in small quantities (as opposed to wholesale). Architects of considerable reputation have long been involved in what might best be called the glorification of retail sales. Louis Sullivan's Carson Pirie Scott and Company Building (Chicago, USA, 1899), located on State Street, is an anthology all to itself of the urban presence of retail architecture. Moscow's GUM or Main Department Store, built from 1890 to1893 by Alexander Pomerantsev and Vladimir Shukov, features a 242-meter-long façade on Red Square, opposite the Kremlin. Even in the time of Soviet rule, when many shelves were poorly stocked, the GUM building placed retail sales near the heart of power. So, too, more recently smaller boutiques have been the object of considerable attention on the part of such nearly mythical architects as Carlo Scarpa, whose restructuring of the Olivetti Showroom on Piazza San Marco (Venice, Italy, 1957–58) was recently cited as an inspiration for Tadao Ando's Punta della Dogana refurbishment (2009) for the François Pinault Foundation. Indeed, it would appear today that only art museums have seen a more extensive presence of star architects than the retail world. Whole neighborhoods in major cities have been filled with shining new buildings dedicated solely to the fine art of selling clothes or other objects. Thus, in Tokyo, along the stretch between Minami Aoyama and Omotesando, leading to Harajuku, buildings by Tadao Ando (Collezione, and other buildings), SANAA (Christian Dior), Kengo Kuma (LVMH), Herzog & de Meuron (Prada), and Toyo Ito (TOD's) are grouped together, rivaled only by nearby Ginza, where Renzo Piano (Hermès) neighbors Massimiliano Fuksas (Armani). Nor is retail architecture merely in the hands of architects. Noted designers such as the late Shiro Kuramata (1934–91), who created boutiques for Issey Miyake in Paris, Tokyo, and New York, lead the way for today's new wave of boutique or store creation.

Figures such as Tom Dixon, Arne Quinze, Jurgen Bey, or Yoshioka Tokujin, known more as designers than architects, are responsible for some of the most outstanding retail spaces of the moment. Retail architecture thus clearly spreads beyond the boundaries of architecture to include what might be termed interior design, but also clearly covers design itself. Some architects or designers working for specific brands are obviously involved in the definition or redefinition of the brand itself. Thus the stunning Prada Store on the corner of Broadway and Prince Street in Manhattan (New York, USA, 1999–2001), former location of the Guggenheim Soho, represented an effort on the part of OMA*AMO/Rem Koolhaas to rethink what might have been considered a somewhat staid retail image. Koolhaas has continued to work with Prada in more recent years, creating such unusual structures as the recent Prada Transformer (Seoul, South Korea, 2008–09). So, too, such inventive figures as Rei Kawakubo (Comme des Garçons) have been deeply involved in their own retail design over the years, calling on architects like Future Systems for the façades or entrances of her Chelsea and Minami Aoyama stores, while using artists and designers for other aspects of the stores.

PRINCESS ZAHA AND SAINT KARL

Though it may be useful to make a clear distinction between such architectural gestures as complete shopping centers and the interiors of boutiques, what makes *Shopping Architecture Now!* interesting is the way in which the traditional barriers between disciplines seem to

1
*Zaha Hadid, Lopez de Heredia
Wine Pavilion, Haro, La Rioja,
Spain, 2001–06*

1

dissolve in the face of retail sales. A noted designer of lights, Ingo Maurer, can be seen here creating his own store in Munich (2008, page 260), without the obvious assistance of architects. The reference to museum architecture as another area where a concentration of well-known architects can be found may be more than skin-deep. Clearly, both museums and brand stores concentrate financial means and seek to draw "customers" in. Although the word "customers" might not be too flattering for museums, even the grand state-run institutions of Old Europe have delved deeply into retailing of their own in recent years. A T-shirt, a catalogue, or a book on Herzog & de Meuron make Tate Modern a going concern nearly as much as admission fees. Retailing itself has broken out of the "box" constituted by boutiques, as is evidenced by Zaha Hadid's recent Mobile Art, Chanel Contemporary Art Container (various locations, 2007–ongoing) that places the creativity of Karl Lagerfeld on a par with that of other reputed artists. If today's creative figures were viewed like the venerated personalities of the past, Zaha Hadid would surely be a princess, and Karl, though still very much in life, something of a saint.

TEMPLES OF THE NEW ORDER

Clearly, the economic difficulties that began in 2008 have caused damage to the world of retailing, but, as this book demonstrates, boutiques and stores continue to spring up, designed by the most creative people available. Retailing, the sale of goods to the ultimate consumer, is in some sense today at the very heart of the system of the developed world. It is not an accident that many of the most spectacular new facilities published here are located in major cities, from Los Angeles to Tokyo. They are built where the money is, where the sales are. The key to any recovery, we are told, is to "consume"—and that is precisely what retailing is all about. At a certain time, critics wondered if museums had not replaced churches as a contemporary place of worship. In the pragmatic, globalized world of today, are the temples of the new order called Dior, Prada, Fauchon, or Chanel? Even brands aimed at a broader audience, such as the Japanese firm Uniqlo, find it useful to call on noted designers in their bid to conquer the retail world. Is retailing the new religion, or perhaps the new battlefield? A bit of both, certainly, and architecture is right in the middle.

ADJAYE AND BOATENG ON SAVILE ROW

The London-based architect David Adjaye has shown considerable flexibility and variety in his built work, and it is not a surprise that he should be interested in retail architecture. The two recent projects published here (Ozwald Boateng Flagship Store, London, UK, 2007, page 46, and Kvadrat Showroom, London, UK, 2008–09, page 52) have different purposes and types of clients. Kvadrat, a Danish textile and wall and ceiling-covering designer, wanted a space not only for sales but also for screenings, discussion groups, and exhibitions. Just as retail spaces are increasingly challenging the traditional limits between architecture and design, so, too, many new spaces seek a multifunctional role that keeps levels of activity high, even if there are days when few clients wander in. The Ozwald Boateng store appears to be more traditional in its concept, and yet the architect has conceived it as a series of shops within the larger shop, each concentrating on a different activity of the brand. Ozwald Boateng, born in 1968 in London, was self-taught as a tailor, but became the Creative Director of Menswear at Givenchy (2003–07). He is one of the "stars" of the London fashion world, which means that the Boateng/Adjaye connection has all the

2
*David Adjaye, Ozwald Boateng
Flagship Store, London, UK, 2007*

2

celebrity quality that one might imagine in retail architecture. David Adjaye states: "The concept and design strategy was to engage with the contemporary and curatorial direction toward which fashion has moved. Rather than just about buying clothes, the store creates experiences and textural and emotional seductions where a range of encounters, from the old to the new, can occur."

David Adjaye was born in 1966 in Dar es Salaam, Tanzania. He studied at the Royal College of Art in London and worked in the offices of David Chipperfield and Eduardo Souto de Moura, before creating his own firm in London in 2000. With works such as the Nobel Peace Center (Oslo, Norway, 2002–05) and the Museum of Contemporary Art/Denver (Denver, Colorado, USA, 2004–07) already to his credit, and the National Museum of African American History and Culture (Smithsonian Institution, Washington, D.C., USA, 2015) underway, David Adjaye is one of the rising stars of contemporary architecture. His work on the Ozwald Boateng or Kvadrat stores is a clear indication of the importance of retail architecture at the moment, and also of the symbiotic relationship that many designer brands have developed with top architects and designers.

FAUCHON GOES FUCHSIA, APPLE GOES TRANSPARENT

The relationship between top designers and well-known brands extends to all areas of commerce—at least the kind that is visible in the chic shopping areas of major cities. Fauchon, the top French food emporium, called on Christian Biecher to redo its stores, which, though always full of wonderful products, were in need of updating. Biecher worked on their Beijing and Paris venues (page 62) and is undertaking other tasks for the firm. With a surprising palette of colors ranging from gold to fuchsia, Biecher also calls on a variety of materials, such as timber, bamboo, and leather, to recall not only the different aspects of the Fauchon stores, but also the broad geographic origins of their products. Using fuchsia like an "electric cord" linking different parts of the store and, indeed, one store to the other, Christian Biecher shows that even an old and highly respected brand can be successfully updated.

Being an old brand is surely not the problem of Apple, the computer manufacturer that has branched out into iPods, iPads, and all manner of other paraphernalia for the digitally connected. On the contrary, the highly stylized and carefully designed aspect of the Apple products makes the architecture of their stores into a statement that must fit in with the ethos developed by Apple director Steven Jobs. The architects Bohlin Cywinski Jackson have marked the presence of Apple in Manhattan with two recent stores, one on Fifth Avenue (767 Fifth Avenue, New York, 2003–06) and the other on the Upper West Side (New York, 2008–09, page 70). These stores share an extremely transparent and relatively simple design that serves to draw in the crowds while ultimately ceding its place to the real "stars," which are of course the products. The lightness of the architecture and its patent modernity are well suited to retailing Apple products, as the ongoing relationship of Bohlin Cywinski Jackson with the firm demonstrates.

SHORT SHELF LIFE FOR YOHJI

Even the most ambitious architectural projects related to the world of fashion can have as brief a shelf life as clothes themselves. The Yohji Yamamoto Store (New York, USA, 2007–08, page 180) on Gansevoort Street in the Meatpacking District of New York was the first architectural project by the promising young Japanese architect Junya Ishigami. It involved cutting an existing building in two and creating a most unusual triangular showroom not far from the art galleries of the Chelsea area. In this instance, the work of the fashion designer Yohji Yamamoto has long existed on the edge of the fashion world and, indeed, in close proximity to art, but the creativity of Yamamoto and Ishigami was unfortunately not a sufficient barrier to the economic problems that have arisen since this store opened. The Yohji Yamamoto store on Gansevoort Street closed early in 2010, lasting just a bit longer than a typical fashion cycle.

The largely ephemeral nature of the relationship between architecture and retailing may in fact be one of the motors of the creativity displayed in this relationship. Some installations play on this ambiguity. Such is the case of the Dr. Martens Pop-Up Store (London, UK, 2009, page 76), a 180-square-meter installation designed by the firm Campaign, working with the creative brand managers Fresh. Dr. Martens shoes are a well-known brand, a sort of "counter-cultural icon," as Campaign put it. Their design made use of the image of a warehouse stockroom, and was installed in just six days using a very large, yellow PVC curtain, construction-site lamps, loading palettes, and shrink-wrapped objects. Here, rather than trying to make quintessentially ephemeral goods appear to be more durable than they are, the brand allowed Campaign to play on the rough and ready image that actually was part of the Dr. Martens ethos already.

BLOWING IN THE WIND

Shopping Architecture Now! does not only evoke what might be more traditionally termed architecture, precisely because the retail field encourages installations and short-term presentations. Two window displays provide different examples of how windows, in the hands of creative designers, can have a clear impact on the interest of passersby, and thus, ultimately, on turnover. The first of these was created by the German firm Liganova for Diesel, first in Germany in 2009, and then elsewhere. These Diesel Interactive Windows (Berlin, page 240) make use of motion-tracking technology that allows passersby to have a "real" impact on the display inside the window. The potential customer in front of the store is permitted "to move virtual objects on a screen by moving his arms and hands, influencing real objects and actions in the window." Sound transducers even allow this action to be accompanied by an appropriate "sound track," thus in a sense bringing those who would normally only look into active contact with the brand.

The Maison Hermès Window Installation (Tokyo, Japan, 2009, page 410) by the noted designer Tokujin Yoshioka took a much more aesthetic and removed approach, with a video of a woman lightly blowing on a real Hermès scarf. Yoshioka speaks of "humor" in describing this window display, but it of course plays on the kind of interaction between video and the "real" world that is often the object of contemporary artworks as well. Not as proactive as the Diesel windows by Liganova, this presentation may well suit the luxury brand Hermès better, of course. Without in any way questioning the longevity of the typical Hermès scarf, Yoshioka places it in motion in an artistic context, blurring boundaries between the real and the imagined.

REM DOES THE CATWALK

The ultimate event of the fashion world is, of course, the carefully choreographed presentation of each collection. Although this is not, strictly speaking, an area where architecture often has its say, brands such as Prada have not hesitated to call on the likes of OMA*AMO/Rem Koolhaas in order to elevate their presentation to artistic or architectural levels not seen frequently in the shows of the competition. As part of an ongoing relationship with the brand, which included the recent Prada Transformer, the Prada Men and Women 2010 Spring/Summer Fashion Shows (Fondazione Prada, Milan, Italy, 2009, page 11) were presented by OMA*AMO. Calling the men's show "A Secret Passage or Love for the Void," the architects and fashion designers immediately set the stage, as it were, introducing ideas that are current in contemporary architecture. A linear catwalk hidden between one edge of an existing room and a new seven-meter-high wall covered in wallpaper showing conversations between male film characters immediately made the case for the interpenetration of fashion, movies, and architecture in the same space, in a way suggesting that men who wear Prada are already the stuff of legend. The women's fashion show included an "abstract wall" with projections of imaginary corridors evoking "mental spaces that combine grand hotels' rich and classic door frames, acid neon lights, trash and abandoned atmospheres, or bright images of crowded beaches," resulting in "a sequence of indefinable settings," according to the architects.

The mutual dependence of architecture and fashion in this instance illustrates the meeting point of two very real concerns. From the point of view of a fashion brand, change is necessary since it incites new sales, and yet the great luxury brands all seek to project an image of timelessness that encourages the fidelity of the clientele. Architects, on the other hand, struggle with the very solidity of their work. A building has an undeniable presence that, at its best, represents precisely the kind of timelessness sought by Prada or Chanel. Both the architect and the fashion designer exaggerate their longevity of course, especially in a world of rapid-pace consumerism, and yet the point where Prada meets OMA is one of mutual satisfaction.

RETAIL GETS CONCRETE

An area of retailing that is dealt with only in a partial way in this volume (see *Architecture Now! Restaurants & Bars*), restaurants and bars are amongst the most active venues for the interaction of commerce and architecture or design. The Amsterdam firm Concrete Architectural Associates has made a considerable reputation designing such interiors as those of the Pearls & Caviar Restaurant (Abu Dhabi, UAE, 2008), the VIP Lounge at Schiphol Airport (Amsterdam, The Netherlands, 2008); the Supperclub (Singapore, 2008), and the De Bijenkorf Kitchen (Amsterdam, The Netherlands, 2008). The principal of Concrete, Rob Wagemans, has a background that partially explains the success of his firm dealing with commissions that do entail a good deal of architectural expertise. Wagemans studied at the Academies of Architecture

3
*OMA*AMO/Rem Koolhaas, Prada Men
and Women 2010 Spring/Summer
Fashion Shows, Fondazione Prada,
Milan, Italy, 2009*

3

in Amsterdam and Utrecht and completed his studies with a master of architecture degree focusing on interior design. One of his recent designs, the Coffee Company Prinsenhof (The Hague, The Netherlands, 2008, page 92), is located in the atrium of an office building and measures just 60 square meters. The steel, glass, and mahogany shell of the coffee shop lifts up 2.5 meters with a hydraulic system at the push of a button. As Concrete states: "The Coffee Company literally becomes part of the atrium. In the evening the shell moves down in order to close up shop." This combination of good design and good architecture is a clear example of what talented creators bring to the world of retailing, above and beyond the simple space required to do business.

A younger and much less well-known figure than Wagemans, the Frenchman Jean-Guillaume Mathiaut, also readily crosses the barrier between architecture and design. Before obtaining his architecture degree in 1999, he worked with the architects François & Lewis (Paris, 1993–98), before becoming an Artistic Director at the Galeries Lafayette (Paris, 2000–05), where he organized exhibitions with the designers Marcel Wanders, Jurgen Bey, Paul Smith, Jakob + MacFarlane, and Ingo Maurer. He created his own firm, Edith Edition, in 2007, and designed the latest Issey Miyake Store in Paris (France, 2008, page 102) in an inner courtyard off the Rue Royale. Mathiaut created monolithic elements in Corian and gave the rather difficult space a large, minimalist glass entry. Within, the atmosphere is inspired by a quarry or an atelier, according to Jean-Guillaume Mathiaut, but, most interestingly, it provides space for art or design installations. Issey Miyake is, of course, known for his creative input that often went beyond fashion to touch on the domain of art in particular. Mathiaut's design for the Rue Royale store seizes on this basic fact of the brand and "exaggerates" the situation, as he says.

ART COMES KNOCKING AT THE DOOR
The idea of crossing barriers is very much at the heart of the recent Balenciaga Flagship Store in London (UK, 2008, page 144). The fashion label's designer, Nicolas Ghesquière, who worked with Jean-Paul Gaultier and Thierry Mugler before joining Balenciaga in 1997, has a reputation for being one of the "super stars" of his profession. Outstanding fashion today seems to have a need to associate itself with outstanding art, design, and architecture, and this is precisely what Ghesquière did when he called on the artist Dominique Gonzalez-Foerster, the architect Martial Galfione, and the lighting designer Benoit Lalloz to work on a number of his stores. Though plasma screens for videos and a musical program specifically written for the space by Christophe Van Huffel mark the London store, the result of this unusual collaboration is above all interesting in and of itself. This is neither specifically a work of art, nor is it pure architecture or design. It is, rather, a subtle blend of each, with an inevitable bow to the fashion of Balenciaga. Though the case is somewhat different, the Balenciaga collaboration does bring to mind such iconic works of the 20th century as the Café L'Aubette, in Strasbourg (1927). Sophie Taeuber-Arp, Jean Arp, and Theo van Doesburg collaborated on the space, which included a tearoom, several bars, function rooms, a ballroom, a cellar nightclub, and a cinema. Though the three participants were best known as artists, Theo van Doesburg (1883–1931), the founder and leader of the De Stijl movement, was involved in painting, writing, poetry, and architecture. Despite its importance as a case of artistic collaboration, Café L'Aubette, completed in 1928, was almost immediately changed because of the disapproval of the café's clients. Dominique Gonzalez-Foerster, who was coinciden-

4

tally born in Strasbourg, is known mainly as a video artist, but she creates installations that inevitably involve the use of space. Might not a Balenciaga store be today's equivalent of the Café L'Aubette?

FASHION FLAGSHIPS

Just as Prada has associated itself with a number of well-known architects ranging from Herzog & de Meuron to Rem Koolhaas, so, too, have other brands understood that there is something to be gained from hiring top designers or architects to imagine new stores. Phillip Lim is an American fashion designer of Chinese origin who won the 2007 Council of Fashion Designers of America Swarovski Award for Womenswear for his work as Creative Director of his firm 3.1 Phillip Lim. Lim has not called on Pritzker Prize-winning architects, but he has certainly made a statement with his recent flagship stores in New York, Los Angeles, and Seoul. The first of these (New York, USA, page 12) was carried forward by Tacklebox LLC and completed in 2007, while the second (Los Angeles, USA, 2007–08, page 278) was the work of a team including Dominic Leong and PARA-Project, together with Office Giancarlo Valle. The third opened in Seoul in 2009 (South Korea, page 220), the work of Leong Leong Architects. The largest of these (Seoul) has 543 square meters of floor space and was created within the volume of a preexisting retail and office building. The architects chose "tactile" materials such as an oak floor inside, as befits a fashion store surely. Whitewashed bricks and worn Douglas fir flooring are seen in the New York store, confirming a mixture of decided modernity in the choice of architects and certain elements of their designs with the idea of preexisting materials or spaces. The implication is one of continuity surely, in an industry that is made up more of breaks with tradition than it is of any real permanence. Contemporary architecture often deals with ephemeral clients or uses for structures by building in "flexibility," but here the name of the game is "change."

GIORGIO IS HERE TO STAY

This is not to say that architecture in its more traditional, solidly built forms does not play a significant role in the retail world. The examples of two projects by the Italian architect Massimiliano Fuksas for the designer Giorgio Armani are clear proof of this point. Indeed, a number of well-known brands have invested in their own buildings in Tokyo, in the Ginza, Omotesando, or Minami Aoyama areas, but Armani's 12-story Ginza Tower (Tokyo, Japan, 2005–07, page 13) stands out even in this ambitious league. With a floor area of 7370 square meters and an overall design that takes into account both exterior and interior, this structure is a statement about the look and feel of Armani goods, including dining, which is represented by the 10th- and 11th-floor restaurant and Privé lounge. An air of exclusivity and high quality is clearly the message, but a building of this size in one of the most expensive areas for construction in the world also speaks volumes about the solidity of the business. Giorgio is here to stay!

A second intervention by Fuksas for Armani, but this time in New York (Emporio Armani Fifth Avenue, New York, New York, USA, 2009, page 130), might be considered somewhat more surprising, although it is less ambitious than the tower in Tokyo. Nonetheless, this store, located in an existing building and retail space, measures 2800 square meters on four floors, a very generous volume considering that it is lo-

5
Massimiliano and Doriana Fuksas,
Armani Ginza Tower, Tokyo, Japan,
2005–07

cated at 56th Street on Fifth Avenue. As is the case in Tokyo, Giorgio Armani seeks out and obtains the most prestigious locations for his stores, another clear signal of the firm's power and place in the fashion world. Here, however, Massimiliano and Doriana Fuksas have created a very unusual rolled calender steel and plastic stairway that seems to consume the center of the store like a large vortex. This stairway goes beyond what might be considered an efficient use of space to make an architectural statement. Like the flowing clothes of Armani, this element seems to actually move through the building, carrying clients up or down in a whirlwind of geometrically complex forms. Although Fuksas did not design the actual building in this instance, there is a clear and present agenda that consists here in placing architecture in the forefront of a retailing operation. This might be a case in which both the client and the architect should be praised for breaking out of the usual mold of "efficient" spaces to dare to be different. The result is successful in spatial terms, but the Giorgio Armani Group will have to determine if it is equally satisfying economically speaking.

CRYSTAL CATHEDRALS

Massimiliano and Doriana Fuksas have also delved into another area of retailing that is by nature closer to traditional types of architecture—the shopping center. The massive (78 000-square-meter) MyZeil Shopping Mall (Frankfurt am Main, Germany, 2009, page 138) includes a shopping mall, movie theater, fitness center, hotel, meeting rooms, offices, and parking areas. One hundred shops neighbor the other facilities, creating a destination that many users may leave very little during a typical day. This kind of multitask space is, of course, quite popular in regions like the Persian Gulf, where scorching outside temperatures make people happy to stay within the same complex for shopping, entertainment, or eating. The architect emphasizes the fluidity of the space, which again is proof that barriers not only between disciplines like design and architecture, but also between different forms of retailing, may be in the process of dissolving, helped along by figures like Fuksas.

Another top international architect, the Polish-born US citizen Daniel Libeskind, has also taken on the challenge of retail architecture in a big way. Two of his recent projects are published in this volume. Winner of the 2003 competition to design the former World Trade Center site in New York, a commission that he later progressively withdrew from, Libeskind completed the noted Jewish Museum Berlin (Germany, 1989–2001), the Imperial War Museum North in Manchester (UK, 2001), as well as extensions of the Denver Art Museum (Colorado, USA, 2006), and of Toronto's Royal Ontario Museum (Canada, 2007). Daniel Libeskind has thus marked the architectural scene more with his museum designs than with any project having to do with retailing, but this is now changing. His Crystals at CityCenter, a 46 000-meter complex in Las Vegas (Nevada, USA, 2006–09, page 234), is part of the even more extensive MGM Mirage CityCenter project. As its name implies, the Crystals evoke a form often seen in Libeskind's designs. "The crystalline and metal clad façade signals to visitors well in advance of arrival that Crystals is not a traditional retail environment," according to Libeskind's firm. The architect was not responsible for the interiors of the complex, and the building was granted LEED® Gold Core & Shell certification from the US Green Building Council, making it the world's largest retail district to receive this recognition for environmental design. CityCenter, much like developments in Dubai, half a world away, has

6

been the object of much speculation in the press about viability in a time of crisis. *The Sunday Times*, in a scorching article about CityCenter ("Vegas puts $9bn on red," February 28, 2010), wrote: "Nothing, not even the Burj Khalifa in Dubai, the world's tallest building, screams 'boom-to-bust' louder." As it happens, Sheikh Mohammed bin Rashid al-Maktoum, the leader of Dubai, is one of the major investors in City-Center. Naturally, it is the overall economic environment that will ultimately determine the success or failure of this ambitious venture, but the reputation of cutting-edge architecture for the retail environment might suffer if the dice rolls the wrong way.

A year earlier, in 2008, Daniel Libeskind completed another large facility, the Westside Shopping and Leisure Center (Bern, Switzerland, 2005–08, page 226). This complex houses 55 shops, 10 restaurants and bars, a hotel, a multiplex movie theater, an indoor water park with a wellness center, as well as housing. Located above a main artery entering Bern (the A1 freeway), the Westside complex is again of a type that challenges assumptions about shopping, blending entertainment, housing, and stores. Amusement parks, multiplex movie theaters, and hotels were, of course, more often stand-alone facilities in the past, but there is an obvious interest in concentrating such activities and encouraging shoppers to do much more than just browse in boutiques. The presence of housing, entertainment, and shopping in the same center implies a very simple logic, one that consists in implying that buying things is now at the center of existence, or, stated in a less unpleasant way, we have truly entered the era of the consumer society. In the case of Westside, the architects stated: "This mixed-use program radically reinvents the concept of shopping, entertainment, and living." Set directly above (the) highway and directly connected with the city's train and transport network, Westside was conceived as a "self-enclosed district." The concept of "self-enclosure" indeed suggests that "residents" may never need to leave Westside, a somewhat unnerving thought. Libeskind designed this complex so that it fits into its urban topography, becoming something of a "natural" phenomenon as it were.

SHOPPING IS GOOD FOR YOU!

The level of concentration and size seen in MyZeil, Crystals, or Westside is surely an indication of a growing aspect of retailing, or perhaps of the economy as a whole. Just as massive groups like LVMH are dominating the luxury-goods market, so, logically, do shopping centers take on an omnivorous nature, sweeping up any available dollars, euros, or yen within their reach. Like the airline industry, which seems to be inhabited by larger and larger firms, with a few "low-cost" carriers nipping at their heels, so, too, retailing is going the way of the old-fashioned industrial trusts in their glory days, with all that that implies for the ways in which goods are presented. While top designer labels such as ones already cited in this text also tend to want to create their own buildings on occasion, they also congregate in complexes like Crystals, where the likes of Louis Vuitton (the LV in LVMH), Bulgari, and Tiffany & Co. are to be seen. It might be noted that the intervention of renowned architects in large shopping complexes is by no means limited to Europe or the United States. The London firm Foreign Office Architects (FOA) completed the 55 000-square-meter Meydan Retail Complex and Multiplex in Ümraniye, Istanbul, Turkey (2007, page 118). Though Meydan may not reach LEED® Gold standards, it was also conceived with a very distinct emphasis on environmental concerns. Shopping is good for you, and naturally good for the planet!

7
HHF, Confiserie Bachmann,
Basel, Switzerland, 2009

Another example of the international proliferation of luxury shopping centers designed by "name" architects is Star Place (Kaohsiung Taiwan, 2006–08, page 356) by the Amsterdam firm UNStudio. Aside from making proficient use of the kinds of voids and column-free spaces that the architects prefer, Star Place relies on a 51.3-meter-high façade made of glass with "projecting horizontal, aluminum-faced lamellas and vertical glass fins that together form a swirling pattern" to draw clients into the sprawling 37 000-square-meter complex. The façade is conceived to be both visible and colorful at night, when local people prefer to shop. The architects have clearly paid careful attention to the overall interior but the "Star" of the project name has a good deal to do with the façade.

BETWEEN A WAREHOUSE AND A SOUK

Concentration, albeit in a less omnivorous mode, is also the object of the Labels 2 building in Berlin (Germany, 2008–09, page 166) by the Swiss architects HHF. With 6630 square meters of floor space, Labels 2 contains areas for 30 different fashion labels. Surely encouraging customers to believe that they are getting a bargain, Labels 2 was designed in harmony with the neighboring Labels 1 building, housed in a former warehouse. Along similar lines, at least insofar as the multi-brand approach is concerned, the Villa Moda (Manama, Bahrain, 2009, page 370) by the noted Dutch designer Marcel Wanders brings together labels ranging from Comme des Garçons to Martin Margiela and includes design objects as well as fashion. Wanders explains: "The brief was simple: to be inspired by the chaos of the souk within a luxury fashion context." Despite the increasingly global approach of fashion, the architects and designers involved in creating sales spaces clearly attempt to add an element of local inspiration to their thoughts in such instances. The topography of urban Bern for Libeskind and the "souk" atmosphere for Wanders are evidence of such ingredients in the developing relationship between the stars of architecture and design with retail sales.

JEWELS IN THE SEA

With all this emphasis on gigantic luxury shopping centers, one might wonder what has happened to one of the most traditional aspects of retail architecture, the small jewel-like boutique, and whether today's economy permits the realization of such stores as the nearly legendary Knize Men's Outfitters (Adolf Loos, Vienna, Austria, 1913). Though the weight of concentrated retailing has undoubtedly taken its toll on city-center shops like Knize, there are a certain number of recent boutiques that show how strong an impact a good designer or architect can have in a limited space. The Belgian-born designer Olivier Lempereur recently created a new store for Pierre Hermé (Pierre Hermé Macarons & Chocolats, Paris, France, 2008, page 214) on Rue Cambon that measures just 25 square meters. This boutique puts an emphasis on dark colors and colored lights above that recall both the varied shades of the macaroons and of their packaging. Even the ceiling was painted in a chocolate color, while the lacquered-bronze finishing of the furnishings also brings to mind the products. The degree of intimacy already implied by the small floor area is emphasized rather than being denied in this instance. The packages of macaroons that Parisians and tourists seek out are worth the wait. Clients find the confirmation of their feeling that these sweets are precious and rare, not only in the size of the store, but naturally in its décor.

8
Francesc Rifé, Pomme Sucre,
Oviedo, Spain, 2009

8

Somewhat along the same lines, Francesc Rifé, who, like Olivier Lempereur, was born in 1969, has designed the first of a series of stores for the master baker Julio Blanco in Oviedo (Spain, 2009, page 292). Pomme Sucre occupies a floor area of 70 square meters divided into two equally sized floors, with the actual sales area occupying just one level. The designer Rifé finds his inspiration in the main ingredients used in the baker's products—flour, eggs, and cocoa—represented in the design by white opal, yellow resin, and smoked mirrors that bring chocolate to mind. The smooth and sophisticated design stands out from neighboring shops and buildings, making it clear to potential customers that this is no ordinary bakery. The products, of course, have to be up to the image created by the designer, but, in this instance, the materials and colors of the bakery obviously announce that high quality can be expected. The association of food and design seen frequently in restaurants also clearly exists in the area of retailing items as potentially ordinary as bread and chocolate. The clients in both cases cited here obviously feel that it is worth spending more on their store in order to project and confirm the image of rising above the ordinary that is part and parcel of their marketing effort.

A third example of a recent carefully designed small retail space, this time for the sale of jewelry, can be found in Pamplona (D Jewelry, Vaillo + Irigaray Architects, Spain, 2006–07, page 364). Working with a space measuring just 50 square meters, the architects sought to evoke the atmosphere of a jewel box, "mysterious, strange, hollow, and weightless, while Oriental and Baroque." Using thick, voluntarily imperfect aluminum plates, they emphasized the narrow and deep space in order to heighten the feeling that a customer might have of discovering something truly precious. While retail spaces this small can easily appear to be ordinary and cramped, the sale of jewelry on this scale obviously does not imply the presence of numerous clients at the same moment, leaving open the option of mystery and discovery.

In all three of the examples cited here, the architects or designers have sought to identify themselves closely with the products concerned, but also with the small premises that they were asked to work with. There is an effect of symbiosis with specific products evident in all three cases that escapes the huge shopping centers of Las Vegas or Istanbul, but, at either end of the spectrum, architects and designers clearly have in mind adding to the value of retailing space. Although in some instances customers may crowd in to see new premises, usually it is clearly difficult to assess the efficiency of an investment in good design. How many more macaroons does Pierre Hermé sell because he chose a designer like Olivier Lempereur to design his boutique? The answer remains largely subjective, but the results must be convincing enough to make many brands across the world seek out the services of the very best designers and architects.

A BLUE HOUSE FOR DROOG

Some of the most interesting recent retail architecture concerns the work of noted designers, who sometimes delve into the sale of their own products, or the products of those close to them. The latter alternative surely corresponds to the work of Makkink & Bey, the husband-and-wife team made up of architect Rianne Makkink and the noted designer Jurgen Bey, who worked for a time with the Dutch group Droog. The Blueprint store in New York (New York, USA, 2009, page 322) was designed by Makkink & Bey in the Soho area of Manhattan for

9
Studio Makkink & Bey, Blueprint,
New York, New York, USA, 2009

Droog. As the designers explain: "Droog's brief to Studio Makkink & Bey was to design an interior that breaks the norms of store design. Droog Design asked for an interior installation to be made of elements that can be purchased. The studio took the brief one step further by blurring architecture, store fittings, and commodities, creating an installation with a multitude of layers—a life of its own." Although advertising hyperbole is the rule in the area of retail sales, it is not an exaggeration to say that Blueprint "breaks the norms of store design." The concept calls for objects of the décor to be purchasable in customized versions so that the client can have a given piece "interpreted" for a given setting. Though real computer-driven customization of consumer goods is not yet an everyday reality, it can be imagined that Blueprint is the first example of a new kind of retailing that will indeed permit customers to select and customize objects that would then be manufactured using digital techniques, for example.

INDUSTRIAL CHIC

Another "star" of contemporary design created the most recent Joseph Store (London, UK, 2009, page 96). Tom Dixon, known for his furniture designs and for his work as head of design for Habitat since 1998, gave a marked industrial appearance to this Joseph Store, despite its location on the very non-industrial Old Bond Street. Using rough plaster and unpolished stone, together with stage projectors, Dixon clearly aimed to create "an entirely unexpected addition" to a traditional London shopping area. It may be that the more "expected" approach to luxury goods, which would be to create a space that also exudes a certain level of refinement, is reaching some of its logical limits. A new solution is thus to press the industrial or warehouse aesthetic in these venues, an inspiration that has obviously also crossed through a good deal of contemporary architecture, in the work of such figures as Rem Koolhaas, for example.

Ingo Maurer, born in 1932, may be the best-known international designer of lights. His work has been exhibited in museums the world over, but his base has always remained in Munich. It is in an industrial building that he has used since the 1970s for storage and manufacturing that he decided to open the new 700-square-meter Ingo Maurer studioshowroomwerkstattatelier (Munich, Germany, 2008, page 260). Maurer intentionally let the industrial atmosphere of the space remain, in particular in the basement area. The sophistication of Ingo Maurer's lights finds a contrast with this storeroom background that strikes a chord with customers, but also in a broader way across the world where similar strategies are used. An obvious advantage of the industrial approach is that it costs a great deal less than a more refined space. Industrial spaces in large cities are often disused or less expensive than "high-street" locales. The potential difficulty with this strategy is that the store needs to be well enough known to draw customers to areas they are not familiar with. Ingo Maurer does not have this problem, but others, often less famous, have made a similar bet.

SKIRTS BLOWING IN THE WIND

At a certain time, the finest architecture was reserved to functions of state or religion, or to those with the means to build a palace. In more recent decades, museums and corporate headquarters joined the ranks of imposing buildings. In this parade of architectural wonders,

10

10
Ingo Maurer,
studioshowroomwerkstattatelier,
Munich, Germany, 2008

retail outlets are surely latecomers, and perhaps the least self-assured. More even than for office space, retail quarters are meant to be profitable, and that rarely takes into account the prestige that goes with calling on a famous architect. And yet, as many of the examples in this book make clear, *Shopping Architecture Now*! has taken on a new dynamism, perhaps an assurance born of a new world in which commerce and retail sales are more global and significant than any single country or belief. It is the rise of unabashed consumerism that is the driving force among today's retail architecture. With vast shopping centers that resemble enclosed cities, offering entertainment, housing, and nourishment close at hand, architecture cannot be far behind. The most innovative architecture frequently serves the interest of the clients, who have the means to realize their dreams. Despite the interest of some of the larger facilities shown here—shopping centers in Taiwan or Las Vegas—retail architecture surely remains one of the more ephemeral manifestations of the built world, changing functions or labels even more frequently than your average Lehman Brothers office. This volatility drives demand for new décors or even buildings, and in a way serves the desire of contemporary architects to be fully engaged in the dynamic, free-flowing atmosphere of parts of today's society. Where architecture seeks sometimes to escape its staid and stolid essence, it meets retailing that frequently longs for more permanence than a pretty skirt blowing in the wind. The "lowly" retailer has progressively assumed a higher and higher place in society, becoming in many ways it driving force. It should be no surprise, then, that designers and architects are flocking to an area that can only expand. Come recession or boom times, priorities may change and budgets may vary, but retail is here to stay and architecture is its willing handmaiden.

Philip Jodidio, Grimentz, Switzerland, March 1, 2010

EINLEITUNG

KAUFEN TUT GUT

Mit dem Begriff *Shopping* wird das Besichtigen von Kaufhäusern und Ladengeschäften bezeichnet sowie das Anschauen und der Kauf von Waren. Das englische Wort *retail* (Einzelhandel) hat französische Ursprünge und geht auf den alten Begriff *retailler* zurück (zuschneiden, beziehungsweise neu zuschneiden oder umschneidern). Im Englischen meint *retail* üblicherweise den Verkauf von Waren an den Endkunden, für gewöhnlich in kleinen Mengen (im Gegensatz zum Großhandel). Schon lange leisten namhafte Architekten ihren Beitrag zu einer regelrechten Glorifizierung des Einzelhandels. Das von Louis Sullivan entworfene Carson Pirie Scott and Company Building, ein Kaufhaus an der State Street in Chicago (1899) ist ein Paradebeispiel für die Präsenz von Einzelhandelsbauten im städtischen Umfeld. Das zwischen 1890 und 1893 von Alexander Pomeranzew und Wladimir Schuchow erbaute Warenhaus GUM in Moskau präsentiert seine 242 m breite Fassade dem Roten Platz und liegt direkt dem Kreml gegenüber. Selbst zu Sowjetzeiten, als viele Regale nur spärlich bestückt waren, war der Einzelhandel dank Warenhaus GUM in unmittelbarer Nähe des Epizentrums der Macht vertreten. Doch auch kleinere Geschäfte wurden mit erheblichem Aufwand gestaltet, etwa von Architekten mit fast mythischem Ruf wie Carlo Scarpa. Sein Umbau der Olivetti-Verkaufsräume am Markusplatz (Venedig, 1957–58) wurde erst kürzlich als Inspiration für Tadao Andos Sanierung der Punta della Dogana (2009) für die François-Pinault-Stiftung zitiert. Tatsächlich hat man den Eindruck, dass heute nur Museen und Kunstinstitutionen mehr Aufmerksamkeit von Stararchitekten erfahren als der Einzelhandel. In den großen Städten der Welt werden ganze Viertel durch beeindruckende Neubauten geprägt, die ausschließlich dem Verkauf von Kunst, Kleidung oder anderen Konsumgütern vorbehalten sind. In Tokio beispielsweise liegen zwischen Minami Aoyama und Omotesando, in Richtung Harajuku, Bauten von Tadao Ando (Collezione und andere), SANAA (Christian Dior), Kengo Kuma (LVMH), Herzog & de Meuron (Prada) oder Toyo Ito (TOD's). Konkurrieren kann hiermit wohl nur das unweit gelegene Ginza-Viertel, wo Neubauten von Renzo Piano (Hermès) und Massimiliano Fuksas (Armani) in trauter Nachbarschaft liegen. Doch die Architektur von Einzelhandelsflächen liegt nicht ausschließlich in den Händen von Architekten. Renommierte Designer, wie Shiro Kuramata (1934–91), der Boutiquen für Issey Miyake in Paris, Tokio und New York realisierte, spielten und spielen eine führende Rolle bei der Umsetzung einer neuen Welle von Boutiquen- und Ladenentwürfen.

Persönlichkeiten wie Tom Dixon, Arne Quinze, Jurgen Bey oder Tokujin Yoshioka, die eher als Designer denn als Architekten bekannt sind, zeichnen für einige der derzeit außergewöhnlichsten Ladenlokale verantwortlich. Folglich umfasst Einzelhandelsarchitektur mehr als nur Architektur im engeren Sinne, sie schließt auch Innenarchitektur und Design mit ein. Einige Architekten und Designer sind für spezifische Firmen tätig und tragen ganz offensichtlich dazu bei, deren Markenimage zu prägen oder gar neu zu definieren. Auch der beeindruckende Prada Store von OMA*AMO/Rem Koolhaas, Ecke Broadway und Prince Street in Manhattan (USA, 1999–2001), am ehemaligen Standort des Guggenheim Soho, war der gezielte Versuch, ein bis dato eher gesetztes Markenimage neu zu erfinden. Koolhaas setzte seine Zusammenarbeit mit Prada in den letzten Jahren fort und realisierte so ungewöhnliche Bauten wie den unlängst entstandenen Prada Transformer (Seoul, Südkorea, 2008–09). Auch innovative Persönlichkeiten wie Rei Kawakubo (Comme des Garçons) haben sich im Laufe der Jahre intensiv mit der Gestaltung ihrer Geschäftsräume auseinandergesetzt. Kawakubo beauftragte Architekten wie Future Systems, um die Fassaden oder Eingangsbereiche ihrer Läden in Chelsea oder Minami Aoyama zu entwerfen, und arbeitete bei anderen Aspekten der Ladengestaltung mit Künstlern und Designern zusammen.

11

PRINZESSIN ZAHA UND DER HEILIGE KARL

Obwohl es sinnvoll scheinen mag, klar zwischen der Architektur ganzer Shoppingcenter und dem Innenausbau kleinerer Läden zu unterscheiden, ist es interessant, wie stark bei Architektur für den Einzelhandel die traditionellen Grenzen zwischen den Disziplinen verschwimmen. Ingo Maurer, ein bekannter Leuchtendesigner, gestaltete seine Geschäftsräume in München (2008, Seite 260) ohne sichtliche Unterstützung von Architekten. Und der Verweis auf die Museumsarchitektur als einem Bereich, in dem besonders viele renommierte Architekten tätig sind, ist tatsächlich mehr als nur oberflächlich relevant. Sowohl Museen als auch Designerboutiquen geht es darum, finanzielle Mittel einzusetzen, um „Kunden" zu gewinnen. Auch wenn der Begriff „Kunde" für ein Museum nicht eben schmeichelhaft klingt, haben sich selbst die großen staatseigenen Museen im Alten Europa intensiv auf eigene Einzelhandelsaktivitäten eingelassen. Der Verkauf von T-Shirts, Katalogen oder Monografien über Herzog & de Meuron fällt für die Tate Modern inzwischen fast ebenso ins Gewicht wie Eintrittsgelder. Dass der Einzelhandel selbst längst nicht mehr althergebrachten Kategorien entspricht, wie sie die klassische Boutique verkörpert, belegt auch Zaha Hadids unlängst realisierter Mobile Art, Chanel Contemporary Art Container (verschiedene Standorte, 2007–), ein Projekt, das Karl Lagerfelds kreative Leistung ebenbürtig neben das Werk anderer namhafter Künstler stellt. Würde man die Kreativen unserer Tage heute ebenso verehren wie große Persönlichkeiten früherer Zeiten, dann wäre Zaha Hadid zweifellos längst Prinzessin und Karl, wenn auch höchst lebendig, so etwas wie ein Heiliger.

NEUE TEMPEL FÜR NEUE GLAUBENSSÄTZE

Zweifellos haben die wirtschaftlichen Schwierigkeiten seit 2008 den Einzelhandel in Mitleidenschaft gezogen. Doch wie dieses Buch belegt, werden nach wie vor neue Läden und Geschäfte eröffnet, gestaltet von den derzeit kreativsten Köpfen. Im Grunde ist der Einzelhandel – der Verkauf von Waren an den Endkunden – zur Zeit das Herzstück des Wirtschaftssystems der entwickelten Welt. Es ist kein Zufall, dass etliche der hier vorgestellten, spektakulären neuen Ladengeschäfte in Großstädten angesiedelt sind, von Los Angeles bis Tokio. Sie werden dort gebaut, wo Geld ist, wo der Verkauf boomt. Der Schlüssel zum Wiederaufschwung, heißt es, sei „Konsum" – eben das ist es ja, worum es im Einzelhandel geht. Es gab Zeiten, als Kritiker fragten, ob Museen den Kirchen nicht inzwischen den Rang als neue Pilgerorte abgelaufen hätten. Doch ist es in unserer heutigen pragmatischen, globalisierten Welt nicht vielmehr so, dass die Tempel Dior, Prada, Fauchon oder Chanel heißen? Selbst Marken, die sich an ein breiteres Publikum wenden, wie die japanische Firma Uniqlo, lassen sich bei ihrem Ziel, die Welt des Einzelhandels zu erobern, von namhaften Designern unterstützen. Ist der Einzelhandel eine neue Religion oder vielleicht der Schauplatz neuer Eroberungszüge? Sicherlich ein bisschen von beidem – und die Architektur ist mittendrin.

ADJAYE UND BOATENG AUF DER SAVILE ROW

David Adjaye, Architekt mit Sitz in London, hat in seinen Bauten ausgeprägte Flexibilität und Vielfältigkeit gezeigt und so dürfte es kaum überraschen, dass ihn auch die architektonische Gestaltung von Läden und Geschäften reizt. Die beiden hier veröffentlichten, unlängst realisierten Projekte (Ozwald Boateng Flagshipstore, London, 2007, Seite 46, und Kvadrat Showroom, London, 2008–09, Seite 52) unterscheiden

12
Peter Marino, Chanel Robertson
Boulevard, Los Angeles, California,
USA, 2008

sich sowohl in ihrer Nutzungsform als auch ihrer Kundengruppe. Kvadrat, ein dänischer Hersteller für Vorhang-, Bezug- und Trennwandstoffe, wollte einen Raum, der nicht nur als Verkaufsraum, sondern auch für Filmvorführungen, Diskussionen und Ausstellungen genutzt werden konnte. Während Einzelhandelsflächen zunehmend die traditionellen Genregrenzen zwischen Architektur und Design hinterfragen, streben zahlreiche neue Verkaufsräume nach Multifunktionalität, die dazu beiträgt, dass selbst an Tagen mit wenig Laufkundschaft ein hohes Level an Aktivität gewährleistet ist. Die Ladenräume des Modemachers Ozwald Boateng geben sich traditioneller in ihrer Konzeption. Allerdings entwarf der Architekt unter dem Dach eines größeren Geschäftsraums gewissermaßen eine ganze Reihe verschiedener Läden, die unterschiedliche Bereiche der Designermarke präsentieren. Ozwald Boateng, 1968 in London geboren, ist Autodidakt. Obwohl er nie eine Schneiderlehre absolvierte, wurde er Kreativdirektor der Herrenlinie bei Givenchy (2003–07). Er gilt als einer der „Stars" der Londoner Modeszene, weshalb die Verbindung Boateng/Adjaye jenen „Celebrity"-Faktor hat, den man sich bei der Gestaltung von Geschäftsräumen wünscht. David Adjaye führt aus: „Konzept und Designstrategie zielen darauf ab, sich auf zeitgenössische, kuratorische Tendenzen einzulassen, in deren Richtung sich die Mode zunehmend entwickelt. Bei diesem Ladenraum geht es nicht nur darum, Kleidung kaufen zu können, sondern darum, Erlebnisse zu schaffen, stofflich und emotional zu verführen, und das Zusammentreffen von Alt und Neu zu ermöglichen."

David Adjaye wurde 1966 in Daressalam, Tansania, geboren. Er studierte am Royal College of Art in London und arbeitete bei David Chipperfield und Eduardo Souto de Moura, bevor er 2000 in London sein eigenes Büro gründete. Mit Projekten wie dem Nobel-Friedenszentrum (Oslo, Norwegen, 2002–05) und dem Museum of Contemporary Art/Denver (Denver, Colorado, 2004–07), die seinen Ruf begründeten, sowie dem derzeit in Planung befindlichen National Museum of African American History and Culture (Smithsonian Institution, Washington D.C., 2015), ist David Adjaye einer der aufgehenden Sterne am Himmel der zeitgenössischen Architektur. Seine Projekte für Ozwald Boateng oder Kvadrat belegen zweifellos, welche Bedeutung die architektonische Gestaltung von Läden und Geschäften derzeit hat, und ebenso, welche symbiotische Beziehung manche Luxusmarken zu herausragenden Architekten und Designern entwickelt haben.

FAUCHON SETZT AUF PINK, APPLE WIRD TRANSPARENT

Die wechselseitige Beziehung von renommierten Designern und namhaften Marken betrifft sämtliche Bereiches des Handels – zumindest jene Bereiche in den gehobenen Einkaufsvierteln der Großstädte, die besondere Sichtbarkeit genießen. Fauchon, Frankreichs größtes Feinschmeckeremporium, beauftragte Christian Biecher, ihre Niederlassungen neu zu gestalten. Zwar führten sie stets beste Ware, hatten aber sehr wohl eine Modernisierung nötig. Biecher gestaltete die Filialen in Peking und Paris (Seite 62) und arbeitet derzeit an weiteren Projekten für die Firma. Neben einer überraschenden Farbpalette von Gold bis Rosa arbeitet Biecher zudem mit den verschiedensten Materialien wie Holz, Bambus und Leder, die nicht nur die unterschiedlichen Aspekte der Fauchon-Filialen reflektieren, sondern auch das breite Spektrum der Herkunftsländer, aus denen die Produkte stammen. Indem Christian Biecher die Farbe Rosa wie einen „roten Faden" einsetzt, der sich durch die verschiedenen Bereiche der Läden zieht, ja sogar die einzelnen Ladenstandorte miteinander verknüpft, beweist der Architekt, dass sich selbst eine alte und hoch angesehene Marke erfolgreich aktualisieren lässt.

Eine alte Marke zu sein ist für Apple sicher kein Problem; der Computerhersteller hat sein Angebot inzwischen auf iPods, iPads und alle möglichen Arten von technischem Zubehör für seine digital vernetzten Kunden ausgeweitet. Im Gegenteil, die stylischen, bis ins Detail durchdesignten Produkte von Apple fordern geradezu, dass auch die Firmenniederlassungen architektonisch ein Statement sind, das dem von Firmengründer Steven Jobs begründeten Markenethos entspricht. In letzter Zeit wurde Apples Präsenz in Manhattan von zwei Filialen geprägt, die von Bohlin Cywinski Jackson entworfen wurden: einer Niederlassung an Fifth Avenue (767 Fifth Avenue, New York, 2003–06), der zweiten an der Upper West Side (New York, 2008–09, Seite 70). Beiden gemeinsam ist die hohe Transparenz und das vergleichsweise schlichte Design, das daraufhin angelegt ist, Kunden anzuziehen und zugleich den wahren „Stars" eine Bühne zu geben – den Produkten selbst. Die lichte Architektur und ihre offenkundige Modernität sind optimal auf den Verkauf der Produkte von Apple abgestimmt, was auch die andauernde Zusammenarbeit von Bohlin Cywinski Jackson und dem Computerhersteller belegt.

KURZE HALTBARKEITSDAUER FÜR YOHJI

In der Modewelt können selbst die ambitioniertesten Bauprojekte von ebenso kurzer „Haltbarkeitsdauer" sein wie die eigentlichen Kollektionen. Der Yohji Yamamoto Store auf der Gansevoort Street (New York, 2007–08, Seite 180) im Meatpacking District war das erste Bauprojekt für Junya Ishigami, einen jungen, vielversprechenden japanischen Architekten. Um den höchst ungewöhnlichen, dreieckigen Showroom zu schaffen, wurde ein bestehender Altbau in zwei Teile geschnitten – das alles unweit des Galerienviertels Chelsea. Zwar hatte sich das kreative Schaffen von Yohji Yamamoto schon lange im Grenzbereich der Mode, im Grunde in allernächster Nähe zur Kunst, bewährt; dennoch war die gebündelte Kreativität von Yamamoto und Ishigami kein ausreichender Schutzwall gegen die Wirtschaftskrise, die seit Eröffnung der Verkaufsraums um sich gegriffen hat. Der Yohji Yamamoto Store auf der Gansevoort Street musste Anfang 2010 schließen und bestand damit kaum länger als ein typischer Zyklus der Modewelt.

Die überaus flüchtige Natur der Beziehung von Architektur und Einzelhandel ist womöglich eine der Triebfedern für die Kreativität, die sich hier spiegelt. Manche Installation in diesem Bereich spielt sogar explizit auf diese Ambiguität an. So etwa der Dr. Martens Pop-Up Store (London, 2009, Seite 76), eine 180 m² große Installation nach einem Entwurf von Campaign in Zusammenarbeit mit der Markenagentur Fresh. Die Schumarke Dr. Martens ist Campaign zufolge eine Art „Ikone der Gegenkultur". Der Entwurf basierte auf dem Konzept eines Lagerraums und wurde in nur sechs Tagen realisiert – montiert aus einem übergroßen gelben PVC-Vorhang, Baustellenleuchten, Frachtpaletten und folienverschweißten Podesten. Statt seine prinzipell vergänglichen Waren haltbarer erscheinen zu lassen, als sie tatsächlich sind, ließ der Auftraggeber zu, dass Campaign mit dem ungehobelten Image spielte, das im Grunde längst Teil des Selbstverständnisses von Dr. Martens war.

BLOWING IN THE WIND

*Shopping Architecture No*w! thematisiert nicht nur, was man gemeinhin unter den Begriff Architektur fassen würde – eben deshalb, weil der Einzelhandelssektor auch Installationen und temporäre Präsentationen fördert. Zwei Schaufenstergestaltungen veranschaulichen, wie

13
Liganova, Diesel Interactive Windows,
Berlin, Germany, 2009

sie in den Händen kreativer Designer spürbaren Einfluss auf das Interesse der Passanten und damit letztendlich auf den Umsatz nehmen können. Das erste Fenster wurde von der Agentur Liganova für Diesel gestaltet, zunächst 2009 in Deutschland und schließlich auch in anderen Ländern. Die interaktiven Fenster für Diesel (Berlin, Seite 240) wurden mithilfe von Motion-Tracking-Technologie realisiert, durch die Passanten die Auslage im Fenster „real" beeinflussen konnten. Die potenziellen Kunden vor dem Geschäft konnten „durch Arm- und Handbewegungen virtuelle Objekte auf einem Bildschirm bewegen und damit die realen Objekte und Geschehnisse im Fenster beeinflussen." Dank Klangwandler wurden die Bewegungen sogar mit einem passenden „Soundtrack" unterlegt. Auf diese Weise wurden Passanten, die sonst bestenfalls einen Blick in das Fenster geworfen hätten, zu direkter Interaktion mit der Marke angeregt.

Der renommiert Designer Tokujin Yoshioka verfolgte mit seiner Schaufensterinstallation für das Maison Hermès in Tokio (2009, Seite 402) einen ästhetischeren und distanzierteren Ansatz. Sein Video zeigte eine Frau, die sanft gegen einen – real im Fenster installierten – Hermès-Schal blies. Yoshioka nennt seine Schaufenstergestaltung „humorvoll", doch natürlich spielt er darüber hinaus mit der Interaktion von Video und „realer" Welt, die auch in der zeitgenössischen Kunst häufig Thema ist. Wenngleich seine Präsentation weniger interaktiv ist als die Diesel-Schaufenster von Liganova, passt sie womöglich ebensogut zur Luxusmarke Hermès. Ohne die Langlebigkeit eines Hermès-Schals in Frage stellen zu wollen, versetzt Yoshioka ihn in Bewegung und rückt ihn in einen künstlerischen Kontext, in dem die Grenzen von Realität und Fantasie verschwimmen.

REM AUF DEM CATWALK
Der ultimative Höhepunkt der Modewelt ist zweifellos die sorgsam choreografierte Präsentation einer jeden Kollektion. Zwar ist dies streng genommen kein Bereich, in dem die Architektur oft etwas zu sagen hätte, doch zögern Firmen wie Prada nicht, Büros wie OMA*AMO/ Rem Koolhaas hinzuzuziehen, um ihre Präsentation künstlerisch oder architektonisch auf ein Niveau zu bringen, das man in den Shows der Mitbewerber nur selten findet. Im Zuge ihrer andauernden Kooperation mit der Modemarke, für die das Büro in letzter Zeit den Prada Transformer realisierte, präsentierte OMA die Schauen der Damen- und Herrenkollektion für die Saison Frühjahr/Sommer 2010 (Fondazione Prada, Mailand, 2009, Seite 11). Die Architekten und Modeschöpfer nannten die Modenschau der Herrenkollektion „A Secret Passage or Love for the Void" (Eine geheime Reise oder die Liebe zur Leere) und thematisierten damit zugleich Ideen, die in der zeitgenössischen Architektur aktuell sind. Ein schnurgerader Catwalk war zwischen der Wand eines Raums der Location und einer eigens hochgezogenen, sieben Meter hohen Wand verborgen. Die Wand war mit Dialogen männlicher Filmdarsteller tapeziert. Damit war ein Bühnenbild geschaffen, das Mode, Film und Architektur in einem Raum verknüpfte und im Grunde suggerierte, dass Männer, die Prada tragen, schon jetzt das Zeug zur Legende haben. Zur Schau der Damenkollektion gehörte unter anderem eine „abstrakte Wand", auf die fiktive Gänge projiziert wurden. Sie beschworen „imaginäre Räume" herauf, „in denen die opulenten, klassizistischen Türrahmen alter Grandhotels neben grellem Neonlicht, Trash und verlassenen Orten oder flirrend-hellen Bildern von dicht bevölkerten Stränden erschienen". Auf diese Weise entstand den Architekten zufolge „eine Sequenz undefinierbarer Orte".

14

14
Dominique Gonzalez-Foerster,
Balenciaga Flagship Store,
London, UK, 2008

Die wechselseitige Abhängigkeit von Architektur und Mode in diesem speziellen Fall veranschaulicht das Zusammentreffen zweier handfester Interessen. Aus Sicht einer Modemarke ist Wandel notwendig, weil er zum erneuten Kauf anregt. Nichtsdestotrotz streben alle großen Luxusmarken nach einem Image von Zeitlosigkeit, das ihnen die Treue ihrer Kunden garantiert. Architekten hingegen kämpfen mit der materiellen Beständigkeit ihres Werks. Ein Bauwerk hat eine nicht zu leugnende Präsenz, die im besten Falle eben jene Zeitlosigkeit repräsentiert, nach der Prada oder Chanel streben. Zweifellos überzeichnen Architekten wie auch Modedesigner ihre Langlebigkeit mitunter, gerade in einer Welt schnelllebigen Konsums. Dennoch ist das Zusammentreffen von Prada und OMA zweifellos eines, das für beide Partner glücklich ist.

MASSIVE PRÄSENZ

Obwohl Restaurants und Bars zum Einzelhandelssektor zählen, werden sie in diesem Band nur ansatzweise behandelt (ausführlicher siehe *Architecture Now! Restaurants & Bars*). Dennoch sind sie zweifellos einer der lebendigsten Schauplätze an der Schnittstelle von Handel und Architektur beziehungsweise Design. Das Amsterdamer Büro Concrete Architectural Associates hat sich einen beachtlichen Ruf mit Interieurs für das Pearls & Caviar Restaurant (Abu Dhabi, 2008), die VIP Lounge am Flughafen Schiphol (Amsterdam, Niederlande, 2008), den Supperclub (Singapur, 2008) oder das Restaurant De Bijenkorf Kitchen (Amsterdam, 2008) gemacht. Rob Wagemans, Seniorpartner bei Concrete, hat einen Hintergrund, der zumindest teilweise den Erfolg erklärt, mit dem seine Firma Aufträge realisiert, die in erheblichem Maß architektonische Expertise erfordern. Wagemans studierte Architektur in Amsterdam und Utrecht und schloss sein Studium mit einem Master in Innenarchitektur ab. Zu seinen jüngeren Projekten zählt die Coffee Company Prinsenhof (Den Haag, 2008, Seite 92). Das Café liegt im Atrium eines Bürogebäudes und hat eine Nutzfläche von nur 60 m². Die Hülle des Coffeeshops aus Stahl, Glas und Mahagoni lässt sich dank eines Hydrauliksystems auf Knopfdruck 2,5 m nach oben fahren. Concrete erklärt: „Die Coffee Company wird buchstäblich zu einem Teil des Atriums. Wenn der Laden abends geschlossen wird, fährt das Gehäuse nach unten." Die Verbindung von gelungenem Design und gelungener Architektur ist ein eindrückliches Beispiel dafür, was talentierte Gestalter für den Einzelhandel tun können – weit über die einfache Schaffung eines Verkaufsraums hinaus.

Eine jüngere, weit weniger bekannte Persönlichkeit als Wagemans, der Franzose Jean-Guillaume Mathiaut, überschreitet die Grenzen zwischen Architektur und Design ebenso leicht. Bevor Mathiaut 1999 sein Architekturstudium abschloss, hatte er bereits für die Architekten François & Lewis (Paris, 1993–98) gearbeitet. Später war er Künstlerischer Leiter bei den Galeries Lafayette (Paris, 2000–05), wo er Ausstellungen mit Designern wie Marcel Wanders, Jurgen Bey, Paul Smith, Jakob + MacFarlane oder Ingo Maurer realisierte. Mit seinem eigenen Büro, Edith Edition, gegründet 2007, gestaltete er den neuesten Issey Miyake Store in Paris (2008, Seite 322) in einem Hof an der Rue Royale. Mathiaut entwarf massive Einbauelemente aus Corian und versah die eher schwierigen Räumlichkeiten mit einem minimalistischen Eingang aus Glas. Atmosphärisch erinnert der Laden Mathiau zufolge an einen Steinbruch oder das Atelier eines Künstlers. Am interessantesten jedoch ist der Aspekt, das hier Raum für Installationen von Künstlern oder Designern geschaffen wird. Schließlich ist Issey Miyake bekannt für seine kreative Energie, die oft über die Grenzen von Mode hinausgeht und gerade auch den künstlerischen Bereich tangiert. Mathiauts Entwurf für das Geschäft an der Rue Royale greift diesen wesentlichen Aspekt der Marke auf und „überzeichnet" die Situation, wie er selbst sagt.

WENN DIE KUNST AN DIE TÜR KLOPFT

Der Gedanke, solche Grenzen überwinden zu wollen, war auch beim unlängst realisierten Flagshipstore für Balenciaga in London (2008, Seite 144) Dreh- und Angelpunkt. Nicolas Ghesquière, Chefdesigner des Modehauses, der vor seinem Einstieg bei Balenciaga 1997 für Jean-Paul Gaultier und Thierry Mugler tätig war, gilt als einer der Superstars seiner Branche. Heutzutage scheint außergewöhnliche Mode das Bedürfnis zu haben, den Schulterschluss mit außergewöhnlicher Kunst, Design und Architektur zu suchen. Dies tat Ghesquière, als er die Künstlerin Dominique Gonzalez-Foerster, den Architekten Martial Galfione sowie den Lichtdesigner Benoit Lalloz hinzuzog, um eine Reihe seiner Läden zu gestalten. Obwohl der Verkaufsraum in London in erster Linie von Plasmabildschirmen dominiert wird, auf denen Videos und Musikprogramme laufen, die Christophe Van Huffel speziell für die Londoner Räume schrieb, ist das Ergebnis dieser ungewöhnlichen Kollaboration vor allem als Konzept interessant. Denn hier handelt es sich weder um ein Kunstwerk, noch um reine Architektur oder reines Design. Vielmehr ist es eine subtile Mischung aus allen dreien, natürlich mit einer Verneigung vor der Mode von Balenciaga. Auch wenn es hier Unterschiede gibt, erinnert die Kollaboration von Balenciaga durchaus an eine Ikone des 20. Jahrhunderts – das Café L'Aubette in Straßburg (1927). Damals hatten Sophie Taeuber-Arp, Jean Arp und Theo van Doesburg gemeinsam einen Ort geschaffen, zu dem ein Teesalon, mehrere Bars, Veranstaltungsräume, ein Ballsaal, ein Nachtclub im Kellergeschoss sowie ein Kino gehörten. Zwar waren die drei Beteiligten in erster Linie als Künstler bekannt, doch Theo van Doesburg (1883–1931), Gründer und Kopf der De Stijl-Bewegung, war als Maler, Autor, Lyriker und Architekt aktiv. Obwohl das 1928 fertiggestellte Café L'Aubette ein bedeutendes Beispiel für künstlerische Kollaboration war, wurde es auf Wunsch der unzufriedenen Cafébesucher fast sofort wieder umgebaut. Dominique Gonzalez-Foerster (die übrigens zufälligerweise in Straßburg geboren wurde), ist in erster Linie als Videokünstlerin bekannt, schafft jedoch ebenso Installationen, die unweigerlich mit der Gestaltung von Raum zu tun haben. Könnte der Balenciaga Store von heute nicht ein zeitgenössisches Pendant zum Café L'Aubette sein?

FLAGSHIPS FÜR DIE MODE

Ebenso wie Prada mit verschiedenen renommierten Architekten zusammenarbeitet – von Herzog & de Meuron bis hin zu Rem Koolhaas – haben auch andere Modehäuser verstanden, dass es durchaus lohnenswert ist, die besten Designer und Architekten zu engagieren, um neue Verkaufsräume zu gestalten. Phillip Lim ist amerikanischer Modedesigner mit chinesischen Wurzeln. 2007 wurde er als Kreativdirektor seiner Firma 3.1 Phillip Lim vom Verband der amerikanischen Modedesigner mit dem Swarovski-Preis für Damenmode ausgezeichnet. Zwar engagierte Lim keine Pritzker-Preisträger, dennoch hat er mit seinen aktuellen Flagshipstores in New York, Los Angeles und Seoul einen starken Eindruck hinterlassen. Der erste Store (New York, Seite 12), ein Entwurf von Tacklebox LLC, konnte 2007 fertiggestellt werden. Die zweite Niederlassung (Los Angeles, 2007–08, Seite 278) war ein Gemeinschaftsprojekt von Dominic Leong und PARA-Project mit Giancarlo Valle. Der dritte Flagshipstore wurde 2009 in Seoul eröffnet (Seite 220) und ist ein Entwuurf von Leong Leong Architects. Der größte dieser

15

15
Massimiliano and Doriana Fuksas,
MyZeil Shopping Mall, Frankfurt,
Germany, 2009

Läden (in Seoul) mit einer Nutzfläche von 543 m² wurde auf einer bereits bestehenden Verkaufsfläche realisiert, zu der ein Bürogebäude hinzugezogen wurde. Die Architekten entschieden sich für „taktile" Materialien wie Eichenholzböden im Interieur, sicherlich eine passende Wahl für ein Modegeschäft. Im New Yorker Store sieht man weiß gestrichene Backsteinmauern und abgenutzte Douglasienböden – eine ausgesprochen moderne Mischung, die den Ansatz der Architekten illustriert, Elemente eigener Entwürfe mit vorhandenen Materialien oder Räumen zu kombinieren. Dies ist zweifellos ein Zeichen für Kontinuität, und das in einer Branche, die eher von Brüchen mit der Tradition lebt als von echter Permanenz. Natürlich hat es die zeitgenössische Architektur oft mit Auftraggebern oder Nutzungszwecken zu tun, die kaum langfristig denken oder konzipiert sind und für die es gilt, „flexibel" zu bauen. Das Schlüsselwort ist „Veränderung".

GIORGIO – GEKOMMEN, UM ZU BLEIBEN

Dies bedeutet jedoch keineswegs, dass Architektur in ihrer traditionelleren, auf Langfristigkeit ausgelegten Form keine entscheidende Rolle im Einzelhandel mehr spielen würde. Zwei Projekte des italienischen Architekten Massimiliano Fuksas für den Designer Giorgio Armani sind ein deutlicher Beleg hierfür. Tatsächlich hat eine ganze Reihe bekannter Modehäuser in Tokio in eigene Gebäude investiert – in den Stadtvierteln Ginza, Omotesando oder Minami Aoyama. Doch selbst in dieser ehrgeizigen Liga hat Armanis 12-stöckiger Ginza Tower (Tokio, Japan, 2005–07, Seite 13) eine ganz eigene Qualität. Mit einer Gesamtfläche von 7370 m² und einem Design, das Außenbau wie Innenraum umfasst, ist dieser Bau ein Statement zum Look von Armani und zu dem Gefühl, das die von ihm gestalteten Produkte vermitteln. Dies schließt sogar Essen und Trinken ein, ein Aspekt, der im 11. und 12. Stock mit einem Restaurant und einer Privé-Lounge vertreten ist. Die hier vermittelte Botschaft ist eindeutig Exklusivität und höchste Qualität. Doch ein Gebäude dieser Größenordnung – in einer der teuersten Regionen der Welt für Bauprojekte – spricht nicht zuletzt auch Bände über die Stabilität des Unternehmens. Keine Frage: Giorgio ist gekommen, um zu bleiben.

Eine weitere architektonische Intervention von Fuksas für Armani, dieses Mal in New York (Emporio Armani Fifth Avenue, 2009, Seite 130), ist vielleicht überraschender, wenn auch etwas bescheidener als das Hochhaus in Tokio. Dennoch hat der in einem bestehenden Geschäftsgebäude gelegene Store eine Gesamtfläche von 2800 m², die sich über vier Etagen verteilen. Ein überaus großzügiges Volumen, bedenkt man die Lage auf der Fifth Avenue auf Höhe der 56th Street. Wie auch in Tokio sucht und erwirbt Giorgio Armani die prestigeträchtigsten Standorte für seine Niederlassungen – ein weiteres deutliches Signal für die Macht der Firma und ihren Status in der Modewelt. Hier realisierten Massimiliano und Doriana Fuksas eine höchst ungewöhnliche Treppe aus Stahl und Kunststoff, die an eine Kalandermaschine erinnert und den gesamten zentralen Bereich des Stores wie ein gewaltiger Strudel in sich hineinzuziehen scheint. Die Treppe geht weit über das hinaus, was man als effiziente Platznutzung bezeichnen würde. Vielmehr ist sie ein architektonisches Statement. Wie die fließende Kleidung von Armani, scheint dieses bauliche Element geradezu durch den Raum zu schwingen und befördert in einem Wirbelwind komplexer geometrischer Formen Kunden hinauf und hinunter. Obwohl Fuksas hier nicht das gesamte Gebäude entwarf, ist dennoch klar die Absicht zu erkennen, die Architektur in den Vordergrund der Verkaufsaktivität zu rücken. In diesem Fall kann man ohne Frage Auftraggeber wie Architek-

*16
Daniel Libeskind, Crystals at
CityCenter, Las Vegas, Nevada,
USA, 2006–09*

16

ten dafür loben, das übliche Muster „effizienter" Raumnutzung durchbrochen zu haben, um etwas Neues zu wagen. In räumlicher Hinsicht ist das Ergebnis zweifellos gelungen. Dennoch wird die Giorgio-Armani-Gruppe für sich entscheiden müssen, ob der Entwurf auch wirtschaftlich erfolgreich ist.

GLÄSERNE KATHEDRALEN

Massimiliano und Doriana Fuksas haben sich darüber hinaus in einen Bereich gewagt, der *per se* größere Nähe zu traditionellen Architekturformen hat – das Einkaufszentrum. Das riesige Shoppingcenter MyZeil (78 000 m², Frankfurt am Main, 2009, Seite 138), umfasst Einkaufszentrum, Kino, Sportstudio, Hotel, Konferenzräume, Büros und Parkflächen. Einhundert Läden liegen in unmittelbarer Nachbarschaft zu den übrigen Einrichtungen. So entsteht ein Ort, den viele Nutzer an einem durchschnittlichen Tag kaum verlassen müssen. Solche Multifunktionsbauten sind besonders in Regionen wie dem Persischen Golf beliebt, wo heiße Außentemperaturen dafür sorgen, dass Besucher froh sind, Einkaufsmöglichkeiten, Freizeiteinrichtungen und Restaurants in ein und demselben Komplex zu finden. In Frankfurt betonten die Architekten besonders das Fließende des Raums. Dies mag ein weiteres Zeichen dafür sein, dass nicht nur die Grenzen zwischen unterschiedlichen Disziplinen, wie Design und Architektur, sondern auch zwischen verschiedenen Einzelhandelsformen in einem Auflösungsprozess begriffen sind, was nicht zuletzt auch durch Persönlichkeiten wie Fuksas gefördert wird.

Auch ein weiterer internationaler Stararchitekt, der in Polen geborene, amerikanische Architekt Daniel Libeskind, hat sich in intensiv mit Einzelhandelsarchitektur auseinandergesetzt. Zwei seiner jüngeren Projekte sind in diesem Band vorgestellt. Libeskind hatte 2003 den Wettbewerb für die Gestaltung des ehemaligen Standorts des World Trade Centers in New York gewonnen – ein Auftrag, von dem er sich später nach und nach distanzierte. Darüber hinaus realisierte Libeskind das renommierte Jüdische Museum Berlin (1989–2001), das Imperial War Museum North in Manchester (2001) sowie Erweiterungsbauten für das Denver Art Museum (Denver, Colorado, 2006) und für das Royal Ontario Museum in Toronto (2007). Dementsprechend hatte Daniel Libeskind die Architekturszene bisher stärker mit Museumsentwürfen als mit Projekten geprägt, die etwas mit dem Einzelhandel zu tun gehabt hätten. Doch dies wird sich nun ändern. Sein Entwurf für das Crystals, ein 46 000 m² großer Komplex in Las Vegas (Nevada, 2006–09, Seite 234), ist Teil des noch größeren CityCenters, einem MGM Mirage-Projekt. Wie schon der Name vermuten lässt, erinnert das Crystals an Formen, die wiederholt in Libeskinds Entwürfen auftauchen. „Die kristalline, metallverblendete Fassade signalisiert den Besuchern schon von weitem, dass das Crystals kein gewöhnliches Einkaufszentrum ist", so Libeskinds Büro. Der Architekt war nicht für die Innengestaltung des Komplexes verantwortlich, der übrigens das LEED® Gold-Zertifikat für Innen- und Außenbau vom US Green Building Council bekam. Es ist die weltweit größte Einkaufsfläche, der diese Auszeichnung für umweltfreundliches Bauen zugedacht wurde. Das CityCenter war, ebenso wie diverse Bauprojekte am anderen Ende der Welt, etwa in Dubai, heftig umstritten. Die Presse fragte, ob solche Projekte in Krisenzeiten noch haltbar seien. In einem scharfen Artikel schrieb *The Sunday Times* über das CityCenter („Vegas mit 9 Milliarden Dollar in der Kreide", 28. Februar 2010): „Nichts – nicht einmal der Burj Khalifa in Dubai, das höchste Gebäude der Welt – symbolisiert den Absturz vom Boom in die Pleite deutlicher [als das CityCenter]." Zufälligerweise ist Scheich Mohammed bin Raschid Al Maktum, Staatsoberhaupt von Dubai, einer der wichtigsten Investoren des CityCenters. Natürlich ist es das ökonomische Gesamtumfeld, das letztendlich über Wohl und Wehe dieses ehrgeizigen Projekts entscheiden wird. Doch der Ruf avangardistischer Toparchitektur im Bereich des Einzelhandels könnte ernstlich beschädigt werden, sollten die Würfel ungünstig fallen.

Ein Jahr zuvor, 2008, hatte Daniel Libeskind einen weiteren Großkomplex realisiert: das Westside Einkaufs- und Freizeitzentrum in Bern (2005–08, Seite 226). Der Komplex umfasst 55 Geschäfte, 10 Restaurants und Bars, ein Hotel, ein Multiplex-Kino, ein Erlebnisbad mit Wellnessbereich sowie Wohnungen. Das Westside überspannt eine der Hauptzufahrtsstraßen nach Bern (die Autobahn A1) und ist damit wieder einmal ein Bautypus, der sämtliche konventionellen Vorstellungen vom Einkaufen hinterfragt und Unterhaltungs-, Wohn- und Gewerbeflächen miteinander verbindet. In der Vergangenheit waren Freizeitparks, Multiplex-Kinos und Hotels eher eigenständige Einrichtungen. Inzwischen versucht man jedoch ganz offensichtlich, solche Aktivitäten zu bündeln und Kunden anzuregen, mehr zu tun, als nur durch Geschäfte zu bummeln. Die Kombination von Wohnungen, Freizeitangeboten und Einkaufsflächen in einem Zentrum folgt einer einfachen Logik, die impliziert, dass Kaufen inzwischen zum Mittelpunkt unserer Existenz geworden ist oder – freundlicher formuliert – dass wir inzwischen vollends im Zeitalter der Konsumgesellschaft angekommen sind. Im Hinblick auf Westside erklären die Architekten: „Das Programm mit gemischter Nutzung ist eine radikale Neuerfindung der Konzepte ‚Shopping‘, ‚Entertainment‘ und ‚Wohnen‘. Das unmittelbar über der Autobahn und mit direktem Anschluss an das Bahn- und Verkehrsnetz der Stadt positionierte Westside-Zentrum wurde als in sich geschlossenes Stadtviertel konzipiert." Das Konzept „Abgeschlossenheit" legt natürlich nahe, dass die „Bewohner" Westside im Grunde überhaupt nicht mehr verlassen müssen, ein wohl eher beunruhigender Gedanke. Libeskind konzipierte den Komplex so, dass er sich in die urbane Topografie fügt und fast so etwas wie ein „natürliches" Phänomen wird.

KAUFEN TUT GUT

Das Ausmaß an Konzentration und Größe, das sich mit Zentren wie MyZeil, dem Crystals oder Westside abzeichnet, ist zweifellos ein Indikator, dass der Einzelhandel – vielleicht sogar die Wirtschaft insgesamt – im Wachsen begriffen ist. So wie große Gruppen wie LVMH den Luxusgütermarkt dominieren, entwickeln sich Einkaufszentren gleichsam zu Allesfressern, um sich alle nur verfügbaren Dollars, Euros oder Yens in ihrer Reichweite einzuverleiben. Wie der Luftverkehr von immer größeren Firmen geprägt wird, denen einige wenige Billigairlines auf den Fersen sind, scheint auch der Einzelhandel dem Vorbild der guten alten Industriekartells nachzueifern – inklusive aller Folgen, die das für die Präsentation der Waren mit sich bringt. Obwohl Topdesigner wie die bereits genannten hin und wieder den Wunsch haben, eigene Bauten zu realisieren, sind sie ebenso in Komplexen wie dem Crystals zu finden, wo Firmen wie Louis Vuitton (das LV im Kürzel LVMH), Bulgari und Tiffany & Co. vertreten sind. Vielleicht ist anzumerken, dass Interventionen namhafter Architekten in großen Einkaufskomplexen keineswegs auf Europa oder die Vereinigten Staaten beschränkt sind. Das Londoner Büro Foreign Office Architects (FOA) etwa realisierte den 55 000 m² großen Shoppingkomplex Meydan im türkischen Ümraniye (2006–07, Seite 118). Zwar entspricht Meydan möglicherweise nicht den LEED® Gold-Standards, dennoch wurde das Zentrum mit besonderem Augenmerk auf Umweltbelange geplant. Kaufen tut gut – natürlich auch unserem Planeten!

17
Moatti et Rivière, Yves Saint Laurent,
Paris, France, 2008

17

Ein weiteres Beispiel für die zunehmende Verbreitung von Luxus-Einkaufscentern weltweit, die von namhaften Architekten gestaltet wurden, ist das Star Place (Kaohsiung Taiwan, 2006–08, Seite 356), ein Entwurf des Amsterdamer Büros UNStudio. Neben reichlich vertretenen räumlichen Aussparungen und stützenfreien Zonen – besonders gern eingesetzten Elementen der Architekten – lebt Star Place in erster Linie von der 51,3 m hohen Glasfassade, mit ihren „horizontal auskragenden, aluminiumbeschichteten Lamellen und vertikalen Glasfinnen, die ein changierendes Musterspiel erzeugen". Die Fassade lockt Besucher in den weitläufigen, über 37 000 m² großen Komplex und wurde so gestaltet, dass sie abends und nachts, wenn die meisten Anwohner einkaufen gehen, farbig leuchtet und weithin sichtbar ist. Die Architekten haben auch den gesamten Innenausbau mit größter Sorgfalt geplant, doch der Name „Star Place" verdankt sich besonders der Fassade.

ZWISCHEN LAGERHAUS UND BASAR

Räumliche Konzentration – wenn auch auf weniger „allesfressende" Weise als oben beschrieben – motiviert auch das Labels 2 (Berlin, 2008–09, Seite 166), ein Projekt der Schweizer Architekten HHF. Mit 6630 m² Gesamtfläche bietet Labels 2 Platz für 30 verschiedene Modemarken. Sicherlich mit der Absicht, dem Kunden das Gefühl zu vermitteln, hier besonders günstig einkaufen zu können, wurde Labels 2 in Anlehnung an das benachbarte Labels 1, das in einem alten Lagerhaus untergebracht ist. Vergleichbar, zumindest was die Kombination verschiedener Modemarken unter einem Dach betrifft, ist die Villa Moda (Manama, Bahrain, 2009, Seite 370) des renommierten niederländischen Designers Marcel Wanders. Das Center bringt verschiedenste Labels, von Comme des Garçons bis zu Martin Margiela, und darüber hinaus Designobjekte und Mode zusammen. Wanders erklärt: „Der Auftrag war einfach: sich vom Gewirr eines Basars inspirieren zu lassen und dies auf den Kontext luxuriöser Mode zu übertragen." Trotz der zunehmenden Globalisierung der Modewelt, geht es den Architekten und Designern bei der Gestaltung von Verkaufsräumen hier ganz offensichtlich darum, lokale Inspiration in ihre Überlegungen mit einfließen zu lassen. Die urbane Topografie Berns bei Libeskind oder die „Basar"-Atmosphäre bei Wanders sind Hinweise darauf, dass solche Aspekte eine Rolle in der immer enger werdenden Beziehung zwischen Stararchitekten beziehungsweise -designern und dem Einzelhandel spielen.

SCHMUCKSTÜCKE

Bei aller Aufmerksamkeit, die riesigen Luxus-Einkaufszentren geschenkt wird, mag man sich fragen, was aus jenen kleinen Juwelen des Einzelhandels geworden ist – den traditionellen kleinen Läden. Man fragt sich, ob die heutige Wirtschaftslage noch Ladengeschäfte wie den legendären Herrenausstatter Knize in Wien (Adolf Loos, 1913) zulässt. Obwohl der Druck durch die zunehmende Konzentration im Einzelhandel sicherlich auch Spuren bei Innenstadtläden wie Knize hinterlässt, gibt es doch eine Reihe von kürzlich entstandenen kleinen Läden und Boutiquen, die beweisen, welch erheblichen Einfluss ein guter Designer oder Architekt auf einen kleinen Raum haben kann. Der in Belgien geborene Designer Olivier Lempereur realisierte unlängst ein neues Ladengeschäft mit nur 25 m² Fläche für Pierre Hermé (Pierre Hermé Macarons & Chocolats, Paris, 2008, Seite 214) auf der Rue Cambon. Das Geschäft wird von dunklen Farben und farbigen Lichtakzenten im oberen Bereich geprägt, Elemente, die an die Farben der Makronen selbst und ihre Verpackung angelehnt sind. Selbst die Decke wurde in einem Schokoladenton gestrichen und auch die mattglänzende Bronzeoptik der Ladeneinrichtung knüpft an die Produktpalette an. Hier wird die Inti-

18

18
Vaillo + Irigaray Architects,
D Jewelry, Pamplona, Spain,
2006–07

mität des kleinen Raums eher betont als kaschiert. Die Makronenschachteln, von Parisern wie von Touristen geliebt, sind es wert, dass man hier warten muss. Die Kunden fühlen sich bestätigt in der Annahme, dass diese süßen Delikatessen etwas Kostbares und Rares sind – nicht nur von der bescheidenen Größe des Ladens, sondern natürlich auch wegen des Décors.

Im Grunde gestaltete Francesc Rifé – wie Olivier Lempereur Jahrgang 1969 – die erste einer Kette von Filialen für den Meisterbäcker Julio Blanco in Oviedo (Spanien, 2009, Seite 292) auf ähnliche Weise. Pomme Sucre hat eine Grundfläche von 70 m², verteilt auf zwei gleich große Etagen, wobei der eigentliche Verkaufsraum nur das Erdgeschoss in Anspruch nimmt. Der Designer findet seine Inspiration in den Hauptzutaten von Backwaren – Mehl, Eier und Kakao – die im Entwurf durch weißes Milchglas, gelben Kunstharz und Rauchglasspiegel vertreten sind, die an Schokolade erinnern. Das elegante, anspruchsvolle Design hebt sich von den Läden und Bauten der Nachbarschaft ab und signalisiert der potenziellen Kundschaft, dass dies keine gewöhnliche Bäckerei ist. Natürlich müssen die Produkte dem vom Designer geschaffenen Image entsprechen. In diesem Fall machen die Materialien und Farben der Bäckerei zweifellos deutlich, dass hier mit herausragender Qualität zu rechnen ist. Das Bündnis von Essen und Trinken und Design, das in Restaurants oft zu beobachten ist, findet sich ganz offensichtlich auch in jenem Bereich des Einzelhandels, der eher alltägliche Waren wie Brot oder Schokolade anbietet. In beiden genannten Fällen waren die Auftraggeber zweifellos überzeugt, dass es sich lohnt, etwas mehr in die Einrichtung der Ladenräume zu investieren, um ein Image zu definieren und betonen, das sich vom Durchschnitt abhebt und integraler Bestandteil des Marketingkonzepts ist.

Ein drittes Beispiel für einen vor kurzem entworfenen kleinen Verkaufsraum, einen Juwelier, ist in Pamplona zu finden (Joyeria D, Vaillo + Irigaray Arquitectos, 2006–07, Seite 364). Die Architekten schufen auf einer Fläche von nur 50 m² eine Atmosphäre, die an ein Schmuckkästchen erinnert, „geheimnisvoll, fremdartig, hohl und schwerelos, dabei zugleich orientalisch und barock". Mit starken, gewollt rohen Aluminiumplatten betonten sie den schmalen, tiefen Raum, und verstärkten so den Eindruck des Kostbaren. Obwohl so kleine Verkaufsräume schnell einfallslos oder beengt wirken können, ist bei Schmuck in dieser Preisklasse nicht damit zu rechnen, dass allzu viele Kunden zeitgleich im Laden sind. Und so geht die gewählte Strategie – den Eindruck zu vermitteln, einem Geheimnis auf der Spur zu sein – hier durchaus auf.

Bei allen drei Beispielen entschieden sich die Architekten beziehungsweise Designer für eine starke Identifizierung mit den fraglichen Produkten und den kleinen Räumlichkeiten, die ihnen zur Verfügung standen. In allen drei Fällen ist geradezu eine Symbiose mit den Produkten zu spüren, die großen Einkaufszentren wie denen in Las Vegas oder Istanbul fehlt. Dennoch geht es Architekten und Designern an beiden Enden des Spektrums darum, die jeweiligen Verkaufsräume aufzuwerten. Auch wenn sich in einigen Fällen die Kunden drängen, um neue Räumlichkeiten in Augenschein zu nehmen, ist es in den meisten Fällen zweifellos schwierig, die Rentabilität von gutem Design zu ermessen. Wieviele Makronen mehr verkauft Pierre Hermé, weil ein Designer wie Olivier Lempereur seine Ladenräume gestaltet hat? Die Antwort auf diese Frage ist in erster Linie subjektiv – dennoch sind die Ergebnisse offenbar überzeugend, schließlich entscheiden sich zahlreiche Marken weltweit, die Unterstützung der allerbesten Designer und Architekten in Anspruch zu nehmen.

EIN BLAUES HAUS FÜR DROOG

Besonders interessante Architektur im Einzelhandelssektor verbindet sich in letzter Zeit oft mit namhaften Designern, die sich mit dem Verkauf ihrer eigenen Produkte oder der Produkte befreundeter Designer befassen. Letzteres trifft zweifellos auf Projekte des Studio Makkink & Bey zu: der Architektin Rianne Makkink und dem renommierten Designer Jurgen Bey, die zugleich Ehe- und Geschäftspartner sind. Bey hatte eine Zeit lang für die niederländische Designgruppe Droog gearbeitet. Vor kurzem realisierten Makkink & Bey den Blueprint Store in Soho (New York, 2009, Seite 322) für Droog. Die Designer führen aus: „Die Vorgabe von Droog an Makkink & Bey lautete, ein Interieur zu gestalten, dass die Normen für die Gestaltung von Ladenräumen auf den Kopf stellt. Droog Design wollte einen Raum als Installation aus Elementen, die man kaufen kann. Unser Studio ging noch einen Schritt weiter und löste die Grenzen von Architektur, Ladeneinrichtung und Waren auf. Wir konzipierten eine Installation aus einer Vielzahl verschiedener Schichten – ein eigenständiges Innenleben." Zwar ist es in der Werbesprache des Einzelhandels durchaus üblich, zu Hyperbeln zu greifen, doch ist es fraglos keine Übertreibung, dass der Blueprint Store „die Normen für die Gestaltung von Ladenräumen auf den Kopf stellt". Das Konzept sieht vor, Teile der Ladeneinrichtung in maßgeschneiderten Versionen kaufen zu können, sodass der Kunde ein bestimmtes Design für einen spezifischen Standort „interpretieren" lassen kann. Obwohl die computergesteuerte Maßanfertigung von Konsumgütern bisher keine alltägliche Realität ist, ist vorstellbar, dass Blueprint zum Vorreiter für ein neuartiges Einzelhandelskonzept wird, das dem Kunden tatsächlich erlaubt, Objekte auszuwählen und zu personalisieren und sie mithilfe digitaler Techniken fertigen zu lassen.

INDUSTRIECHIC

Ein weiterer „Star" der zeitgenössischen Designszene, Tom Dixon, gestaltete die neuesten Geschäftsräume für das Modelabel Joseph (London, 2009, Seite 96). Dixon ist besonders für seine Möbelentwürfe und als Chefdesigner bei Habitat (seit 1998) bekannt. Er verlieh dem Joseph Store, trotz seiner Lage auf der alles andere als industriellen Old Bond Street, einen ausgesprochen industriellen Look. Dixon arbeitete mit Rauputz, unpoliertem Stein und Bühnenscheinwerfern, ganz offensichtlich mit der Absicht, für einen „absolut unerwarteten Neuzugang" in der traditionellen Londoner Einkaufsgegend zu sorgen. Könnte es sein, dass die „erwartungsgemäße" Strategie bei Luxusgütern – Räumlichkeiten zu schaffen, die ein gewisses Maß an Finesse vermitteln – langsam an ihre Grenzen stößt? Ein neuer Lösungsansatz ist, an solchen Orten stärker auf Industrie- beziehungsweise Lagerhausästhetik zu setzen. Diese Inspiration dürfte sich einem Großteil zeitgenössischer Architektur verdanken, etwa im Werk solcher Persönlichkeiten wie Rem Koolhaas.

Ingo Maurer, geboren 1932, ist der vermutlich international bekannteste Designer von Leuchten. Seine Entwürfe waren bereits in Museen in aller Welt zu sehen, dennoch ist sein Schaffensmittelpunkt stets München geblieben. Maurer entschied sich, sein 700 m² großes studioshowroomwerkstattatelier (München, 2008, Seite 260) in einem Industriegebäude zu eröffnen, das er bereits seit den 1970er-Jahren als Lager und Fertigungsstätte nutzt. Er behielt den industriellen Charakter der Räume bewusst bei, insbesondere im Untergeschoss. Dass Mauerers anspruchsvolle Leuchten mit dem Lagerhausflair kontrastieren, gefällt den Kunden, trifft jedoch auch darüber hinaus einen Nerv,

19

19
*Tom Dixon, Joseph Store
London, UK, 2009*

denn solche Strategien werden inzwischen weltweit eingesetzt. Ein auf der Hand liegender Vorteil des industriellen Ansatzes sind die geringen Kosten im Vergleich zu anspruchsvolleren Räumen. In Großstädten stehen Industrieflächen oft leer und sind weniger kostspielig als Ladenräume an den einschlägigen Einkaufsstraßen. Die potenzielle Schwierigkeit bei dieser Strategie ist natürlich, dass der Bekanntheitsgrad des Geschäfts hoch genug sein muss, um Kunden in Gegenden zu ziehen, die ihnen unbekannt sind. Ingo Maurer hat mit diesem Problem nicht zu kämpfen, doch andere, weniger prominente Einzelhändler müssen sich dieser Frage stellen.

RÖCKE IM WIND

Es gab eine Zeit, da war anspruchsvolle Architektur allein staatlichen oder kirchlichen Institutionen vorbehalten oder denjenigen, die über ausreichend finanzielle Mittel verfügten, um sich Schlösser zu bauen. Doch in den vergangenen Jahrzehnten haben sich auch Museen und Firmenzentralen in die oberste Liga beeindruckender Bauten eingereiht. In diesem Reigen architektonischer Wunder sind Einzelhandelsbauten ohne Frage Nachzügler und vielleicht auch die am wenigsten selbstbewussten. Mehr noch als Büroflächen müssen Einzelhandelsflächen profitabel sein. Doch nur selten wird der Prestigegewinn einkalkuliert, der entsteht, wenn ein berühmter Architekt engagiert wird. Allerdings: Wie zahlreiche Beispiele in diesem Buch belegen, hat die zeitgenössische Architektur im Einzelhandel an Dynamik gewonnen. Vielleicht verdankt sich diese Sicherheit einer neuen Welt, in der Kommerz und Einzelhandel inzwischen von globalerer Reichweite und Bedeutung sind als ein einzelnes Land oder Glaubenssystem. Es ist der Aufstieg eines vorbehaltlosen Konsumverhaltens, der sich als Antrieb unserer heutigen Einzelhandelsarchitektur erweist. Wo weitläufige Einkaufszentren wie autonome Städte wirken, mit Freizeitangeboten, Wohnraum und Gastronomie in unmittelbarer Reichweite, kann die Architektur nicht weit sein. Zweifellos ist sie oft dort am innovativsten, wo sie Interessen von Auftraggebern vertritt, die über die nötigen Mittel verfügen, ihre Träume zu realisieren. Trotz der faszinierenden Großprojekte in diesem Band – Einkaufszentren in Taiwan oder Las Vegas – ist die Architektur des Einzelhandels ohne Frage eines der flüchtigsten Phänomene der gebauten Welt, in der Nutzung oder Namen immer öfter wechseln. Diese Flüchtigkeit steigert die Nachfrage nach neuer Innenausstattung oder gar neuen Bauten. In gewisser Weise kommt diese Nachfrage dem Wunsch zeitgenössischer Architekten entgegen, sich ganz auf die dynamische, fließende Atmosphäre unserer Zeit einzulassen. Während die Architektur mitunter wünscht, sie könnte sich von ihrem eher gesetzten, mitunter schwerfälligen Image lösen, trifft sie nun auf den Einzelhandel, der sich oft mehr Langlebigkeit wünscht, als ein hübscher Rock im Wind verspricht. Die einst „kleinen" Kaufleute beanspruchen einen immer wichtigeren Platz in unserer Gesellschaft und sind in gewisser Weise sogar zu ihrem Motor geworden. So ist es kaum überraschend, dass Designer und Architekten in einen Bereich strömen, der im Grunde nur wachsen kann. Ob Rezession oder Boom – selbst bei sich wandelnden Prioritäten und Budgets – der Einzelhandel ist ein Phänomen von Dauer, in deren Dienst sich die Architektur nur zu gern stellt.

Philip Jodidio, Grimentz, Schweiz, 1. März 2010

INTRODUCTION

LE SHOPPING, C'EST CE QU'IL VOUS FAUT !

Le shopping se définit aujourd'hui comme l'activité qui consiste à se rendre dans des magasins, des boutiques et des centres commerciaux, pour regarder et acheter. Le terme de détail, comme dans commerce de détail, vient du verbe détailler, couper en morceaux. En économie de la consommation, c'est vendre en petites quantités au consommateur final, par opposition au commerce de gros. Des architectes réputés se sont depuis longtemps intéressé à la mise en avant - ou à la mise en scène - de la vente au détail. L'immeuble Carson Pirie Scott and Company de Louis Sullivan à Chicago (1899) sur State Street est à lui seul une anthologie de la présence urbaine de l'architecture commerciale. Les grands magasins du GUM à Moscou, édifiés entre 1890 et 1893 par Alexander Pomerantsev et Vladimir Shukoff, étirent leur façade de 242 mètres de long sur la Place Rouge, face au Kremlin. Même au temps des soviets, alors que ses rayonnages étaient très mal achalandés, le GUM symbolisait le commerce face au cœur du pouvoir. Plus récemment, des boutiques sensiblement plus petites ont fait l'objet d'interventions remarquables de la part d'architectes aussi mythiques que Carlo Scarpa, dont la restructuration du showroom Olivetti, place Saint-Marc à Venise (1957–58), fut récemment citée comme une source d'inspiration de la rénovation de la Punta della Dogana (Fondation François Pinault, Venise, 2009) par Tadao Ando. En fait, on pourrait penser aujourd'hui que les musées d'art seulement ont bénéficié des interventions des vedettes de l'architecture, plus que les points de vente. Des quartiers entiers de grandes villes se remplissent de nouveaux immeubles étincelants, exclusivement consacrés à l'art de la vente de vêtements et d'autres accessoires. Ainsi, à Tokyo, entre Minami Aoyama et Omotesando en direction d'Harajuku, les immeubles de Tadao Ando (Collezione, et d'autres), SANAA (Christian Dior), Kengo Kuma (LVMH), Herzog & de Meuron (Prada) et Toyo Ito (TOD'S) rivalisent avec le quartier de Ginza où Renzo Piano (Hermès) voisine avec Massimiliano Fuksas (Armani). Mais l'architecture commerciale n'est pas uniquement confiée à des architectes. Des designers de renom comme Shiro Kuramata (1934–91), qui a créé des boutiques pour Issey Miyake à Paris, Tokyo et New York, ont ouvert la voie à la nouvelle vague actuelle de boutiques et de magasins.

Des personnalités comme Tom Dixon, Arne Quinze, Jurgen Bey ou Tokujin Yoshioka, plus connus comme designers qu'architectes, sont à l'origine de quelques-uns des plus extraordinaires lieux de vente actuels. L'architecture commerciale dépasse ainsi largement les frontières de l'architecture en général pour intégrer ce que l'on pourrait appeler de l'architecture intérieure, mais qui couvre également à l'évidence le design. Certains architectes ou designers qui travaillent régulièrement pour la même marque, participent à la définition ou la redéfinition de celles-ci. Par exemple, l'étonnant Prada Store à l'angle de Broadway et de Prince Street à Manhattan (1999–2001), ancien siège du Guggenheim Soho, était une tentative de OMA*AMO/Rem Koolhaas de repenser l'image d'une entreprise qui semblait un peu trop sage. Koolhaas a poursuivi sa collaboration avec Prada au cours de ces dernières années et a créé des structures étonnantes comme le Prada Transformer à Séoul (2008–09). D'autres personnalités très créatives comme Rei Kawakubo (Comme des Garçons) se sont beaucoup impliquées dans la concep-tion de leurs points de vente, faisant appel à des architectes comme Future Systems pour les façades ou les entrées de leurs magasins de Chelsea ou de Minami Aoyama, mais aussi à des artistes et des designers.

PRINCESS ZAHA ET SAINT KARL

S'il est pertinent d'établir une distinction entre une opération architecturale d'envergure comme un centre commercial et l'aménagement intérieur d'une boutique, *Shopping Architecture Now!* s'intéresse à la manière dont les barrières traditionnelles entre ces disciplines semblent se dissoudre dans le commerce de détail. Célèbre designer de luminaires, Ingo Maurer, a ainsi créé son propre magasin à Munich (208, page 260) sans l'assistance d'un architecte. La référence à l'architecture muséale, autre domaine sur lequel se concentrent aujourd'hui les architectes de renom, n'est peut-être pas superficielle. Il est clair que les musées et les magasins de marques attirent vers eux d'importants moyens financiers et cherchent à capter des « clients ». Le terme de « client » sera jugé peu flatteur par les musées, mais, depuis quelques années déjà, même les grandes institutions muséales étatiques de la vieille Europe ont plongé dans le marketing commercial. Un T-shirt, un catalogue ou un livre sur Herzog & de Meuron font maintenant partie des activités commerciales de la Tate Modern, autant que les billets d'entrée. Les points de vente eux-mêmes se sont éloignés de la typologie de la « boîte » longtemps adoptée par les boutiques, comme le montre le récent Mobile Art, Chanel Contemporary Art Container (divers lieux, 2007–) de Zaha Hadid, qui place la créativité de Karl Lagerfeld à égalité avec celle d'artistes réputés. Si les personnalités de la création actuelle étaient aussi vénérées que dans le passé, Zaha Hadid serait certainement une princesse et Karl, toujours très vivant, une sorte de saint.

LES TEMPLES D'UN ORDRE NOUVEAU

La crise économique, qui a débuté en 2008, a provoqué de multiples dommages dans le monde de la vente, mais comme ce livre le démontre, des boutiques et des magasins conçus par les plus grands créateurs continuent à surgir chaque jour. La vente de biens au consommateur final est aujourd'hui au cœur même du système économique du monde développé. Ce n'est pas par accident que beaucoup des points de vente les plus spectaculaires publiés ici sont situés dans de grandes villes, de Los Angeles à Tokyo. Ils ouvrent là où est l'argent, là où l'on vend. La solution à la sortie de crise est, nous dit-on, dans la « consommation », et c'est précisément la tâche du commerce de détail. À un certain moment, les critiques se demandaient si les musées n'avaient pas remplacé les églises dans leur fonction culturelle. Dans le monde globalisé et pragmatique d'aujourd'hui, les temples de l'ordre nouveau seraient-ils Dior, Prada, Fauchon ou Chanel ? Même les marques destinées au plus grand public comme l'entreprise japonaise Uniqlo jugent bon de faire appel à des designers connus pour conquérir leur marché. Le commerce est-il une nouvelle religion, ou un nouveau champ de bataille ? Un peu des deux, sans doute, et l'architecture se situe juste à la jonction.

ADJAYE ET BOATENG SUR SAVILE ROW

Aujourd'hui londonien, l'architecte David Adjaye a déjà fait preuve d'une souplesse et d'une diversité considérables dans son travail et il n'est donc pas surprenant qu'il se soit intéressé à l'architecture de la distribution. Ses deux projets récents publiés ici, (page 52 le magasin amiral d'Ozwald Boateng, Londres, 2007, page 46, et le showroom Kvadrat, Londres, 2008–09), visent des objectifs et une clientèle différents. Kvadrat, fabricant danois de revêtements textiles pour meubles, murs et plafonds, souhaitait disposer d'un lieu non seulement pour

20
Studio Arne Quinze (SAQ),
Ferrer, Nieuwpoort-Bad,
Belgium, 2008

20

présenter sa gamme mais aussi faire des tests, accueillir des discussions de groupe et tenir des expositions. Comme l'architecture commerciale remet de plus en plus souvent en cause les limites traditionnelles entre architecture et design, beaucoup de ces nouveaux lieux de vente s'efforcent de remplir un rôle diversifié pour maintenir un certain niveau d'activité, même lorsque les clients se font rares. Le magasin Ozwald Boateng semble plus traditionnel dans son concept, bien que l'architecte l'ait conçu comme une collection de boutiques dans un magasin plus vaste, chacune consacrée à une des activités de la marque. Ozwald Boateng, né à Londres en 1968, est un tailleur autodidacte, devenu directeur de création de la ligne homme de Givenchy (2004–07). Il est l'une des stars du milieu de la mode londonien, ce qui signifie que son association avec Adjaye avait tout pour attirer l'attention des médias. Selon David Adjaye : « Le concept et la stratégie de conception ont été de se confronter à l'orientation contemporaine et muséale récemment prise par la mode. Plutôt qu'un simple endroit où acheter des vêtements, le magasin est un lieu d'expériences de séduction variées, à travers des textures et des émotions, dans lequel toute une gamme de rencontres, de types anciens ou nouveaux, peuvent se dérouler. »

David Adjaye, né en 1966 à Dar es-Salam en Tanzanie, a fait ses études au Royal College of Art à Londres et travaillé chez David Chipperfield et Eduardo Souto de Moura avant d'ouvrir sa propre agence à Londres en 2000. À travers des réalisations comme le Centre Nobel de la Paix (Oslo, 2002–05), le Musée d'art contemporain de Denver (Denver, Colorado, 2004–07) ou le Musée national de l'histoire et de la culture afro-américaines (Smithsonian Institution, Washington, en chantier–2015), il est devenu l'une des vedettes montantes de l'architecture contemporaine. Son travail sur les magasins Ozwald Boateng et Kvadrat est un témoignage de l'importance actuelle prise par l'architecture commerciale et de la relation symbiotique que beaucoup de marques de créateurs ont développée avec de grands architectes ou designers.

FAUCHON OPTE POUR LE FUCHSIA, APPLE POUR LA TRANSPARENCE

Les relations entre les grands designers et les marques célèbres s'étendent à tous les secteurs du commerce, du moins ceux que l'on peut remarquer dans les élégants quartiers de shopping des grandes villes. Fauchon, la grande épicerie parisienne, a fait appel à Christian Biecher pour rénover ses magasins, qui, bien que débordant toujours de merveilleux produits, avaient besoin d'être remis au goût du jour. Biecher a travaillé, entre autres interventions, sur les points de vente de Pékin et de Paris (page 62). Imaginant une palette de couleurs surprenantes – de l'or au fuchsia –, il a déployé une multiplicité de matériaux comme le bois, le bambou et le cuir, qui rappellent non seulement les différents aspects des boutiques Fauchon, mais aussi la diversité géographique de ses produits. Le fuchsia est comme un « fil électrique » qui relie les différentes parties des magasins, et ceux-ci entre eux. Christian Biecher démontre ici qu'une marque, aussi ancienne et respectée soit-elle, peut être modernisée avec succès.

Être une marque ancienne n'est évidemment pas le problème d'Apple, le fabricant d'ordinateur qui s'est imposé à travers les iPods, iPhones, iPads et toute la panoplie du numérique. Au contraire, l'extrême qualité du design des produits Apple l'oblige en quelque sorte à donner à chacune de ses boutiques une présence architecturale en accord avec la philosophie de Steven Jobs, le fondateur de l'entreprise.

Les architectes de Bohlin Cywinski Jackson ont imposé la présence de la marque à Manhattan à travers deux boutiques récentes, l'une sur la Cinquième Avenue (767 Fifth Avenue, New York, 2003–06), l'autre dans l'Upper West Side (2008–09, page 70). Ces points de vente et d'information partagent une conception relativement simple reposant sur un principe de transparence qui attire les foules, tout en sachant à un certain moment laisser aux produits toute leur place. La légèreté de cette architecture et sa modernité patente sont bien adaptées à la vente des produits Apple, comme le prouve d'ailleurs la poursuite de la relation entre Bohlin Cywinski Jackson et la firme de Cupertino.

ROTATION ACCÉLÉRÉE CHEZ YOHJI

Même les projets architecturaux les plus ambitieux de l'univers de la mode peuvent connaître une durée d'existence aussi courte que les vêtements qu'ils mettent en valeur. Le magasin Yohji Yamamoto (New York, 2007–08, page 180) sur Gansevoort Street dans le quartier du Meatpacking a été le premier chantier du jeune et très prometteur architecte japonais Junya Ishigami. Il a découpé en deux un bâtiment existant et a créé un showroom triangulaire extrêmement curieux, non loin des galeries de Chelsea. L'œuvre du styliste Yamamoto, depuis toujours à l'avant-garde de la mode, est proche de l'univers de l'art, mais sa créativité et celle d'Ishigami n'ont pas suffi à les protéger des difficultés économiques apparues depuis l'ouverture de ce point de vente. La boutique a fermé début 2010 et n'aura guère duré plus qu'un cycle des saisons de la mode.

La nature très éphémère de la relation entre l'architecture et la distribution pourrait bien être le moteur de la créativité déployée dans ce secteur. Certaines installations jouent de cette ambiguïté. C'est le cas du magasin temporaire de Dr. Martens (Londres, 2009, page 76), une installation de 180 mètres carrés conçue par l'agence Campaign en collaboration avec le spécialiste des marques Fresh. Les chaussures Dr. Martens sont une marque très connue, une sorte « d'icône de la contre-culture », comme l'explique Campaign. Leur projet, qui utilise l'image d'un entrepôt de stockage à l'aide de projecteurs de chantier, des palettes de chargement, d'objets emballés et d'un très grand rideau de PVC jaune, a été mis en place en six jours à peine. Plutôt que d'essayer de faire passer des produits essentiellement éphémères pour plus durables qu'ils ne le sont, la marque a joué sur l'image brute et décontractée qui fait partie de sa personnalité.

BLOWING IN THE WIND

Shopping Architecture Now! n'évoque pas seulement ce qui est traditionnellement qualifié d'architecture, car le secteur du commerce de détail encourage précisément des installations et des présentations à courte durée de vie. Deux interventions montrent comment des vitrines, confiées à des designers créatifs, peuvent exercer un impact réel sur le passant et finalement sur le chiffre d'affaires du magasin. La première a été imaginée par l'agence allemande Liganova pour la marque Diesel, d'abord en Allemagne en 2009, puis dans d'autres pays. Ces vitrines interactives (Berlin, page 240) utilisent une technologie de repérage des mouvements qui permet aux passants d'influer sur ce qui se trouve dans la vitrine. Le client potentiel peut « déplacer des objets virtuels sur un écran en bougeant ses mains et ses bras, influencer des objets et des actions dans la vitrine ». Des transducteurs sonores permettent d'accompagner ces interventions d'une bande sonore appropriée. Au lieu de simplement regarder, le passant entre ainsi en contact actif avec la marque.

*21
Sinato, Duras Ambient Funabashi,
Funabashi, Chiba, Japan, 2008*

21

L'installation d'une vitrine de la maison Hermès à Tokyo (2009, page 402) par le fameux designer Tokujin Yoshioka relève d'une approche beaucoup plus esthétique et distanciée autour d'une femme soufflant légèrement sur un carré Hermès. Yoshioka parle « d'humour » pour décrire cette vitrine, mais il s'agit bien d'un jeu interactif entre la vidéo et le monde « réel », technique souvent utilisée dans l'art contemporain. Pas aussi proactive que les vitrines Diesel de Liganova, cette présentation est sans doute mieux adaptée à la grande marque de luxe. Sans remettre en question la longévité d'un carré Hermès, Yoshioka le met en mouvement dans un contexte artistique qui brouille les frontières entre le réel et l'imaginaire.

REM SUR LE PODIUM

Comme on le sait, le grand événement périodique de l'univers de la mode est la présentation quasi chorégraphiée de chaque collection. Bien que ce ne soit pas à strictement parler un domaine dans lequel l'architecture ait beaucoup à dire, des marques comme Prada n'ont pas hésité à faire appel à des intervenants célèbres, dont OMA*AMO/Koolhaas, pour propulser leurs défilés à des niveaux artistiques ou architecturaux rarement observés. OMA*AMO a organisé les défilés de mode féminine et masculine printemps/été 2010 (Fondazione Prada, Milan, 2009, page 11) dans le cadre de sa longue relation avec la marque illustrée par le récent Prada Transformer. En intitulant le défilé homme « Passage secret, ou l'amour du vide », les architectes et les stylistes donnaient d'emblée le ton en introduisant des concepts par ailleurs courants en architecture contemporaine. Un podium rectiligne aménagé entre un mur existant et un autre – spécialement construit, de sept mètres de haut, recouvert de papier peint montrant des conversations entre des personnages de film – illustrait l'interpénétration de la mode, du cinéma et de l'architecture en un même espace, pour suggérer que les hommes qui portent du Prada sont de l'étoffe dont on fait les légendes. Le défilé femme comprenait un « mur abstrait » sur lequel des projections de corridors imaginaires évoquaient « des espaces mentaux combinant les embrasures de portes classiques surdécorées des grands hôtels, des néons de tonalités acides, des atmosphères de lieux trash ou des images hypercolorées de plages envahies par la foule », pour produire « une succession de cadres indéfinissables ».

L'interdépendance de l'architecture et de la mode se manifeste au point de rencontre de deux préoccupations très réelles. Du point de vue de la marque, le changement est nécessaire puisqu'il provoque de nouvelles ventes, même si les grands labels de luxe cherchent à projeter une image d'intemporalité qui encourage la fidélité de la clientèle. D'un autre côté, les architectes sont confrontés avec la durabilité même de leurs réalisations. Un bâtiment possède une présence indéniable qui, porté au meilleur de lui-même, illustre précisément cette intemporalité recherchée par Prada ou Chanel. L'architecte comme le styliste de mode exagèrent cet aspect de longévité, en particulier dans un monde rythmé par une consommation effrénée, mais arrivent cependant – comme dans le cas de Prada et d'OMA – à trouver un terrain d'entente pour leur plus grande satisfaction mutuelle.

CONCRÈTEMENT COMMERCIAL

Domaine partiellement abordé dans ce volume (voir *Architecture Now! Restaurants & Bars*), le secteur des bars et des restaurants est l'un des terrains de rencontre les plus actifs entre le commerce, l'architecture et le design. L'agence d'Amsterdam Concrete Architectural As-

22

23

22 + 23
OMA*AMO/Rem Koolhaas, Prada
Transformer, Seoul, South Korea,
2008–09

sociates s'est fait une réputation remarquée à travers des projets comme le restaurant Pearls & Caviar (Abou Dhabi, EAU, 2008), le salon VIP de l'aéroport de Schiphol (Amsterdam, 2008), le Supperclub (Singapour, 2008) et le restaurant De Bijenkorf Kitchen (Amsterdam, 2008). La formation de Rob Wagemans, qui dirige Concrete, explique en partie le succès de cette agence dans des projets qui exigent une excellente expertise architecturale. Wagemans a étudié l'architecture à Amsterdam et à Utrecht et achevé ses études par un mastère d'architecture intérieure. L'une de ses récentes réalisations, la Coffee Company Prinsenhof (La Haye, 2008, page 92), installée dans l'atrium d'un immeuble de bureaux, ne mesure que 60 mètres carrés. Cette *coffee shop* est contenue dans une cage d'acier et d'acajou qui se soulève de 2,5 mètres en appuyant sur un bouton déclenchant des vérins hydrauliques. Comme l'explique Wagemans : « La Coffee Company fait alors littéralement partie de l'atrium. Le soir, la cage redescend pour fermer la boutique. » Cette combinaison de design efficace et de bonne architecture est un exemple de ce que des créateurs de talent peuvent apporter à l'univers du commerce de détail, en dépassant l'idée d'un simple espace nécessaire à l'activité de la vente.

Une personnalité plus jeune et bien moins connue que Wagemans est le Français Jean-Guillaume Mathiaut, qui a déjà franchi les frontières entre l'architecture et le design. Avant d'obtenir son diplôme d'architecte en 1999, il a travaillé pour l'agence d'architecture François & Lewis (Paris, 1993–98), puis est devenu directeur artistique pour les Galeries Lafayette (Paris, 2000–05) où il a organisé des expositions avec Marcel Wanders, Jurgen Bey, Paul Smith, Jakob + MacFarlane et Ingo Maurer. Il a créé son agence, Édith Édition, en 2007, et conçu le dernier magasin d'Issey Miyake à Paris (2008, page 102) dans une cour intérieure de la rue Royale. Pour ce projet, il a imaginé des éléments monolithiques en Corian et éclairé cet espace assez difficile par une entrée en verre de style minimaliste. À l'intérieur, l'atmosphère s'inspire d'une carrière ou d'un atelier, selon Mathiaut, mais laisse de la place pour des installations artistiques ou de design. Issey Miyake, qui l'a choisi, est connu pour son apport créatif qui va souvent au-delà de la mode pour toucher à l'art. Le projet de Mathiaut pour le magasin de la rue Royale s'est emparé du caractère de la marque et en a « exagéré la situation », comme il l'explique.

QUAND L'ART FRAPPE À LA PORTE

L'idée de franchir les barrières est précisément au cœur du récent magasin amiral de Balenciaga à Londres (2008, page 144). Le couturier Nicolas Ghesquière, qui a travaillé avec Jean-Paul Gaultier et Thierry Mugler avant d'entrer chez Balenciaga en 1997, est aujourd'hui l'une des « superstars » de sa profession. La haute couture semble avoir le besoin de s'associer avec des œuvres d'art, de design et d'architecture tout aussi exceptionnelles, ce qui a précisément été la volonté de Ghesquière lorsqu'il a fait appel à l'artiste Dominique Gonzalez-Foerster, à l'architecte Martial Galfione et au designer d'éclairage Benoit Lalloz pour intervenir sur quelques-uns des magasins Balenciaga. Des écrans vidéo plasma et un programme musical spécialement composé pour l'espace par Christophe Van Huffel signalent ce magasin londonien, le résultat de cette collaboration inhabituelle étant intéressant en soi et au-delà. Ce n'est ni vraiment une œuvre d'art, ni une réalisation d'architecture ou de design pur, mais plutôt un subtil mélange qui rend hommage au style Balenciaga. Quoiqu'un peu différent, ce travail en commun rappelle certaines œuvres iconiques du XXᵉ siècle comme le café l'Aubette à Strasbourg (1927). Sophie Taeuber-Arp, Jean

Arp et Theo van Doesburg avaient travaillé ensemble sur ce complexe qui comprenait un salon de thé, plusieurs bars, des salles de réunions, une salle de bal, un night-club en sous-sol et un cinéma. Les trois participants étaient surtout connus pour leur œuvre artistique, mais Theo van Doesburg (1883–1931), fondateur et un des principaux animateurs du mouvement De Stijl, intervenait aussi comme peintre, écrivain, poète et architecte. Malgré son importance et l'exemplarité de cette collaboration artistique, l'Aubette, achevée en 1928, fut presque immédiatement modifiée pour ne pas avoir réussi à convaincre la clientèle du café. Dominique Gonzalez-Foerster, qui par coïncidence est née à Strasbourg, est surtout connue comme vidéaste, mais crée des installations qui ont des répercussions directes sur l'espace. Un magasin Balenciaga ne pourrait-il être notre équivalent contemporain de l'Aubette ?

MAGASINS AMIRAUX DE LA MODE

De même que Prada s'est associée à un certain nombre d'architectes célèbres, de Herzog & de Meuron à Rem Koolhaas, d'autres marques ont elles aussi compris qu'elles pouvaient gagner à engager de grands architectes ou designers pour imaginer leurs nouveaux lieux de vente. Phillip Lim est un styliste de mode américain d'origine chinoise, qui a remporté, en 2007, le prix Swarovski de la mode féminine décerné par le Conseil des stylistes de mode américains pour le travail réalisé pour sa marque, 3.1 Phillip Lim. Lim n'a pas appelé un prix Pritzker, mais a certainement su faire parler de lui par ses récents magasins de New York, Los Angeles et Séoul. Le premier, à New York (page 12), œuvre de Tacklebox LLC, a été achevé en 2007, tandis que le second à Los Angeles (2007–08, page 278) est signé d'une équipe comprenant Dominic Leong, PARA-Project et l'Office Giancarlo Valle. Le troisième, ouvert à Séoul en 2009 (page 220), est dû à Leong Leong Architects. Le plus grand des trois mesure 543 mètres carrés et a été aménagé dans un immeuble de bureaux et de commerces existant. Les architectes ont choisi des matériaux « tactiles » – comme un plancher en chêne –, ce qui convient certainement à un magasin de mode. Les murs de briques passés à la chaux et le sol en sa pin de Douglas patiné de la boutique new-yorkaise confirment l'option d'un mix entre la modernité – dans le choix des architectes et de certains éléments de leur travail – et l'idée de conserver des matériaux ou des volumes préexistants. Il s'agit ici de rechercher une continuité dans une activité davantage vouée aux ruptures avec la tradition qu'à la quête de permanence. L'architecture contemporaine qui est souvent confrontée à des clients ou des usages éphémères répond par la « flexibilité », traduite ici plutôt dans un concept de « changement ».

L'INAMOVIBLE GIORGIO

Tout ceci ne veut pas dire que l'architecture sous sa forme construite traditionnelle ne joue pas un rôle important dans le commerce de détail, comme le montrent deux réalisations de l'architecte italien Massimiliano Fuksas pour le couturier Giorgio Armani. Un certain nombre de marques très connues ont édifié leurs propres immeubles à Tokyo dans les quartiers de Ginza, d'Omotesando ou de Minami-Aoyama, mais la tour Ginza de douze niveaux réalisée pour Armani (Tokyo, 2005–07, page 13) se singularise au sein de ce club d'ambitieux. Par son importance, 7370 mètres carrés de surfaces de planchers, et sa conception qui englobe l'intérieur comme l'extérieur, cet immeuble exprime le style et l'esprit de la production d'Armani, y compris dans le restaurant qui occupe le onzième et douzième niveau et le salon « Privé ». Le mes-

24

24
*Leong Leong, 3.1 Phillip Lim Flagship
Store, Seoul, South Korea, 2009*

sage tourne entièrement autour de d'exclusivité et de la qualité. Un bâtiment de ces dimensions dans l'un des quartiers les plus chers du monde en dit également beaucoup sur la solidité et la pérennité de l'empire Armani.

Une seconde intervention de Fuksas pour Armani, mais à New York cette fois (Emporio Armani Fifth Avenue, 2009, page 130), est peut-être encore plus surprenante, quoique moins ambitieuse que la tour tokyoïte. Implanté dans un immeuble existant, ce magasin mesure 2800 mètres carrés répartis sur quatre niveaux, volume généreux, même pour la Cinquième Avenue. Comme à Tokyo, Giorgio Armani a cherché et trouvé pour cette implantation un des sites les plus prestigieux, autre indication de la puissance et de la place de la marque dans l'univers de la mode. Massimiliano et Doriana Fuksas ont créé un très étonnant escalier en acier laminé et plastique qui semble occuper le centre des lieux à la manière d'un énorme vortex. Cet élément plastique va au-delà des notions classiques d'efficacité dans l'utilisation de l'espace pour se transformer en composant architectural majeur. Comme les vêtements fluides d'Armani, il semble évoluer à travers l'immeuble entraînant les clients dans un tourbillon de formes de géométrie complexe. Si Fuksas n'a pas conçu l'ensemble de l'immeuble, son intervention architecturale vient occuper le premier plan dans ce concept de magasin. On pourrait féliciter l'architecte et son client d'avoir osé la différence et la rupture avec le moule habituel de « l'efficacité spatiale ». Le résultat est là, spatialement réussi, mais il reste à voir s'il est aussi satisfaisant en termes de ventes.

CATHÉDRALES DE CRISTAL

Massimiliano et Doriana Fuksas se sont également intéressés à un autre domaine de la distribution qui est par nature plus proche des types architecturaux traditionnels : le centre commercial. Leur massif MyZeil de 78 000 mètres carrés (Francfort, 2009, page 138) comprend un centre commercial, un cinéma, un centre de remise en forme, un hôtel, des salles de réunions, des bureaux et des parkings. Tout autour, une centaine de magasins font de ce lieu une sorte de « destination » qui peut occuper les visiteurs pendant toute une journée. Ce type d'espace multitâche est assez répandu dans des régions comme les pays du golfe Persique où les températures extérieures font que l'on a plaisir à rester dans un même complexe pour faire ses courses, se distraire et manger. L'architecte a mis l'accent sur la fluidité de l'espace, ce qui là encore est une preuve que les barrières, non seulement entre l'architecture et le design, mais aussi entre différentes formes de commerce, sont peut-être en cours de dissolution, grâce à des interventions comme celle de Fuksas.

Un autre grand architecte international, l'Américain d'origine polonaise Daniel Libeskind a également abordé le problème de l'architecture du commerce de détail avec générosité. Deux de ses récents projets sont publiés dans cet ouvrage. Gagnant du concours de 2003 pour la reconstruction du site du World Trade Center à New York, opération dont il s'est progressivement retiré, Libeskind a réalisé le très remarqué Musée juif de Berlin (1989–2001), l'Imperial War Museum North à Manchester (2001), les extensions du Denver Art Museum (Colorado, 2006) et du Royal Ontario Museum à Toronto (2007). Il a donc davantage marqué l'actualité architecturale par ses interventions dans le domaine des musées que dans celui du commerce, mais ceci est en train de changer. Son Crystals à CityCenter, un complexe de

46 000 mètres carrés pour Las Vegas (2006–09, page 234), fait partie du projet encore plus vaste du MGM Mirage CityCenter. Comme son nom l'implique, le Crystals évoque une forme souvent présente dans les projets de Libeskind. « La façade habillée de verre et de métal signale bien à l'avance aux visiteurs que Crystals n'est pas un environnement classique de centre commercial », précise l'agence. L'architecte n'a pas été chargé des aménagements intérieurs du complexe et l'ensemble bénéficie, pour son noyau central et sa coque, d'une certification LEED® « Or » accordée par le US Green Building Council, ce qui en fait la plus grande installation commerciale à recevoir ce label environnemental. Comme pour beaucoup de projets en cours à Dubaï par exemple, le CityCenter a été l'objet de multiples spéculations sur sa viabilité en période de crise. *The Sunday Times*, dans un article décapant sur CityCenter (« Vegas mise 9 milliards de dollars sur le rouge », 28 février 2010) écrivait même : « Rien, même le Burj Khalifa à Dubaï, l'immeuble le plus haut du monde, n'évoque davantage le phénomène de "bulle" ». Comme par hasard, le cheik Mohammed bin Rashid Al Maktoum, le souverain de Dubaï, est l'un des principaux investisseurs dans ce projet. C'est évidemment l'environnement économique global qui déterminera au final le succès ou l'échec de cette ambitieuse entreprise, mais la réputation de l'architecture d'avant-garde dans le secteur du commerce risque de souffrir si les dés ont été jetés trop loin.

Un an plus tôt, Daniel Libeskind avait achevé un autre projet, le centre commercial et de loisirs Westside à Berne (Suisse, 2005–09, page 226), qui regroupe 55 boutiques, 10 restaurants et bars, un hôtel, un multiplexe de salles de cinéma, un parc aquatique couvert, un centre sportif et des logements. Situé au-dessus de l'une des principales voies d'accès à la capitale suisse (l'autoroute A1), le Westside défie lui aussi les idées reçues sur le shopping, en mélangeant divertissements, logements et magasins. Les parcs d'attractions, les complexes multisalles de cinéma et les hôtels étaient naguère des installations généralement autonomes, mais il peut être intéressant de concentrer ces activités pour proposer aux consommateurs une offre plus complète. La réunion d'activités diverses dans le même ensemble implique une logique très simple qui veut que la consommation soit au centre de l'existence ou, sous une forme moins critique, que nous soyons maintenant totalement plongés dans l'ère de la consommation. Dans le cas du Westside, l'architecte a expliqué : « Ce programme mixte réinvente radicalement le concept de shopping, de divertissement et de vie. Implanté directement au-dessus de l'autoroute et en lien direct avec le réseau de trains et de transports en commun de la ville, Westside a été conçu comme un quartier fermé. » Cette notion de fermeture suggère que les « résidants » pourraient n'avoir jamais besoin de quitter le quartier, pensée assez préoccupante en soi. Libeskind a adapté le complexe à la topographie urbaine pour en faire une sorte de phénomène « naturel ». Dans la mesure du possible.

LE SHOPPING, C'EST CE QU'IL VOUS FAUT !

Le niveau de concentration et la taille observés dans MyZeil, Crystals ou Westside est certainement un indicateur de l'une des caractéristiques de plus en plus importantes du commerce de détail et de l'économie dans son ensemble. De même que des groupes géants comme LVMH dominent le marché des produits de luxe, les centres commerciaux adoptent logiquement une attitude littéralement omnivore, captant tout ce qui peut leur rapporter de l'argent. Comme l'industrie aéronautique contrôlée par des groupes de plus en plus gigantesques, aux talons desquels jappent quelques transporteurs *low-cost*, le commerce emprunte à son tour le parcours des trusts industriels du temps de leur

25

gloire, avec tout ce que cela implique dans la façon dont les produits son présentés. Tandis que des marques de créateurs comme celles déjà citées dans ce texte font construire leurs propres immeubles quand elles le peuvent, elle se regroupent également à l'occasion dans des complexes comme Crystals, où l'on retrouve Louis Vuitton, Bulgari et Tiffany. Il faut noter que l'intervention d'architectes de renom dans ces grands ensembles commerciaux ne se limite pas à l'Europe et aux États-Unis. L'agence londonienne Foreign Office Architects (FOA) a ainsi livré les 55 000 mètres carrés du complexe de commerces et de cinémas de Meydan à Ümraniye (Istanbul, Turquie, 2007, page 118). Si Meydan ne répond pas aux standards LEED® « Or », il met néanmoins l'accent sur les préoccupations environnementales. Si le shopping est bien pour vous, il doit l'être aussi pour la planète !

Un autre exemple de la prolifération internationale des centres commerciaux de luxe conçus par de grands noms est le Star Place (Kaohsiung, Taïwan, 2006–08, page 356), dû à l'agence amstellodamoise UNStudio. Mettant en œuvre ce jeu habile de vides et d'espaces sans colonnes que les architectes néerlandais apprécient, Star Place présente une façade de 51,3 mètres de haut en verre à « lamelles d'aluminium se projetant horizontalement et ailettes verticales en verre qui forment un motif tourbillonnant » pour attirer les clients dans ce complexe de 37 000 mètres carrés. La façade est conçue pour être à la fois visible et colorée la nuit, moment où les Taïwanais aiment faire leurs courses. Les architectes ont aménagé l'intérieur avec le plus grand soin, mais le côté « Star » présent dans le nom de cette réalisation doit surtout beaucoup à sa façade.

ENTRE SOUK ET ENTREPÔT

Bien que sur un mode un peu moins omnivore, la concentration est également le thème des immeubles Labels 2 à Berlin (2008–09, page 166) des architectes suisses HHF. D'une surface de 6630 mètres carrés, Labels 2 regroupe une trentaine de marques de mode. Sans doute pour laisser penser aux clients qu'ils obtiendront de meilleurs prix, Labels 2 a été conçu en harmonie avec le Labels 1 voisin, logé dans un ancien entrepôt. Selon une approche similaire, du moins pour l'offre multimarque, la Villa Moda (Manama, Bahreïn, 2009, page 370) du fameux designer néerlandais Marcel Wanders réunit des labels allant de Comme des Garçons à Martin Margiela, et propose des produits aussi bien de mode que de design. Selon Wanders : « Le brief était simple : s'inspirer du chaos du souk dans un contexte de mode de luxe. » Malgré l'approche de plus en plus globale de la mode, les architectes et les designers, qui créent des lieux de vente, tentent à l'évidence d'ajouter à chaque fois un élément d'inspiration locale à leur réflexion. La topographie de la ville de Berne pour Libeskind ou l'atmosphère de souk de Wanders illustrent une véritable tendance dans la relation en plein développement entre les stars de l'architecture, celles du design et l'univers du commerce.

DES JOYAUX DANS LA MER

Quand on observe l'importance accordée aux centres commerciaux de luxe, on peut se poser des questions sur le sort d'un des aspects les plus traditionnels du commerce de détail : la petite boutique. L'économie actuelle permet-elle encore de réaliser des magasins com-

26
UNStudio, Star Place, Kaohsiung,
Taiwan, 2006–08

26

me le légendaire tailleur Knize d'Adolf Loos (Vienne, 1913) ? Si la concentration commerciale a eu de lourdes conséquences sur les boutiques de centre-ville comme Knize, un certain nombre de petits magasins récents montrent l'impact que peut encore avoir l'intervention d'un bon designer ou architecte sur un espace limité. Le designer d'origine belge Olivier Lempereur a récemment créé un nouveau point de vente pour Pierre Hermé rue Cambon à Paris (Macarons & Chocolats Pierre Hermé, 2008, page 214) qui ne dépasse pas 25 mètres carrés. Cette boutique joue sur les couleurs sombres et les éclairages de couleurs variées qui rappellent les macarons et leur conditionnement. Même le plafond de couleur chocolat et certains détails en bronze laqué du mobilier rappellent le produit. Le degré d'intimité qu'entraîne naturellement la petitesse de l'espace est mis en valeur plutôt que dissimulé. Les clients trouvent ici la confirmation du sentiment de préciosité et de rareté donné par le célèbre macaron, aussi bien dans les dimensions du magasin que dans son décor.

Dans un esprit assez similaire, le designer Francesc Rifé qui, comme Olivier Lempereur, est né en 1969, a conçu le premier d'une série de magasins pour le maître pâtissier Julio Blanco à Oviedo (Espagne, 2009, page 292). Pomme Sucre occupe 70 mètres carrés divisés en deux niveaux de dimensions égales, la partie vente se trouvant au rez-de-chaussée. Rifé a pris son inspiration dans les principaux ingrédients de la pâtisserie – la farine, les œufs et le cacao – représentés dans sa réalisation par des résines blanches opalescentes et jaunes, et des miroirs fumés qui évoquent le chocolat. Sophistiqué et lisse, ce projet se détache du style des boutiques et immeubles du voisinage, signalant ainsi aux passants qu'il ne s'agit pas d'une pâtisserie ordinaire. Les produits se doivent maintenant d'être à la hauteur de l'image créée par le designer, mais ici tout proclame, à travers les couleurs et les matériaux, que l'on peut s'attendre à bénéficier du plus haut niveau de qualité possible. L'association d'aliments et de design souvent remarquée dans les restaurants se retrouve également dans des produits aussi ordinaires que le pain et le chocolat. Les deux pâtissiers cités ici ont compris l'intérêt d'investir davantage dans leur lieu de vente pour projeter et confirmer l'image d'une qualité hors de l'ordinaire qui fait partie intégrante de leur politique commerciale.

Un troisième exemple d'intervention particulièrement originale dans le même secteur des petites surfaces de vente est offert par une bijouterie de Pampelune (Joaillerie D, Vaillo + Irigaray Architects, Espagne, 2006–07, page 364). Intervenant sur un espace de 50 mètres carrés à peine, les architectes ont cherché à évoquer l'atmosphère d'un coffret à bijoux « mystérieux, étrange, profond et impondérable, tout en étant oriental et baroque ». À l'aide de plaques d'aluminium d'aspect volontairement imparfait, ils ont mis en valeur l'étroitesse et la profondeur du volume pour renforcer chez le client le sentiment de découverte de quelque chose d'authentiquement précieux. Alors que les petites boutiques paraissent facilement banales et encombrées, la vente de bijoux à cette échelle, qui n'attire généralement pas la présence de nombreux acheteurs au même moment, a permis de jouer avec le mystère de la découverte.

Dans ces trois exemples, les architectes ou les designers ont cherché à s'identifier étroitement au produit concerné, mais aussi avec la taille réduite des lieux. On note dans ces trois cas un effet de symbiose avec la spécificité du produit, à mille lieues des vastes centres commerciaux de Las Vegas ou d'Istanbul. D'un côté comme de l'autre, cependant, architectes et designers ont voulu accroître la valeur et l'impact

27

27
*Olivier Lempereur, Pierre Hermé
Macarons & Chocolats, Paris,
France, 2008*

de ces points de vente. Si dans certains cas, les clients se pressent en masse pour découvrir ces nouveaux lieux, la plupart du temps, il est difficile de juger de l'effet d'un investissement dans un projet bien conçu. Combien de macarons supplémentaires Pierre Hermé vend-il pour avoir choisi un designer comme Olivier Lempereur ? La réponse est en grande partie subjective, mais les résultats doivent être suffisamment convaincants pour que de nombreuses marques à travers le monde cherchent à s'attacher les meilleurs architectes et designers.

MAISON BLEUE POUR DROOG

Certains des projets d'architecture commerciale les plus intéressants concernent des interventions de designers réputés qui s'attaquent à la vente de leur propre production ou à des produits proches. Cette seconde alternative correspond certainement au travail de Makkink & Bey, couple marié composé de l'architecte Rianne Makkink et d'un designer célèbre, Jurgen Bey, qui a travaillé un temps pour le groupe néerlandais Droog. C'est justement pour Droog qu'ils ont conçu le magasin Blueprint à Manhattan (2009, New York, page 322) dans le quartier de Soho. Comme ils l'expliquent : « Le brief de Droog était de concevoir un intérieur en rupture avec les normes du design traditionnel pour les points de vente. Droog Design a demandé que l'installation soit réalisée à partir d'éléments facilement accessibles sur le marché. Nous sommes allés encore plus loin en mélangeant la perception de ce qui est architecture, équipement du magasin et éléments techniques, pour créer une installation à strates multiples, qui possède sa propre vie. » Bien que l'hyperbole publicitaire soit de règle dans l'activité commerciale, il n'est pas exagéré de dire que Blueprint « rompt avec les normes de la conception de magasins ». Le concept s'appuie sur l'idée d'objets du décor que l'on peut acheter dans des versions adaptées, afin que les clients achètent une pièce « interprétée » pour un cadre donné. Si la personnalisation pilotée par ordinateur des biens de consommation n'est pas encore une réalité quotidienne, on peut penser que Blueprint est le premier exemple d'un nouveau type de vente au détail qui permettra aux clients de choisir et de personnaliser des objets qui pourront ensuite être fabriqués à l'aide de techniques numériques, par exemple.

CHIC INDUSTRIEL

Une autre « star » du design contemporain a signé le dernier des magasins Joseph à Londres (2009, page 96). Tom Dixon, connu pour ses meubles et son travail à la tête d'Habitat depuis 1998, a donné un aspect résolument industriel à ce « Joseph Store », bien qu'il soit situé dans une rue qui n'évoque en rien l'usine : Old Bond Street. À grand renfort de plâtre, de pierre brute et de projecteurs de théâtre, Dixon a voulu créer « un ajout entièrement inattendu » à cette artère de shopping londonienne si traditionnelle. L'approche plus « attendue » pour des produits de luxe qui aurait consisté à créer un espace marqué d'un certain niveau de raffinement a-t-elle atteint d'une certaine façon ses limites ? Une solution nouvelle consiste donc à convoquer l'esthétique de l'usine ou de l'entrepôt, source d'inspiration déjà présente dans de nombreuses réalisations architecturales contemporaines, par exemple chez Rem Koolhaas.

Ingo Maurer, né en 1932, est peut-être le designer de luminaires le plus connu au monde. Son œuvre a été exposée par des musées sur toute la planète, mais il a toujours maintenu sa base à Munich. Installé dans un bâtiment industriel qu'il utilise depuis les années 1970 pour

28
Marcel Wanders, Villa Moda
Manama, Bahrain, 2009

28

fabriquer et entreposer ses créations, le nouveau studioshowroomwerkstattatelier Ingo Maurer (Munich, Allemagne, 2008, page 260) mesure 700 mètres carrés. Maurer a intentionnellement conservé l'atmosphère industrielle, en particulier dans la partie située en sous-sol. La sophistication de ces lampes et luminaires contraste avec ce décor de salle de stockage qui interpelle les clients, mais correspond de façon plus générale à un type de stratégie déjà adopté dans cet univers. L'avantage évident de cette approche est d'être nettement moins coûteuse qu'un aménagement spatial plus raffiné. Dans les grandes villes, les espaces industriels sont souvent abandonnés et moins chers que les emplacements dans les rues commerçantes. La difficulté de cette stratégie est que la marque doit être suffisamment connue pour attirer les clients vers des quartiers où ils n'ont pas l'habitude de se rendre. Si Ingo Maurer ne connaît pas ce problème, d'autres, souvent moins fameux, ont quand même tenté ce pari.

UNE JOLIE PETITE ROBE DANS LA VITRINE

À une certaine époque, les meilleures interventions architecturales étaient réservées aux fonctions officielles, religieuses ou de pouvoirs politique ou financier. Au cours de ces dernières décennies, les musées et les sièges sociaux d'entreprises ont rejoint les rangs des adeptes d'une architecture de haute qualité. Dans cette parade de prestige, les points de vente sont assurément de nouveaux venus, peut-être encore assez peu sûrs d'eux. Plus encore que les bureaux, les magasins sont censés être rentables, ce qui prend rarement en compte l'apport du prestige d'un architecte célèbre. Cependant, comme le montrent beaucoup d'exemples cités dans cet ouvrage, l'architecture commerciale actuelle a trouvé un dynamisme nouveau et même une assurance qui s'appuient sur l'importance de plus en plus globale des activités commerciales. C'est la montée d'un consumérisme triomphant qui en est la force d'impulsion. L'architecture ne pouvait pas ne pas s'intéresser à ces immenses centres commerciaux qui ressemblent à des villes toutes équipées, proposant leurs propres formules de logement, de divertissement et d'alimentation. L'architecture la plus novatrice sert fréquemment les intérêts de clients qui possèdent les moyens de réaliser leurs rêves. Malgré l'intérêt évident de certaines réalisations présentées ici – les centres commerciaux de Taïwan ou de Las Vegas entre autres – l'architecture commerciale reste néanmoins l'une des manifestations les plus éphémères de l'univers du construit à travers des changements de fonctions ou de marques de plus en plus fréquents. Cette volatilité entraîne des demandes de décors ou même de bâtiments nouveaux, et, d'une certaine façon, correspond au désir des architectes contemporains de s'engager pleinement dans la dynamique de flux de certains aspects de la société actuelle. Alors que l'architecture cherche parfois à échapper à son essence – l'immuable et le solide –, elle va à la rencontre de l'univers du commerce de détail qui recherche davantage de permanence que la simple présence d'une jolie petite robe dans une vitrine. Le commerçant prend peu à peu une part grandissante dans la société, et devient, à de nombreux égards, une de ses forces d'impulsion. Il n'est donc pas étonnant que les architectes et les designers se précipitent vers un domaine qui ne peut que se développer. Récession ou expansion, les priorités peuvent changer et les budgets varier, mais le commerce est bien présent, et l'architecture est devenue sa servante. Volontaire.

Philip Jodidio, Grimentz, Suisse, 1er mars 2010

DAVID ADJAYE

Adjaye/Associates
23–28 Penn Street, London N1 5DL, UK

Tel: +44 20 77 39 49 69 / Fax: +44 20 77 39 34 84
E-mail: info@adjaye.com / Web: www.adjaye.com

DAVID ADJAYE was born in 1966 in Dar es Salaam, Tanzania. He studied at the Royal College of Art in London (M.Arch, 1993), and worked in the offices of David Chipperfield and Eduardo Souto de Moura, before creating his own firm in London in 2000. He is widely recognized as one of the leading architects of his generation in the United Kingdom, in part because of the talks he has given in various locations such as the Architectural Association, the Royal College of Art, and Cambridge University, as well as Harvard, Cornell, and the Universidad de Luisdad in Lisbon. His office employs a staff of 35, and some of his key works are: a house extension (Saint John's Wood, 1998); studio/home for Chris Ofili (1999); the SHADA Pavilion (2000, with artist Henna Nadeem); Siefert Penthouse (2001); Elektra House (2001); and a studio/gallery/home for Tim Noble and Sue Webster (2002), all in London. Recent work includes the Nobel Peace Center (Oslo, Norway, 2002–05); Bernie Grant Performing Arts Center (London, 2001–06); Stephen Lawrence Center (London, 2004–06); a visual-arts building for the London-based organizations inIVA/Autograph at Rivington Place (London, 2003–07); the Museum of Contemporary Art/Denver (Denver, Colorado, USA, 2004–07); Ozwald Boateng Flagship Store (London, 2007, published here); the Sclera Pavilion (Size + Matter, London Design Festival, London, 2008); and Kvadrat Showroom (London, 2008–09, also published here), all in the UK unless stated otherwise. Current work includes the Moscow School of Management/SKOLKOVO (Moscow, Russia, 2011); the African Contemporary Arts Center (Lisbon, Portugal, to be completed in 2012); and the National Museum of African American History and Culture (Smithsonian Institution, Washington, D.C., USA, to be completed in 2015).

DAVID ADJAYE wurde 1966 in Daressalam, Tansania, geboren. Er studierte am Royal College of Art in London (M.Arch, 1993) und arbeitete für David Chipperfield und Eduardo Souto de Moura, bevor er 2000 in London sein eigenes Büro gründete. Er gilt weithin als einer der führenden Architekten seiner Generation in Großbritannien, unter anderem wegen seiner Vorträge an so verschiedenen Institutionen wie der Architectural Association, dem Royal College of Art, der Universität Cambridge, der Harvard und der Cornell University sowie der Universidad de Luisdad in Lissabon. Sein Büro beschäftigt 35 Mitarbeiter, zu seinen wichtigsten Projekten zählen eine Hauserweiterung (Saint John's Wood, 1998), ein Atelier/Haus für Chris Ofili (1999), der SHADA Pavilion (2000, mit der Künstlerin Henna Nadeem), das Siefert Penthouse (2001), das Elektra House (2001), sowie ein Atelier/Galerie/Haus für Tim Noble und Sue Webster (2002), alle in London. Zu seinen jüngeren Arbeiten gehören das Friedensnobelpreis-Zentrum (Oslo, Norwegen, 2002–05), das Bernie Grant Performing Arts Center (London, 2001–06), das Stephen Lawrence Center (London, 2004–06), ein Haus für Bildende Künste für die Londoner Organisation inIVA/Autograph am Rivington Place (London, 2003–07), das Museum of Contemporary Art/Denver (Denver, Colorado, USA, 2004–07), der Ozwald Boateng Flagshipstore (London, 2007, hier vorgestellt), der Sclera-Pavillon (Size + Matter, London Design Festival, London, 2008) und der Kvadrat Showroom (London, 2008–09, ebenfalls hier vorgestellt), alle in Großbritannien, sofern nicht anders angegeben. Aktuelle Projekte sind u.a. die Moscow School of Management/SKOLKOVO (Moskau, Russland, 2011), das Zentrum für zeitgenössische afrikanische Kunst (Lissabon, Portugal, Fertigstellung 2012) sowie das National Museum of African American History and Culture (Smithsonian Institution, Washington D.C., USA, Fertigstellung 2015).

DAVID ADJAYE est né en 1966 à Dar es-Salam en Tanzanie. Après des études au Royal College of Art à Londres (M. Arch., 1993), il travaille auprès de David Chipperfield et d'Eduardo Souto de Moura, avant de créer sa propre agence à Londres en 2000. Il est considéré comme un des plus brillants architectes de sa génération au Royaume-Uni, en partie du fait des conférences qu'il a données dans diverses enceintes comme l'Architectural Association, le Royal College of Art et l'université de Cambridge, mais aussi Harvard, Cornell et l'Universidad de Luisdad à Lisbonne. Son agence emploie 35 collaborateurs. Parmi ses réalisations les plus notables : extension d'une maison (Saint John's Wood, 1998) ; studio/maison pour Chris Ofili (1999) ; le pavillon SHADA (2000, avec l'artiste Henna Nadeem) ; la Siefert Penthouse (2001) ; la maison Elektra (2001) et un studio/galerie/résidence pour Tim Noble et Sue Webster (2002), le tout à Londres. Plus récemment, il a réalisé le Centre Nobel de la Paix (Oslo, Norvège, 2002–05) ; le Bernie Grant Performing Arts Center (Londres, 2001–06) ; le Stephen Lawrence Center (Londres, 2004–06) ; un bâtiment pour les arts plastiques pour inIVA/Autograph à Rivington Place (Londres, 2003–07) ; le Museé d'art contemporain de Denver (Denver, Colorado, 2004–07) ; le magasin amiral d'Ozwald Boateng (Londres, 2007, publié ici) ; le pavillon Sclera (Size + Matter, Londres Design Festival, Londres, 2008) ; et le showroom Kvadrat (Londres, 2008–09, également publié ici). Parmi ses travaux actuels figurent l'École de gestion de Moscou/SKOLKOVO (Moscou, Russie 2011) ; le Centre des arts contemporains africains (Lisbonne, achèvement prévu en 2012) et le Museé national de l'histoire et de la culture afro-americaines (Smithsonian Institution, Washington, achèvement prévu en 2015).

OZWALD BOATENG FLAGSHIP STORE

London, UK, 2007

Address: 30 Savile Row, London W1S 3PT, UK, +44 20 74 37 20 30, www.ozwaldboateng.co.uk
Area: 594 m². Client: Ozwald Boateng / Bespoke Couture Ltd. Cost: not disclosed
Collaboration: Lucy Tilley, Carly Sweeney, Rosie Pattison

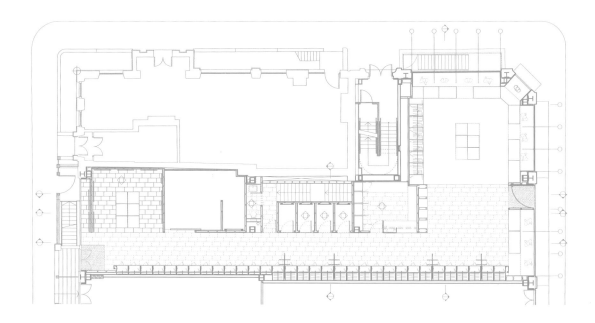

OZWALD BOATENG opened his first store on Vigo Street in London in 1994, and has based his business on Savile Row since 2002. He was the Creative Director of Givenchy's Menswear from 2003 to 2007. The flagship store designed by David Adjaye includes a ready-to-wear space, accessories display area, and a gallery. The basement area houses offices for staff as well as the tailors' and designers' studios. The store is conceived as a series of "shops within shops," each with a different identity. The architects have contrasted spaces such as the white cube gallery area with the more "plush" accessories chamber. The architect states: "The concept and design strategy was to engage with the contemporary and curatorial direction toward which fashion has moved. Rather than just about buying clothes, the store creates experiences and textural and emotional seductions, where a range of encounters, from the old to the new, can occur."

1994 eröffnete **OZWALD BOATENG** sein erstes Geschäft auf der Vigo Street in London, seit 2002 hat er seinen Sitz auf der Savile Row. Von 2003 bis 2007 war er Kreativdirektor der Herrenlinie bei Givenchy. Der von David Adjaye gestaltete Flagshipstore umfasst einen Prêt-à-porter-Bereich, Präsentationsflächen für Accessoires und eine Galerie. Im Untergeschoss sind Büros sowie die Schneider- und Designerwerkstätten untergebracht. Das Geschäft wurde nach einem „Shop im Shop"-Prinzip gestaltet, wobei jeder Bereich seinen eigenen Charakter hat. Es entstanden kontrastreiche Räume, etwa die „White Cube"-Galerie oder der „gemütlichere" Bereich für Accessoires. Der Architekt führt aus: „Konzept und Designstrategie zielen darauf ab, sich auf zeitgenössische, kuratorische Tendenzen einzulassen, in deren Richtung sich die Mode zunehmend entwickelt. Bei diesem Ladenraum geht es nicht nur darum, Kleidung kaufen zu können, sondern darum, Erlebnisse zu schaffen, stofflich und emotional zu verführen, und das Zusammentreffen von Alt und Neu zu ermöglichen."

OZWALD BOATENG, directeur de la création de la ligne homme de Givenchy de 2003 à 2007, a ouvert sa première boutique dans Vigo Street à Londres en 1994, et s'est installé sur Savile Row en 2002. Son magasin principal, conçu par David Adjaye, comprend un espace pour le prêt-à-porter, une zone pour les accessoires et une galerie. Le sous-sol contient des bureaux et les ateliers des tailleurs et stylistes. Le magasin a été conçu comme une succession de « boutiques dans la boutique », chacune possédant son identité propre. Par exemple, les architectes ont fait contraster le cube blanc de la partie galerie avec la pièce des accessoires de traitement plus luxueux. Selon Adjaye : « Le concept et la stratégie de conception ont été de se confronter à l'orientation contemporaine et muséale récemment prise par la mode. Plutôt qu'un simple endroit où acheter des vêtements, le magasin est un lieu d'expériences de séduction variées, à travers des textures et des émotions, dans lequel toute une gamme de rencontres, de types anciens ou nouveaux, peuvent se dérouler. »

The plan above shows the relatively simple L-shaped configuration of the space. A long, open passage gives an immediate sense of the depth of the space, with the changing rooms in the center.

Der Grundriss oben macht die vergleichsweise einfache, L-förmige Konfiguration des Ladenlokals deutlich. Ein langer, offener Gang vermittelt sofort einen Eindruck von der Tiefe des Raums, in dessen Mitte sich die Umkleiden befinden.

Le plan ci-dessus montre la configuration en L relativement simple des lieux. Un long passage ouvert laisse percevoir la profondeur du magasin. Les salons d'essayage sont au centre.

Warm colors contrast with the clothing on display. The cases and mannequins are intentionally clear and simple while extraneous objects or furnishings are kept to the useful minimum.

Warme Farben bilden einen Kontrast zur präsentierten Mode. Vitrinen und Modepuppen wurden bewusst klar und schlicht gehalten. Objekte oder Möbel wurden auf ein sinnvolles Minimum reduziert.

Les couleurs chaudes du décor contrastent avec celles des vêtements présentés. Les vitrines et les mannequins sont de formes volontairement simples. Le nombre des meubles et des objets est limité au minimum nécessaire.

Left page, dark, repetitive alcoves display carefully arranged shirts or jackets. Spotlighting highlights the objects and allows the architecture to be strongly present while not interfering with the function of the shop.

Linke Seite: Akkurat arrangierte Hemden und Sakkos werden in dunklen, sich rhythmisch wiederholenden Wandnischen präsentiert. Spotbeleuchtung betont die Objekte gezielt und verschafft der Architektur merkliche Präsenz, ohne die Funktionalität des Ladens zu beeinträchtigen.

Page de gauche : un alignement de niches de couleur sombre présente les vestes ou les chemises disposées avec soin. L'éclairage par spots met en valeur les articles et permet à l'architecture d'affirmer sa forte présence sans interférer avec la vente.

An upholstered couch or wooden table bring more of a club-like atmosphere to the space, while mirrors or lighting accentuate the fundamental modernity of the architecture.

Ein Ledersofa und ein Tisch aus Holz geben dem Raum die Atmosphäre eines exklusiven Clubs. Zugleich unter-streichen Spiegel die ausgeprägte Modernität der Architektur.

Un canapé de cuir et une table en bois évoquent l'atmosphère d'un club, même si les miroirs ou l'éclairage accentuent le sentiment de modernité de l'architecture.

KVADRAT SHOWROOM

London, UK, 2008–09

Address: 10 Shepherdess Walk, London N1 7LB, UK
+44 20 73 24 55 55, www.kvadrat.dk
Area: 346 m². Client: Kvadrat. Cost: not disclosed
Collaboration: Peter Saville, Alice Asafu-Adjaye, Joanna Malitzki

This showroom, intended as a "design hub" as opposed to being a conventional space, was created in an existing Victorian mixed-use block in Shoreditch, North London. According to the architect, it is "a space for stimulation and the incubation of design ideas within the Kvadrat core values and philosophy of color, warmth, and nature." **KVADRAT** is a Danish company that creates textiles and wall and ceiling coverings. Its British staff is located in the mezzanine level of the building. The hall-like space of the showroom is marked by a central staircase framed with 13 four-meter-high glass panels. The glass balustrade of the stairway colors the space both during the day and at night. Screenings, discussions, and special projects or installations imagined by Peter Saville, the Creative Director of Kvadrat, as well as occasional guest curators serve to animate the space beyond its more regular sales function. David Adjaye comments: "A concept that is deliberately responsive to the natural and artificial lighting conditions, the resulting space thrives on creativity and social interaction and is an example of a successful relationship between architect and a cultured, free-thinking, and supportive client."

Dieser Showroom wurde nicht so sehr als konventioneller Verkaufsraum, sondern vielmehr als „Design-Hotspot" konzipiert und ist in einem viktorianischen Altbau mit Wohn- und Gewerbeflächen im Nordlondoner Bezirk Shoreditch untergebracht. Der Architekt sieht das Projekt als „einen Ort, an dem Designideen entstehen und sich entwickeln können – in Einklang mit den zentralen Werten und der Philosophie von Kvadrat: Farbe, Wärme und Natur." **KVADRAT** ist ein dänischer Hersteller für Vorhang-, Bezug- und Trennwandstoffe. Die Mitarbeiter der britischen Dependance arbeiten im Mezzaningeschoss des Gebäudes. Eine zentrale Treppe dominiert den hallenartigen Showroom mit 13 vier Meter hohen Glastafeln – die gläsernen Seitenpaneele der Treppe tauchen den Raum tagsüber wie nachts in farbiges Licht. Neben seiner regulären Funktion als Verkaufsraum dient der Showroom auch als Veranstaltungsort für Filmvorführungen, Diskussionen, Sonderprojekte oder Installationen, die von Peter Saville, Kreativdirektor bei Kvadrat, oder Gästen kuratiert werden. David Adjaye erklärt: „Dieser Ort wurde so konzipiert, dass er bewusst auf die natürliche und künstliche Lichtsituation reagiert und von Kreativität und sozialer Interaktion profitiert. Er ist ein Beispiel für die gelungene Zusammenarbeit zwischen einem Architekten und einem kultivierten, freidenkenden und kooperativen Auftraggeber."

Ce showroom qui se veut un « club de design », par opposition à l'idée de point de vente conventionnel, a été créé à l'intérieur d'un immeuble mixte victorien de Shoreditch, dans le nord de Londres. Selon l'architecte : « Il s'agit d'un espace de stimulation et d'incubation des concepts de design qui sont au cœur des valeurs essentielles et de la philosophie **KVADRAT** de la couleur, de la chaleur et de la nature. » Kvadrat est une société danoise de textiles et de revêtements pour murs et plafonds. Le personnel travaille à l'entresol de l'immeuble. Le showroom aux dimensions de grand hall est animé par un escalier central contenu dans une cage composée de treize panneaux de verre de quatre mètres de haut. Le garde-corps également en verre participe à l'ambiance chromatique aussi bien de jour que de nuit. La salle accueille des projections, des débats et des projets ou installations imaginés par Peter Saville, directeur de la création de Kvadrat, ainsi que des spécialistes invités à venir animer cet espace en dehors de ses fonctions commerciales classiques. Pour David Adjaye : « À travers ce concept qui répond frontalement aux conditions particulières de l'éclairage naturel et artificiel des lieux, ce volume se prêtant à la créativité et aux interactions sociales est un exemple de relation réussie entre un architecte et un client cultivé et ouvert qui a su le soutenir. »

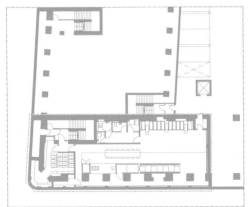

The essentially rectangular spaces are laid out on two floors as the plans show above. The presence of the Victorian structure is not denied inside, quite the contrary, but lighting and colors immediately create an atmosphere as seen in the image on the right page.

Die prinzipiell rechteckigen Räume verteilen sich über zwei Ebenen, wie die Etagengrundrisse oben zeigen. Das Interieur kaschiert die viktorianische Bausubstanz durchaus nicht, ganz im Gegenteil, zugleich schaffen Beleuchtung und Farbe sofort Atmosphäre, wie rechts zu sehen.

Les espaces à peu près rectangulaires s'étagent sur deux niveaux, comme le montrent les plans ci-dessus. À l'intérieur, l'existence du bâtiment victorien n'est pas niée – au contraire – mais l'éclairage et les couleurs créent une atmosphère différente, comme le montre la photographie à droite.

David Adjaye makes subtle use of lighting and colors, or the lack there-of, to give a distinctive feeling to the showroom. Purity of line contrasts here with the walls of the preexisting structure.

David Adjaye arbeitet auf subtile Wei-se mit Licht und Farben, oder ihrem Fehlen. So gewinnt der Showroom ein ganz eigenes Flair. Klare Linien kon-trastieren mit dem Mauerwerk des Altbaus.

David Adjaye utilise avec subtilité l'éclairage et les couleurs – ou leur absence – pour créer une atmosphère particulière dans ce showroom. La pureté de ligne des nouveaux aména-gements contraste avec les murs du bâtiment ancien.

Colored glass animates the stairway, while extremely simple furnishings emphasize the modernity of the function of the space.

Farbiges Glas gibt der Treppe Lebendigkeit, während besonders schlichte Einbauten die moderne Funktionalität der Räume betonen.

L'escalier est dynamisé par des panneaux de verre de couleur tandis que des meubles extrêmement simples magnifient la modernité fonctionnelle de cet espace.

APA

APA
25 Lexington Street
Soho
London W1F 9AH
UK

Tel: + 44 20 74 39 42 90
Fax: + 44 20 74 39 42 91
E-mail: info@apalondon.com
Web: www.apalondon.com

Born in London in 1968, Angus Pond attended the Portsmouth School of Architecture (B.A., Dip.Arch / RIBA Parts 1 and 2), the RMIT in Melbourne (Diploma), and the Architectural Association in London (AA, RIBA Part 3), before working in the offices of Nicholas Grimshaw (1992–93) and Future Systems (1994–2001), both in London. At Future Systems, he worked on Selfridges Birmingham (UK), and Comme des Garçons stores in New York, Paris, and Tokyo. He created his own firm, Angus Pond Architects (**APA**), in London in 2001. Sarah Jayne Backen was born in Manchester, UK, in 1980 and attended the University of Nottingham (B.Arch, RIBA Part 1), the Royal College of Art (M.Arch, RIBA Part 2), and the AA (RIBA Part 3), before working for Stephenson Bell (2000) and Future Systems (2001–02), and joining APA in 2003 as an Associate. Work by APA since 2007 includes Established & Sons Limited Gallery (2007); Established & Sons Headquarters (2008); the Stella McCartney Flagship Store (Paris, France, 2008–09, published here); Adidas by Stella McCartney (Beijing, Tokyo, Paris, London, and Berlin, 2008–09); the store concept for Adidas Women (various locations, 2009–12); and Stratford City Marks & Spencer department store (Stratford City 2012 Olympic Site, London, 2011 completion), all in the UK unless stated otherwise.

Angus Pond wurde 1968 in London geboren und studierte an der Portsmouth School of Architecture (B.A., Dipl. Arch/RIBA Part 1 und 2), am RMIT in Melbourne (Diplom) und der Architectural Association in London (AA, RIBA Part 3). Anschließend war er für Nicholas Grimshaw (1992–93) und Future Systems (1994–2001) tätig, beide in London. Bei Future Systems arbeitete er u.a. an Projekten wie dem Kaufhaus Selfridges in Birmingham und den Comme des Garçons Stores in New York, Paris und Tokio. 2001 gründete er in London sein eigenes Büro, Angus Pond Architects (**APA**). Sarah Jayne Backen wurde 1980 in Manchester, Großbritannien, geboren und studierte an der University of Nottingham (B.Arch, RIBA Part 1), dem Royal College of Art (M.Arch, RIBA Part 2) und der AA (RIBA Part 3), bevor sie für Stephenson Bell (2000) und Future Systems (2001–02) tätig war. 2003 schloss sie sich APA als Partnerin an. Seit 2007 realisierte das Team u.a. die Established & Sons Limited Gallery (2007), das Hauptbüro von Established & Sons (2008), einen Flagshipstore für Stella McCartney (Paris, Frankreich, 2008–09, hier vorgestellt), Adidas by Stella McCartney (Peking, Tokio, Paris, London und Berlin, 2008–09), ein Ladenkonzept für Adidas Women (verschiedene Standorte, 2009–12) sowie das Kaufhaus Marks & Spencer in Stratford City (Stratford City, Olympiagelände 2012, London, Fertigstellung 2011), alle in Großbritannien, sofern nicht anders vermerkt.

Né à Londres en 1968, Angus Pond a étudié à la Portsmouth School of Architecture (B. A., Dip. Arch. / RIBA Part 1 et 2), au RMIT à Melbourne (diplômé), et à l'Architectural Association de Londres (AA, RIBA Part 3), avant de travailler pour Nicholas Grimshaw (1992–93) et Future Systems (1994–2001) à Londres. Chez Future Systems, il est intervenu sur le projet du grand magasin Selfridges à Birmingham et les boutiques Comme des Garçons de New York, Paris et Tokyo. Il a créé sa propre agence, Angus Pond Architects (**APA**), à Londres en 2001. Sarah Jayne Backen, née à Manchester en 1980 a étudié à l'université de Nottingham (B. Arch. RIBA Part 1), au Royal College of Art (M. Arch. RIBA Part 2), et à l'AA (RIBA Part 3), avant de travailler pour Stephenson Bell (2000) et Future Systems (2001–02), puis de rejoindre APA en 2003 comme associée. Parmi les interventions de l'agence depuis 2007 : la galerie d'Established & Sons Limited (2007) ; le siège d'Established & Sons (2008) ; le magasin amiral de Stella McCartney (Paris, 2008–09, publié ici) ; Adidas by Stella McCartney (Pékin, Tokyo, Paris, Londres et Berlin, 2008–09) ; le concept de magasin Adidas Women (divers lieux, 2009–12) et le grand magasin Marks & Spencer de Stratford City (Stratford City, site des J.O. de 2012 à Londres, achèvement prévu en 2011).

STELLA MCCARTNEY FLAGSHIP STORE

Paris, France, 2008–09

Address: 114–121 Galerie de Valois, Jardin du Palais Royal, 75001 Paris, France, www.stellamccartney.com
Area: 270 m². Client: Stella McCartney Ltd. Cost: not disclosed
Collaboration: Buzzoni (furniture manufacturer, Italy)

Set on two floors, this store features furniture designed by APA and manufactured by Buzzoni (Italy). The walls are in Japanese ash veneer panels with brass trim and detailing. Bronze-colored veined marble, cast bronze, dark gray carpets, and white ceramic tiles are amongst the other materials used. The **STELLA MCCARTNEY FLAGSHIP STORE** occupies eight of the 141 limestone arches that form the inner arcade of the Palais Royal. As the architects state: "The existing site parameters have determined the design response in terms of specific historical reference, materiality, craftsmanship, and detail." The existing ceiling was restored with gold leaf, while the architects added three brass *Rain* sculptures made of mirror-polished stainless-steel rods with polished and cast brass shards and mirror-polished stainless-steel hanging rails to give a modern rhythm to the space. Indeed, the work of APA in this instance is a careful balance between the very modern world of Stella McCartney's fashion and the strong tradition of the architecture of the Palais Royal.

Das über zwei Etagen verteilte Ladenlokal ist mit Einbauten von APA ausgestattet, die in Italien von Buzzoni gefertigt wurden. Die Wände wurden mit Furnierplatten aus japanischer Esche vertäfelt, Einbauelemente und -details sind aus Messing gearbeitet. Weitere Materialien sind Marmor mit bronzefarbener Maserung, Gussbronze, dunkelgrauer Teppichboden und weiße Keramikfliesen. Der **STELLA MCCARTNEY FLAGSHIPSTORE** belegt acht der insgesamt 141 Sandstein-Arkaden im Innenhof des Palais Royal. Die Architekten führen aus: „Das räumliche Umfeld beeinflusste unsere Herangehensweise an den Entwurf, sowohl im Hinblick auf spezifische historische Bezüge, als auch hinsichtlich der Materialien, Verarbeitung und baulichen Details." Die alte Decke wurde mit Blattgold restauriert. Einen modernen Rhythmus gewinnt der Raum durch die drei *Rain*-Skulpturen aus hochglanzpoliertem Stahlrohr und polierten Splitterteilen aus Gussmessing, die die Architekten als neues Element entwarfen. Die Kleiderstangen aus hochglanzpoliertem Stahlrohr wurden in die Installation integriert. Tatsächlich gelingt es APA bei diesem Projekt, ein sorgsam austariertes Gleichgewicht zwischen dem zeitgenössischen Mode-Universum Stella McCartneys und der beeindruckenden, traditionellen Architektur des Palais Royal zu finden.

Implanté sur deux niveaux, ce magasin se distingue par des meubles conçus par APA et fabriqués par Buzzoni (Italie). Les murs sont habillés de panneaux plaqués de frêne du Japon à finitions de laiton. Parmi les autres matériaux figurent un marbre veiné de couleur bronze, le bronze, des moquettes gris sombre et des carrelages de céramique blanche. Le **STELLA MCCARTNEY FLAGSHIP STORE** occupe huit des 141 arches de pierre des arcades des jardins du Palais-Royal à Paris. L'architecte précise : « Les paramètres du site ont déterminé notre réponse en termes de références historiques spécifiques, de choix des matériaux, de type de travail artisanal et de détails. » Le plafond existant a été restauré à la feuille d'or et les architectes ont installé trois sculptures *Rain* en tiges d'acier inoxydable poli miroir, avec plaquettes de laiton poli et rails suspendus en acier inoxydable poli miroir, pour donner un rythme moderne à cet espace. Le travail d'APA représente un équilibre calculé entre l'univers très moderne du style Stella McCartney et la force de la présence architecturale historique du Palais-Royal.

The modernity of the store contrasts with the arcades of the enclosed garden of the Palais Royal. A good part of the space is visible from the outside, inviting passersby to come in.

Der moderne Store ist ein Kontrast zu den Arkaden am Jardin du Palais Royal. Ein Großteil der Räume ist von außen einsehbar und lädt Passanten zum Eintreten ein.

La modernité du magasin contraste avec les arcades des jardins du Palais-Royal. Une bonne partie de l'espace est visible de l'extérieur, ce qui invite les passants à entrer.

The arcades of the Palais Royal are visible outside the storefront in the image to the right. Below, wood finishes or other cladding give warmth to the space and immediately create a kind of intimacy.

Rechts im Bild lassen sich die Arkaden durch das Schaufenster ausmachen. Unten: Holzoberflächen und weitere Verblendmaterialien geben dem Raum Wärme und schaffen eine intime Atmosphäre.

Image de droite : les arcades du Palais Royal se devinent devant la vitrine. Ci-dessous, les finitions en bois et divers habillages confèrent une certaine chaleur à cet espace et créent une sorte d'intimité immédiate.

To the right, a sculptural element is used to present Stella McCartney's creations in the middle of the space. Its complexity contrasts with the smooth wooden walls.

Rechts: Ein skulpturales Element mitten im Raum dient zur Präsentation der Mode und ist in seiner Komplexität ein Kontrast zu den glatten Holzwänden.

À droite, un élément sculptural sert également à suspendre des vêtements au milieu du magasin. Sa complexité contraste avec le traitement des murs parés de bois.

Horse patterns or a quilted design (with the shoe, to the right) imply a certain continuity with Parisian elegance despite the fundamentally contemporary nature of Stella McCartney's clothes.

Trotz des dezidiert zeitgenössischen Profils der Mode Stella McCartneys, knüpfen Pferdemotive und eine Steppstruktur (rechts, hinter dem Schuh) in gewisser Weise an die Pariser Eleganz an.

Un motif de cheval et un effet de matelassage (avec chaussure, à droite) dessinent une certaine continuité avec l'élégance parisienne malgré la nature fondamentalement contemporaine du style de Stella McCartney.

CHRISTIAN BIECHER

CBA/Christian Biecher & Associés
14 Rue Crespin du Gast
75011 Paris
France

Tel: +33 1 49 29 69 39
Fax: +33 1 49 29 69 30
E-mail: info@biecher.com
Web: www.biecher.com

CHRISTIAN BIECHER received his diploma as an architect from the École d'Architecture de Paris-Belleville in 1989. He worked as a designer for Bernard Tschumi Architects (Paris, New York, 1986–92) and was an Assistant Professor at Columbia University Graduate School of Architecture (1990–97). He created his own firm in Paris in 1992, and, more recently, his current firm CBA (Christian Biecher & Associés) in 1997. He won the Maison & Objet "Designer of the Year" Award in 2001. Aside from the Fauchon restaurant and store (Beijing, China, 2006–07), he has also designed spaces for the same firm in Paris (France, 2007, published here), Tokyo, and Casablanca (2010). Biecher has also worked recently on interior design and furniture for Harvey Nichols stores in Hong Kong (China), Dublin (Ireland), and Bristol (UK), and has designed numerous objects for such manufacturers as Christofle, Poltrona Frau, and Baccarat. He is currently working on the Starship, a building for retail space and offices in Prague (Czech Republic); the interior design of the Hôtel Chambon de la Tour (Uzès, France); and the refurbishment of the former Budapest Stock Exchange into a center for retail, offices, and restaurants.

CHRISTIAN BIECHER schloss sein Studium 1989 als Diplomarchitekt an der École d'Architecture de Paris-Belleville ab. Er arbeitete als Planer bei Bernard Tschumi Architects (Paris, New York, 1986–92) und war Assistenzprofessor am Graduiertenprogramm für Architektur der Columbia University (1990–97). 1992 gründete er sein erstes eigenes Büro in Paris, 1997 schließlich sein derzeitiges Büro CBA (Christian Biecher & Associés). 2001 wurde er von der Messe Maison & Objet als „Designer des Jahres" ausgezeichnet. Neben einem Restaurant und einer Filiale für Fauchon in Peking (2006–07), gestaltete er für denselben Auftraggeber Filialen in Paris (Frankreich, 2007, hier vorgestellt), Tokio und Casablanca (2010). Darüber hinaus übernahm Biecher Raumgestaltung und Einrichtungen für Dependancen des Kaufhauses Harvey Nichols in Hongkong (China), Dublin (Irland) und Bristol (Großbritannien) und entwarf Objekte für Hersteller wie Christofle, Poltrona Frau und Baccarat. Derzeit arbeitet Biecher an Starship, einem Büro- und Geschäftsgebäude in Prag, der Innenarchitektur für das Hôtel Chambon de la Tour (Uzès, Frankreich) sowie dem Umbau der ehemaligen Börse in Budapest als gemischt genutztes Gebäude mit Ladenflächen, Büros und Restaurants.

CHRISTIAN BIECHER est diplômé de l'École d'architecture de Paris-Belleville (1989). Il a travaillé comme designer chez Bernard Tschumi Architects (Paris, New York, 1986–92) et a été professeur assistant à la Graduate School of Architecture de l'université Columbia (New York, 1990–97). Il a créé une première agence à Paris en 1992 et son agence actuelle CBA (Christian Biecher & Associés) en 1997. Il a été élu « Designer de l'année » au salon Maison & Objet en 2001. En dehors du magasin et restaurant Fauchon de Pékin (2006–07), il a également entièrement rénové le magasin d'origine de la marque à Paris (2007, publié ici), puis ceux de Tokyo et de Casablanca (2010). Biecher a également travaillé récemment sur l'aménagement intérieur et le mobilier des magasins Harvey Nichols à Hong Kong, Dublin (Irlande) et Bristol (Royaume-Uni) et conçu de nombreux objets pour des fabricants comme Christofle, Poltrona Frau ou Baccarat. Il travaille actuellement sur le projet Starship, un immeuble de bureaux et de commerces à Prague ; l'aménagement intérieur de l'Hôtel Chambon de la Tour (Uzès, France) et la transformation de l'ancienne bourse de Budapest en centre de commerces, de bureaux et de restaurants.

MAISON FAUCHON

Paris, France, 2007

*Address: 24–26 and 39 Place de la Madeleine, 75008 Paris, France,
+33 1 70 39 38 00, www.fauchon.com//en/#/our-addresses/paris-madeleine
Area: 800 m² (plus 80 m² patio). Client: Fauchon SAS. Cost: not disclosed
Collaboration: Céline Trétout, Xiao Dai, Régis Botta, Alexander Bartzsch,
Pascal Schaller, Alexis Coussement*

Christian Biecher works with a pastel palette and smooth surfaces to emphasize the fine foods sold by Fauchon. There is certainly an emphasis on the precious aspect of the food that is not typical of other stores.

Christian Biecher arbeitet mit einer Palette aus Pastellfarben und glatten Oberflächen, um das Delikatessensortiment von Fauchon zur Geltung zu bringen. Zweifellos wird hier der kostbare Aspekt der Lebensmittel hervorgehoben, was bei anderen Geschäften eher untypisch ist.

Christian Biecher a travaillé sur une palette de tons pastel et de surfaces polies pour mettre en valeur la qualité des produits vendus par Fauchon. Cette emphase mise sur l'aspect précieux des aliments est assez originale.

The exterior of the store with its smooth, dark surface makes the rose tones visible in the image above all the more inviting. A drawing (right) shows the three levels of the store.

Die Außenfront des Geschäfts mit ihren glatten dunklen Oberflächen lässt die Rosatöne oben im Bild umso einladender wirken. Eine Zeichnung (rechts) zeigt alle drei Etagen des Ladens.

La façade de verre sombre du magasin fait ressortir la séduction des tons roses visibles dans l'image ci-dessus. À droite, une coupe montre les trois niveaux du magasin.

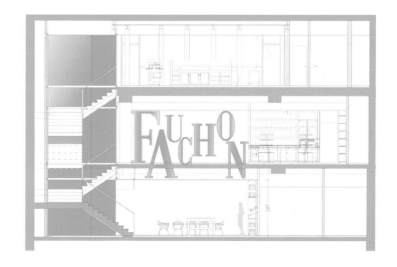

Located at 26 and 30 Place de la Madeleine in Paris, **FAUCHON** may be the best-known high-quality food store in the world. Christian Biecher explains that he was inspired by the desire to create rooms with different atmospheres. He created a "gold" space for the bakery, pastry, and coffee bar. Biecher states: "The 'gold' echoes the golden pastries and breads and fills the space with brightness and luster." The 300-square-meter restaurant is colored silver, and, as the designer states, the "luminous and crystalline 'silver' melts into a pale pink evoking subtle Parisian elegance." Finally, a combination of black, white, and gray marks the grocery, catering, and wine-cellar areas. The use of timber, bamboo, and leather makes reference to the wide geographical origins of the products sold by Fauchon. Much as he did in the Beijing outlet of the same company, Christian Biecher calls on a rose or fuchsia color that he uses "like an electrical cord … the thread that links the different spaces celebrating the Fauchon brand."

FAUCHON, gelegen an der Place de la Madeleine in Paris, ist der vielleicht bekannteste Delikatessenhändler der Welt. Christian Biecher führt aus, was ihn inspirierte, Räume mit verschiedenen Stimmungen zu schaffen – etwa einen „goldenen" Bereich für Bäckerei, Patisserie und Café: „Das ,Gold' spiegelt die goldbraunen Kleingebäcke und Brote und füllt den Raum mit Licht und Glanz." Das 300 m² große Restaurant ist in Silber gehalten, wo „das leuchtende, kristalline ,Silber' mit einem dezenten, blassen Rosa verschmilzt, dem Inbegriff subtiler Pariser Eleganz." Eine Kombination aus Schwarz, Weiß und Grau prägt die Lebensmittelabteilung, die Cateringabteilung und den Weinkeller. Materialien wie Holz, Bambus und Leder spielen auf das breite Spektrum der Herkunftsländer an, aus denen Fauchon sein Warenangebot bezieht. Wie bei der Fauchon-Niederlassung in Peking greift Biecher auf ein Rosa beziehungsweise Magenta zurück, das sich wie „ein roter Faden, eine Hauptleitung durch die verschiedenen Abteilungen zieht" und zugleich „eine Hommage an die Marke Fauchon" ist.

Situé 26 et 30 place de la Madeleine à Paris, **FAUCHON** est peut-être l'épicerie fine la plus célèbre du monde. Christian Biecher a expliqué qu'il avait désiré créer des salles d'atmosphères différentes. Il a ainsi imaginé un volume « or » pour la pâtisserie et le bar à café. « L'or vient en écho au doré des pâtisseries et des pains et emplit le volume de son éclat et de son lustre », explique le designer. Le restaurant de 300 m² est couleur argent : « L'argent lumineux et cristallin fusionne avec un rose très pâle qui évoque la subtilité de l'élégance parisienne. » Une combinaison de noir, de blanc et de gris met en valeur l'épicerie, le traiteur et la cave à vin. Le recours au bois, au bambou et au cuir fait référence aux origines géographiques variées des produits commercialisés par Fauchon. En grande partie comme il l'a fait pour le magasin Fauchon de Pékin, Christian Biecher s'est appuyé sur le rose ou le fuchsia, une couleur utilisée « comme un câble électrique … c'est un lien qui relie les différents espaces de célébration de la marque Fauchon. »

The carefully arranged rows of products allow full visibility while continuing to emphasize the exceptional nature of the items on display.

Die akkurat aufgereihten Produkte sorgen für optimale Übersichtlichkeit und unterstreichen zusätzlich die Exklusivität des Warenangebots.

Les alignements impeccables des produits assurent leur parfaite visibilité tout en mettant en valeur leur nature d'exception.

To the right floor plans show the careful compartmentalized division of the spaces. Above, lighting and ceiling design echo the floor pattern, while a pink counter recalls the designer's predilection for hot colors.

Die Grundrisse rechts zeigen die präzise Gliederung des Raums. Beleuchtung und Deckengestaltung (oben) wirken wie ein Spiegelbild des Bodenmusters. Ein magentafarbener Tresen unterstreicht die Vorliebe des Architekten für leuchtende Farben.

À droite, plans du compartimentage des espaces. Au-dessus, le design du plafond et de son éclairage renvoie à la mosaïque du sol. Le comptoir rose rappelle la prédilection du designer pour les couleurs chaudes.

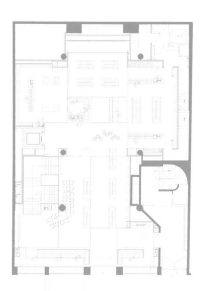
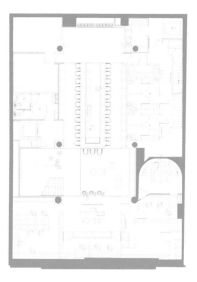

The designer has chosen more muted tones for the bar space, but the same clean elegance seen elsewhere is very much present here.

Im Barbereich entschied sich der Architekt für zurückhaltendere Töne. Doch wie in den übrigen Räumen prägt zweifellos eine klare Eleganz das Bild.

Christian Biecher a choisi des couleurs plus sourdes pour le bar tout en conservant la même élégante simplicité.

A floor plan shows the dining area
and bar space. Below, the dining
room. Though pink highlights are visible near the columns and elsewhere,
Biecher has chosen shades of silver
and gray for the main tones.

Ein Etagengrundriss zeigt den
Bar- und Restaurantbereich. Unten
der Speiseraum. Obwohl auch hier –
an den Säulen und anderen Bereichen
– Akzente in Rosa zu finden ist,
konzentriert sich Biecher in erster
Linie auf Silber- und Grautöne.

Plan du niveau de la salle à manger
et du bar. Ci-dessous, la salle à manger. Si quelques touches de rose sont
encore apparentes ici et là, Biecher y
a privilégié l'argent et le gris en couleurs principales.

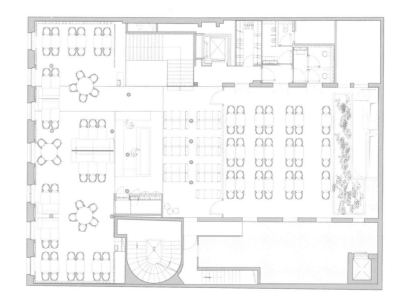

Apple Store ▶

BOHLIN CYWINSKI JACKSON

Bohlin Cywinski Jackson
49 Geary Street, Suite 300 / San Francisco, CA 94108 / USA
Tel: +1 415 989 2100 / Fax: +1 415 989 2101
E-mail: info_request@bcj.com / Web: www.bcj.com

BOHLIN CYWINSKI JACKSON was founded in 1965 by Peter Bohlin and Richard Powell in Wilkes-Barre, Pennsylvania. Peter Bohlin received a B.Arch from Rensselaer Polytechnic Institute (1959) and an M.Arch from Cranbrook Academy of Art (1961). Today the principals are Peter Bohlin (left), Bernard Cywinski, Jon Jackson (center), Dan Haden, Frank Grauman, William Loose, Randy Reid, Karl Backus (right), Gregory Mottola, Roxanne Sherbeck, Robert Miller, and Raymond Calabro. The firm has additional offices in Pittsburgh, Philadelphia, Seattle, and San Francisco. In 1994, the practice received the Architecture Firm Award from the American Institute of Architects and has received over 425 regional, national, and international design awards. Peter Bohlin won the 2010 Gold Medal of the AIA. Significant work includes the Forest House (Cornwall, Connecticut, 1975); Software Engineering Institute (Pittsburgh, Pennsylvania, 1987); Headquarters of Pixar Animation Studios (Emeryville, California, 2001); Liberty Bell Center Independence National Historical Park (Philadelphia, Pennsylvania, 2003); and Seattle City Hall (Washington, Bassetti local architect). In 2008, they completed the Visitor Activity Center at Pocono Environmental Education Center (PEEC), listed by the AIA as one of the "Top Ten Green Buildings" for that year. Current work includes the Williams College Faculty Buildings and Library (Williamstown, Massachusetts, 2008 and 2012); Marcus Nanotechnology Research Center, Georgia Institute of Technology (Atlanta, Georgia, 2009); California Institute of Technology Chemistry Building (Pasadena, California, 2010); Peace Arch US Port of Entry (Blaine, Washington, 2012), all in the USA; and the prototype and a series of high-profile retail stores for Apple Inc.—for example, the Apple Store on Upper West Side in New York (New York, USA, 2008–09, published here)—in various locations worldwide.

BOHLIN CYWINSKI JACKSON wurde 1965 von Peter Bohlin und Richard Powell in Wilkes-Barre, Pennsylvania, gegründet. Peter Bohlin schloss sein Studium mit einem B.Arch am Rensselaer Polytechnic Institute (1959) und einem M.Arch an der Cranbrook Academy of Art (1961) ab. Partner des Büros sind heute Peter Bohlin (links), Bernard Cywinski, Jon Jackson (Mitte), Dan Haden, Frank Grauman, William Loose, Randy Reid, Karl Backus (rechts), Gregory Mottola, Roxanne Sherbeck, Robert Miller und Raymond Calabro. Das Büro hat weitere Niederlassungen in Pittsburgh, Philadelphia, Seattle und San Francisco. 1994 wurde die Firma mit dem Architecture Firm Award des American Institute of Architects ausgezeichnet und darüber hinaus mit über 425 regionalen, nationalen und internationalen Designpreisen geehrt, so auch der Goldmedaille des AIA im Jahr 2010. Bedeutende Projekte sind u.a. Forest House (Cornwall, Connecticut, 1975), das Software Engineering Institute (Pittsburgh, Pennsylvania, 1987), die Zentrale der Pixar Animationsstudios (Emeryville, Kalifornien, 2001), der Liberty Bell Center Independence National Historical Park (Philadelphia, Pennsylvania, 2003) und das Rathaus in Seattle (Washington, Architekten vor Ort: Bassetti). 2008 konnte das Besucherzentrum am Pocono Environmental Education Center (PEEC) fertiggestellt werden, das im selben Jahr vom AIA in die Top Ten „Grüne Bauten" aufgenommen wurde. Aktuelle Projekte sind u.a. Fakultätsgebäude und eine Bibliothek für das Williams College (Williamstown, Massachusetts, 2008 und 2012), das Marcus-Forschungszentrum für Nanotechnologie am Georgia Institute of Technology (Atlanta, Georgia, 2009), das Chemiegebäude am California Institute of Technology (Pasadena, Kalifornien, 2010), der US-amerikanische Grenzübergang Peace Arch (Blaine, Washington, 2012), alle in den USA, sowie der Prototyp und eine Reihe prominenter Flagshipstores für Apple – z.B. der Apple Store auf der Upper West Side in New York (2008–09, hier vorgestellt) – an verschiedenen Standorten weltweit.

L'agence **BOHLIN CYWINSKI JACKSON** a été fondée en 1965 par Peter Bohlin et Richard Powell à Wilkes-Barre (Pennsylvanie). Peter Bohlin est diplômé B. Arch. du Rensselaer Polytechnic Institute (1959) et M. Arch. de la Cranbrook Academy of Art (1961). Les associés actuels sont Peter Bohlin (à gauche), Bernard Cywinski, Jon Jackson (au milieu), Dan Haden, Frank Grauman, William Loose, Randy Reid, Karl Backus (à droite), Gregory Mottola, Roxanne Sherbeck, Robert Miller et Raymond Calabro. L'agence possède des bureaux à Pittsburgh, Philadelphie, Seattle et San Francisco. En 1994, elle a reçu le prix de l'agence d'architecture de l'American Institute of Architects et, depuis, plus de 425 distinctions régionales, nationales et internationales, ainsi que la médaille d'or du AIA en 2010. Parmi ses réalisations les plus significatives : la maison Forêt (Forest House, Cornwall, Connecticut 1975) ; le Software Engineering Institute (Pittsburgh, Pennsylvanie, 1987) ; le siège des Pixar Animation Studios (Emeryville, Californie, 2001) ; le Liberty Bell Center dans l'Independance National Historical Park (Philadelphie, Pennsylvanie, 2003) ; et l'hôtel de ville de Seattle (avec l'architecte local Bassetti). En 2008, l'agence a achevé le Centre d'activités des visiteurs du Centre de formation à l'environnement de Pocono (PEEC), désigné par l'AIA comme l'un des « dix plus importants bâtiments écologiques de l'année ». Ses interventions actuelles, en diverses adresses dans le monde, comprennent entre autres la bibliothèque et les bâtiments des enseignants de Williams College (Williamstown, Massachusetts, 2008 et 2012) ; le Centre de recherches sur les nanotechnologies Marcus du Georgia Institute of Technology (Atlanta, Georgia, 2009) ; le bâtiment de la chimie du California Institute of Technology (Pasadena, Californie, 2010) ; le péage d'entrée du parc de l'Arche de la paix (Blaine, Washington, 2012) et le prototype puis la réalisation d'une série de magasins de prestige pour Apple Computer, tel le Apple Store sur Upper West Side (New York, 2008–09, publié ici).

APPLE STORE

Upper West Side, New York, New York, USA, 2008–09

*Address: 1981 Broadway, Upper West Side, New York, NY 10023, USA,
+1 212 209 3400, www.apple.com/retail/upperwestside
Area: 1951 m². Client: Apple Inc. Cost: not disclosed. Collaboration: Eckersley O'Callaghan, Buro Happold*

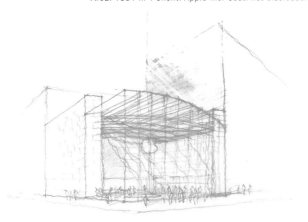
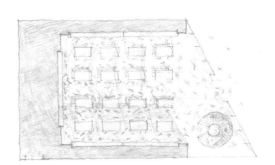

The vast glazed space of the Apple Store contrasts with the more mineral and closed appearance of neighboring buildings, at the same time as it carries on with the style established by the architects for the earlier Apple Store on Fifth Avenue.

Der mächtige verglaste Baukörper des Apple Store kontrastiert mit den steinernen, geschlossen wirkenden Nachbarbauten und knüpft zugleich stilistisch an das Erscheinungsbild des etwas älteren Apple Store auf der Fifth Avenue an, der von denselben Architekten gestaltet wurde.

L'énorme volume vitré de l'Apple Store contraste avec l'aspect plus minéral et fermé des immeubles voisins. Il reprend le style établi par les architectes pour l'Apple Store antérieur de la Cinquième Avenue.

Located at 1981 Broadway on the corner of 67th Street, this new **APPLE STORE** echoes the earlier one erected at 767 Fifth Avenue (2003–06) by the same architects. As was the case with the glass cube on Fifth Avenue (9.75 meters per side—length, width, and height), this Apple Store confidently juxtaposes its transparent angled glass façades with the rather massive stone structures nearby. The architects have created an inviting interior space "simply organized by the rhythm of steel trusses and a grid of product display tables." As is the case on Fifth Avenue, a spiral staircase descends to the lower level, which in this instance is dedicated to accessories and a learning space. "Recalling the glass façade above," state the architects, "stainless-steel panels reflect the borrowed light and provide a sleek backdrop to the spiral stair." Given the careful attention paid by Apple to the design of its own products, the creation of an Apple Store almost inevitably involves cutting-edge design and a lightness that the architects have certainly mastered in this instance as they did on Fifth Avenue.

Der neue **APPLE STORE** am Broadway 1981, Ecke 67th Street, wirkt wie das Echo des kaum älteren Stores an der Fifth Avenue 767 (2003–06) derselben Architekten. Wie schon der Glaskubus an der Fifth Avenue (mit je 9,75 m in Länge, Breite und Höhe) sucht der jüngere Apple Store mit seiner kantigen Glasfassade selbstbewusst den Kontrast zu den massiven Steinbauten ringsum. Die Architekten gestalteten einen einladenden Innenraum, indem sie ganz schlicht „den Rhythmus der Stahlträger festlegten und die Präsentationstische zu einem Raster anordneten". Wie an der Fifth Avenue führt eine Wendeltreppe ins Untergeschoss, das hier dem Verkauf von Zubehör und einem Lernbereich vorbehalten ist. „Anknüpfend an die Glasfassade," erklären die Architekten, „spiegeln hier Edelstahlplatten das indirekte Licht und bilden zugleich eine elegante Kulisse für die Wendeltreppe." Angesichts des hohen Stellenwerts, den das Design der Produkte bei Apple hat, ist bei der Gestaltung eines Apple Stores unweigerlich Spitzendesign und eine Leichtigkeit gefragt, der die Architekten hier – wie an der Fifth Avenue – offensichtlich meisterhaft gerecht werden.

Située au 1981 Broadway à l'angle de la 67e Rue, ce nouvel **APPLE STORE** fait suite au précédent érigé 767 Cinquième Avenue (2003–06) par les mêmes architectes. Comme pour le cube de verre de la Cinquième Avenue de 9,75 mètres de côté, les nouvelles installations juxtaposent sans gêne apparente leurs façades de verre transparentes à celles de pierre et de brique des immeubles massifs qui les entourent. Les architectes ont créé un volume intérieur séduisant, « simplement structuré par le rythme des poutrelles d'acier et la trame des tables de présentation des produits ». Comme sur la Cinquième Avenue, un escalier en spirale descend vers le sous-sol, consacré ici aux accessoires et à la formation. « Rappelant les façades en verre qui les dominent », expliquent les architectes, « des panneaux en acier inoxydable reflètent la lumière naturelle et constituent un fond sur lequel se détache l'escalier. » Le soin porté par Apple au design de ses produits se retrouve dans la conception avant-gardiste des Apple Stores placées sous le signe d'une légèreté que les architectes ont une fois de plus parfaitement maîtrisée.

Clear, geometric lines characterize the lower level sales space with its carefully aligned wooden tables (also visible on the floor plan to the right).

Klare geometrische Formen prägen den Verkaufsraum im Untergeschoss mit seinen präzise ausgerichteten Tischen (zu sehen auch auf dem Etagengrundriss rechts).

Le niveau inférieur qui est consacré à la vente se caractérise par la netteté de ses lignes, dans l'alignement des grandes tables de bois (visibles sur le plan de droite).

Apple Computer's image of clean, sharp product design blends seamlessly with Bohlin Cywinski Jackson's scheme for the store, where light and transparency are the themes.

Apples Image als Hersteller von klarem, innovativem Design fügt sich nahtlos in Bohlin Cywinski Jacksons Storekonzept, bei dem Licht und Transparenz eine Schlüsselrolle spielen.

L'image du design Apple – des produits d'avant-garde d'une grande lisibilité fonctionnelle – s'accorde naturellement avec les plans de Bohlin Cywinski Jackson qui ont choisi une thématique de légèreté et de transparence.

CAMPAIGN

Campaign
Unit 16 Perseverance Works
25–27 Hackney Road
London E2 8DD
UK

Tel: + 44 20 70 33 38 40
E-mail: someone@campaigndesign.co.uk
Web: www.campaigndesign.co.uk

CAMPAIGN founder and Creative Director Philip Handford was born in 1972. He obtained a B.A. in Interior Architecture from Brighton University and worked with the London consultancies Imagination and Barber Osgerby, before establishing Campaign in January 2009. As he explains: "The studio is hands-on in exploring different media and methods in order to tell unique and engaging brand stories, developing integrated brand experiences through interior architecture, graphic and interactive design." Recent projects include the Dr. Martens Pop-Up Store in Spitalfields (London, UK, 2009, published here) and a temporary installation for Dunhill during New York Fashion Week (New York, USA, 2010).

Philip Handford, Gründer und Kreativdirektor von **CAMPAIGN**, wurde 1972 geboren. Er schloss sein Innenarchitekturstudium an der Universität Brighton mit einem B.A. ab und arbeitete für die Londoner Agenturen Imagination und Barber Osgerby, bevor er im Januar 2009 Campaign gründete. Er erklärt: „Das Studio lotet in der Praxis die verschiedensten Medien und Methoden aus, um das unverwechselbare und faszinierende Profil einer Marke zu vermitteln. Durch Innenarchitektur, Grafikdesign und interaktives Design werden ganzheitliche Markenerlebnisse entwickelt." Jüngste Projekte sind u.a. der Dr. Martens Pop-Up Store in Spitalfields (London, Großbritannien, 2009, hier vorgestellt) und eine temporäre Installation für Dunhill während der New Yorker Fashion Week (New York, USA, 2010).

Le fondateur et directeur de la création de **CAMPAIGN**, Philip Handford, né en 1972 a reçu son B. A. en architecture intérieure de l'université de Brighton et a travaillé pour les agences londoniennes Imagination et Barber Osgerby, avant de fonder l'agence en janvier 2009. « Le studio est très impliqué dans l'exploration des différents médias et méthodes qui lui permettent d'établir un discours de marque original et motivant et de développer des expériences intégrées grâce à l'architecture intérieure, au graphisme et au design interactif », explique Philip Handford. Parmi ses récents projets figurent une boutique éphémère Dr. Martens à Spitalfields (Londres, 2009, publiée ici) et une installation temporaire pour Dunhill prévue pour la Semaine de la mode à New York (2010).

DR. MARTENS POP-UP STORE
London, UK, 2009

Address: Unit SP 1F, Old Spitalfields Market, London E1 6EW, UK,
+44 20 73 75 29 43, www.drmartens.com
Area: 180 m². Client: Dr. Martens. Cost: € 17 000. Collaboration: Neil Sharman (Design Director Interiors),
Aaron Richardson (Design Director Graphics), Nese Halil (Marketing Director)

Created in Germany by Klaus Maertens and Herbert Funck, Dr. Martens shoes have been manufactured in the United Kingdom by R. Griggs Group Ltd. since 1960. The design workshop Campaign was commissioned to design a **POP-UP STORE FOR DR. MARTENS** in Old Spitalfields Market, in London's East End. Working with the creative brand managers Fresh, Campaign put an emphasis on an image that corresponded to that of the product. As they say: "Inspired by Dr. Martens' heritage and attitude that catapulted it from a working-class essential to a counter-cultural icon, the store has been designed with a no-frills aesthetic using inexpensive industrial materials, readily available and quick to assemble." This analysis led Campaign to be inspired by the image of a warehouse stockroom, permitting them to build the project in just six days at the fraction of the cost of a normal store. Yellow and white fluorescent lighting is used, while an 18 x 3.5-meter bright yellow PVC curtain divides the space and recalls the brand's trademark yellow color. A Gypframe metal wall system is used for display, together with construction-site lamps, loading palettes, and shrink-wrapped salvaged furniture. Signage was stenciled with spray paint on the glass façades, concrete flooring, and shrink-wrapped objects.

Schuhe von **DR. MARTENS**, zunächst in Deutschland von Klaus Maertens und Herbert Funck entwickelt, werden seit 1960 von der R. Griggs Group Ltd. in Großbritannien produziert. Campaign erhielt den Auftrag, einen **POP-UP STORE** für das Unternehmen in Old Spitalfields Market im Londoner East End zu entwerfen. Gemeinsam mit der Markenagentur Fresh entwickelte Campaign einen Auftritt für die Marke, der dem Image des Produkts entspricht. Die Designer erklären: „Inspiriert von der Geschichte der Firma Dr. Martens und der Philosophie, durch die die Marke von einem Nutzartikel für Arbeiter zu einer Ikone der Gegenkultur katapultiert worden war, konzipierten wir den Store mit einer schnörkellosen Ästhetik. Es wurden kostengünstige, industrielle Materialien verwendet, die leicht zu beschaffen und schnell zu installieren waren." Vor diesem Hintergrund ließ Campaign sich von der Atmosphäre eines Lagerhauses anregen, sodass das Projekt in nur sechs Tagen zu einem Bruchteil der Kosten eines regulären Ladenlokals realisiert werden konnte. Gelbe und weiße Leuchtstoffröhren kamen zum Einsatz, ein 18 x 3,5 m großer gelber PVC-Vorhang gliedert den Raum und greift mit der Farbe Gelb ein Markenzeichen der Firma auf. Für die Präsentation der Waren wurden Regale aus den Metallteilen eines Trockenbausystems, Baustellenleuchten, Transportpaletten und in Folie eingeschweißte Objekte verwendet. Schließlich wurden Schriftzüge und Logos mit Schablonen auf die Glasfassaden, den Betonboden und die verschweißten Objekte gesprayt.

Créées en Allemagne par Klaus Maertens et Herbert Funck, les chaussures Dr. Martens sont fabriquées en Grande-Bretagne par le R. Griggs Group Ltd. depuis 1960. L'agence de design Campaign a été chargée de concevoir cette boutique éphémère, **LE DR. MARTENS POP-UP STORE** à l'Old Spitalfields Market, dans l'East End de Londres. En collaboration avec l'agence de gestion de marques Fresh, Campaign a misé sur une image qui corresponde à celle du produit. Comme elle l'explique : « Inspiré par le patrimoine de la marque Dr. Martens et son style qui a catapulté un article pour ouvriers au rang d'icône de la contre-culture, ce magasin a été conçu dans un esprit de recherche esthétique, sans fioritures, en utilisant des matériaux bon marché, disponibles et faciles à assembler. » Cette analyse a conduit à jouer sur l'image d'un stock d'entrepôt, ce qui a permis par ailleurs de réaliser le projet en six jours à peine pour une fraction du prix qu'aurait demandé un magasin normal. L'éclairage est jaune et blanc, et l'espace divisé par un rideau en PVC jaune vif de 18 x 3,5 mètres qui rappelle la couleur jaune de la marque. Un système de rangement mural Gypframe permet de présenter les chaussures dans un décor de lampes de chantier, de palettes de transport et de mobilier de récupération enveloppé de film plastique. La signalétique a été reproduite au pochoir et à la bombe sur les façades en verre, les sols en béton et les éléments de mobilier emballés.

The clever use of yellow PVC curtains more frequently found in an industrial environment gives the store an air of strong design that combines with practicality for shoppers.

L'utilisation habile de rideaux en PVC jaune, plus couramment trouvés dans un environnement industriel, confère un style affirmé au magasin qui reste néanmoins d'utilisation très pratique.

Der geschickte Einsatz eines PVC-Vorhangs, sonst eher in der Industrie üblich, gibt dem Laden sein markantes Designprofil und wahrt zugleich die Funktionalität für die Kunden.

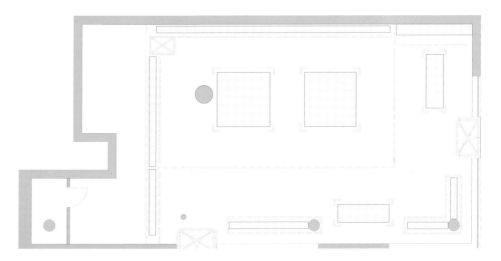

The use of shipping pallets and hanging industrial-type lights emphasizes the temporary nature of the installation as well as a ruggedness that suits the image of the client.

Transportpaletten und hängende Industrieleuchten betonen das Temporäre der Installation und wirken zugleich eher derb, was an das Image des Auftraggebers anknüpft.

Le recours à des palettes d'expédition et à des éclairages suspendus de type industriel renforce l'aspect temporaire de l'installation mais aussi le sentiment de robustesse attaché à l'image de marque de Dr. Martens.

Hanging work-site lights, perforated metal shelves, or a standing sign contribute to the "rough-and-ready" appearance of the sales space.

Hängende Baustellenlampen, Regale aus Lochblech und ein Werbeschild streichen die provisorische Optik des Verkaufsraums heraus.

Les éclairages de chantier, les rayonnages en tôle perforée ou un panneau triangulaire de signalétique contribuent à l'aspect « brut de décoffrage » de ce point de vente.

ARTHUR CASAS

Studio Arthur Casas SP
Rua Itápolis 818
01245–000 São Paulo, SP
Brazil

Tel: +55 11 2182 7500
Fax: +55 11 3663 6540
E-mail: sp@arthurcasas.com
Web: www.arthurcasas.com

ARTHUR CASAS was born in 1961 and graduated as an architect from the Mackenzie University of São Paulo, Brazil, in 1983. He has concentrated on both interiors and constructions, developing residential and commercial projects with a distinctive vocabulary of forms. He has participated in two Biennials of Architecture in São Paulo, in 1997 and 2003, and in the Buenos Aires Biennial, in 2003 and 2005. In 2008, Arthur Casas won the prestigious Red Dot Design Award, in Germany, for developing creative cutlery and dinner-set lines for Riva. His completed commercial projects include the Natura Store (Paris, France, 2005); Alexandre Herchcovitch store (Tokyo, Japan, 2007); Huis Clos Store (São Paulo, 2008); Cidade Jardim Mall (São Paulo, 2008); Zeferino store, Rua Oscar Freire (São Paulo, 2008, published here); Kosushi Restaurant (São Paulo, 2008); C-View Bar and C-House Restaurant, Affinia Hotel (Chicago, Illinois, USA, 2008); C-House Restaurant, Affinia Hotel (Chicago, Illinois, USA, 2008); KAA Restaurant (São Paulo, 2008); and the Jack Vartanian Store (New York, New York, USA, 2008), all in Brazil unless stated otherwise.

ARTHUR CASAS wurde 1961 geboren und schloss sein Studium 1983 an der Mackenzie University in São Paulo, Brasilien, ab. Er konzentriert sich gleichermaßen auf Innenarchitektur und Bauprojekte und entwickelt Wohn- und Gewerbebauten in einer unverwechselbaren Formensprache. Er war auf zwei Architekturbiennalen in São Paulo (1997 und 2003) vertreten sowie auf der Biennale in Buenos Aires (2003 und 2005). 2008 erhielt Casas für die Entwicklung einer kreativen Besteck- und einer Geschirrlinie für die Firma Riva den renommierten deutschen Red Dot Design Award. Zu seinen realisierten Bauten zählen Natura (Paris, Frankreich, 2005), Alexandre Herchcovitch (Tokio, Japan, 2007) und Huis Clos (São Paulo, 2008); ebenso das Einkaufszentrum Cidade Jardim (São Paulo, 2008), die Zeferino-Filiale auf der Rua Oscar Freire (São Paulo, 2008, hier vorgestellt), das Restaurant Kosushi (São Paulo, 2008), die Bar C-View und das Restaurant C-House im Affinia Hotel (Chicago, Illinois, USA, 2008), das Restaurant KAA (São Paulo, 2008) und der Jack Vartanian Store (New York, USA, 2008), alle in Brasilien sofern nicht anders angegeben.

Né en 1961, **ARTHUR CASAS** est diplômé en architecture de l'université Mackenzie à São Paulo (Brésil, 1983). Il se consacre à la fois à l'aménagement intérieur et à l'architecture et met en œuvre dans ses projets résidentiels ou commerciaux un vocabulaire formel personnel. Il a participé à deux Biennales d'architecture de São Paulo – 1997 et 2003 –, et à la Biennale de Buenos Aires en 2003 et 2005. En 2008, ses lignes de couverts et de services de table pour Riva ont remporté le prestigieux prix allemand Red Dot Design Award. Parmi ses projets d'architecture commerciale réalisés : le magasin Natura (Paris, 2005) ; le magasin Alexandre Herchcovitch (Tokyo, 2007) ; le magasin Huis Clos (São Paulo, 2008) ; le Cidade Jardim Mall (São Paulo, 2008) ; le magasin Zeferino, rue Oscar Freire (São Paulo, 2008, publié ici) ; le restaurant Kosushi (São Paulo, 2008) ; le bar C-View et le restaurant C-House, l'hôtel Affinia (Chicago, Illinois, 2008) ; le restaurant KAA (São Paulo, 2008) et le magasin Jack Vartanian (New York, 2008), tous au Brésil sauf mention contraire.

ZEFERINO

São Paulo, São Paulo, Brazil, 2008

Address: Rua Oscar Freire 924, 01426–001 São Paulo, SP, Brazil, +55 11 3846 7519, zeferino.com.br
Area: 96 m². Client: Zeferino Shoe Store. Cost: not disclosed

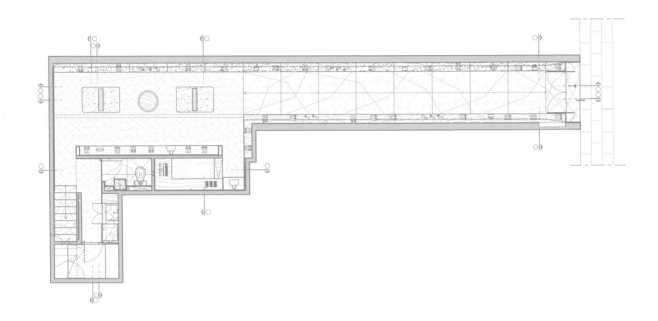

This shoe and accessories store is located at 924 Rua Oscar Freire in São Paulo. *Pierre grise* limestone with a hammered finish and black-and-beige carpet were used for the floors. Milled freijo wood and cement panels clad the walls, while the same wood covers the ceiling. Freijo (*Cordia alliodora*) is a tropical flowering tree whose wood is used for boat decking, furniture and cabinetry, as well as guitars. The architect states: "The tiny width of the lot (two meters) was what gave personality to the project. It forms a wooden box, with ramps, and angled ceilings at the same inclination as the floor. Mirrors give it a perspective and a sensation of a much bigger space." The glass façade of the entrance to the store emphasizes this boxlike design as well as the ceiling height. The transparency of the entrance contrasts with the willfully closed wooden surfaces of the interior.

Das Geschäft für Schuhe und Accessoires liegt auf der Rua Oscar Freire 924 in São Paulo. Die Böden wurden aus gehämmerten *Pierre grise*-Sandstein und schwarzem und beigem Teppich gestaltet. Die Wände sind mit geschliffenem Freijo-Holz und Zementplatten vertäfelt, auch die Decken wurden mit demselben Holz verkleidet. Freijo (*Cordia alliodora*) ist ein tropischer, blühender Baum, dessen Holz für Boots-, Möbel- und Gitarrenbau sowie Intarsienarbeiten verwendet wird. Der Architekt erklärt: „Seinen Charakter erhielt das Projekt durch das extrem schmale Grundstück (nur zwei Meter). Der Raum ist im Grunde eine hölzerne Box mit Rampen und schrägen Decken, die mit der Neigung des Bodens korrespondieren. Spiegel geben dem Raum Perspektive und lassen den Eindruck entstehen, er sei weitaus größer." Die Glasfassade mit Eingang unterstreicht den boxartigen Charakter ebenso wie die hohen Decken. Die Transparenz des Eingangsbereichs kontrastiert bewusst mit den geschlossenen Oberflächen des Innenraums.

Ce magasin de chaussures et d'accessoires est installé 924 rue Oscar Freire à São Paulo. Les sols sont en pierre grise martelée et moquette noire et beige. Les murs sont habillés de panneaux en bois de freijo usiné et de béton. Le même bois recouvre le plafond. Le freijo (*Cordia alliodora*) est un arbre tropical à fleurs dont le bois est utilisé pour les ponts de bateaux, le mobilier, la menuiserie mais aussi dans la fabrication de guitares. Pour l'architecte : « La faible largeur des lieux (deux mètres) donne au projet toute sa personnalité. C'est une boîte en bois, animée par des rampes et des plafonds qui suivent la pente du sol. Des miroirs créent une perspective et donnent la sensation d'un espace beaucoup plus vaste. » La façade de verre qui constitue l'entrée du magasin renforce cette impression de boîte tout en mettant en valeur la hauteur du plafond. Sa transparence contraste avec l'impression fermée donnée par l'habillage de bois des surfaces intérieures.

As the plan above and the photo to the right show, the Zeferino store has an extremely narrow layout, particularly near the entrance. The designer uses this quirky shape to create long, low display shelves.

Wie der Grundriss oben und die Aufnahme rechts belegen, sind die Ladenräume von Zeferino extrem schmal und lang, insbesondere im Eingangsbereich. Der Architekt nutzt den ungewöhnlichen Grundriss ideal durch lange, niedrige Regale.

Comme le montrent le plan ci-dessus et la photo de droite, la boutique Zeferino est extrêmement étroite, en particulier au niveau de l'entrée. Le designer a profité de ce volume un peu bizarre pour y insérer de chaque côté de très longs présentoirs pour les produits.

Setting shoes and bags up on small pedestals like works of art in a narrow gallery, the designer makes the most of the shape of the space, while the muted brown to tan color scheme allows the products to stand out.

Durch die Präsentation der Schuhe und Taschen auf kleinen Podesten – wie Kunstwerke in einer schmalen Galerie – nutzt der Architekt die Form des Raums optimal. Eine Farbpalette in gedeckten Braun- bis Honigtönen hebt die Produkte hervor.

En plaçant les chaussures et les sacs sur de petits socles – comme des œuvres d'art –, le designer tire le meilleur parti possible de la forme de l'espace. La gamme de couleurs brun-jaune mates fait ressortir les produits.

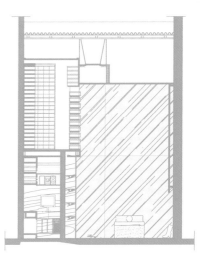

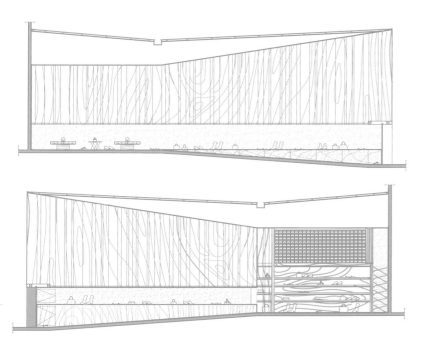

COLLI+GALLIANO

COLLIDANIELARCHITETTO
Via Sannio 61
00183 Rome
Italy

Tel: +39 6 97 61 04 47
Fax: +39 6 97 61 04 48
E-mail: mail@collidaniela.com
Web: www.collidaniela.com

LUCA GALLIANO ARCHITETTO
Via Cesare Beccaria 23
00196 Rome
Italy

Tel: +39 647 62 09
Fax: +39 647 72 76
E-mail: lucagalliano.studio@gmail.com
Web: www.lucagalliano.com

DANIELA COLLI was born in Piombino, Italy, in 1966, graduated from the Faculty of Architecture of the University of Florence, and completed a postgraduate course at City & Guilds in London. She worked with several offices in Rome, including that of Massimiliano Fuksas. She has been a consultant for Grandi Stazioni S.p.A. since 1998, working on the restructuring of the Rome Termini, Turin Porta Nuova, Genoa Brignole, and Genoa Principe railway stations. **LUCA GALLIANO** was born in Turin, Italy, in 1964 and graduated from the Faculty of Architecture in Rome. He has worked as a consultant with the Style Centre of Lotus Engineering (Norfolk, UK). He has also been a consultant for Grandi Stazioni S.p.A. since 1998. Having created their firm Colli+Galliano in 2005, the partners decided to separate in 2009, creating two new firms, ColliDanielArchitetto and Luca Galliano Architetto. Their work includes the Vyta Boulangerie Italiana (Rome, 2008, published here); Il Palazzetto Restaurant and Wine Bar (Rome, 2008); W.O.K. Restaurant and Bar (Rome, 2009), and the Moroni House (Rome, 2009), all in Italy.

DANIELA COLLI wurde 1966 in Piombino, Italien, geboren. Sie schloss ihr Studium an der Universität Florenz ab und absolvierte ein Postgraduiertenprogramm am City & Guilds in London. Sie arbeitete für verschiedene Büros in Rom, u.a. für Massimiliano Fuksas. Seit 1998 ist sie Beraterin für Grandi Stazioni S.p.A. und an der Sanierung der Bahnhöfe Roma Termini, Torino Porta Nuova, Genova Brignole und Genova Principe beteiligt. **LUCA GALLIANO** wurde 1964 in Turin, Italien, geboren und schloss sein Studium an der Fakultät für Architektur in Rom ab. Er war als Berater für das Style Centre von Lotus Engineering (Norfolk, Großbritannien) tätig. Auch er arbeitet seit 1998 als Berater für Grandi Stazioni S.p.A. Einige Jahre nach Gründung ihres Büros Colli+Galliano (2005) beschlossen die Partner 2009, wieder getrennte Wege zu gehen und gründeten eigene Büros – ColliDanielArchitetto und Luca Galliano Architetto. Zu ihren Projekten zählen die Vyta Boulangerie Italiana (Rom, 2008, hier vorgestellt), das Restaurant mit Weinbar Il Palazzetto (Rom, 2008), Restaurant und Bar W.O.K. (Rom, 2009) sowie das Haus Moroni (Rom, 2009), alle in Italien.

DANIELA COLLI, née à Piombino (Italie) en 1966, est diplômée de la Faculté d'architecture de l'université de Florence, études qu'elle a complétées à l'Institut City & Guilds à Londres. Elle a travaillé dans plusieurs agences à Rome, dont celle de Massimiliano Fuksas. Elle est consultante pour Grandi Stazioni S.p.A. depuis 1998, travaillant à la restructuration des gares de Rome Termini, Turin Porta Nuova, Gênes Brignole et Gênes Principe. **LUCA GALLIANO**, né à Turin en 1964 est diplômé de la Faculté d'architecture de Rome. Il a été consultant pour le Centre de style de Lotus Engineering (Norfolk, Angleterre) et l'est pour Grandi Stazioni S.p.A. depuis 1998. Après avoir fondé l'agence Colli+Galliano en 2005, les deux associés se sont séparés en 2009 pour créer deux agences ColliDanielArchitetto and Luca Galliano Architetto. Parmi leurs réalisations : la Boulangerie italiana Vyta (Rome, 2008, publiée ici) ; le restaurant et bar à vins Il Palazzetto (Rome, 2008) ; le restaurant et bar W.O.K. (Rome, 2009) et la Maison Moroni (Rome, 2009), toutes en Italie.

VYTA BOULANGERIE ITALIANA

Rome, Italy, 2008

Address: Galleria Centrale, Termini Station, Rome, Italy, +39 06 47 78 68 21, www.retailgroup.it
Area: 150 m². Client: Retail Group S.p.A. Cost: € 300 000

Located in Rome's Termini Station, this bakery is meant to be "totally projected toward the outside, and separated from it by a simple black portal." Oak is used on the floor and ceiling while black Corian furnishings contrast with the warmth of the wood. A decorative wall covering symbolizes "the surface and fragrance of bread crust," while a large counter serves as the "essential exhibition structure." Tables and chairs are set in a more intimate space, while compact black display alcoves are used to show wines and oils from the different regions of Italy. The architects state: "There is maximum design uniformity that slides unobtrusively into the busy station, while allocating ample room for the people waiting to depart, creating a relaxing ambience closely linked to the traditions that are hidden behind the minimalist lines—making Vyta a valid alternative to the world of fast food, and promoting good food culture."

Die Bäckerei im Bahnhof Roma Termini wurde so konzipiert, dass sich „ihre gesamte Wirkung nach außen richtet, sie jedoch durch ein schlichtes schwarzes Portal vom Außenraum abgegrenzt ist". Für Böden und Decken wurde Eiche verwendet, schwarze Einbauten aus Corian kontrastieren mit der Wärme des Holzes. Die dreidimensionale Wandstruktur versinnbildlicht „die Oberfläche und den Duft einer Brotkruste". Der große Tresen dient „im Wesentlichen als Präsentationsfläche". Tische und Stühle wurden zu intimeren Bereichen angeordnet, kompakte schwarze Wandvitrinen dienen der Präsentation von Weinen und Ölen aus den verschiedenen Regionen Italiens. Die Architekten erklären: „Das Design ist von größtmöglicher Geschlossenheit und integriert sich unaufdringlich in den Bahnhof. Zugleich bietet die Bäckerei großzügig Platz für wartende Reisende. Sie ist ein entspannendes Umfeld, das hinter der minimalistischen Anmutung dennoch der Tradition verbunden ist. Damit ist Vyta eine echte Alternative zur Welt des Fastfood und Botschafter einer gesunden Esskultur."

Implantée dans la gare Termini à Rome, cette boulangerie se veut « totalement projetée vers l'extérieur dont elle n'est séparée que par un simple portique noir ». Une partie des murs est parée de chêne dont la couleur chaleureuse contraste avec un habillage et des meubles en Corian noir. Le parement décoratif des murs latéraux illustre « la surface craquelée et l'odeur de la croûte de pain » tandis qu'un important comptoir fait office de « principale structure de présentation des produits ». Au fond, des tables et des chaises ont été installées dans un espace plus intime tandis que de petites alcôves noires permettent de présenter des vins et des huiles de diverses régions d'Italie. « L'objectif d'unité visé dans ce projet s'est aisément intégré dans l'atmosphère affairée de la gare. La boulangerie offre un espace généreux aux voyageurs en attente et crée une atmosphère décontractée, étroitement liée aux traditions alimentaires mises en valeur par le style minimaliste. Vyta devient une alternative séduisante au monde du fast food, et promet une culture alimentaire plus saine. »

The black gateway of the bakery seems appropriate for setting off the space of the station from the shop interior. Refinement is evident in the design and in the signage, for example.

Der schwarz gerahmte Eingangsbereich der Bäckerei ist ein wirkungsvolles Mittel, um die Bahnhofszone vom Ladenraum abzusetzen. Die Hochwertigkeit des Entwurfs zeigt sich im Design ebenso wie etwa in der Gestaltung der Beschilderung.

La façade noire de la pâtisserie semble une bonne solution pour séparer nettement le hall de la gare de l'intérieur du magasin. Le raffinement du projet est évident dans ses aménagements et sa signalétique.

The long shallow curve of the plan gives a certain dynamism to the design, perhaps recalling a curving railway platform, while maintaining the degree of elegance sought by the client.

La longue courbe du plan crée une certaine dynamique (peut-être pour rappeler un quai de gare incurvé), tout en maintenant le niveau d'élégance recherché par le client.

Der lange, flache Schwung des Grundrisses verleiht dem Entwurf Dynamik und mag manche an einen geschwungenen Bahnsteig erinnern. Zugleich wird die vom Auftraggeber gewünschte Eleganz erzielt.

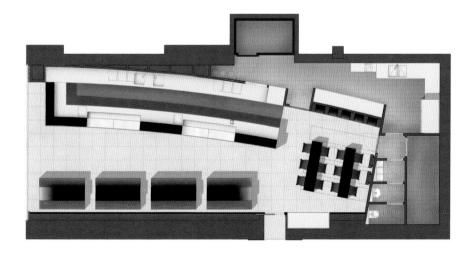

CONCRETE

Concrete Architectural Associates
Rozengracht 133 III
1016 LV Amsterdam
The Netherlands

Tel: +31 20 520 02 00
Fax: +31 20 520 02 01
E-mail: info@concreteamsterdam.nl
Web: www.concreteamsterdam.nl

Rob Wagemans was born in 1973. He created the interior design office **CONCRETE** Architectural Associates in 1997 with Gilian Schrofer and Erik van Dillen. Wagemans studied at the Academies of Architecture in Amsterdam and Utrecht and completed his studies with an M.Arch degree focusing on interior design. The firm, with a staff of 30, includes interior designers, product, communication, and graphic designers, as well as architects. It is divided into three divisions—Concrete Architectural Associates, Concrete Reinforced, and Studio Models + Monsters. Concrete worked with the architects UNStudio on the Mercedes-Benz Museum shops and restaurants (Stuttgart, Germany, 2006), while recent work includes the CitizenM Hotel at Schiphol Airport (Amsterdam, The Netherlands, 2008); the Pearls & Caviar Restaurant (Abu Dhabi, UAE, 2008); VIP Lounge at Schiphol Airport (Amsterdam, The Netherlands, 2008); the Supperclub (Singapore, 2008); the De Bijenkorf Kitchen (Amsterdam, The Netherlands, 2008); Coffee Company Prinsenhof (The Hague, The Netherlands, 2008, published here); and the Finca Pangola Eco Lodge (Costa Rica, 2009). Current work includes the W Hotel (Leicester Square, London, UK, 2010); and the 280-room W Hotel (Amman, Jordan, in progress).

Rob Wagemans wurde 1973 geboren. 1997 gründete er mit Gilian Schrofer und Erik van Dillen die gemeinsame Firma **CONCRETE** Architectural Associates, ein Büro für Innenarchitektur. Wagemans studierte Architektur in Amsterdam und Utrecht und schloss sein Studium mit einem M.Arch (Schwerpunkt Innenarchitektur) ab. Das Büro beschäftigt 30 Mitarbeiter, darunter Innenarchitekten, Produkt-, Kommunikations- und Grafikdesigner sowie Architekten. Die Firma gliedert sich in drei Bereiche: Concrete Architectural Associates, Concrete Reinforced und Studio Models + Monsters. Mit den Architekten von UNStudio arbeitete Concrete an den Museumsshops und -Restaurants des Mercedes-Benz Museums (Stuttgart, Deutschland, 2006). Jüngere Projekte sind u.a. das CitizenM Hotel am Flughafen Schiphol (Amsterdam, Niederlande, 2008), das Pearls & Caviar Restaurant (Abu Dhabi, VAE, 2008), die VIP Lounge am Flughafen Schiphol (Amsterdam, Niederlande, 2008), der Supperclub (Singapur, 2008), das Restaurant De Bijenkorf Kitchen (Amsterdam, Niederlande, 2008), die Coffee Company Prinsenhof (Den Haag, Niederlande, 2008, hier vorgestellt) und die Finca Pangola Eco Lodge (Costa Rica, 2009). Zu ihren aktuellen Projekten zählen das W Hotel am Leicester Square (London, Großbritannien, 2010) sowie das 280 Betten große W Hotel (Amman, Jordanien, im Bau).

Rob Wagemans, né en 1973, a créé l'agence d'architecture intérieure **CONCRETE** Architectural Associates en 1997, avec Gilian Schrofer et Erik van Dillen. Wagemans a étudié aux Académies d'architecture d'Amsterdam et d'Utrecht, études récompensées d'un M. Arch. d'architecture intérieure. L'agence, qui compte trente collaborateurs, réunit des architectes d'intérieur, des designers produits et de communication, des graphistes ainsi que des architectes, répartis en trois départements : Concrete Architectural Associates, Concrete Reinforced, et Studio Models + Monsters. Concrete a travaillé avec l'agence d'architecture UNStudio sur les boutiques et restaurants du musée Mercedes-Benz (Stuttgart, Allemagne, 2006). Plus récemment ont été réalisés : l'hôtel CitizenM (aéroport de Schiphol, Amsterdam, 2008) ; le restaurant Pearls & Caviar (Abou Dhabi, EAU, 2008) ; le salon VIP de l'aéroport de Schiphol (Amsterdam, 2008) ; le Supperclub (Singapour, 2008) ; le restaurant De Bijenkorf Kitchen (Amsterdam, 2008, publié ici) ; La Coffee Company Prinsenhof (La Hague, Pays-Bas, 2008, publiée ici) et le Finca Pangola Eco Lodge (Costa Rica, 2009). Parmi les projets en cours : l'hôtel W (Leicester Square, Londres, 2010) ; et l'hôtel W de 280 chambres (Amman, Jordanie, en chantier).

COFFEE COMPANY PRINSENHOF

The Hague, The Netherlands, 2008

*Address: Prinses Beatrixlaan 614, 2595 BM The Hague, The Netherlands,
+31 70 347 01 22, www.coffeecompany.nl/location
Area: 60 m². Client: Coffee Company b.v. Amsterdam. Cost: not disclosed*

This project was designed in eight weeks and built in just six. It is located in the atrium of the Prinsenhof office building in the Hague. This unusual, open location was the basis for the design. The shell of the coffee shop lifts up 2.5 meters at the push of a button. As Concrete states: "The **COFFEE COMPANY** literally becomes part of the atrium. In the evening the shell will move down in order to close up shop." The shell is made of a steel frame and steel tensile bars clad with mahogany boards 8 or 7.5 meters long. The hydraulic lifting system employs four 150 x 150-millimeter columns. A laser security system stops the movement of the shell if any person or object is directly beneath it. The counter and cabinet are made of plywood and Winckelmans tiles, with a Belgian ground freestone counter top. The tabletop is made of shaved azobe wood, sanded and finished with oil, while the railing is made of steel girders and strips surfaced in mahogany.

Das Projekt wurde in nur acht Wochen entworfen und nur sechs Wochen gebaut. Es liegt im Atrium des Bürogebäudes Prinsenhof in Den Haag – ein ungewöhnlicher, offener Standort, der Ausgangspunkt des Entwurfs war. Das Rahmengestell des Coffeeshops lässt sich per Knopfdruck 2,5 m in die Höhe fahren. Concrete erklärt: „Die **COFFEE COMPANY** wird buchstäblich zu einem Teil des Atriums. Abends lässt sich das Gehäuse nach unten fahren, um den Laden zu schließen." Das Gehäuse besteht aus einem Stahlrahmen mit Stahlzugstäben und ist mit 8 m bzw. 7,5 m langen Mahagonileisten verblendet. Das hydraulische System arbeitet mit vier Hubsäulen mit einer Stärke von je 150 x 150 mm. Ein Lasersicherheitssystem stoppt den Hubmechanismus des Gehäuses, sollte sich eine Person oder ein Gegenstand darunter befinden. Tresen und Einbauten sind aus Furnierplatten gearbeitet, die Fliesen stammen von Winckelmans, die Arbeitsplatte besteht aus geschliffenem belgischen Werkstein. Die Tischplatten aus Azobé wurden geschliffen und geölt. Das umlaufende Geländer wurde aus Stahlstreben und Mahagoni gefertigt.

Ce projet conçu en huit semaines a été réalisé en six. Il se trouve dans l'atrium de l'immeuble de bureaux du Prinsenhof à La Haye. L'idée de base est l'ouverture totale. La coque ou cage qui délimite l'espace de ce petit café se soulève de 2,5 mètres en appuyant sur un bouton. Comme l'explique Concrete : « La **COFFEE COMPANY** fait alors littéralement partie de l'atrium. Le soir, la cage redescend et referme le café. » Elle est constituée d'un cadre d'acier et de barreaux d'acier ductile sur lesquels sont fixées des lattes d'acajou de 7,5 ou 8 mètres de long. Le système de levage hydraulique est intégré dans des colonnes de section carrée de 15 x 15 cm. Un système de sécurité à laser arrête le mouvement de descente si une personne ou un objet se trouvent sur la trajectoire de la cage. Le comptoir et les rangements sont en contreplaqué et carrelage Winckelmans, et le plan de travail en grès belge. La table est en azobé raboté, sablé et huilé tandis que le garde-corps est en barreaux d'acier à barre d'appui en acajou.

The wooden cage around the coffee shop sets it off from its environment while maintaining the openness required to attract clients.

Der Holzkäfig um den Coffeeshop hebt ihn von seinem Umfeld ab und gewährleistet zugleich die nötige Transparenz, um Kunden anzuziehen.

La cage de bois détache ce café de son environnement et le singularise, tout en le laissant suffisamment ouvert pour attirer la clientèle.

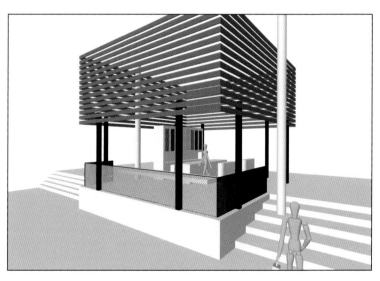

Simple furniture designs, warm wood, and some bright colors characterize the interior. The drawing to the left shows the wooden shell in the open position, but it slides down to close off the shop at night.

Schlichte Möbel, warmes Holz und einige farbige Akzente prägen das Interieur. Die Zeichnung links zeigt das Holzgerüst in geöffnetem Zutand, es lässt sich herunterfahren, wenn der Shop abends geschlossen wird.

Un mobilier simple, du bois de couleur chaude et quelques touches de couleurs vives personnalisent l'intérieur. Le dessin de gauche montre la cage en position ouverte. Elle descend pour refermer le café pendant la nuit.

TOM DIXON

Design Research Studio
Wharf Building
Portobello Dock
344 Ladbroke Grove
London W10 5BU
UK

Tel: + 44 20 74 00 05 00
Fax: + 44 20 74 00 05 01
E-mail: contact@designresearchstudio.net
Web: www.designresearchstudio.net

TOM DIXON was born in 1959 in Sfax, Tunisia, and moved to the United Kingdom as a child. He began designing furniture in his twenties without formal training. Amongst his many well-known furniture designs, the S-bend Chair, Kitchen Chair, and Bird chaise longue have been fabricated by Capellini since the 1990s. Tom Dixon has taught at the Royal College of Art, Kingston Polytechnic, and Plymouth University, and was appointed head of design for Habitat in 1998. He is the Creative Director of Tom Dixon (established by Tom Dixon and David Begg in 2002) and of Artek, the furniture design company founded in 1935 by Alvar Aalto. Dixon is also the Creative Director of the interior design firm Design Research Studio, which "is an interior design practice specializing in high-concept interiors, large-scale installations, and architectural design." Work of the Design Research Studio includes Tokyo Hipsters Club (Tokyo, Japan, 2006); Shoreditch House, a club created by Nick Jones (London, 2007); Paramount Club, located on the top three floors of Centrepoint (London, 2008); the Joseph Store published here (London, 2009); Circus (London, 2010); and the Tazmania Ballroom (Central district, Hong Kong, China, 2010), all in the UK unless stated otherwise.

TOM DIXON wurde 1959 in Sfax, Tunesien, geboren und siedelte als Kind mit seiner Familie nach Großbritannien um. Mit Mitte zwanzig begann er ohne formelle Ausbildung mit dem Entwerfen von Möbeln. Seit den 1990er-Jahren wurden zahlreiche bekannt gewordene Entwürfe, wie der Stuhl „S-bend", „Kitchen Chair" oder die Chaiselongue „Bird", von Capellini gefertigt. Tom Dixon lehrte am Royal College of Art, der Kingston Polytechnic und der Universität Plymouth und wurde 1998 Chefdesigner bei Habitat. Er ist Kreativdirektor seiner Firma Tom Dixon (2002 von Tom Dixon und David Begg gegründet) sowie bei Artek, des 1935 von Alvar Aalto gegründeten Möbelherstellers. Darüber hinaus ist Dixon Kreativdirektor von Design Research Studio, „einem Büro für Innenarchitektur, das sich auf perfekt durchkonzeptionierte Interieurs, Großinstallationen und architektonische Gestaltung spezialisiert hat". Zu den Projekten von Design Research Studio zählen der Tokyo Hipsters Club (Tokio, Japan, 2006), Shoreditch House, ein von Nick Jones entworfener Club (London, 2007), der Paramount Club auf den obersten drei Etagen des Centrepoint-Hochhauses (London, 2008), der hier vorgestellte Joseph Store (London, 2009), das Circus (London, 2010) sowie der Tazmania Ballroom (Central District, Hongkong, China, 2010), alle in Großbritannien, sofern nicht anders angegeben.

TOM DIXON, né en 1959 à Sfax en Tunisie, est arrivé en Angleterre encore enfant. Il a commencé à dessiner des meubles à partir de l'âge de 20 ans sans avoir reçu de formation pratique. Parmi ses modèles les plus connus figurent la chaise S-bend, la Kitchen chair et la chaise longue Bird fabriquées par Capellini depuis les années 1990. Il a enseigné au Royal College of Art, à la Kingston Polytechnic, à l'université de Plymouth et a été nommé responsable du design d'Habitat en 1998. Il est directeur de la création de Tom Dixon (agence fondée par lui et David Begg en 2002), d'Artek, entreprise de fabrication de mobilier fondée en 1935 par Alvar Aalto, ainsi que de l'agence d'architecture intérieure Design Research Studio, « spécialisée dans les aménagements intérieurs de conception sophistiquée, les installations à grande échelle et la conception architecturale ». Parmi les réalisations du Design Research Studio figurent le Hipsters Club (Tokyo, 2006) ; la Shoreditch House, club créé par Nick Jones (Londres, 2007) ; le Paramount Club, qui occupe les trois derniers niveaux de la tour Centrepoint (Londres, 2008) ; le magasin Joseph publié ici (Londres, 2009) ; le Circus (Londres, 2010) et le Tazmania Ballroom (Central district, Hong Kong, 2010), tous au Royaume-Uni sauf mention contraire.

JOSEPH STORE

London, UK, 2009

Address: 23 Old Bond Street, London W1S 4PZ, UK,
+44 20 76 29 37 13, www.joseph.co.uk
Area: 280 m². Client: not disclosed. Cost: not disclosed

Rough wood textures or visible utilities conduits mark the interior space, as do furniture or display stands designed by Tom Dixon.

Die Textur von rauem Holz und offen liegende Versorgungsleitungen prägen den Innenraum, ebenso wie die von Tom Dixon entworfenen Möbel und Ladeneinbauten.

L'espace est marqué par la texture brute des bois utilisés, la présence des conduites techniques, et bien sûr par les meubles et présentoirs dessinés par Tom Dixon.

Located on Old Bond Street in London, this **JOSEPH STORE** opened in May 2009. Tom Dixon states: "Joseph allowed us to create something unique that we wanted to do, to go in and be very not Bond Street. I think that the minimal aspect that Joseph has used is still very legitimate, but it is something that has been copied widely. What we tried to do was maintain the monochrome aspect but to bring in texture. The shop is now full of really quite intense texture and relief." With its industrial look, the store indeed differs from anything else on Bond Street. Rough plaster and unpolished stone mark the space as do metal ceiling covers and balustrades, together with projectors more often found in stage work. The designers conclude: "Metallic finishes and mechanized clothes rails provide more features. The result is an entirely unexpected addition to London's most refined and elegant fashion district."

Der **JOSEPH STORE** auf der Old Bond Street in London wurde im Mai 2009 eröffnet. Tom Dixon führt aus: "Joseph ermöglichte uns, etwas Einzigartiges umzusetzen – auf der Bond Street zu sein und dennoch so gar nicht die Bond Street zu verkörpern. Ich glaube, dass der minimalistische Ansatz, den Joseph verfolgt, nach wie vor durchaus legitim ist; allerdings wurde er weithin kopiert. Was wir hingegen versucht haben, ist das Monochrome beizubehalten, dafür aber Texturen einzubringen. Der Store ist jetzt voller starker Texturen und reliefartiger Oberflächen." Mit seinem industriellen Look unterscheidet sich der Laden tatsächlich von allen anderen auf der Bond Street. Grobputz und unpolierter Stein prägen den Raum, ebenso wie die Deckenpaneele und Geländer aus Metall oder die Scheinwerfer, die sonst in Theatern zu finden sind. Die Planer fassen zusammen: "Metallische Oberflächen und technisch anmutende Kleiderstangen sind weitere Charakteristika. Das Ergebnis ist eine absolut überraschende Bereicherung für Londons feinste und eleganteste Einkaufsmeile."

Situé dans Old Bond Street à Londres, le **JOSEPH STORE** a ouvert ses portes en mai 2009. Pour Tom Dixon : « Joseph nous a permis de créer quelque chose d'unique que nous voulions faire, être dans Bond Street, sans faire trop Bond Street. Je pense que le style minimaliste privilégié par Joseph reste très légitime, mais a été largement copié. Nous avons essayé d'en maintenir l'aspect monochrome, tout en apportant une texture. Le magasin exprime maintenant un relief et des textures assez intenses. » Par son style industriel, ce point de vente diffère certainement du style de Bond Street. Le plâtre brut et la pierre non polie personnalisent l'espace, de même que les revêtements de plafonds et les garde-corps métalliques ou les projecteurs que l'on trouve habituellement plutôt sur les scènes de théâtre. Dixon conclut : « Les finitions métalliques et les rails motorisés qui présentent les vêtements sont également des éléments nouveaux. Le tout apporte une contribution surprenante à l'un des quartiers de boutiques de mode les plus élégants et les plus raffinés de Londres. »

Whether they serve as small display stands or tables, the round lines of the furniture and its muted monochromatic palette fit into the shop perfectly. Right, a series of bent metal bands covers a stairway.

Utilisés comme tables ou petits présentoirs, les petits meubles ronds et la palette chromatique mate conviennent parfaitement à l'atmosphère du magasin. À gauche, des barres de métal plié isolent une cage d'escalier.

Ob nun als kleine Präsentationspodeste oder Tische im Einsatz – die geschwungenen Formen der Möbel und ihre gedämpfte monochrome Palette fügen sich ideal in das Interieur. Links die von Metallbändern eingefasste Treppe.

There is an almost archaic or organic feeling about the cylindrical changing booths, contrasting with the fine metal display structure in the foreground.

Die zylindrischen Umkleiden haben beinahe etwas Archaisches, Organisches und kontrastieren mit dem filigranen Metallregal im Vordergrund.

Les cabines d'essayage cylindriques projettent une impression d'archaïsme ou d'organicité qui contraste avec la finesse du présentoir au premier plan.

EDITH

Edith and 3Cabanes
9 Impasse Maire
77300 Fontainebleau
France

Tel: +33 678 19 20 80
E-mail: contact@edithedition.com
Web: www.edithedition.com / www.3cabanes.com

JEAN-GUILLAUME MATHIAUT received his architecture degree in 1999 (DPLG, Paris la Seine). He was a Creative Director with the architects François & Lewis (Paris, 1993–98) before becoming an Artistic Director at the Galeries Lafayette (Paris, 2000–05), where he organized exhibitions with Marcel Wanders, Jurgen Bey, Paul Smith, Jakob + MacFarlane, and Ingo Maurer. He created Edith Edition in 2007. His work has been exhibited at the Van Alen Institute (New York, Greenport Waterfront, 1996), and at the Pavillon de l'Arsenal in Paris (Génération transculturelle, 2000). He has designed furniture for the Paris graphic designers Antoine + Manuel, and Florence Doléac, who has also done installations in the Issey Miyake Boutique published here (Paris, 2008). Mathiaut has also designed a number of contemporary huts that have been exhibited at the Château de Fontainebleau (Château Flight, France, 2009–10).

JEAN-GUILLAUME MATHIAUT schloss sein Architekturstudium 1999 ab (DPLG, Paris la Seine). Er war Kreativdirektor im Architekturbüro François & Lewis (Paris, 1993–98), ehe er als Künstlerischer Leiter bei den Galeries Lafayette (Paris, 2000–05) Ausstellungen mit Designern wie Marcel Wanders, Jurgen Bey, Paul Smith, Jakob + MacFarlane und Ingo Maurer realisierte. 2007 gründete er Edith Edition. Seine Entwürfe waren am Van Alen Institute (New York, Greenport Waterfront, 1996) und im Pavillon de l'Arsenal in Paris (Génération transculturelle, 2000) zu sehen. Mathiaut entwarf Möbel für die Pariser Grafikdesigner Antoine + Manuel und für Florence Doléac, die auch Installationen für die hier vorgestellte Issey Miyake Boutique (Paris, 2008) gestaltete. Darüber hinaus entwarf Mathiaut mehrere moderne Hütten, die im Château de Fontainebleau (Château Flight, Frankreich, 2009–10) zu sehen waren.

JEAN-GUILLAUME MATHIAUT est diplômé en architecture (DPLG, Paris-Val de Seine). Il a été chef de projet à l'agence d'architecture François & Lewis (Paris, 1993–98), avant de devenir directeur artistique des Galeries Lafayette (Paris, 2000–05), où il a organisé des expositions pour Marcel Wanders, Jurgen Bey, Paul Smith, Jakob + MacFarlane et Ingo Maurer. Il a fondé Edith Edition en 2007. Son travail a été exposé au Van Alen Institute (New York, Greenport Waterfront, 1996) et au Pavillon de l'Arsenal à Paris (Génération transculturelle, 2000). Il a conçu des meubles pour les graphistes parisiens Antoine + Manuel et Florence Doléac, qui a également réalisé des installations pour la boutique Issey Miyake publiée ici (Paris, 2008). Mathiaut a également conçu des cabanes contemporaines, exposées au château de Fontainebleau (France, 2009–10).

ISSEY MIYAKE STORE

Paris, France, 2008

Address: 11 Rue Royale, 75008 Paris, France +33 1 48 87 01 86, www.isseymiyake.co.jp
Area: 420 m². Client: Issey Miyake. Cost: € 1.8 million

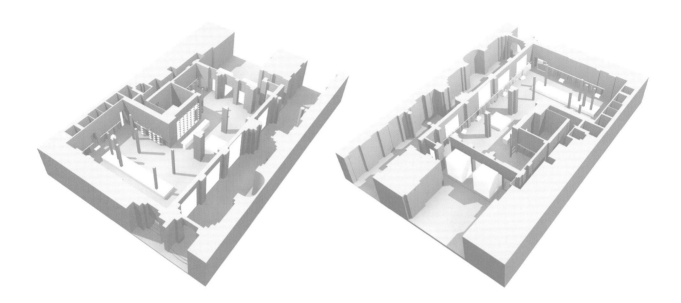

Located in an interior courtyard at 11 Rue Royale in Paris near the Concorde, the new **ISSEY MIYAKE STORE** was described at its opening on October 1, 2008, as a space dedicated to contemporary creation, "both didactic and dynamic." The original building was erected in the 17th and 18th centuries, and modified successively in the 1930s and the 1960s, with a variety of different ceiling heights that intrigued the architect. He describes his approach as being related to the concepts of a quarry and an atelier usable in different ways. "The idea," says Jean-Guillaume Mathiaut, "was to create an address and to exaggerate the existing situation, avoiding any sense of being closed in." Conceived and carried out in just five months, the interior design exudes a somewhat industrial feeling, with an obvious will to remove "parasitic" elements that might have distracted attention from the space itself. Not visible from the Rue Royale, the store is marked by a large, minimalist glass entry. Monolithic white Corian changing rooms form blocks near the entrance that are one of the main elements of the design, together with a vast 12-meter-long table intended for the display of the work of young creators and other furnishing elements also crafted in Corian. Issey Miyake has always worked in close collaboration with artists and this store, which covers the variety of the different lines and objects created by and for the Japanese designer, is one of his most successful and intriguing spaces.

Der neue **ISSEY MIYAKE STORE** liegt in einem Innenhof der Rue Royale 11 unweit der Place de la Concorde. Am Tag der Eröffnung, dem 1. Oktober 2008, wurde der Laden als Schauplatz zeitgenössischen, „didaktischen wie dynamischen" kreativen Schaffens beschrieben. Der ursprüngliche Altbau stammt aus dem 17. und 18. Jahrhundert und wurde in den 1930er- und 1960er-Jahren nach und nach umgebaut. Die verschiedenen Deckenhöhen faszinierten den Architekten. Sein Ansatz ist nach eigener Aussage vergleichbar mit einem Steinbruch oder einem Atelier, die man auf verschiedene Weisen nutzen kann. „Mein Gedanke war", so Jean-Guillaume Mathiaut, „eine Adresse zu schaffen, die vorhandene Raumsituation zu überzeichnen und dabei jedes Gefühl von Beengung zu vermeiden." Das Interieur, in nur fünf Monaten geplant und umgesetzt, wirkt in gewisser Weise industriell. Dabei ging es auch darum, alle „parasitären" Elemente zu entfernen, die vom eigentlichen Raum hätten ablenken können. Der von der Rue Royale nicht einsehbare Laden kündigt sich mit einem großen minimalistischen Entrée aus Glas an. Die Umkleidekabinen – monolithische weiße Corian-Blöcke – liegen unweit des Eingangs und sind eines der Hauptelemente des Entwurfs. Dasselbe gilt für den 12 m langen Tisch, auf dem Entwürfe junger Designer und Künstler präsentiert werden, ebenso wie für weitere Einbauten aus Corian. Issey Miyake arbeitet seit jeher eng mit Künstlern zusammen und dieser Laden, in dem die gesamte Bandbreite seiner verschiedenen Modelinien und auch Objekte zu sehen sind, die von und für den japanischen Designer entworfen wurden, ist eine seiner gelungensten und faszinierendsten Niederlassungen.

Située dans une cour intérieure au 11 rue Royale à Paris près de la place de la Concorde, la nouvelle **BOUTIQUE ISSEY MIYAKE** a été décrite lors de son ouverture, le 1er octobre 2008, comme un espace dédié à la création contemporaine « à la fois didactique et dynamique ». L'immeuble datant des XVIIe et XVIIIe siècles a été modifié dans les années 1930 et 1960 et la variété de hauteur de ses plafonds a intrigué l'architecte. Il décrit son approche s'apparentant aux concepts de carrière et d'atelier utilisables de multiples façons : « L'idée, a été de créer une vraie adresse et d'exagérer la situation de l'existant, en évitant tout sentiment d'enfermement. » Conçu et réalisé en cinq mois seulement, l'aménagement intérieur, d'aspect un peu industriel, traduit la volonté de supprimer les éléments « parasites » qui auraient pu distraire de la perception de l'espace. Invisible de la rue Royale, le magasin se signale cependant par une importante entrée en verre de style minimaliste. À proximité de celle-ci, des blocs monolithiques en Corian brun servent de cabines d'essayage. Ils constituent l'une des principales composantes du projet, de même que la table de 12 mètres de long, qui sert de présentoir aux travaux de jeunes créateurs, ou les éléments meublants, également en Corian. Issey Miyake a toujours travaillé en collaboration étroite avec des artistes et ce magasin, qui présente diverses lignes de vêtements et d'objets créées par ou pour le styliste japonais, est l'un de ses points de ventes les plus étranges et les plus réussis.

Located at the back of a courtyard on the chic Rue Royale in Paris, the boutique has intentionally been given an industrial appearance, emphasizing modernity over the more staid street leading from the Concorde to the Madeleine.

Die im hinteren Bereich eines Innenhofs an der eleganten Rue Royale gelegene Boutique in Paris hat bewusst einen industriellen Look. Hier erhält die Moderne Vorrang vor dem gesetzteren Flair der Straße, die von der Place de la Concorde zur Madeleine führt.

Située au fond d'une cour donnant sur l'élégante rue Royale à Paris, la boutique a volontairement pris cet aspect industriel qui affirme sa modernité par rapport au style classique de la rue menant de la place de la Concorde à celle de la Madeleine.

Two images show the boutique empty and two with merchandise in place. The coldness of the architectural design leaves a place of honor to the clothing.

Die zwei Ansichten zeigen die Boutique einerseits leer, andererseits mit Ware. Die kühle Architektur räumt der Mode einen Ehrenplatz ein.

Deux images montrant la boutique vide et achalandée. La froideur voulue de l'architecture laisse toute leur importance aux vêtements.

CARLOS FERRATER/OAB

Carlos Ferrater Partnership / OAB
Barcelona
C/Balmes 145 bajos
08008 Barcelona
Spain

Tel: +34 93 238 51 36
Fax: +34 93 416 13 06
E-mail: oab@ferrater.com
Web: www.ferrater.com

CARLOS FERRATER LAMBARRI was born in Barcelona, Spain, in 1944 and received his diploma from the Barcelona ETSAB (1971) and his doctorate from the same institution in 1987. He created his current office, **OAB**—Office of Architecture in Barcelona—with Xavier Martí, Lucía Ferrater, and Borja Ferrater in 2006. His work includes three city blocks in the Olympic Village (1992); the Hotel Rey Juan Carlos I (1992); Botanical Garden (1999); Catalonia Convention Center (2000); the Scientific Botanical Institute (2002); MediaPro Office complex (2008); and the Mandarin Oriental Hotel on the Passeig de Gracia (2010), all in Barcelona. He also designed an Intermodal Station (Zaragoza, 2003); an Auditorium (Castellón, 2004); the Royal Golf Club (Sabadell, 2004); the Aquileia Tower (Venice, Italy, 2008); the Science Park in Granada (2008); West Beach Promenade (Benidorm, 2009); and an office complex in Paris (France, 2010), all in Spain unless stated otherwise. His son, Borja Ferrater, was born in Barcelona in 1978. He studied biology from 1994 to 1997 at Temple University (Philadelphia) and the University of Navarre (Pamplona). He graduated as a licensed architect from the University of Catalonia (UIC, Barcelona, 2005). Lucia Ferrater Arquer, the daughter of Carlos Ferrater, was born in Barcelona in 1971. She graduated in 1997 from the ETSAB of Barcelona and became an Associate Architect in the Carlos Ferrater Studio in 1998. They both worked on the Roca Barcelona Gallery (Barcelona, 2008–09, published here).

CARLOS FERRATER LAMBARRI wurde 1944 in Barcelona geboren und absolvierte sein Diplom an der Technischen Fachhochschule für Architektur Barcelona (ETSAB, 1971), wo er 1987 auch promovierte. 2006 gründete er sein aktuelles Büro, **OAB** – Office of Architecture in Barcelona, mit Xavier Martí, Lucía Ferrater und Borja Ferrater. Zu seinen Projekten zählen zahlreiche Bauten in Barcelona, darunter drei Häuserblöcke im Olympischen Dorf (1992), das Hotel Rey Juan Carlos I (1992), der Botanische Garten (1999), das Katalanische Messezentrum (2000), das Botanische Institut (2002), der MediaPro Bürokomplex (2008) und das Mandarin Oriental am Passeig de Gracia (2010). Außerdem entwarf er den Umsteigebahnhof Las Delicias (Saragossa, 2003), ein Auditorium (Castellón, 2004), den Königlichen Golfclub (Sabadell, 2004), den Torre Aquileia (Venedig, Italien, 2008), den Wissenschaftspark in Granada (2008), die Strandpromenade West (Benidorm, 2009) und einen Bürokomplex in Paris (Frankreich, 2010), alle in Spanien, sofern nicht anders angegeben. Sein Sohn, Borja Ferrater, wurde 1978 in Barcelona geboren. Er studierte von 1994 bis 1997 Biologie an der Temple University (Philadelphia) und der Universität Navarra (Pamplona). Er schloss sein Studium als zertifizierter Architekt an der Universität von Katalonien ab (UIC, Barcelona, 2005). Lucía Ferrater Arquer, die Tochter von Carlos Ferrater, wurde 1971 in Barcelona geboren. Sie schloss ihr Studium 1997 an ETSAB in Barcelona ab und wurde 1998 Partnerin bei Carlos Ferrater Studio. Gemeinsam arbeiteten die beiden an der Roca Barcelona Gallery (Barcelona, 2008–09, hier vorgestellt).

CARLOS FERRATER LAMBARRI, né à Barcelone en 1944, est diplômé de l'École d'architecture de Barcelone (ETSAB, 1971) et docteur de la même institution (1987). Il a fondé son agence actuelle, **OAB** (Office of Architecture in Barcelona), avec Xavier Martí, Lucía Ferrater et Borja Ferrater en 2006. Parmi ses réalisations à Barcelone : trois blocs d'immeubles pour le village olympique (1992) ; l'hôtel Rey Juan Carlos I (1992) ; le jardin botanique (1999) ; le Centre de congrès de Catalogne (2000) ; L'Institut de botanique scientifique (2002) ; l'immeuble de bureaux MediaPro (2008) et l'hôtel Mandarin Oriental sur le Passeig de Gracia (2010). Il a également conçu la gare intermodale de Zaragoza-Delicias (2003) ; un auditorium (Castellón, 2004) ; le Golf Club royal (Sabadell, 2004) ; la tour Aquileia (Venise, 2008) ; le Parc des sciences à Grenade (2008) ; la promenade de la plage Ouest (Benidorm, 2009) et un immeuble de bureaux à Paris (2010). Son fils, Borja Ferrater, né à Barcelone en 1978, a étudié la biologie de 1994 à 1997 à Temple University (Philadelphia), puis à l'université de Navarre (Pampelune). Il est architecte licencié, diplômé de l'université de Catalogne (UIC, Barcelone, 2005). Lucía Ferrater Arquer, fille de Carlos Ferrater, née en 1971 à Barcelone, est diplômée de l'ETSAB de Barcelone (1997) et est architecte associée du Carlos Ferrater Studio depuis 1998. Tous deux ont travaillé sur le projet de la Galerie Roca Barcelona (Barcelone, 2008–09, publiée ici).

ROCA BARCELONA GALLERY

Barcelona, Spain, 2008–09

Address: C/ Joan Guell 211–213, 08028 Barcelona, Spain,
+34 93 366 1212, www.roca.com.es/rocabarcelonagallery/rocabarcelonagallery/en
Area: 2029 m². Client: Roca Sanitaria S.A. Cost: not disclosed

Roca describes itself as "the world leader in bathroom spaces" and this gallery as "a brand experience centre which will host exhibitions and social and cultural activities."

Roca versteht sich selbst als „weltweit führenden Badausstatter" und diese Galerie als „Marken-Erlebniscenter für Ausstellungen und gesellschaftliche und kulturelle Aktivitäten".

Roca se présente comme « le leader mondial de la salle de bains » et cette galerie comme « un centre de découverte de la marque qui accueillera des expositions et des activités sociales et culturelles ».

The architects state clearly that "in the very first stages of conceiving the institutional headquarters of Roca (or **ROCA BARCELONA GALLERY**) the architectural design was already understood as a tool for disseminating a brand and the company behind it." This headquarters building is also intended as a museum for the brand and a "platform for social events that involve the business world." Surrounded by other buildings, the Gallery is distinguished by its small size and its clean lines. Despite its apparent simplicity, the building is indeed "eye-catching" as the architects affirm. An essential element in this strategy is the skin made of a succession of planes of glass set at a ninety-degree angle vis-à-vis the façade. The architects state: "It was light, both natural daylight and artificial nightlight, that went on to become the main protagonist. In this way we obtained a totally ambiguous façade that appears as a solid sort of element by day and a liquid one by night, both heavy and light, rough and smooth, and it is difficult at times to recognize if its character is transparent, translucent or opaque." Interior space continues the impression of ambiguity created by the façade with motion detectors, loudspeakers, and projectors that emphasize movement, conceived by the architects in collaboration with specialists in each area. The floors are treated in slightly reflective ceramics, while the ceiling is clad in stainless steel and foam tetrahedrons cover the walls, creating a "weightless space."

Die Architekten machen unmissverständlich klar, dass „die architektonische Gestaltung der Zentrale von Roca (oder auch **ROCA BARCELONA GALLERY**) schon in der Anfangsphase des Entwurfsprozesses eindeutig als Instrument verstanden wurde, um die Marke und die dahinter stehende Firma zu promoten". Die Firmenniederlassung soll außerdem als Firmenmuseum und als „Plattform für gesellschaftliche Events dienen, bei denen sich die Geschäftswelt trifft". Die von anderen Bauten umgebene Gallery unterscheidet sich schon durch ihre geringere Größe und ihre klaren Linien. Trotz seiner Schlichtheit zieht der Bau durchaus die Blicke auf sich, wie die Architekten betonen. Dies verdankt sich im wesentlichen der Strategie, die Gebäudehaut aus Glasscheiben zu gestalten, die im 90°-Winkel zur Fassade installiert wurden. Die Architekten erklären: „Das Licht – das natürliche Tageslicht ebenso wie das künstliche Licht bei Nacht – wurde zum Hauptdarsteller. Auf diese Weise haben wir eine vollkommen mehrdeutige Fassade geschaffen, die tagsüber massiv, nachts jedoch wie flüssig wirkt; schwer und leicht, rau und glatt zugleich. Manchmal ist es schwer auszumachen, ob sie transparent, transluzent oder opak ist." In den Innenräumen setzt sich der Eindruck der Mehrdeutigkeit fort: hier allerdings durch Bewegungsmelder, Lautsprecher und Projektoren, die Bewegungen akzentuieren und von den Architekten in Zusammenarbeit mit Fachleuten entwickelt wurden. Auf den Böden wurden matt reflektierende Fliesen verlegt, die Decken mit Edelstahl verblendet, Tetraeder aus Schaumstoff überziehen die Wände – so entstand ein scheinbar „schwereloser" Raum.

Les architectes précisent que « dès les tout premiers stades de la conception, le projet architectural du siège institutionnel de Roca (**ROCA BARCELONA GALLERY**) a été considéré comme un moyen de faire connaître la marque et l'entreprise dont elle est l'expression ». Cet immeuble est également un musée de la marque et « une plate-forme pour événements du monde des affaires ». Entourée d'autres immeubles, la galerie se distingue par ses dimensions réduites et la rigueur de ses lignes. Malgré sa simplicité apparente, le bâtiment « attire les regards », notent ses auteurs. Un des éléments stratégiques essentiels est une peau extérieure composée de panneaux de verre posés à 90° par rapport à la façade. « La lumière, aussi bien naturelle le jour qu'artificielle la nuit, est devenue la principale protagoniste du projet. Nous avons ainsi obtenu une façade totalement ambiguë, qui semble massive le jour et liquide la nuit, à la fois lourde et légère, brute et lisse, au point qu'il est même parfois difficile de percevoir si elle est transparente, translucide ou opaque », expliquent les architectes. Le volume intérieur développe cette impression d'ambiguïté par des détecteurs de mouvement, des haut-parleurs et des projecteurs qui mettent en valeur les déplacements, conçus et installés par les architectes en collaboration avec des spécialistes de chacun de ces domaines. Les sols sont en carrelage de céramique, légèrement réfléchissants, tandis que le plafond est habillé d'acier inoxydable et les murs revêtus de tétraèdres de mousse pour créer une impression « d'espace impondérable ».

The intervention of OAB certainly places an emphasis on strict architectural volumes as opposed to any overt identification of the brand.

Die Intervention von OAB betont zweifellos die recht strengen architektonischen Volumina, ohne die Marke allzu offensichtlich in den Vordergrund zu rücken.

L'intervention d'OAB a résolument mis l'accent sur des volumes architecturaux rigoureux, indépendant de toute identification ouverte à la marque.

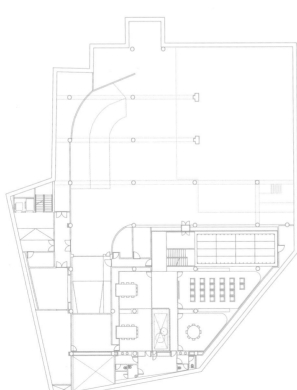

Showroom spaces resemble a
museum more than a typical bathroom display. The mostly light-colored
fixtures are contrasted with a dark
environment in which architecture
and lighting form the space.

Der Showroom wirkt eher museal
als wie ein typischer Ausstellungsraum für einen Badausstatter. Die
zumeist farbigen Leuchten schaffen
Kontraste zum dunklen Umfeld, in
dem Architektur und Licht gleichermaßen raumgestaltend wirken.

Les salles du showroom font
davantage penser à celles d'un musée qu'à une exposition de sanitaires.
Généralement de couleur claire, les
éléments présentés contrastent avec
l'environnement sombre créé par l'architecture et l'éclairage étudié.

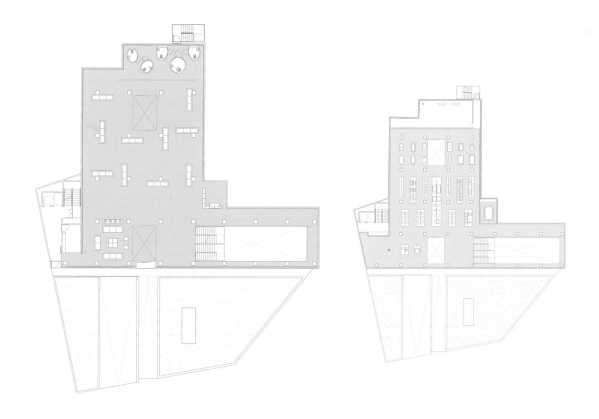

FOREIGN OFFICE ARCHITECTS

Foreign Office Architects (FOA)
55 Curtain Road
London EC2A 3PT
UK

Tel: +44 20 70 33 98 00
Fax: +44 20 70 33 98 01
E-mail: press@f-o-a.net
Web: www.f-o-a.net

FOREIGN OFFICE ARCHITECTS is led by architects Farshid Moussavi and Alejandro Zaera-Polo, and is "known for combining technical innovation with design excellence." Farshid Moussavi received her M.Arch degree from Harvard GSD. She worked for the Renzo Piano Building Workshop (Genoa, 1988) and for OMA, before establishing Foreign Office Architects in 1993. Educated at the ETSA of Madrid and Harvard GSD, Alejandro Zaera-Polo worked with OMA in Rotterdam at the same time as Farshid Moussavi. Together they completed the Yokohama International Port Terminal (Yokohama, Japan, 1995–2002); Dulnyouk Publishers (Paju City, South Korea, 2005); La Rioja Technology Transfer Center (Logroño, Spain, 2007); Carabanchel Social Housing (Madrid, Spain, 2007); Meydan Retail Complex and Multiplex (Istanbul, Turkey, 2006–07, published here); and the John Lewis Department Store and Cineplex (Leicester, UK, 2006–08, also published here). Ongoing work includes Ravensbourne College of Design and Communication (London, UK, 2010); Museum of Contemporary Art (Cleveland, Ohio, USA, completion date to be determined); Watermark WestQuay Commercial and Residential Development (Southampton, UK, completion date to be determined); and the Birmingham New Street Station (Birmingham, UK, 2014).

FOREIGN OFFICE ARCHITECTS arbeitet unter der Leitung der Architekten Farshid Moussavi und Alejandro Zaera-Polo und ist „bekannt dafür, technische Innovation mit herausragendem Design zu verbinden". Farshid Moussavi absolvierte ihren M.Arch an der Harvard GSD. Sie arbeitete für Renzo Piano Building Workshop (Genua, 1988) und OMA, bevor sie 1993 Foreign Office Architects gründete. Alejandro Zaera-Polo studierte an der ETSA Madrid sowie der Harvard GSD und arbeitete zur gleichen Zeit wie Farshid Moussavi bei OMA in Rotterdam. Gemeinsam konnten sie Projekte realisieren wie das Terminal im Internationalen Hafen von Yokohama (Yokohama, Japan, 1995–2002), ein Verlagsgebäude für Dulnyouk (Paju City, Südkorea, 2005), das La Rioja Technologietransfer-Center (Logroño, Spanien, 2007), Sozialbauten in Carabanchel (Madrid, 2007), den Shoppingkomplex Meydan mit Multiplex-Kino (Istanbul, Türkei, 2006–07, hier vorgestellt) sowie das Kaufhaus John Lewis mit Cineplex (Leicester, Großbritannien, 2006–08, ebenfalls hier vorgestellt). Derzeit in Arbeit sind das Ravensbourne College of Design and Communication (London, 2010), das Museum of Contemporary Art (Cleveland, Ohio, USA, Datum der Fertigstellung noch offen), der Einkaufs- und Wohnkomplex Watermark WestQuay (Southampton, Großbritannien, Datum der Fertigstellung noch offen) und der Bahnhof New Street in Birmingham (Birmingham, Großbritannien, 2014).

L'agence **FOREIGN OFFICE ARCHITECTS**, dirigée par les architectes Farshid Moussavi et Alejandro Zaera-Polo, est réputée « combiner l'innovation technique et l'excellence de conception ». Farshid Moussavi a obtenu son M. Arch. de la Harvard GSD. Elle a travaillé pour le Renzo Piano Building Workshop (Gênes, 1988) et pour OMA, avant de fonder Foreign Office Architects en 1993. Formé à l'ETSA de Madrid et à la Harvard GSD, Alejandro Zaera-Polo a travaillé pour OMA à Rotterdam au même moment que Farshid Moussavi. Ensemble, ils ont réalisé le terminal international du port de Yokohama (Japon, 1995–2002) ; le siège des éditions Dulnyouk (Paju City, Corée du Sud, 2005) ; le centre de transfert de technologies de la Rioja (Logroño, Espagne, 2007) ; des logements sociaux à Carabanchel (Madrid, 2007) ; le centre commercial et multiplexe de cinéma de Meydan (Istanbul, Turquie, 2006–07, publié ici) et le grand magasin et Cineplex John Lewis (Leicester, Angleterre, 2006–08, également publié ici). Actuellement, ils travaillent sur les projets du Collège de design et de communication de Ravensbourne (Londres, 2010) ; le Musée d'art contemporain de Cleveland (Ohio, date d'achèvement non fixée) ; l'ensemble commercial et résidentiel de Watermark WestQuay (Southampton, Angleterre, date d'achèvement non fixée) et la gare de New Street à Birmingham (Angleterre, 2014).

MEYDAN RETAIL COMPLEX AND MULTIPLEX

Ümraniye, Istanbul, Turkey, 2006–07

*Address: M1 Meydan, Alisveris Merkezi, Çakmak Mah. Metro Group Sok. No. 243 34770, Ümraniye, Istanbul, Turkey,
+90 216 526 0101, www.m1meydan.com.tr
Area: 55 000 m². Client: Metro Group AG. Cost: € 34 million*

This complex is located in a suburban area of the Asian part of Istanbul. It is set near an Ikea store and future residential lots. By placing parking areas below grade, the architects were able to create a generous urban square in the center of the plan. Foreign Office Architects sought to "organize the retail volumes as an extension of the surrounding topography rather than as sheds deployed onto an asphalt platform." Anticipating the future development of the urban context, the architects have "continuously connected" the complex "with the urban space beyond." The green roofs of the shopping center serve to give park space to an area badly in need of it, and also to improve the energy efficiency of the buildings. Ventilation, including in the car park, is natural, and solar panels power public lighting. For the first time in Turkey, heating and cooling comes from boreholes rather than a traditional mechanical system. "Lastly," conclude the architects, "through its geometry and placement on the site, the scheme maximizes natural shading and creation of wind shelters, using architectural massing to change and improve the local environment instead of mechanical reparative measures."

Der Komplex liegt in einem Vorort auf der asiatischen Seite Istanbuls, unweit einer Ikea-Niederlassung und einer geplanten Wohnsiedlung. Indem die Architekten die Parkplätze unter Tage verlegten, gelang es, einen großzügigen urbanen Platz im Herzen der Anlage zu schaffen. Foreign Office Architects ging es darum, „die Baukörper des Einkaufskomplexes als Fortsetzung der Topografie des Umfelds zu organisieren, statt als ‚Gebäudeschuppen' auf einer asphaltierten Plattform." Sie planten die künftige Entwicklung des urbanen Kontexts bereits ein und „banden" den Komplex entsprechend „konsequent an den angrenzenden städtischen Raum an". Die begrünten Dächer des Einkaufszentrums verhelfen dem Umfeld zu einem dringend benötigten Park und verbesserten zugleich die Energieeffizienz der Bauten. Die Belüftung, einschließlich die des Parkhauses, ist natürlich. Solarpaneele liefern Energie für die Beleuchtung der öffentlichen Bereiche. Heizwärme und Kühlung werden aus geothermischen Bohrlöchern bezogen statt aus einem herkömmlichen Lüftungssystem – ein Novum für die Türkei. „Schließlich", resümieren die Architekten, „werden die natürliche Bildung von Schatten- und Windschattenzonen durch die Geometrie und Anordnung der Baukörper auf dem Grundstück maximiert. So wird die architektonische Baumasse genutzt, um die lokale Umwelt zu verändern und zu verbessern, statt sie später mit mechanischen Mitteln wiederherzustellen."

Ce complexe est situé dans une banlieue d'Istanbul sur la côte asiatique, près d'un magasin Ikea, et non loin d'un projet de lotissements résidentiels. En implantant les parkings en sous-sol, les architectes ont pu dégager l'emplacement d'une importante place au centre du projet. FOA a cherché à « organiser les volumes consacrés au commerce comme une extension de la topographie locale plutôt qu'à la manière habituelle qui consiste à répartir des hangars sur une plate-forme asphaltée ». Anticipant les développements futurs de son contexte, le complexe « est en permanence connecté à l'espace urbain qui l'entoure ». Les toits végétalisés du centre commercial apportent une sensation d'espace vert à une banlieue qui en manque cruellement, et améliorent l'efficacité énergétique des bâtiments. La ventilation, y compris celle des parkings, est naturelle et l'éclairage public est alimenté par des panneaux solaires. Pour la première fois en Turquie, le chauffage et le refroidissement proviennent de forages plutôt que d'un système mécanique conventionnel. « Enfin », concluent les architectes, « par sa géométrie et son implantation sur le site, ce schéma optimise l'ombre naturelle et crée des zones protégées du vent ; c'est la structuration du plan masse, et non des procédés mécaniques compensateurs, qui permet de modifier et d'améliorer l'environnement local. »

Faithful to the rather geological style that they have often employed, FOA here introduces continuity and a green consciousness to the retail shopping environment.

Dem vergleichsweise geologischen Ansatz treu bleibend, den FOA oft verfolgt, setzen die Architekten hier räumliche Kontinuität und Umweltbewusstsein im Kontext eines Shoppingumfelds um.

Fidèle au style assez géologique qu'ils ont souvent employé, les architectes de FOA introduisent ici dans l'univers du commerce de détail un esprit de continuité et de conscience écologique assez rares.

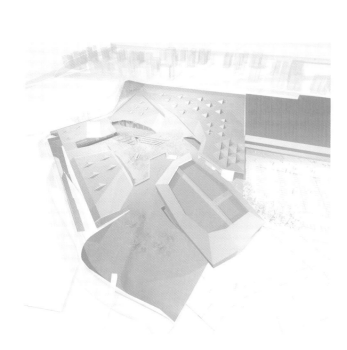

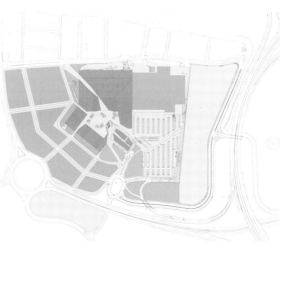

The roofs of the complex sometimes slope down to ground level or rise up to allow for double-height glazing (below).

Die Dächer des Komplexes sind zum Teil bis zum Boden hinuntergezogen oder schwingen sich hoch auf, sodass eine doppelgeschossige Verglasung möglich wird (unten).

La toiture du complexe descend parfois jusqu'au sol ou se relève pour laisser place à des murs de verre double-hauteur (ci-dessous).

An inner courtyard (above) might resemble an urban park more than a shopping-center space. Section drawings show how the parking areas are situated at ground level below the enveloping shell of the complex.

Der Innenhof (oben) wirkt eher wie ein Stadtpark als wie das Gelände eine Shoppingcenters. Querschnitte illustrieren die Lage der Parkflächen im Erdgeschoss unter der Gebäude-hülle des Komplexes.

La cour intérieure (ci-dessus) ressemble davantage à un parc urbain qu'à un centre commercial. Les coupes montrent l'implantation des parkings au rez-de-chaussée sous l'enveloppe du complexe.

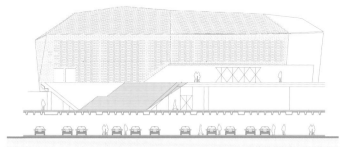

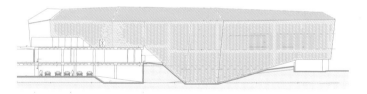

JOHN LEWIS DEPARTMENT STORE AND CINEPLEX

Leicester, UK, 2006–08

Address: 2 Bath House Lane, Highcross, Leicester LE1 4SA, UK,
+44 11 62 42 57 77, www.johnlewis.com/Shops/DSShop.aspx?Id=38
Area: 34 000 m². Client: Hammerson PLC. Cost: £44 million

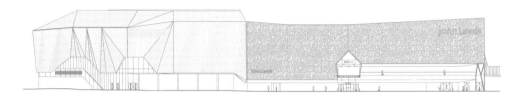

Playing on the irregular reflectivity of the surface cladding, the architects give an almost evanescent impression of the John Lewis Department Store, creating a sculptural object that is recognizable yet not typical of retail design.

Indem sie mit den unregelmäßigen Spiegeleffekten der Gebäudehülle spielen, lassen die Architekten das John-Lewis-Kaufhaus fast ephemer wirken. So entsteht ein skulpturales Objekt mit Wiedererkennungswert – eine eher untypische Einzelhandels-architektur.

Jouant de la réflexion irrégulière de la lumière sur l'habillage des façades du grand magasin John Lewis, FOA donne une quasi impression d'éva-nescence à cet objet sculptural forte-ment identifiable bien que non typi-que de l'architecture commerciale.

This complex, which is part of a larger city-center regeneration plan, borders Vaughan Way to the northwest and the Shires Shopping Center to the southeast. The architects have sought new ways to relate the building to its urban context, in particular cladding the store with a double-glazed façade, forming a kind of "net curtain" that allows natural light into the buildings, and offers a controlled transparency between the store interiors and the city. Thus, the façade allows the store to reconfigure its interiors without compromising on its exterior appearance. The four-panel pattern with varying densities used by the architects recalls those in the 200-year-old textile archives of John Lewis, and intentionally creates a moiré effect when seen from street level. Farshid Moussavi states: "At a time of online shopping, we thought there should be something special about a physical department store." The curtain idea is also extended to the 12-theatre Cineplex to give it continuity with the store, but here becomes "an opaque stainless-steel rain screen," pleated and treated with a mirror finish.

Der Komplex entstand im Zuge eines Verjüngungsplans für das Stadtzentrum von Leicester und grenzt im Nordwesten an den Vaughan Way und im Südosten an das Shires Shoppingcenter. Den Architekten ging es darum, den Bau auf neue Weise in Bezug zu seinem urbanen Kontext zu setzen. Dafür arbeiteten sie insbesondere mit einer Doppelglasfassade, die wie eine Gardine Tageslicht in das Gebäude lässt und von außen kontrolliert transparent wirkt. Die Planung des Innenraums ermöglicht räumliche Neukonfigurationen, ohne Eingriffe in die Fassade zu erfordern. Das von den Architekten entworfene Fassadenmuster, das sich über vier Paneele erstreckt und von unterschiedlicher Dichte bzw. Transparenz ist, greift Muster aus den 200 Jahre alten Textilarchiven von John Lewis auf und erzeugt bewusst einen Moirée-Effekt, der von der Straße aus sichtbar wird. Farshid Moussavi erklärt: „In Zeiten des Onlineshoppings meinen wir, dass ein reales Warenhaus etwas Besonderes haben sollte." Um sich in das Gesamtbild des Kaufhauses zu fügen, wurde das Vorhang-Prinzip auf das Cineplex mit seinen zwölf Kinos ausgeweitet. Hier jedoch ist er zu einem „opaken Wandschirm aus Edelstahl" gefaltet und auf Spiegelhochglanz poliert.

Ce complexe, qui fait partie d'un vaste plan de rénovation du centre-ville, s'étend en bordure de Vaughan Way au nord-ouest et du centre commercial des Shires au sud-est. Les architectes ont recherché de nouvelles façons de relier une opération de ce type au contexte urbain, en particulier par l'habillage extérieur d'une façade d'un double-vitrage qui forme une sorte de « rideau-filet », permettant à la lumière naturelle de pénétrer dans les bâtiments et d'installer une transparence contrôlée entre l'intérieur des magasins et la ville. Ainsi, la façade permet-elle à ce centre commercial de pouvoir reconfigurer son organisation interne sans remettre en cause son aspect extérieur. Le motif utilisé, en quatre panneaux et de densités variées, rappelle des échantillons de tissus vieux de deux siècles trouvés dans les archives de John Lewis. Ils créent un effet volontaire de moirage sensible de la rue. Farshid Moussavi précise : « À l'époque du shopping par internet, nous avons pensé qu'un grand magasin devait offrir quelque chose de spécial dans sa dimension physique. » L'idée de rideau a été étendue au multiplexe de douze salles de cinéma pour assurer une continuité avec le magasin, mais il est traité cette fois comme « un écran opaque de protection contre la pluie en acier inoxydable », plié et poli comme un miroir.

An elaborate arabesque pattern inspired by textiles in the John Lewis archives lightens the structure and gives an impression that might be likened to lacework from a distance.

Ein kunstvolles Arabeskenmuster, angeregt von Stoffentwürfen aus den John-Lewis-Archiven, gibt dem Bau Leichtigkeit und wirkt von weitem fast wie Spitze.

Un motif d'arabesques élaborées inspiré de tissus tirés des archives de John Lewis allège la structure en donnant, de loin, une impression de dentelle.

Cut-out patterns and an irregular metallic cage-like passage move clearly away from any notion of strict geometric alignments.

Scherenschnittartige Muster und unregelmäßige, käfigähnliche Gänge aus Metall sind zweifellos weit entfernt von streng geometrischer Linienführung.

Des motifs découpés et un passage en forme de cage métallique irrégulière montrent que l'on est loin des stricts alignements géométriques.

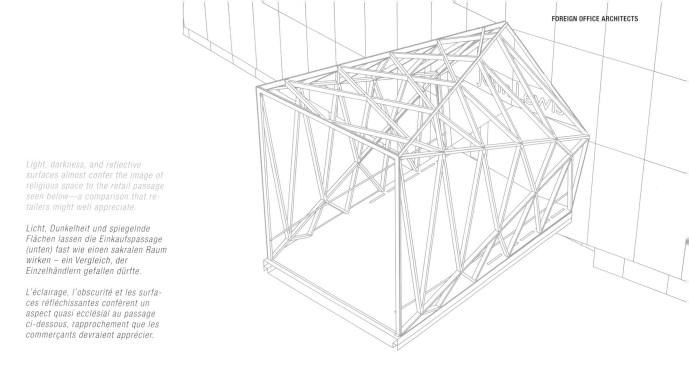

Light, darkness, and reflective surfaces almost confer the image of religious space to the retail passage seen below—a comparison that retailers might well appreciate.

Licht, Dunkelheit und spiegelnde Flächen lassen die Einkaufspassage (unten) fast wie einen sakralen Raum wirken – ein Vergleich, der Einzelhändlern gefallen dürfte.

L'éclairage, l'obscurité et les surfaces réfléchissantes confèrent un aspect quasi ecclésial au passage ci-dessous, rapprochement que les commerçants devraient apprécier.

MASSIMILIANO AND DORIANA FUKSAS

Massimiliano and Doriana Fuksas
Piazza del Monte di Pietà 30 / 00186 Rome / Italy

Tel: +39 06 68 80 78 71 / Fax: +39 06 68 80 78 72
E-mail: office@fuksas.it / Web: www.fuksas.it

MASSIMILIANO FUKSAS was born in 1944 in Rome, Italy. He received his degree in Architecture at the "La Sapienza" University of Rome in 1969. He created Granma (1969–88) with Anna Maria Sacconi, and opened an office in Paris in 1989. He won the 1999 Grand Prix d'Architecture in France, and has written the architecture column of the Italian weekly *L'Espresso* since 2000. He was the Director of the 7th Architecture Biennale in Venice (1998–2000). He has worked with Doriana Mandrelli Fuksas since 1985. She attended the Faculty of Architecture at the "La Sapienza" University of Rome and has been responsible for design in the firm since 1997. The presence in France of Massimiliano Fuksas was notably marked by his work at the Mediatheque in Rézé (1987–91); the National Engineering School in Brest (ENIB ISAMOR, 1990–92); the Maison des Arts at the Michel de Montaigne University in Bordeaux (1992–95); and the Maximilien-Perret High School Alfortville near Paris (1995–97). His Cor-ten steel entrance for the caves at Niaux (1988–93) shows, as did the Maison des Arts in Bordeaux, that Fuksas has a sustained interest in contemporary sculpture and art. More recently, Fuksas completed the Ferrari Research Center (Maranello, Italy, 2001–04); Fiera Milano (Rho-Pero, Milan, Italy, 2002–05); Zenith Strasbourg (Eckbolsheim, Strasbourg, France, 2003–07); the Armani Ginza Tower (Tokyo, Japan, 2005–07); a church in Foligno (Italy, 2001–09); Emporio Armani Fifth Avenue (New York, New York, USA, 2009, published here); and MyZeil Shopping Mall (Frankfurt am Main, Germany, 2009, also published here). Upcoming work includes the Peres Peace Center (Jaffa, Israel); Molas Golf Resort (Pula, Italy); Euromed Center in Marseille (France); and the French National Archives (Pierrefitte near Paris, France).

MASSIMILIANO FUKSAS wurde 1944 in Rom geboren und schloss sein Architekturstudium an der Universität Rom „La Sapienza" ab. Gemeinsam mit Anna Maria Sacconi gründete er Granma (1969–88) und eröffnete 1989 ein Büro in Paris. 1999 wurde er in Frankreich mit dem Grand Prix d'Architecture ausgezeichnet und schreibt seit 2000 eine Architekturkolumne für die italienische Wochenzeitschrift *L'Espresso*. Er war Direktor der 7. Architekturbiennale von Venedig (1998–2000). Seit 1985 arbeitet er mit Doriana Mandrelli Fuksas zusammen. Sie studierte an der Fakultät für Architektur an der „La Sapienza" in Rom und ist seit 1997 verantwortlich für die Entwürfe des Büros. In Frankreich machte sich Massimiliano Fuksas insbesondere mit Projekten wie der Mediathek in Rézé (1987–91) einen Namen sowie der Nationalen Hochschule für Bauingenieurwesen (ENIB ISAMOR, 1990–92), der Maison des Arts an der Universität Michel de Montaigne in Bordeaux (1992–95) oder der Maximilien-Perret-Schule in Alfortville bei Paris (1995–97). Der vom Büro aus Cor-ten-Stahl gestaltete Eingangsbereich zu den Höhlen von Niaux (1988–93) belegt ebenso wie die Maison des Arts in Bordeaux, dass Fuksas ein anhaltendes Interesse für zeitgenössische Skulptur und Kunst hat. In jüngerer Zeit konnte Fuksas das Ferrari-Forschungszentrum (Maranello, Italien, 2001–04), die Fiera Milano (Rho-Pero, Mailand, 2002–05), das Zenith Strasbourg (Eckbolsheim, Frankreich, 2003–07), den Armani Ginza Tower (Tokio, 2005–07), eine Kirche in Foligno (Italien, 2001–09), Emporio Armani Fifth Avenue (New York, USA, 2009, hier vorgestellt) und das Einkaufszentrum MyZeil (Frankfurt am Main, 2009, ebenfalls hier vorgestellt) fertigstellen. Geplante Projekte sind u.a. das Peres-Friedenszentrum (Haifa, Israel), der Molas Golf Resort (Pula, Italien), das Euromed Center in Marseille (Frankreich) sowie das Französische Nationalarchiv (Pierrefitte bei Paris).

MASSIMILIANO FUKSAS, né en 1944 à Rome est diplômé d'architecture de l'université romaine La Sapienza (1969). Il crée l'agence Granma (1969–88) avec Anna Maria Sacconi, et ouvre un bureau à Paris en 1989. En 1999, il remporte le Grand Prix d'architecture français. Il est l'auteur d'une rubrique d'architecture pour l'hebdomadaire italien *L'Espresso* publiée depuis 2000. Il a été directeur de la VIIe Biennale d'architecture de Venise (1998–2000) et travaille avec Doriana Mandrelli Fuksas depuis 1985. Celle-ci a également étudié à la faculté d'architecture de l'université romaine La Sapienza et est responsable du design à l'agence depuis 1997. La présence en France de Massimiliano Fuksas a été marquée par plusieurs réalisations comme la médiathèque de Rézé (1987–91) ; l'École nationale des ingénieurs de Brest (ENIB ISAMOR, 1990–92) ; la Maison des Arts à l'université Michel de Montaigne à Bordeaux (1992–95) ; et le collège Maximilien Perret à Alfortville près de Paris (1995–97). Son entrée en acier Corten réalisée pour les grottes de Niaux (1988–93) montre, comme la Maison des Arts de Bordeaux, son intérêt soutenu pour l'art et la sculpture contemporains. Parmi ses réalisations plus récentes : le Centre de recherches Ferrari (Maranello, Italie, 2001–04) ; la Foire de Milan (Rho-Pero, Milan, 2002–05) ; le Zenith de Strasbourg (Eckbolsheim, Strasbourg, 2003–07) ; la tour Ginza pour Armani (Tokyo, 2005–07) ; une église à Foligno (Italie, 2001–09) ; l'Emporio Armani Fifth Avenue (New York, 2009, publié ici) ; et le centre commercial MyZeil (Francfort, 2009, également publié ici). L'agence travaille actuellement au Centre Perez pour la Paix (Jaffa, Israël) ; le Golf de Molas Resort (Pula, Italie) ; le Centre Euromed à Marseille et les Archives nationales de France (Pierrefitte, près de Paris).

EMPORIO ARMANI FIFTH AVENUE

New York, New York, USA, 2009

Address: 717 Fifth Avenue, New York, NY 10022, USA,
+1 212 207 1902, www.armani5thavenue.com
Area: 2800 m². Client: Giorgio Armani Group. Cost: not disclosed

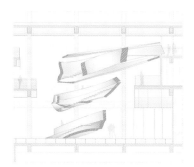

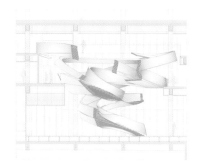
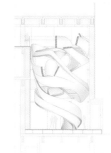

The central stairway is the strongest architectural feature of the Emporio Armani on Fifth Avenue. The sinuous, irregular forms of the stairway occupy the very center of the store.

Die Haupttreppe ist das beeindruckendste architektonische Element in den Räumen von Emporio Armani an der Fifth Avenue. Die geschwungenen, unregelmäßigen Formen der Treppe dominieren das Zentrum des Stores.

L'escalier central est l'élément architectural le plus fort de l'Emporio Armani de la Cinquième Avenue. De forme sinueuse irrégulière, il occupe le centre même du magasin.

This is the third **ARMANI STORE** designed by Doriana and Massimiliano Fuksas after Hong Kong Charter House and Tokyo Ginza Tower (page 13). It is located on the corner of 56th Street on Fifth Avenue, a highly visible location. The store occupies four different levels, including basement space, linked by a vortex-type staircase specifically designed for this location. The staircase is made of rolled calender steel clad in plastic. Lacquered wood panels also create a sense of continuity in the interior space. Black ceilings and fairly dark spaces contrast with the winding white ribbon of the central stairway. A café-restaurant offering a view of Fifth Avenue and the southern edge of Central Park completes the experience generated by the space. Writing about the restaurant, the architects state: "The colors and materials utilized are the same as in the rest of the showroom, but with new and different suggestions. The space becomes recreational. A line of light on the floor leads to the entrance of the restaurant, underlining the sensuality of the bends of the wall. A virtual curtain enlivens the passage and, just like a theater... the show begins!"

Dies ist die dritte **ARMANI-BOUTIQUE**, die Doriana und Massimiliano Fuksas entworfen haben, nach dem Hong Kong Charter House und dem Tokyo Ginza Tower (Seite 13). An der Ecke 56th Street und Fifth Avenue ist sie mehr als prominent gelegen. Der Store erstreckt sich über vier Ebenen, einschließlich Untergeschoss, die durch eine Treppe verbunden sind. Sie wirkt wie ein Strudel und wurde eigens für diesen Ort entworfen. Die Treppe aus gewalztem, kalandriertem Stahl wurde mit Kunststoff ummantelt. Auch lackierte Holzpaneele unterstreichen die Kontinuität des Interieurs. Schwarze Decken und vergleichsweise dunkle Räume kontrastieren mit dem sich schlängelnden weißen Band der Haupttreppe. Ein Café und Restaurant mit Blick auf die Fifth Avenue und die südliche Spitze des Central Park rundet das Raumerlebnis ab. Die Architekten schreiben über das Restaurant: „Materialien und Farben sind dieselben wie im übrigen Showroom, wenn auch mit neuen und anderen Wirkungen. Der Raum wird zum Ort der Entspannung. Ein Lichtband im Boden führt zum Eingang des Restaurants und betont die Sinnlichkeit der geschwungenen Wände. Der Weg gewinnt zusätzliche Lebendigkeit durch einem virtuellen Vorhang, wie in einem Theater ... und die Vorstellung beginnt!"

C'est le troisième **MAGASIN ARMANI** conçu par Doriana et Massimiliano Fuksas après celui de Hong Kong (Charter House) et la tour Ginza à Tokyo (page 13). Il occupe une position très en vue à l'angle de la 56e Rue et de la Cinquième Avenue. Le magasin s'étend sur quatre niveaux dont un en sous-sol, reliés par une sorte d'escalier-vortex en acier laminé satiné habillé de plastique. Des panneaux de bois créent un sentiment de continuité dans le volume intérieur. Les plafonds noirs et les espaces assez sombres contrastent avec le ruban blanc torsadé de l'escalier. Un café-restaurant offrant une vue sur la Cinquième Avenue et l'extrémité sud de Central Park complète cette expérience spatiale. Selon les architectes : « Les couleurs et les matériaux utilisés sont les mêmes que dans le reste du showroom, mais mis en œuvre selon des propositions nouvelles différentes. L'espace devient récréatif. Une ligne de lumière au sol conduit vers l'entrée du restaurant et souligne la sensualité de la courbure des murs. Un rideau virtuel anime le passage. Comme dans un théâtre ... le spectacle commence ! »

Although images give an almost "alien" impression of the presence of the stairway, it ties together the space and contrasts its organic swirls to the more traditional areas that surround it.

Obwohl die Treppe auf diesen Aufnahmen geradezu fremdartig wirkt, hält sie den Raum zusammen und kontrastiert dank ihrer organischen Schwünge mit den angrenzenden, traditioneller gestalteten Bereichen.

Si les images donnent l'impression d'une présence « venue d'ailleurs », cet escalier est le lien qui unifie ce vaste volume et contraste par ses tourbillons organiques avec les espaces plus traditionnels qui l'entourent.

The stairway seems to float in the relatively confined space of the store. Images below show the Emporio Armani from across Fifth Avenue at night, and the upper-level dining space.

Die Treppe scheint in der vergleichsweise engen Raumhülle des Stores zu schweben. Unten eine nächtliche Ansicht des Geschäfts von der gegenüberliegenden Straßenseite der Fifth Avenue, sowie das Restaurant im Obergeschoss.

L'escalier semble suspendu dans l'espace relativement confiné du magasin. Les images ci-dessous montrent le magasin Emporio Armani la nuit, vu de la Cinquième Avenue, et le restaurant du niveau supérieur.

The ribs of the stairway give an almost abstract vision in the image above, yet the structure is perfectly rational in its function. Plans below show how the interior space is orchestrated around the stairs.

Die Rippen der Treppe wirken auf der Aufnahme oben fast abstrakt, dabei ist die Anlage in ihrer Funktionalität vollkommen rational. Die Grundrisse unten illustrieren, wie der Innenraum um die Treppe herum organisiert wurde.

Les nervures de l'escalier créent une image presque abstraite bien qu'il soit parfaitement rationnel par rapport à sa fonction. Les plans ci-dessous montrent l'orchestration de l'espace intérieur autour de l'escalier.

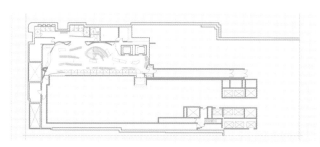

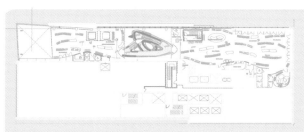

MYZEIL SHOPPING MALL

Frankfurt am Main, Germany, 2009

Address: Zeil 106, 60313 Frankfurt am Main, Germany,
+46 69 21 65 77 02, www.myzeil.de
Area: 78 000 m². Client: Palais Quartier GmbH & Co.KG. Cost: €135 million
Collaboration: Speirs and Major Associates (Lighting Consultants)

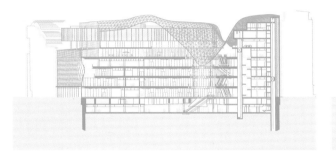
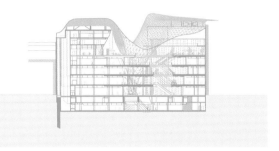

Fuksas makes use of vertiginous openings and protrusions from the upper part of the structure in a gesture that recalls his Fiera Milano (Rho-Pero, Milan, Italy, 2002–05).

Fuksas arbeiten mit schwindelerregenden Öffnungen und Ausbuchtungen in bzw. aus der oberen Gebäudezone – eine Geste, die an den Entwurf der Architekten für die Fiera Milano (Rho-Pero, Mailand, 2002–05) erinnert.

Partant de la partie supérieure, Fuksas met en œuvre des ouvertures et des protrusions vertigineuses dans un geste qui rappelle sa Foire de Milan (Rho-Pero, Milan, 2002–05).

Located on the "Zeil", an important shopping street in Frankfurt, this complex includes a shopping mall, movie theater, fitness center, hotel, meeting rooms, offices, and parking areas. The considerable site area is 105 000 square meters. The commercial space containing more than 100 shops is located between the ground and fourth levels, while the movie theater, sports center, and restaurants are set on the fourth floor, where there is a separate entrance. The architects state: "The project's structure was inspired by a fluid form connecting the Zeil … to the reconstituted Thurn und Taxis Palace. Fluid paths encourage circulation of visitors to the various levels, while a series of voids allows natural light into the entire complex as required." The architects have differentiated the appearance of the building according to the urban environment, although a steel-and-glass translucent skin "envelops and deforms the entire building." As they explain: "The façade running along the Zeil embodies a sense of leisure time, entertainment, and relaxation. The other side is where the entrances to the hotel and offices are located. The hotel lobby, reconstructed inside the Thurn und Taxis, is set near the art gallery and the most upmarket shops in the mall." Office space is acceded to through a 27.5-meter-high entrance on Große Eschenheimer Strasse.

Der auf der Zeil, einer Haupteinkaufsstraße von Frankfurt gelegene Komplex, umfasst ein Einkaufszentrum, ein Kino, ein Fitnessstudio, ein Hotel, Konferenzräume, Büros und Parkflächen. Die beeindruckende Baufläche beträgt 105 000 m². Die Verkaufsflächen mit über 100 Geschäften verteilt sich vom Erdgeschoss bis in das 3. Obergeschoss; Kino, Fitnessstudio und Restaurants befinden sich im 4. Obergeschoss, wo es einen separaten Eingang gibt. Die Architekten erklären: „Strukturell wurde das Projekt durch eine fließende Linie bestimmt, durch die die Zeil … mit dem wiederaufgebauten Palais Thurn und Taxis verbunden ist. Fließende Pfade regen den Verkehrsfluss der Besucher auf den verschiedenen Ebenen an. Eine Reihe von Lichthöfen lässt, wie gewünscht, Tageslicht in den gesamten Komplex." Die Architekten gestalteten das Erscheinungsbild des Baus entsprechend dem urbanen Umfeld, wenngleich eine transluzente Außenhaut aus Stahl und Glas „das gesamte Gebäude umhüllt und zu verformen scheint". Sie führen aus: „Die Fassade zur Zeil hin signalisiert Freizeit, Unterhaltung und Entspannung. Zur anderen Seite hin liegen die Eingänge zum Hotel und den Büros. Die im Palais Thurn und Taxis gelegene Hotellobby befindet sich unweit der Kunstgalerie und den exklusivsten Geschäften des Einkaufszentrums." Die Büros werden über einen 27,5 m hohen Eingang an der Große Eschenheimer Straße erschlossen.

Situé dans la « Zeil », une principale rue commerçante de Francfort, ce complexe comprend un centre commercial, un cinéma, un centre de remise en forme, un hôtel, des salles de réunions, des bureaux et des parkings. L'ensemble occupe la surface considérable de 105 000 m². Les commerces comptent plus de cent boutiques entre le rez-de-chaussée et le troisième étage, tandis que le cinéma, la salle de sport et les restaurants occupent le quatrième niveau, accessible par une entrée séparée. « La structure du projet vient d'une idée de forme fluide qui connecterait le Zeil … au Palais Thurn und Taxis reconstruit. Des cheminements fluides encouragent la circulation des visiteurs entre les différents niveaux, tandis qu'une succession de vides laisse entrer la lumière naturelle dans le complexe, comme il était souhaité. » Les architectes ont différencié l'aspect du bâtiment en fonction de l'environnement urbain, mais une peau translucide en verre et acier « enveloppe et déforme le bâtiment tout entier » … « La façade qui court le long du Zeil donne un sentiment de loisirs, de divertissement et de détente. L'entrée de l'hôtel et des bureaux se trouve de l'autre côté. Le hall de réception de l'hôtel, reconstruit à l'intérieur du Palais Thurn und Taxis est à côté de la galerie d'art et des boutiques le plus haut de gamme du complexe. » Les bureaux disposent d'une entrée de 27,5 mètres de haut sur la Große Eschenheimer Straße.

Building on more traditionally formed base structures, the architect adds a web of glazed extrusions to the top of the shopping complex.

Auf einen eher traditionellen Unterbau setzen die Architekten ein Netz aus verglasten Einstülpungen.

S'appuyant sur des structures de base de formes plus traditionnelles l'architecte a recouvert le complexe commercial d'un réseau d'extrusions de verre.

The interior of the center renders
coherent the use of the bulbous forms
on the roofs—irregular openings are
used to channel the escalators from
floor to floor.

L'intérieur du centre est en
cohérence avec les formes bulbeuses
de la couverture : des ouvertures de
formes irrégulières laissent passer
les escalators d'un niveau à l'autre.

Das Nutzungskonzept im Innenraum
des Centers knüpft konsequent an
die bauchigen Formen der Dachkon-
struktion an – in den unregelmäßigen
Öffnungen wurden Rolltreppen
untergebracht, die die einzelnen
Ebenen verbinden.

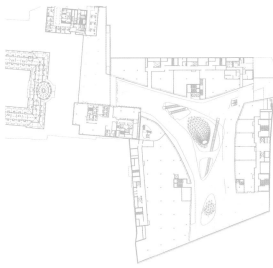

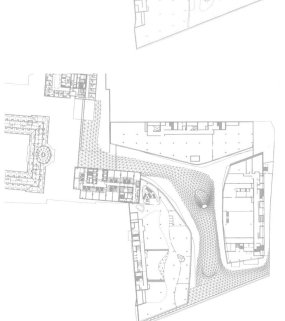

Balenciaga Flagship Store ▶

DOMINIQUE GONZALEZ-FOERSTER

Poste 9.3
5 Rue de Charonne
75011 Paris
France

Tel: +33 1 53 36 09 81
E-mail: poste.9@wanadoo.fr

DOMINIQUE GONZALEZ-FOERSTER was born in 1965 in Strasbourg, France. She is one of the best-known French contemporary artists, a recipient of the 1996–97 Mies van der Rohe Award (Krefeld), and of the 2002 Marcel Duchamp Award (Paris). Her recent solo exhibitions include one at the Centre Pompidou (Paris, France, 2002); Kunsthalle Zürich (Zurich, Switzerland, 2004); Musée d'Art Moderne de la Ville de Paris/ARC (Paris, France, 2007); a project for the Turbine Hall (Tate Modern, London, UK, 2008); and shows at the MUSAC (Museo de Arte Contemporáneo de Castilla y Léon, Spain, 2008). **MARTIAL GALFIONE** was born in 1973 in Dijon, France. He received a DNSEP degree from the École Nationale d'Art de Cergy Pontoise (1996) and his architecture degree from the École nationale supérieure d'Architecture Paris La Villette (2006). He worked on "Sainte Bazeille," a temporary archeological museum (Utrecht, The Netherlands, 2005, in collaboration with Gonzalez-Foerster and Benoit Lalloz), and on the Balenciaga Paris show in collaboration with Dominique Gonzalez-Foerster (Musée des arts décoratifs, Paris, France, 2006). **BENOIT LALLOZ** was born in 1961 and studied haute couture (École Lainé, Paris) as well as management and the lighting of monuments, for such events as the 2008 Balenciaga fashion show (Paris). Together they worked on the Balenciaga Flagship Store (London, UK, 2008, published here).

DOMINIQUE GONZALEZ-FOERSTER wurde 1965 in Straßburg, Frankreich, geboren. Sie ist eine der bekanntesten zeitgenössischen Künstlerinnen Frankreichs und wurde 1996–97 mit dem Mies van der Rohe Preis (Krefeld) sowie 2002 mit dem Marcel Duchamp Preis (Paris) geehrt. Zu ihren jüngsten Einzelausstellungen zählen Schauen am Centre Pompidou (Paris, 2002), der Kunsthalle Zürich (Zürich, 2004), dem Musée d'Art Moderne de la Ville de Paris/ARC (Paris, 2007), ein Projekt für die Turbinenhalle der Tate Modern (London, 2008) und eine Ausstellung am MUSAC (Museo de Arte Contemporáneo de Castilla y Léon, Spanien, 2008). **MARTIAL GALFIONE** wurde 1973 in Dijon, Frankreich, geboren. Er schloss sein Studium mit einem DNSEP an der École Nationale d'Art de Cergy Pontoise (1996) ab und absolvierte einen Architekturabschluss an der École nationale supérieure d'Architecture Paris La Villette (2006). Er arbeitete am Projekt „Sainte Bazeille", einem temporären Archäologiemuseum (Utrecht, Niederlande, 2005, eine Kollaboration mit Gonzalez-Foerster und Benoit Lalloz) sowie, ebenfalls mit Dominique Gonzalez-Foerster, an einer Modenschau für Balenciaga in Paris (Musée des arts décoratifs, Paris, 2006). **BENOIT LALLOZ** wurde 1961 geboren und studierte Haute Couture (École Lainé, Paris) sowie Management und Beleuchtung, u.a. für Events wie die Balenciaga Modenschau 2008 (Paris). Das Team arbeitete gemeinsam am Balenciaga Flagshipstore (London, 2008, hier vorgestellt).

DOMINIQUE GONZALEZ-FOERSTER, née en1965 à Strasbourg, est l'une des artistes françaises les plus connues. Elle a reçu le prix Mies van der Rohe 1996–97 (Krefeld) et le prix Marcel Duchamp 2002 (Paris). Elle a récemment exposé au Centre Pompidou (Paris, 2002) ; à la Kunsthalle de Zurich (2004) ; au Musée d'art moderne de la Ville de Paris / ARC (2007) ; au MUSAC (Museo de Arte Contemporáneo de Castilla y Léon, Espagne, 2008) ; et a occupé le Turbine Hall de la Tate Modern à Londres (2008). **MARTIAL GALFIONE**, né en 1973 à Dijon, est diplômé de l'École nationale d'art de Cergy Pontoise (1996) et diplômé en architecture de l'École nationale supérieure d'architecture de Paris La Villette (2006). Il a travaillé sur le projet de « Sainte Bazeille », musée d'archéologie temporaire (Utrecht, Pays-Bas, 2005, en collaboration avec D. Gonzalez-Foerster et B. Lalloz), et sur le défilé Balenciaga en collaboration avec Dominique Gonzalez-Foerster (Musée des arts décoratifs, Paris, 2006). **BENOIT LALLOZ**, né en 1961, a étudié la couture à l'École Lainé à Paris ainsi que la gestion et l'éclairage de monuments, et a participé au défilé Balenciaga 2008, à Paris. Ensemble, ils ont travaillé sur le projet du magasin amiral de Balenciaga à Londres (2008, publié ici).

BALENCIAGA FLAGSHIP STORE

London, UK, 2008

*Address: 12 Mount Street, London W1K 2RD, UK,
+44 20 73 17 44 00, www.balenciaga.com/int/en/Default.aspx?nav=/stores/store-locator
Area: 150 m². Client: Balenciaga. Cost: not disclosed*

This is an unusual project in that it is the result of a collaboration between a noted artist (Dominique Gonzalez-Foerster), an architect (Martial Galfione), and a specialist in lighting (Benoit Lalloz). As well as the 2006 Balenciaga Paris exhibition at the Musée des arts décoratifs, the team has worked on **BALENCIAGA** stores in Paris, New York, Hong Kong, Milan, and Los Angeles, as well as the London store published here. In each instance, they have collaborated closely with the Creative Director of Balenciaga, Nicolas Ghesquière. In the specific case of the London store, the project was carried out with Thomas Powell, who was responsible for the construction, and Christophe Van Huffel, a musician and composer who created a sound track for this flagship store. Located at 12 Mount Street, the shop features an interior that includes plasma screens, silver walls, and white changing rooms. The ceiling is covered with lights, while brightly colored sculptural elements complement the white clothing rails. In this instance, it would seem that the interest of the artistic realization, clearly the result of a close collaboration, has taken a welcome precedence over pure marketing decisions.

Dieses ungewöhnliche Projekt ist das Resultat einer Kollaboration zwischen einer renommierten Künstlerin (Dominique Gonzalez-Foerster), einem Architekten (Martial Galfione) und einem Lichtspezialisten (Benoit Lalloz). Neben der Balenciaga-Ausstellung 2006 am Musée des arts décoratifs in Paris arbeitete das Team auch an den **BALENCIAGA** Stores in Paris, New York, Hong Kong, Mailand und Los Angeles sowie der hier vorgestellten Londoner Niederlassung. In sämtlichen Fällen kooperierten sie eng mit dem Kreativdirektor von Balenciaga, Nicolas Ghesquière. Im speziellen Fall des Londoner Stores wurde das Projekt gemeinsam mit Thomas Powell realisiert, der für den Bau zuständig war, und Christophe Van Huffel, einem Musiker und Komponisten, der einen eigenen Soundtrack für den Flagshipstore schuf. Der an der Mount Street 12 gelegene Store wurde mit Plasmabildschirmen, silbernen Wänden und weißen Umkleidekabinen ausgestattet. Die Decke ist durchgehend mit Leuchtkörpern durchzogen, leuchtend farbige skulpturale Elemente bilden ein Pendant zu den weißen Kleiderständern. Hier scheint es geradezu, als habe das Interesse an der künstlerischen Gestaltung – ganz offensichtlich das Ergebnis einer engen Zusammenarbeit – erfreulicherweise Vorrang vor Marketingüberlegungen gehabt.

Ce projet est inhabituel en ce qu'il résulte d'une collaboration entre une artiste célèbre (Dominique Gonzalez-Foerster), un architecte (Martial Galfione) et un spécialiste de l'éclairage (Benoit Lalloz). En dehors de l'exposition sur **BALENCIAGA** au Musée des arts décoratifs à Paris en 2006, l'équipe a travaillé sur les magasins de la marque à Paris, New York, Hong Kong, Milan et Los Angeles, ainsi que sur celui de Londres présenté dans ces pages. À chaque fois, ils ont œuvré en collaboration étroite avec le directeur de la création de Balenciaga, Nicolas Ghesquière. Dans le cas précis de Londres, le projet a également fait appel à Thomas Powell, responsable du chantier, et Christophe Van Huffel, musicien et compositeur qui a créé une bande-son originale. Situé 12 Mount Street, le magasin se signale par ses murs argentés, ses salons d'essayage intégralement blancs et ses écrans plasma. Le plafond est entièrement lumineux et des éléments sculpturaux très colorés mettent en valeur les rail de présentations blancs des vêtements. Il semble que l'intérêt de la nature artistique de ce projet – certainement l'aboutissement d'une collaboration étroite – a pris le pas sur de purs choix de marketing.

Shown here without any merchandise, the Balenciaga Flagship Store in London makes use of ample color, decorative elements, and integrated hanging space to create something of a riot of impressions.

Im Balenciaga Flagshipstore in London, hier noch ohne Waren, kommen reichlich Farben, dekorative Elemente und Hängevorrichtungen zum Einsatz. So entsteht ein fast exzessiver Raumeindruck.

Vide ici de toute marchandise, la boutique Balenciaga de Londres utilise des couleurs fortes, des compositions décoratives et des systèmes d'accrochage des vêtements intégrés qui provoquent une confusion d'impressions.

Neil Barrett Flagship Store ▶

ZAHA HADID

Zaha Hadid Architects
Studio 9 / 10 Bowling Green Lane / London EC1R OBQ / UK
Tel: +44 20 72 53 51 47 / Fax: +44 20 72 51 83 22
E-mail: press@zaha-hadid.com / Web: www.zaha-hadid.com

ZAHA HADID studied architecture at the Architectural Association in London (AA) beginning in 1972 and was awarded the Diploma Prize in 1977. She then became a partner of Rem Koolhaas in OMA and taught at the AA. She has also taught at Harvard, the University of Chicago, in Hamburg, and at Columbia University in New York. In 2004, Zaha Hadid became the first woman to win the Pritzker Prize. Well-known for her paintings and drawings, she has had a substantial influence, despite earlier having built relatively few buildings. She completed the Vitra Fire Station (Weil am Rhein, Germany, 1990–94); and exhibition designs such as that for "The Great Utopia" (Solomon R. Guggenheim Museum, New York, 1992). Significant competition entries include her design for the Cardiff Bay Opera House (1994–96); the Habitable Bridge (London, 1996); and the Luxembourg Philharmonic Hall (1997). More recently, Zaha Hadid has entered a phase of active construction with such projects as the Bergisel Ski Jump (Innsbruck, Austria, 2001–02); Lois & Richard Rosenthal Center for Contemporary Art (Cincinnati, Ohio, USA, 1999–2003); Phaeno Science Center (Wolfsburg, Germany, 2001–05); the Central Building of the new BMW Assembly Plant in Leipzig (Germany, 2005); Ordrupgaard Museum Extension (Copenhagen, 2001–05); Lopez de Heredia Wine Pavilion (Haro, Spain, 2001–06); Mobile Art, Chanel Contemporary Art Container (various locations, 2007–); Home House (London, 2007–08); Atelier Notify (Paris, 2007–08, published here); and the Neil Barrett Flagship Store (Tokyo, 2008, also published here). She has recently completed the MAXXI, the National Museum of 21st Century Arts (Rome, 1998–2009); Burnham Pavilion (Chicago, Illinois, USA, 2009); and the JS Bach/Zaha Hadid Architects Chamber Music Hall (Manchester, UK, 2009). Current projects include the Guangzhou Opera House (Guangzhou, China, 2006–10) and the Sheik Zayed Bridge (Abu Dhabi, UAE, 2005–10).

ZAHA HADID studierte ab 1972 an der Architectural Association (AA) in London und erhielt 1977 den Diploma Prize. Anschließend wurde sie Partnerin von Rem Koolhaas bei OMA und unterrichtete an der AA. Darüber hinaus lehrte sie in Harvard, an der Universität von Chicago, in Hamburg sowie an der Columbia University in New York. 2004 wurde Zaha Hadid als erste Frau mit dem Pritzker-Preis ausgezeichnet. Hadid wurde besonders durch ihr malerisches und zeichnerisches Werk bekannt. Obwohl nur wenige ihrer frühen Entwürfe realisiert wurden, zählt sie zu den einflussreichsten Vertreterinnen ihrer Zunft. Realisiert wurden u.a. die Feuerwache für Vitra (Weil am Rhein, Deutschland, 1990–94) und Ausstellungsarchitekturen wie „The Great Utopia" (Solomon R. Guggenheim Museum, New York, 1992). Zu ihren wichtigsten Wettbewerbsbeiträgen zählen der Entwurf für das Cardiff Bay Opera House (1994–96), die Habitable Bridge (London, 1996) und die Philharmonie in Luxemburg (1997). In jüngerer Zeit begann eine Phase des aktiven Bauens für Hadid, etwa mit der Skisprungschanze Bergisel (Innsbruck, Österreich, 2001–02), dem Lois & Richard Rosenthal Center for Contemporary Art (Cincinnati, Ohio, 1999–2003), dem Phaeno Wissenschaftszentrum (Wolfsburg, 2001–05), dem Zentralgebäude des neuen BMW-Werks in Leipzig (2005), dem Anbau für das Museum Ordrupgaard (Kopenhagen, 2001–05), dem Lopez de Heredia Weinpavillon (Haro, Spanien, 2001–06), dem Mobile Art, Chanel Contemporary Art Container (verschiedene Standorte, 2007–), dem Home House (London, 2007–08), dem Atelier Notify (Paris, 2007–08, hier vorgestellt) sowie dem Neil Barrett Flagshipstore (Tokio, 2008, ebenfalls hier vorgestellt). Unlängst fertig gestellt wurde das MAXXI Nationalmuseum für Kunst des 21. Jahrhunderts in Rom (1998–2009), der Burnham Pavilion (Chicago, Illinois, 2009) und die JS Bach / Zaha Hadid Architects Chamber Music Hall (Manchester, 2009). Aktuelle Projekte sind u.a. das Opernhaus in Guangzhou (Guangzhou, China, 2006–10) sowie die Scheich-Zajed-Brücke (Abu Dhabi, VAE, 2005–10).

ZAHA HADID a étudié à l'Architectural Association (AA) de Londres de 1972 à 1977, date à laquelle elle a reçu le Prix du diplôme. Elle est ensuite devenue partenaire de Rem Koolhaas à OMA, et a enseigné à l'AA ainsi qu'à Harvard, à l'université de Chicago, à Hambourg et à l'université Columbia. En 2004, elle a été la première femme à remporter le prix Pritzker. Connue pour ses peintures et dessins, elle a exercé dès le départ une réelle influence, même si elle n'a que peu construit au début. Parmi ses réalisations : un poste d'incendie pour Vitra (Weil am Rhein, Allemagne, 1990–94), et des projets pour des expositions comme *La Grande Utopie* au Solomon R. Guggenheim Museum (New York, 1992). Elle a participé à de nombreux concours, dont les plus importants sont le projet pour l'Opéra de la baie de Cardiff (Pays-de-Galles, 1994–96) ; un pont habitable (Londres, 1996) et la salle de concerts philharmoniques de Luxembourg (1997). Plus récemment, elle est entrée dans une phase active de grands chantiers avec des réalisations comme le tremplin de ski de Bergisel (Innsbruck, Autriche, 2001–02) ; le Lois & Richard Rosenthal Center for Contemporary Art (Cincinnati, Ohio, 1999–2003) ; le musée scientifique Phaeno (Wolfsburg, Allemagne, 2001–05) ; le bâtiment central de la nouvelle usine BMW de Leipzig (2005) ; l'extension du musée Ordrupgaard (Copenhague, 2001–05) ; le pavillon du vin Lopez de Heredia (Haro, Espagne, 2001–06) ; le pavillon Mobile Art, Chanel Contemporary Art Container (divers lieux, 2007–) ; la Maison Home (Londres, 2007–08) ; l'atelier Notify (Paris, 2007–08) et le magasin amiral Neil Barrett (Tokyo, 2008), les deux publiés ici. Elle a récemment achevé le Musée national des arts du XXIe siècle (MAXXI, Rome, 1998–2009) ; le pavillon Burnham (Chicago, Illinois, 2009) et le JS Bach/Zaha Hadid Architects Music Hall (Manchester, 2009). Parmi ses projets récents figurent l'Opéra de Guangzhou (Chine, 2006–10) et le pont Cheikh Zayed (Abou Dhabi, EAU, 2005–10).

NEIL BARRETT FLAGSHIP STORE

Tokyo, Japan, 2008

Address: 3–17–6 Minami Aoyama, Minato-ku, Tokyo 107–0062, Japan, + 3 5474 0051, www.neilbarrett.com
Area: furniture dimensions/ground floor: h 3 m; w 2.6 m; l 15.8 m; footprint 2 m² / first floor: h 2.8 m; w 3.7 m; l 8.4 m; footprint 2.2 m²
Client: Neil Barrett. Cost: not disclosed

In this unusual project, the architects prefer to indicate the dimensions of the furniture in smooth white Corian that they designed for the **NEIL BARRETT FLAG-SHIP STORE** rather than its floor area. They state: "Rather than defining a single room or space, our design creates a circular passage, allowing the customer to experience the space in multiple ways and interpretations. Furniture staged in key points throughout the store creates the spatial concept of a narrow enclosure changing to an open condition. In two formal elements the design shifts between architecture and sculpture, where a compact mass of surface layers unravel and fold to form the shelving display and seating." The ground-floor furniture is conceived as "strong, masculine and dynamic" as opposed to the "more fluid contour lines" of the "feminine" first-floor design. The white thermoformed furniture, designed with 3D computer models, is contrasted with the black glossy floor and fair-faced concrete of the store.

Bei diesem ungewöhnlichen Projekt ziehen die Architekten es vor, nicht etwa die Nutzfläche, sondern die Dimensionen der Ladeneinbauten aus glattem, weißem Corian anzugeben, die sie für den **FLAGSHIPSTORE VON NEIL BARRETT** entworfen haben. Sie erklären: „Statt einen einzelnen Raum oder Bereich zu definieren, entsteht durch unseren Entwurf eine kreisförmige Passage, die dem Kunden erlaubt, den Raum auf zahlreiche Weisen zu erleben und zu interpretieren. Die an Schlüsselpunkten im Store positionierten Einbauten lassen ein Raumkonzept entstehen, bei dem sich schmale umbaute Bereiche zu einem offenen Raum wandeln. Mit seinen zwei formalen Elementen changiert der Entwurf zwischen Architektur und Skulptur. Ein kompaktes Volumen aus mehreren Schichten blättert sich auf und wird zu Präsentationsflächen und Sitzmöglichkeiten." Die Einbauten im Erdgeschoss wurden „stark, maskulin und dynamisch" konzipiert, im Gegensatz zu den „fließenderen Konturen" im „weiblichen" ersten Stock. Die weißen thermoplastisch geformten Einbauten, die mithilfe digitaler 3D-Modelle entworfen wurden, kontrastieren mit dem glänzend schwarzen Boden und den hellen Sichtbetonflächen des Ladens.

Pour présenter ce projet très inhabituel, le **MAGASIN AMIRAL NEIL BARRETT**, les architectes préfèrent fournir les dimensions des éléments de mobilier en Corian blanc lisse qu'ils ont conçus au lieu de la surface au sol et précisent : « Plutôt que se contenter de définir un volume ou une salle uniques, notre projet crée un cheminement circulaire qui permet au client de faire l'expérience de l'espace de multiples façons et d'entrevoir des interprétations variées. Le mobilier est installé à des points stratégiques selon un concept spatial d'espace clos étroit se modifiant en évoluant pour accéder à un état d'ouverture. Au moyen de deux formes importantes, le projet passe de l'architecture à la sculpture, quand la masse compacte de strates se défait, se plie et se replie pour former des étagères de présentation et un siège. » Le mobilier du rez-de-chaussée « massif, masculin et dynamique » contraste avec les « lignes plus fluides » de l'étage consacré à la femme. Les meubles en matériau thermoformé fluide, dessinés par ordinateur à partir de modèles en 3D, se détachent sur le sol noir brillant et le béton lissé des murs.

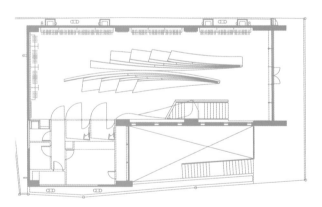

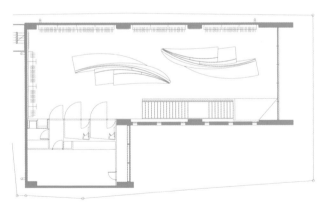

Zaha Hadid appropriates the rectangular, or L-shaped, space by adding her own flowing white forms to the center of each sales space.

Zaha Hadid macht sich den rechteckigen bzw. L-förmigen Raum zu eigen, indem sie ihre eigenen fließenden weißen Formen ins Zentrum der jeweiligen Verkaufsräume setzt.

Zaha Hadid s'est approprié l'espace rectangulaire en forme de L en y insérant un flux de formes blanches qui traverse chaque partie du magasin.

The exterior of the building located in Minami Aoyama is nearly minimalist, allowing the Corian forms of Hadid's interior design to stand out in contrast.

Der Außenbau des Stores in Minami Aoyama wirkt fast minimalistisch und lässt die Corian-Einbauten in Hadids Interieur umso stärker als Kontrast wirken.

L'extérieur du petit immeuble du quartier de Minami Aoyama est d'allure presque minimaliste, ce qui permet aux formes en Corian dessinées par Hadid de créer un contraste puissant.

Neil Barrett states: "I chose Zaha Hadid because I believe she embodies the crossover between art and architcture."

Neil Barrett erklärt: „Ich entschied mich für Zaha Hadid, weil ich glaube, dass sie den Brückenschlag zwischen Kunst und Architektur verkörpert."

« J'ai choisi Zaha Hadid parce que je crois qu'elle incarne un passage entre l'art et l'architecture », explique Neil Barrett.

ATELIER NOTIFY

Paris, France, 2007–08

Address: 1/3 Rue Saint-Hyacinthe, 75001 Paris, France
Area: 500 m². Client: Crystal Denim SAS. Cost: not disclosed

The concept of this project, located on the Rue Saint-Hyacinthe in the first arrondissement of Paris, involves allowing customers to view each step in the creation of garments made of denim. The architects state: "Like an installation, the space is constructed with an elegant sculpture-like gesture, organizing the interior and creating differentiated spaces. Its surface cuts through the façade and slabs to allow natural light to flow down to the basement. It also contains the main stairs bringing guests to the heart of the atelier, establishing an effective connectivity between ground and basement levels." Storage and display units are embedded in intentionally thickened walls. The façade is designed to emphasize a fluid transition between exterior and interior in the "seamless" style of Zaha Hadid. The unusual aspect of this unbuilt work is the conjugation of production and more typical retail activities.

Teil des Konzepts dieses Projekts auf der Rue Saint-Hyacinthe im 1. Arrondissement von Paris war es, den Kunden Einblick in sämtliche Fertigungsschritte der Jeansmode des Labels zu geben. Die Architekten schreiben: „Der Raum wird, wie eine Installation, durch eine elegante, skulpturenartige Geste definiert, die den Innenraum gliedert und separate Bereiche entstehen lässt. Ihr Volumen durchbricht Fassade und Bodenplatte, sodass Tageslicht in das Untergeschoss strömen kann. Außerdem umfängt sie die Haupttreppe, über die Besucher ins Herz des Studios gelangen und bildet so eine wirkungsvolle Verbindung zwischen Erd- und Untergeschoss." Stauraum und Präsentationsflächen sind in die eigens hierfür besonders tief geplanten Wände integriert. Die Fassade wurde so gestaltet, dass der fließende Übergang zwischen Außen- und Innenraum im für Zaha Hadid so typischen „nahtlosen" Stil akzentuiert wird. Das Ungewöhnliche an diesem nicht realisierten Projekt ist die Verknüpfung von Produktion und eher klassischen Verkaufsfunktionen.

Le concept de ce projet d'atelier prévu pour la rue Saint-Hyacinthe dans le 1er arrondissement de Paris vise à offrir aux clients une vision de toutes les étapes de la confection de vêtements en denim. Selon les architectes : « À la manière d'une installation, l'espace naît d'un geste sculptural élégant, qui organise l'intérieur en générant des volumes différenciés. À l'avant, il vient découper la façade de l'immeuble en s'incurvant pour que la lumière naturelle pénètre jusqu'au sous-sol. L'escalier principal intégré conduit les visiteurs jusqu'au cœur de l'atelier, créant une connexion efficace entre le rez-de-chaussée et le sous-sol. » Les éléments de présentation et de rangement sont intégrés dans les murs dont l'épaisseur a été augmentée. La façade facilite la transition fluide entre l'extérieur et l'intérieur dans le style « lisse » de Zaha Hadid. L'aspect surprenant de ce projet (non réalisé) tient aussi à la conjugaison de la production et de la vente au détail.

These computer images give an impression of the flowing space of the design, which includes not only walls and ceilings, but also the furnishings.

Die Computersimulationen vermitteln den fließenden Raumeindruck des Entwurfs, der nicht nur Wände und Decken, sondern ebenso die Einbauten umfasst.

Ces images numériques rendent l'impression d'un espace traité comme un flux de formes, qui englobe aussi bien les murs que les plafonds et les meubles.

Zaha Hadid's design appears to break down the traditional relationships of spatial orientation to create volumes that are truly her own.

Zaha Hadids Entwurf scheint mit den traditionellen Prinzipien räumlicher Orientierung zu brechen, um Volumina zu realisieren, die ganz und gar ihre Handschrift tragen.

Le projet de Zaha Hadid rompt avec les relations traditionnelles de l'orientation spatiale pour créer des volumes profondément originaux.

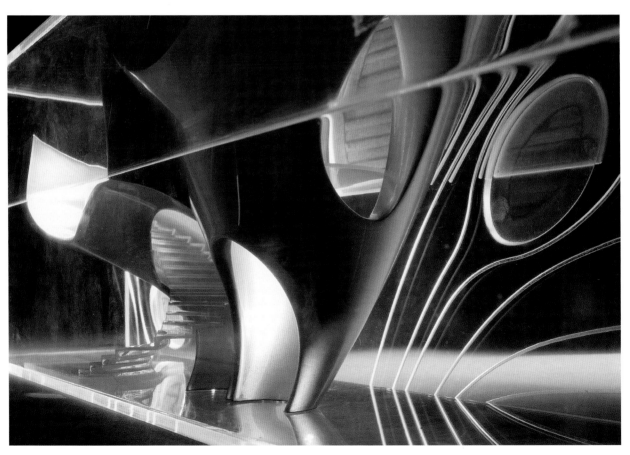

HEATHERWICK STUDIO

Heatherwick Studio
356–364 Gray's Inn Road
London WC1X 8BH
UK

Tel: +44 20 78 33 88 00
Fax: +44 20 78 33 84 00
E-mail: studio@heatherwick.com
Web: www.heatherwick.com

Thomas Heatherwick founded **HEATHERWICK STUDIO** in 1994. The firm deals in architecture, sculpture, urban infrastructure, product design, exhibition design, and "strategic thinking." Its 25-member team is led by the Director Thomas Heatherwick. Born in London in 1970, Heatherwick studied three-dimensional design at Manchester Metropolitan University, and completed his studies at the Royal College of Art in London. Heatherwick Studio has three Associate Directors: Fred Manson, architect and former Director of Environment for the London Borough of Southwark; Ron Packman, principal, Packman Lucas; and Maisie Rowe, a landscape architect. The studio's work includes the Rolling Bridge (Paddington Basin, London, 2005); La Maison Unique (New York, New York, USA, 2006, published here); East Beach Café (Littlehampton, 2005–07); Paperhouse (London, 2009, also published here); 16 Creative Units for the Aberystwyth Arts Center at the University of Wales in Aberystwyth (Wales, 2009); and the UK Pavilion at Expo 2010 in Shanghai (China, 2010). Current projects include a monastic building in Sussex; the Pacific Place Shopping Center (Hong Kong, China, in progress); and a power station in Teesside, all in the UK unless stated otherwise. The studio is also involved in designing the new Routemaster bus in London.

Thomas Heatherwick gründete **HEATHERWICK STUDIO** 1994. Das Büro beschäftigt sich mit Architektur, Skulptur, städtischer Infrastruktur, Produktdesign, Ausstellungsdesign und „strategischem Denken". Das 25-köpfige Team arbeitet unter der Leitung von Thomas Heatherwick. Heatherwick wurde 1970 in London geboren, studierte 3D-Design an der Manchester Metropolitan University und schloss sein Studium am Royal College of Art in London ab. Heatherwick Studio hat drei außerordentliche Direktoren: Fred Manson, Architekt und ehemaliger Umweltbeauftragter für den Londoner Bezirk Southwark, Ron Packman, Direktor von Packman Lucas, und Maisie Rowe, Landschaftsarchitektin. Zu den Projekten des Teams zählen die Rolling Bridge (Paddington Basin, London, 2005), La Maison Unique (New York, 2006, hier vorgestellt), East Beach Café (Littlehampton, 2005–07), Paperhouse (London, 2009, ebenfalls hier vorgestellt), 16 Ateliers für das Aberystwyth Arts Center an der Universität Wales in Aberystwyth (Wales, 2009) sowie der Britische Pavillon für die Expo 2010 in Shanghai (China). Aktuelle Projekte sind u.a. ein Klostergebäude in Sussex, das Pacific Place Shoppingcenter (Hongkong, China, in Arbeit) und ein Kraftwerk in Teesside, alle in Großbritannien, sofen nicht anders angegeben. Das Studio ist außerdem am Entwurf für die neuen Routemaster-Busse in London beteiligt.

Thomas Heatherwick a fondé **HEATHERWICK STUDIO** en 1994. L'agence se consacre à l'architecture, à la sculpture, aux infrastructures urbaines, au design produit, à la conception d'expositions et à la recherche stratégique. L'équipe de 25 collaborateurs est dirigée par Thomas Heatherwick. Né à Londres en 1970, celui-ci a étudié la conception tridimensionnelle à la Manchester Metropolitan University puis au Royal College of Art de Londres. Heatherwick Studio est animé par trois directeurs associés : Fred Manson, architecte et ancien directeur de l'environnement pour le *borough* londonien de Southwark ; Ron Packman, directeur de l'agence d'ingénierie Packman Lucas et Maisie Rowe, architecte-paysagiste. Parmi leurs réalisations : le Rolling Bridge (Pont roulant, Paddington Basin, Londres, 2005) ; La Maison Unique (New York, 2006, publiée ici) ; l'East Beach Café (Littlehampton, 2005–07) ; la Paperhouse (Londres, 2009, publiée ici) ; 16 unités de création pour l'Aberystwyth Arts Center de l'université du Pays de Galles à Aberystwyth (2009) et le pavillon britannique pour Expo 2010 à Shanghaï (2010). Actuellement, l'agence travaille à un projet de bâtiment monastique dans le Sussex (G.-B.) ; au centre commercial Pacific Place (Hong Kong, en cours) ; à une centrale électrique à Teesside (G.-B.), ainsi qu'au design d'un nouveau bus Routemaster pour les transports publics londoniens.

LA MAISON UNIQUE

New York, New York, USA, 2006

Address: 132 Spring Street, New York, NY 10012, USA,
+1 212 343 7444, www.longchamp.com
Area: 910 m². Client: Longchamp. Cost: not disclosed
Collaboration: Shawmut Design and Construction, Atmosphere Design Group LLC

The store is seen here with a décor designed by the Belgian artist Jean-Luc Moerman, which is not a part of the permanent design created by Thomas Heatherwick.

Der Store in einer Ansicht, die das vom belgischen Künstler Jean-Luc Moerman gestaltete Interieur zeigt, das nicht zum Grundentwurf von Thomas Heatherwick gehört.

Le magasin présente ici un décor conçu par l'artiste belge Jean-Luc Moerman. Il ne fait pas partie de l'aménagement permanent mis en place par Thomas Heatherwick.

Section drawings below make clear how Heatherwick has linked one level to another with the flowing bands of the 55-ton staircase.

Querschnitte (unten) verdeutlichen, wie Heatherwick die einzelnen Ebenen durch die fließenden Metallbänder der 55 Tonnen schweren Treppeanlage miteinander verbindet.

Les coupes ci-dessous montrent comment Heatherwick a relié les deux niveaux au moyen des 55 tonnes de bandeaux d'acier de l'escalier.

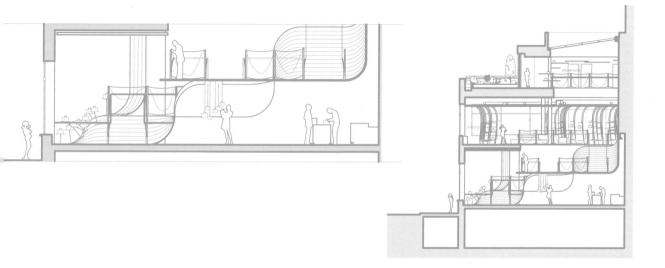

This store is located at 132 Spring Street in the Soho area of Manhattan. An unusual aspect of the project is that it is located above ground level, where other stores were installed. An issue for the architect was thus finding a way to draw people from the street up one floor. A third story was added to the building and a shaft topped by a glass skylight was punched through the structure. The solution proposed by Thomas Heatherwick consisted in creating what he calls a "landscape" made up of 28 hot-rolled steel ribbons that cascade through the core of the building, "creating a topography of walkways, landings that connect the street level to the main store on the second floor." Weighing no less than 55 tons, the staircase took six months to complete. A sliced, laminated timber ceiling that allows glimpses of the service conduits of the building marks the main retail space. Aerospace windscreen technology was employed in the design of the unique panels for the balustrade. Movable lights and display stands are attached to the stair structure using super-strength magnets. Longchamp called on the Belgian artist Jean-Luc Moerman to decorate the store for its 60th anniversary, in 2008.

Der Laden liegt an der Spring Street 132 in Soho, Manhattan. Ein ungewöhnlicher Aspekt ist der Umstand, dass die Hauptverkaufsfläche über dem Straßenniveau liegt, wo sich die übrigen Läden der Gegend befinden. Eine Herausforderung des Architekten war es also, die Kunden von der Straße in das obere Geschoss zu locken. Das Gebäude wurde um ein zweites Obergeschoss aufgestockt, ein Schacht mit einem gläsernen Oberlicht durchschneidet den Bau. Thomas Heatherwick entwickelte eine „Landschaft" aus 28 warmgewalzten Stahlbändern, die sich wie ein Wasserfall durch das Zentrum des Gebäudes ziehen. „So entstand eine Topografie aus Schneisen und Treppenabsätzen, die die Straßenebene an das eigentliche Geschäft im ersten Stock anbindet." Die Fertigung der 55 t schweren Treppenanlage nahm sechs Monate in Anspruch. Der Hauptverkaufsraum wird von der durchbrochenen Decke aus Schichtholz dominiert, durch die man einen Blick in die Versorgungsleitungen des Gebäudes erhaschen kann. Die ungewöhnlichen Glassegmente des Treppengeländers wurden mithilfe einer Technik gefertigt, die in der Produktion von Windschutzscheiben im Flugzeugbau üblich ist. Bewegliche Lichtspots und filigrane Podeste sind mit besonders starken Magneten an der Treppenkonstruktion montiert. Anlässlich des 60. Firmenjubiläums 2008 beauftragte Longchamp den belgischen Künstler Jean-Luc Moerman mit der Innengestaltung des Stores.

Ce magasin situé 132 Spring Street dans le quartier de Soho à Manhattan, présente la caractéristique inhabituelle de se trouver en étage au-dessus d'un rez-de-chaussée dans lequel étaient déjà installés d'autres magasins. Un des enjeux était donc de trouver une façon d'inciter les clients à monter de la rue à l'étage. Un troisiè-me niveau a été ajouté à l'immeuble et un puits de lumière fermé par une verrière, percé à travers les différents niveaux. La solution proposée par Heatherwick a consisté à créer ce qu'il appelle un « paysage », composé de 28 rubans d'acier laminé qui descendent en cascade du magasin jusqu'au niveau de la rue. Cet escalier qui ne pèse pas moins de 55 tonnes a nécessité six mois de travaux. Le plafond découpé en bois lamellé-collé qui laisse entrevoir les conduits techniques de l'immeuble définit la partie principale du magasin. Une technologie issue de l'aéronautique a été employée pour dessiner les panneaux de verre du garde-corps. Des éclairages mobiles et des éléments de présentation sont reliés à la structure de l'escalier par des aimants ultra puissants. Pour décorer le magasin à l'occasion de son soixantième anniversaire en 2008, la marque Longchamp a fait appel à l'artiste belge Jean-Luc Moerman.

The considerable height of the stairway gives a feeling of open space, accentuated by a skylight. A plan shows the essentially rectangular form of the store.

Die beachtliche Höhe der Treppenanlage lässt den Raum offen wirken, was durch ein Oberlicht unterstrichen wird. Ein Grundriss zeigt die im Kern rechteckige Form des Ladenlokals.

La hauteur considérable de l'escalier donne l'impression d'un espace ouvert, effet qu'accentue une verrière. Le plan du magasin est quasi rectangulaire.

The superimposed, curving forms of the stairway and display surfaces recall topographical survey lines, and in this instance they are cleverly adapted to showing products (right photo on left page).

Die einander überlagernden, geschwungenen Formen der Treppe und Präsentationsflächen wirken wie topografische Geländelinien und sind geschickt auf die Präsentation der Produkte zugeschnitten (linke Seite, rechte Abbildung).

Les courbes en cascade de l'escalier et les plans de présentation des produits font penser à des courbes de niveaux. Elles semblent bien adaptées à la présentation des produits (page de gauche, photo de droite).

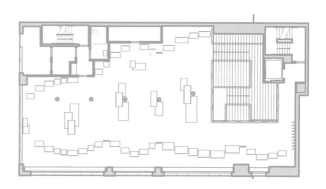

PAPERHOUSE

London, UK, 2009

Address: Sloane Square, London SW1W, UK
Footprint: 2.4 m x 1.9 m. Client: Royal Borough of Kensington & Chelsea
Cost: not disclosed. Collaboration: Manage Ltd., 2D3D, TALL Engineers

The architects were commissioned by the Royal Borough of Kensington & Chelsea to improve the design of local kiosks intended for the sale of newspapers. They state: "The studio wanted to design a kiosk without flat surfaces on the outside that looks good by night as well as day, with a different kind of opening and closing mechanism to make the vendor's life easier." Completed in February 2009, the first of these new newsstands is located in Sloane Square. The shape of the structures is intended to make them resistant to vandalism, such as graffiti, but also to allow a more efficient stocking of magazines on the inside. Toughened glass is used on the top of the roof to allow daylight in. The structure, made with wood and an external cladding of patinated brass, opens by rotating the front sections outwards, avoiding the flat rolling shutters employed on earlier designs seen in London.

Der Londoner Stadtteil Kensington & Chelsea hatte die Architekten beauftragt, die Gestaltung der Zeitungskioske vor Ort zu optimieren. Die Architekten erklären: „Das Studio wollte einen Kiosk ohne plane Flächen an der Außenfront gestalten, der nachts ebenso gut aussieht wie am Tage und über einen neuartigen Mechanismus zum Öffnen und Schließen verfügt, der dem Händler den Alltag erleichtern würde." Der erste dieser neuen Zeitungskioske wurde 2009 fertiggestellt und steht am Sloane Square. Die Form des Kiosks wurde so konzipiert, dass er gegen Vandalismus wie Graffiti geschützt ist und zugleich das effiziente Präsentieren der Zeitschriften im Innenraum ermöglicht. Durch gehärtetes Glas im Dach fällt Tageslicht in das Häuschen. Geöffnet wird der Kiosk aus Holz und einer Außenverblendung aus patiniertem Messing, indem die vorderen Wandpaneele nach außen gefahren werden. So werden die flachen Rollläden, die man von an früheren Kiosktypen in London kennt, vermieden.

C'est le *borough* royal de Kensington & Chelsea qui a demandé à Heatherwick d'améliorer le design des kiosques à journaux locaux. « L'agence souhaitait un kiosque sans façade externe plane, qui ait aussi bon aspect le jour que la nuit, et soit doté d'un système d'ouverture original et d'un mécanisme de fermeture qui facilite la vie du vendeur de journaux », explique Heatherwick. Achevé en février 2009, le premier de ces stands se dresse sur Sloane Square. La forme imaginée rend l'édicule plus résistant au vandalisme – comme les graffitis – mais permet également un stockage intérieur plus efficace des magazines. Une partie de la toiture est en verre de sécurité pour laisser pénétrer l'éclairage naturel. En bois habillé de cuivre patiné, la petite construction s'ouvre en faisant pivoter vers l'extérieur les deux sections avant, ce qui élimine les volets roulants habituellement utilisés à Londres dans ce type de kiosque.

Images show the Paperhouse in various degrees of openness of closure—bringing to mind an organic form, and above all a practical one for newspaper sales in an urban setting.

Die Ansichten zeigen das Paperhouse unterschiedlich stark geöffnet. Die Formen wirken organisch, sind jedoch vor allem pragmatisch auf den Verkauf von Zeitungen und Zeitschriften in einem urbanen Umfeld zugeschnitten.

Ces trois photos montrent le kiosque fermé, entrouvert et ouvert. Cette forme organique semble pratique pour la présentation et la vente de journaux dans un contexte urbain.

HHF

HHF architects
Allschwiler Str. 71A / 4055 Basel / Switzerland

Tel: +41 61 756 70 10 / Fax: +41 61 756 70 11
E-mail: info@hhf.ch / Web: www.hhf.ch

HHF ARCHITECTS was founded in 2003 by Tilo Herlach, Simon Hartmann, and Simon Frommenwiler. Tilo Herlach was born in 1972 in Zurich, Switzerland. He studied architecture at the ETH Zurich and at the EPFL in Lausanne (1992–98). He subsequently worked with d-company in Bern (2001–03), and with Rolf Furrer Architekten (Basel, 2003). Simon Hartmann was born in 1974 in Bern, Switzerland, and studied architecture at the EPFL, Technical University of Berlin and the ETH (1994–2003). From 1997 to 2003, he worked with Nicola di Battista in Rome, A.B.D.R., Garofalo & Miura, Steuerwald + Scheiwiller Architekten, Basel, and Rolf Furrer Architekten, in Basel. Hartmann has been a teaching assistant at the ETH Studio Basel, working with Jacques Herzog, Pierre de Meuron, Roger Diener, and Marcel Meili since 2002, and head of teaching there since 2005. Since 2009, he has been Professor at the HTA in Fribourg, Switzerland. Simon Frommenwiler was born in London, UK, in 1972. He attended the ETH in Zurich (1994–2000), and worked subsequently with Bearth & Deplazes, Chur, ARchos Architecture, Basel, and Skidmore, Owings & Merrill, New York. Frommenwiler has been a teaching assistant working with Harry Gugger at the EPFL in Lausanne since 2005. HHF have recently worked on the Jinhua Sculpture Park Baby Dragon (Jinhua, China, 2006); "Ono" Bar-Café-Lounge (Basel, Switzerland, 2006); SonVida Housing (Bottmingen, Switzerland, 2003–07); Artfarm, showroom and storage for art (Clinton, New York, USA, 2006–08); Tsai Residence (Ancram, New York, USA, 2006–08); Cafeteria Kirschgarten High School (Basel, Switzerland, 2006–08); Dune House (Ordos, Inner Mongolia, China, 2008–09); Labels 2 (Berlin, Germany, 2008–09, published here); and Confiserie Bachmann (Basel, Switzerland, 2009).

HHF wurde 2003 von Tilo Herlach, Simon Hartmann und Simon Frommenwiler gegründet. Tilo Herlach, 1972 in Zürich geboren, studierte Architektur an der ETH Zürich und der EPFL in Lausanne (1992–98). Anschließend arbeitete er für d-company in Bern (2001–03) und Rolf Furrer Architekten in Basel (2003). Simon Hartmann wurde 1974 in Bern geboren und studierte Architektur an der EPFL, der TU Berlin und der ETH Zürich (1994–2003). Von 1997 bis 2003 arbeitete er für Nicola di Battista in Rom, A.B.D.R., Garofalo & Miura, Steuerwald + Scheiwiller Architekten, Basel, und Rolf Furrer Architekten in Basel. Hartmann war ab 2002 Lehrassistent am ETH Studio Basel, wo er mit Jacques Herzog, Pierre de Meuron, Roger Diener und Marcel Meili zusammenarbeitete, seit 2005 leitet er dort die Lehre. Seit 2009 ist er Professor an der HTA in Fribourg, Schweiz. Simon Frommenwiler wurde 1972 in London geboren. Nach seinem Studium an der ETH Zürich (1994–2000) war er für Bearth & Deplazes in Chur, ARchos Architecture in Basel, und Skidmore, Owings & Merrill in New York tätig. Frommenwiler ist seit 2005 Lehrassistent bei Harry Gugger an der EPFL in Lausanne. In letzter Zeit arbeitete HHF am „Baby Dragon" im Skulpturenpark Jinhua (Jinhua, China, 2006), der Bar-Café-Lounge „Ono" (Basel, Schweiz, 2006), dem Wohnbauprojekt SonVida (Bottmingen, Schweiz, 2003–07), der Artfarm, einem Ausstellungraum und Lager für Kunst (Clinton, New York, USA, 2007–08), der Tsai Residence (Ancram, New York, USA, 2006–08), der Kirschgarten Schulcafeteria (Basel, Schweiz, 2006–08), dem Dune House (Ordos, Innere Mongolei, China, 2008–09), Labels 2 (Berlin, 2008–09, hier vorgestellt) und der Confiserie Bachmann (Basel, Schweiz, 2009).

L'agence **HHF** architects a été fondée en 2003 par Tilo Herlach, Simon Hartmann et Simon Frommenwiler. Tilo Herlach, né en 1972 à Zurich, a étudié l'architecture à l'ETH à Zurich et à l'EPFL à Lausanne (1992–98). Il a ensuite travaillé pour la d-company à Berne (2001–03) et Rolf Furrer Architekten (Bâle, 2003). Simon Hartmann, né en 1974 à Berne, a étudié l'architecture à l'EPFL, à l'Université technique de Berlin et à l'ETH (1994–2003). De 1997 à 2003, il a travaillé pour Nicola di Battista à Rome, A.B.D.R., Garofalo & Miura, Steuerwald + Scheiwiller Architekten (Bâle), et Rolf Furrer Architekten à Bâle. Il a été assitant enseignant à l'ETH Studio de Bâle, en compagnie de Jacques Herzog, Pierre de Meuron, Roger Diener et Marcel Meili depuis 2002, et est devenu directeur de l'enseignement en 2005. Il est professeur à l'HTA de Fribourg depuis 2009. Simon Frommenwiler, né à Londres en 1972 a étudié à l'ETH à Zurich (1994–2000), puis a travaillé pour Bearth & Deplazes (Chur), ARchos Architecture (Bâle) et Skidmore, Owings & Merrill à New York. Il est enseignant assistant et travaille avec Harry Gugger à l'EPFL à Lausanne depuis 2005. HHF est récemment intervenue sur le projet du Parc de sculpture de Jinhua, Baby Dragon (Jinhua, Chine, 2006) ; le Ono Bar-Café-Lounge (Bâle, 2006) ; les logements SonVida (Bottmingen, Suisse, 2003–07) ; le showroom et entrepôt d'art Artfarm (Clinton, New York, 2006–08) ; la résidence Tsai (Ancram, New York, 2006–08) ; la cafétéria du collège du Kirschgarten (Bâle, 2006–08) ; la maison Dune (Ordos, Mongolie intérieure, Chine, 2008–09) ; les magasins Labels 2 (Berlin, 2008–09, publiés ici) et la confiserie Bachmann (Bâle, 2009).

LABELS 2

Berlin, Germany, 2008–09

Address: Stralauer Allee 12, 10245 Berlin, Germany, www.labelsberlin.de/eng/labels_berlin2/labels_berlin2.php
Area: 6630 m². Client: Labels Projektmanagement GmbH & Co. KG. Cost: not disclosed

The architects won a 2007 competition for a fashion industry showroom space in Berlin. **LABELS 2** contains space for 30 different fashion labels. An event area and a restaurant are located on the ground floor. The design concept is related to the neighboring Labels 1 structure, which is housed in former warehouse space. The exposed concrete structure of the new building is designed with supporting panels "perforated by sinuous curves that are positioned at intervals of 9.625 meters." Pre-fabricated green concrete elements fan out, shading the glazing beneath. Plumbing is embedded in the exposed concrete serving to heat or cool the load-bearing structure. The main entrance is on the west side of the building, while the small restaurant is accessible on the Spree River side. Within, a steel spiral staircase links the floors. The showrooms, each with its own water and electrical connections, are located on the upper floors. A large rooftop terrace overlooks the Spree. The building has a 1537-square-meter footprint.

2007 konnten die Architekten einen Wettbewerb für einen Mode-Showroom in Berlin für sich entscheiden. **LABELS 2** bietet 30 verschiedenen Model-Labels Raum. Im Erdgeschoss befinden sich ein Eventbereich und ein Restaurant. Das Designkonzept knüpft an das benachbarte Labels 1 an, das in einem ehemaligen Speichergebäude untergebracht ist. Die Sichtbetonkonstruktion des Neubaus hat tragende Wandplatten, die von „geschmeidigen Schwüngen durchbrochen werden, die in Intervallen von 9,625 m platziert wurden". Vorgefertigte Platten aus grüntonigem Beton sind der Verglasung vorgehängt und spenden Schatten. Die Wasserleitungen wurden in den Sichtbeton integriert, um Wärme bzw. Kälte an die tragende Konstruktion abzugeben. Während der Haupteingang an der Westseite des Gebäudes liegt, liegt der Eingang zu dem kleinen Restaurant an der Spreeseite. Im Innern des Baus verbindet eine Stahlwendeltreppe die Geschosse. Die Showrooms wurden mit eigenen Wasser- und Stromanschlüssen versorgt und liegen auf den oberen Etagen. Eine große Dachterrasse bietet Blick auf die Spree. Das Gebäude hat eine Grundfläche von 1537 m².

Les architectes ont remporté le concours pour ce centre d'exposition de l'industrie de la mode à Berlin en 2007. **LABELS 2** réunit 30 marques différentes. Un espace événementiel et un restaurant occupent le rez-de-chaussée. Son concept est à rapprocher de celui de l'immeuble voisin de Labels 1, logé dans d'anciens entrepôts. La structure en béton apparent du nouvel immeuble de 1537 m² d'emprise au sol se compose de dalles porteuses « découpées de courbes sinueuses positionnées à 9,625 mètres d'intervalle ». Des éléments en béton préfabriqué vert ont été déployés sur la façade pour protéger le mur-rideau de verre du soleil. Un réseau de tuyaux inséré dans le béton sert à réchauffer ou rafraîchir la structure porteuse. L'entrée principale se trouve sur la façade ouest tandis que l'on accède au petit restaurant par le quai sur la Spree. Les différents niveaux intérieurs sont reliés par un escalier d'acier en spirale. Conçus comme des unités autonomes, les showrooms se répartissent dans les niveaux supérieurs. En toiture, une vaste terrasse donne sur la Spree.

With its rectangular form, the building stands out in good part due to the slightly irregular exterior cladding pattern, which might bring waves to mind.

Das Gebäude mit seiner rechteckigen Grundform fällt vor allem durch seine unregelmäßige Fassadenverblendung auf, deren Muster an Wellen erinnert.

De forme rectangulaire, le bâtiment se détache du voisinage en grande partie grâce à son habillage extérieur irrégulier en forme de vagues.

The building is strictly geometric, but the uneven exterior forms give it a dynamic presence on the waterfront.

Der Bau ist streng geometrisch gehalten, doch die unregelmäßige Gebäudefront am Ufer der Spree gibt ihm eine gewisse Dynamik.

L'immeuble est strictement orthogonal, mais son parement extérieur lui assure une présence dynamique au bord de la Spree.

Generous interior arches bring
daylight and open space to the
building, while such touches as the
unusual spiral staircase seen on this
page signal that talented architects
have worked to give the space a
dynamic aspect.

Großzügige Bögen im Innenraum
lassen Licht einfallen und schaffen
offene Räume. Details wie die ungewöhnliche Wendeltreppe auf dieser
Seite belegen, dass hier talentierte
Architekten am Werk waren, die dem
Raum Dynamik geben.

Les grandes arches intérieures se
prêtent au plan ouvert généreusement
éclairé. Des détails comme le curieux
escalier en spirale reproduit sur cette
page montrent comment ces architectes de talent réussissent à dynamiser
l'espace.

  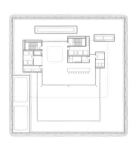

The open spaces work well for the display of clothing, but blocks are also added for boutique space, as can be seen on the right. Exposed ducts highlight a rather industrial feeling.

Die offenen Räume eignen sich gut für die Präsentation von Mode. Zusätzlich wurden Raumboxen eingefügt, wie rechts zu sehen. Die offen liegenden Versorgungs-leitungen unterstreichen die Industrieatmosphäre.

L'espace ouvert fonctionne efficace-ment pour la présentation de vêtements, mais des blocs ont été délimités pour certaines boutiques (à droite). La tuyauterie apparente don-ne un certain air de style industriel.

SOPHIE HICKS

SH Architects Ltd
17 Powis Mews
London W11 1JN
UK

Tel: + 44 20 77 92 26 31
Fax: + 44 20 77 27 33 28
E-mail: mail@sophiehicks.com
Web: www.sophiehicks.com

SOPHIE HICKS studied at the Architectural Association in London (AA, 1987–93). She founded SH Architects Ltd. in London in 1990. In recent years, she has worked on the architecture of Chloé stores worldwide, including flagship stores in Paris, Tokyo, Hong Kong, Los Angeles, and New York (2006). Over 100 stores in this chain have been developed to date. Sophie Hicks developed the concept and design of the "Miró, Calder, Giacometti, Braque: Aimé Maeght and His Artists" exhibition at the Royal Academy of Arts (London, 2008). She was the architect of the Yohji Yamamoto flagship store in Paris (2008, published here), and has more recently worked on the design development of properties in central London.

SOPHIE HICKS studierte an der Architectural Association (London, 1987–93). 1990 gründete sie ihr Büro SH Architects Ltd. in London. In den letzten Jahren arbeitete sie an der architektonischen Gestaltung der Chloé Stores in aller Welt, darunter die Flagshipstores in Paris, Tokio, Hongkong, Los Angeles und New York (2006). Für diese Kette wurden bis dato 100 Stores realisiert. Außerdem entwickelte Sophie Hicks Konzept und Design der Ausstellung „Miró, Calder, Giacometti, Braque: Aimé Maeght and His Artists" an der Royal Academy of Arts (London, 2008). Sie ist die Architektin des Yohji Yamamoto Flagshipstore in Paris (2008, hier vorgestellt) und arbeitete in jüngster Zeit an Entwürfen für Bauprojekte im Zentrum von London.

SOPHIE HICKS a étudié à l'Architectural Association (Londres, 1987–93) et fondé SH Architects Ltd. à Londres en 1990. Au cours de ces dernières années, elle a travaillé sur l'architecture intérieure des magasins Chloé dans le monde entier, ce qui représente une centaine de boutiques, sans compter les magasins amiraux de Paris, Tokyo, Hong Kong, Los Angeles et New York (2006). Elle a mis au point le concept de l'exposition de la Royal Academy of Arts : « Miró, Calder, Giacometti, Braque: Aimé Maeght and His Artists » (Londres, 2008). Elle a réalisé l'architecture du magasin amiral de Yohji Yamamoto à Paris (2008, publié ici) et a plus récemment travaillé sur la conception d'appartements dans le centre de Londres.

YOHJI YAMAMOTO

Paris, France, 2008

Address: 4 Rue Cambon, 75001 Paris, France, +33 1 40 20 00 71, www. yohjiyamamoto.co.jp
Area: 600 m². Client: Yohji Yamamoto, Y's France SARL. Cost: not disclosed
Collaboration: Arup Lighting, Nomura Co. Ltd. (Shojigami paper sculpture),
Miyazaki Mokuzai Kyogo Co. Ltd. (wood sculpture)

The new **YOHJI YAMAMOTO** boutique is located on the corner of Rue Cambon in the first arrondissement of Paris. Sophie Hicks states: "The world of Yohji Yamamoto has its roots in Japan, but is also closely associated with Paris. Yohji Yamamoto has said: 'I am aware of Paris, a part of it, yet apart as well.' We hope to create a shop for Yohji which is absolutely in his image and which floats in Paris, making delicate connections with the luxurious world outside while preserving a Japanese feeling of calm and integrity." A part of the atmosphere of the store is embodied by a white Japanese Shojigami (shoji screen paper) folded into birdlike shapes and suspended in the windows, forming a large-scale translucent sculpture. Wooden chestnut veneer sculptures echo the bird theme on the entrance wall. White concrete with marble chips is used for the floors and staircase. Mannequins and furniture are white, again bringing to mind the image of Yamamoto's work floating in Paris.

Die neue **YOHJI YAMAMOTO** Boutique liegt an der Ecke Rue Cambon im 1. Arrondissement von Paris. Sophie Hicks führt aus: „Die Welt von Yohji Yamamoto hat seine Wurzeln in Japan, ist aber auch mit Paris eng verbunden. Yohji Yamamoto sagte einmal: ‚Ich nehme Paris wahr, bin ein Teil der Stadt und doch getrennt von ihr.' Wir hoffen, dass es uns gelingt, einen Laden für Yohji zu gestalten, der ein perfektes Spiegelbild seiner selbst ist und in Paris zu schweben scheint; der subtil Anknüpfungen an die benachbarte Luxuswelt sucht und dennoch eine japanische Ruhe und Integrität wahrt." Die Atmosphäre des Stores wird unter anderem durch den weißen japanischen *shojigami* (einem *shoji*, Wandschirm, aus Papier) verkörpert, der zu vogelähnlichen Formen gefaltet ist, in den Fenstern hängt und zu einer großformatigen, transluzenten Skulptur wird. Skulpturen aus Kastanienfurnier an der Wand des Eingangsbereichs greifen das Vogelmotiv auf. Für Böden und Treppen und wurde weißer Beton mit Marmoreinschluss verwendet. Modepuppen und Einbauten sind ebenfalls weiß und beschwören tatsächlich den Eindruck herauf, Yamamotos Werk würde in Paris schweben.

La nouvelle boutique **YOHJI YAMAMOTO** est située à un angle de la rue Cambon dans le 1er arrondissement de Paris. Pour Sophie Hicks : « Le monde de Yohji Yamamoto prend ses racines au Japon, mais est aussi étroitement lié à Paris. Il a d'ailleurs déclaré : " Je suis conscient de Paris, j'en fais partie, tout en ne lui appartenant pas vraiment. " Nous voulons créer pour Yohji une boutique qui soit absolument à son image, comme un objet flottant, qui entretiendrait de délicates connexions avec le monde du luxe tout en préservant une qualité japonaise de calme et d'intégrité. » Une partie de l'atmosphère du magasin s'incarne dans un *shojigami* blanc (écran de papier *shoji*) replié en forme d'oiseau et suspendu dans les vitrines pour former une sculpture transparente de grand format. Des sculptures en bois plaqué de noyer rappellent ce thème ornithologique dans le hall d'entrée. Au sol et dans l'escalier, le béton blanc est constellé d'éclats de marbre. Les mannequins et le mobilier sont également blancs, ce qui confirme une atmosphère de mode en état de suspension.

A prestigious corner location not far from the Rue de Rivoli, and on the Rue Cambon, was used by the designers in an unusual way, attracting attention without necessarily making the brand very evident.

Die Architekten nutzten die prestige-trächtige Ecklage an der Rue de Rivoli/Rue Cambon auf ungewöhnliche Weise. Sie lenken Aufmerksamkeit auf den Laden, ohne die Marke zu offensichtlich zu bewerben.

À un angle de la prestigieuse rue Cambon près de la rue de Rivoli, le magasin attire l'attention sans s'astreindre à mettre la marque en avant.

On the right page, a stairway and a
view of the store window from the
exterior, where artistic forms take
precedence over the display of
clothing.

Rechts eine Treppe und eine Außenansicht des Schaufensters, in dem
kunstvolle Formen Vorrang vor der
Präsentation der Mode haben.

Page de droite, un escalier et une vue
extérieure de la vitrine dans laquelle
une installation artistique prend la
préséance sur la présentation des
vêtements.

The designer has employed white and
simplified surfaces to great effect,
especially given the mainly 19th
century architecture of the street and
building concerned.

Im Kontext der überwiegend aus
dem 19. Jahrhundert stammenden
Nachbarbauten und dem Gebäude
selbst, arbeitete die Architektin
höchst wirkungsvoll mit weißer
Farbe und schlichten Oberflächen.

Hicks a tiré l'effet maximum des
plans verticaux allongés peints en
blanc, une réussite dans le cadre
de style XIXe siècle de la rue et de
l'immeuble.

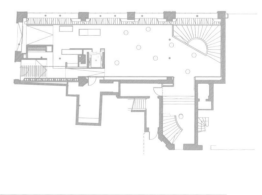

JUNYA ISHIGAMI

junya.ishigami+associates
1–2–6 Tuttle Building 5F
Bunkyo-ku, Suido
Tokyo 112–0005
Japan

Tel: +81 3 5840 9199
Fax: +81 3 5840 9299
E-mail: ii@jnyi.jp
Web: www.jnyi.jp

JUNYA ISHIGAMI was born in Kanagawa, Japan, in 1974. He studied at the Tokyo National University of Fine Arts and Music in the Architecture Department, graduating in 2000. He worked in the office of Kazuyo Sejima & Associates (now SANAA) from 2000 to 2004, establishing junya.ishigami+associates in 2004. Given his age, his list of projects is not long, but he has designed a number of tables, including one 9.5 meters long and 3 millimeters thick made of prestressed steel, and undertaken a project for the Hotel Kaiyo, as well as one for housing (2007). Aside from the Kanagawa Institute of Technology KAIT Workshop (Kanagawa, Japan, 2007–08), he has designed a New York store for Yohji Yamamoto (New York, USA, 2007–08, published here) in the so-called Meatpacking District, and participated in the 2008 Venice Architecture Biennale (Japanese Pavilion, Venice, Italy). Despite his limited number of completed works, with the Kanagawa Institute of Technology KAIT Workshop, Junya Ishigami has emerged as one of the more significant young Japanese architects.

JUNYA ISHIGAMI wurde 1974 in Kanagawa, Japan, geboren. Er studierte an der Fakultät für Architektur der Staatlichen Kunst- und Musikhochsschule Tokio, wo er 2000 seinen Abschluss machte. Zwischen 2000 und 2004 arbeitete er für Kazuyo Sejima & Associates (inzwischen SANAA) und gründete 2004 sein Büro junya. ishigami+associates. Angesichts seines Alters ist seine Projektliste nicht lang, dennoch hat Ishigami bereits mehrere Tische entworfen, darunter den 9,5 m langen „Table" aus 3 mm starkem Spannstahl, sowie ein Projekt für die Kaiyo Hotel- und Wohnanlage (2007). Neben dem Werkstattgebäude für das Kanagawa Institute of Technology (KAIT; Kanagawa, Japan, 2007–08) gestaltete er einen Yohji Yamamoto Store im New Yorker Meatpacking District (2007–08, hier vorgestellt) und war 2008 auf der Architekturbiennale in Venedig vertreten (Japanischer Pavillon). Trotz der geringen Anzahl gebauter Projekte hat sich Junya Ishigami mit dem Werkstattgebäude des Kanagawa Institute of Technology als einer der maßgeblichen jungen japanischen Architekten etabliert.

JUNYA ISHIGAMI, né à Kanagawa au Japon, a étudié l'architecture à l'Université nationale des Beaux-Arts et de la Musique de Tokyo dont il est sorti diplômé en 2000. Il a travaillé chez Kazuyo Sejima & Associates (aujourd'hui SANAA) de 2000 à 2004 et a créé son agence, junya.ishigami+associates en 2004. Son jeune âge explique la brièveté de sa liste de réalisations : il a dessiné un certain nombre de tables dont une de 9,5 mètres de long et 3 mm d'épaisseur en acier précontraint (Table) et réalisé un projet pour l'hôtel Kaiyo ainsi que des logements (2007). En dehors d'installations pour l'Institut de technologie de Kanagawa (Japon, 2007–08), il a conçu un magasin à New York pour le couturier japonais Yohji Yamamoto (2007–08, publié ici) dans le quartier du Meatpacking. Il a participé à la Biennale d'architecture de Venise en 2008 (pavillon japonais, Italie). Malgré ce nombre limité de réalisations, Ishigami est sans doute depuis l'Institut de technologie de Kanagawa l'un des jeunes architectes japonais les plus prometteurs.

YOHJI YAMAMOTO NEW YORK GANSEVOORT STREET STORE

New York, New York, USA, 2007–08

Address: 1 Gansevoort Street, New York, NY 10014–1601, USA, +1 212 966 3615, www.yohjiyamamoto.co.jp
Area: 188 m². Client: Yohji Yamamoto. Cost: not disclosed
Collaboration: Ralph Sobel (Architect), Engineers Network (Structural Engineers),
Jack Stone Engineers (Mechanical Engineers)

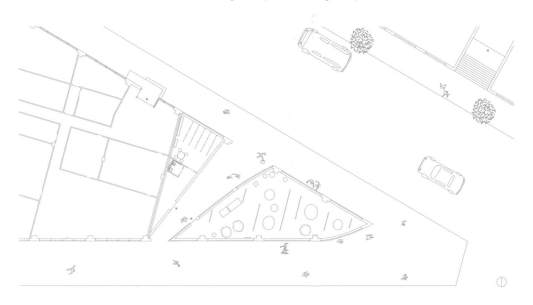

Located at 1 Gansevoort Street near Hudson and West 13th Streets in lower Manhattan in the Meatpacking District, this unusual store was created in the sharply angled structure formerly occupied by an industrial shop and a modeling agency. Junya Ishigami, in fact, cut the existing red-brick structure in half, reserving one part for the single-space showroom and the other for storage and offices. The interior is white to a point that recalls a number of nearby Chelsea art galleries. The unusual geometry of the building and the sparse exhibition of Yamamoto's trademark clothes make for an unexpected experience, especially given the rather drab nature of the architectural environment. The architect added angles to the structure, such as the leading edge of an essentially triangular gallery space, emphasizing the geometry. Unfortunately, this store closed in January 2010, illustrating the highly ephemeral nature not only of the fashion business but also of the architecture associated with it.

Dieser ungewöhnliche Store an der Gansevoort Street 1 – unweit der Kreuzung Hudson und West 13th Street im Meatpacking District in Lower Manhattan – befand sich in einem spitz zulaufenden Gebäude, in dem früher eine Werkstatt und eine Modelagentur untergebracht waren. Tatsächlich hatte Junya Ishigami den bestehenden roten Ziegelbau buchstäblich entzweigeschnitten und einen Teil dem Showroom vorbehalten, der aus einem einzigen Raum bestand. Der zweite Teil des Gebäudes war Lager und Büros vorbehalten. Das Interieur war so schlicht weiß, dass man unwillkürlich an die nahe gelegenen Galerien in Chelsea erinnert wurde. Durch die außergewöhnliche geometrische Form des Gebäudes und die sparsame Präsentation der Mode Yamamotos entstand ein überraschendes Raumerlebnis – umso mehr wegen des tristen architektonischen Umfelds. Der Architekt hatte dem Raum zusätzliche Winkel hinzugefügt, etwa die dominierende Spitze der dreieckigen Galerie, und deren Geometrie damit zusätzlich akzentuiert. Bedauerlicherweise musste der Store im Januar 2010 geschlossen werden, was deutlich macht, wie extrem flüchtig nicht nur die Modewelt, sondern auch die mit ihr assoziierte Architektur ist.

Au 1 Gansevoort Street, près de l'Hudson Street et de la 13e Rue Ouest, dans le quartier du Meatpacking (bas Manhattan), cette curieuse boutique s'est installée dans un petit bâtiment tout en angles aigus, anciennement occupé par un atelier industriel et une agence de mannequins. En fait, Junya Ishigami a coupé en deux le bâtiment de briques en réservant une partie au showroom qui l'occupe intégralement et l'autre au stockage et aux bureaux. L'intérieur est totalement blanc, ce qui rappelle un certain nombre de galeries d'art du quartier de Chelsea tout proche. La surprenante géométrie du bâtiment et le mode de présentation très simple des vêtements de Yamamoto créent les conditions d'une expérience assez curieuse, en particulier dans un environnement architectural assez sinistre. L'architecte a renforcé l'étrange géométrie d'origine du bâtiment en multipliant les angles, en particulier dans le showroom à peu près triangulaire. Malheureusement, le magasin a fermé ses portes en janvier 2010, ce qui confirme la nature hautement éphémère de la mode mais aussi de l'architecture qui lui sert de faire-valoir.

Making use of an existing building that he cut in two, Ishigami created a striking ground-level exhibition space for Yohji Yamamoto in the Meatpacking District of Manhattan.

Ishigami nutzte ein vorhandenes Gebäude, das er buchstäblich entzwei schnitt und schuf so einen eindrucksvollen, ebenerdigen Showroom für Yohji Yamamoto im Meatpacking District von Manhattan.

Utilisant un bâtiment existant qu'il a découpé en deux, Ishigami a créé pour Yohji Yamamoto dans le quartier du Meatpacking à Manhattan un étonnant espace d'exposition.

Within its unusual envelope, the store offered relatively simple hangars to display clothing, with a generous band of windows looking out onto the neighborhood.

Der Store mit seiner ungewöhnlichen Raumhülle war mit eher einfachen Kleiderstangen für die Präsentation der Mode ausgestattet. Ein großzügiges Fensterband bot Ausblick in die Nachbarschaft.

Dans cette enveloppe inhabituelle, le magasin possède un système de suspension des vêtements relativement simple, derrière un généreux bandeau de baies ouvrant sur la rue.

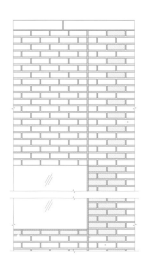
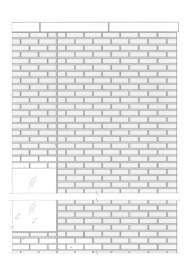

LOK JANSEN

Lok Jansen
2–28–24–402 Kyonan-cho
Musashino-shi
Tokyo 180–0023
Japan

Tel: +81 90 7551 7671
E-mail: lok@lokjansen.com
Web: www.lokjansen.com

LOK JANSEN was born in 1972 in the Netherlands. He attended the Delft University of Technology, where he obtained an M.Sc. in architecture (2002). After receiving a grant from the Japanese government, he graduated from the Tokyo Institute of Technology (M.Sc. 2001). He works in the area of illustration, visuals, and architecture for such clients as Prada (*Lookbooks*, FW 2007, SS 2008, SS 2009, FW 2009, SS 2010); Premsela Dutch Platform for Design and Fashion (editorial illustration); OMA*AMO/ Rem Koolhaas ("Image of Europe Exhibition," a 62-meter-long panorama illustrating the history of Europe, commissioned by the European Union); and Jan Jansen Shoes, for which he did the concept design and development of the interior of the Jan Jansen store (Amsterdam, The Netherlands, 2007, published here).

LOK JANSEN wurde 1972 in den Niederlanden geboren. Er studierte an der TU Delft, wo er einen M.Sc. in Architektur absolvierte (2002). Mit einem Stipendium der japanischen Regierung graduierte er zudem am Tokyo Institute of Technology (M.Sc. 2001). Jansen arbeitet in den Bereichen Illustration, Visuals und Architektur für Kunden wie Prada (*Lookbooks*, FW 2007, SS 2008, SS 2009, FW 2009, SS 2010), Premsela Dutch Platform for Design and Fashion (Illustration von redaktionellen Beiträgen), OMA*AMO/Rem Koolhaas (Ausstellung „Image of Europe", ein 62 m langes Panorama mit Illustrationen zur Geschichte Europas, im Auftrag der EU) und Jan Jansen Shoes, wo er das Konzeptdesign und die Koordination der Innengestaltung des Jan Jansen Store übernahm (Amsterdam, 2007, hier vorgestellt).

LOK JANSEN, né en 1972 aux Pays-Bas, a étudié l'architecture à l'Université de technologie de Delft (M.Sc. en architecture, 2002). Grâce à une bourse du gouvernement japonais, il a également étudié à l'Institut de technologie de Tokyo (M.Sc., 2001). Il intervient dans les domaines de l'illustration, de la création visuelle et de l'architecture, pour des clients comme Prada (*Lookbooks*, FW 2007, SS 2008, SS 2009, FW 2009, SS 2010) ; Premsela, Dutch Platform for Design and Fashion (illustration éditoriale) ; OMA*AMO/Rem Koolhaas (exposition «Image d'Europe», panorama de 62 mètres de long illustrant l'histoire de l'Europe, commande de l'Union européenne) et la boutique de chaussures Jan Jansen Shoes pour laquelle il a mis au point le concept général et l'aménagement intérieur du magasin Jan Jansen (Amsterdam, 2007, publié ici).

JAN JANSEN ATELIER
Amsterdam, The Netherlands, 2007

Address: Vijzelstraat 111, Amsterdam 1017 HH, The Netherlands, +31 20 625 13 50, www.janjansenshoes.com
Area: 40 m². Client: Jan Jansen Shoes. Cost: not disclosed

JAN JANSEN is a maker of customized, handmade shoes that allows customers to select colors and materials for each part of the shoe. Lok Jansen states: "For this we thought a luxurious but relaxed atmosphere was called for—something seemingly effortless, like a well executed sketch." The work was carried out by several artists who freelance as carpenters, painters, or electricians to augment their income. The design was essentially done within the space itself, using full-scale drawings and mockups. The orange-red vermillion color was chosen for its capacity to change dramatically, depending on the light that shines on it. According to Lok Jansen, the materials used include "MDF, duct tape and lots of latex."

JAN JANSEN stellt handgemachte Schuhe nach Wunsch her: Der Kunde kann Farben und Materialien für jeden einzelnen Bestandteil des Schuhs wählen. Lok Jansen erklärt: „Wir meinten, dass eine luxuriöse, aber auch entspannte Atmosphäre hier das richtige wäre – etwas scheinbar Müheloses, wie eine gekonnt hingeworfene Zeichnung." Realisiert wurde das Projekt in Zusammenarbeit mit mehreren Künstlern, die zusätzlich frei als Tischler, Maler oder Elektriker arbeiten, um etwas dazu zu verdienen. Der Entwurf entstand im Grunde direkt vor Ort – mithilfe von Zeichnungen und Attrappen in Originalgröße. Für die orange-zinnoberrote Farbe entschied man sich, weil sie je nach Lichteinfall dramatisch unterschiedlich wirkt. Lok Jansen zufolge sind die Hauptmaterialien „MDF, Klebeband und jede Menge Latex".

JAN JANSEN est un chausseur qui fabrique à la main des modèles sur mesure. Ses clients peuvent choisir les matériaux et les coloris de chaque partie de leurs souliers. Lok Jansen précise : « Nous avons pensé qu'il était nécessaire de créer une atmosphère à la fois luxueuse et détendue – quelque chose qui paraisse naturel, comme un croquis bien exécuté. » Le travail a été réalisé par des artistes faisant office de menuisiers, peintres ou électriciens pour améliorer leurs revenus. Le projet a été réalisé sur place à l'aide de dessins et de maquettes grandeur nature. Le rouge vermillon orangé a été retenu pour sa capacité à réagir en fonction des modifications de l'éclairage. Les principaux matériaux sont « le médium, le ruban adhésif et des masses de latex ».

This very small retail space makes use of color and form to attract customers and to signal the presence of unexpected designs.

Der ausgesprochen kleine Verkaufsraum nutzt Farbe und Formen, um Kunden anzuziehen und auf das überraschende Design aufmerksam zu machen.

Ce très petit point de vente utilise la couleur et la forme pour attirer les clients et signaler ses surprenantes créations de chaussures.

JOUIN MANKU

Agence Jouin Manku
8 Passage de la Bonne Graine / 75011 Paris / France

Tel: +33 1 55 28 89 20 / Fax: +33 1 58 30 60 70
E-mail: agence@jouinmanku.com / Web: www.jouinmanku.com

Born in Nantes, France, in 1967, **PATRICK JOUIN** studied at the École Nationale Supérieure de Création Industrielle (ENSCI) in Paris and received his diploma in 1992. He worked in 1992 as a designer at the Compagnie des Wagons-Lits, and for the two following years at Tim Thom, Thomson Multimedia, under Philippe Starck, who was then Artistic Director of the brand. From 1995 to 1999, Patrick Jouin was a designer in Philippe Starck's Paris studio. He has designed numerous objects and pieces of furniture, while his architectural work includes the Alain Ducasse au Plaza Athénée Restaurant (Paris, 2000); 59 Poincaré Restaurant (Paris, 2000); Plastic Products Factory (Nantes, 2001); Plaza Athénée Bar (Paris, 2001); Spoon Byblos Restaurant (Saint-Tropez, 2002); Chlösterli Restaurants and Club, Spoon des Neiges Restaurant (Gstaad, Switzerland, 2004); Terrasse Montaigne, Plaza Athénée (Paris, 2005); and the Gilt Restaurant and Bar (New York, New York, USA, 2005), all in France unless stated otherwise. **SANJIT MANKU** was born in 1971 in Nairobi, Kenya. He received his B.Arch degree from Carleton University (Ottawa, Canada, 1995) and was a designer in the office of Yabu Pushelberg (New York, 1996–2001). Sanjit Manku joined Patrick Jouin in 2001 and became a partner in 2006. During this period, he has worked on interior and architecture projects, including the Mix restaurants in New York (2003) and Las Vegas (2004), as well as private houses in London and Kuala Lumpur (Malaysia, 2004–08), and hotels in England and France. Recently, Jouin Manku have completed Van Cleef & Arpels (Paris, 2006, published here); Alain Ducasse at the Dorchester (London, UK, 2007); Le Jules Verne, Eiffel Tower (Paris, 2007); the Auberge de l'Ill (Illhaeusern, 2007); and the Silvera Showroom (Paris, 2009, also published here), all in France unless stated otherwise.

PATRICK JOUIN, 1967 in Nantes, Frankreich, geboren, studierte an der École Nationale Supérieure de Création Industrielle (ENSCI) in Paris und erwarb sein Diplom 1992. Im selben Jahr arbeitete er als Designer für die Compagnie des Wagons-Lits, in den folgenden zwei Jahren für Tim Thom, Thomson Multimedia unter der Leitung von Philippe Starck, der damals Artdirector der Marke war. Zwischen 1995 und 1999 war Patrick Jouin als Designer in Philippe Starcks Pariser Büro tätig. Er entwarf zahlreiche Objekte und Möbel. Zu seinen architektonischen Arbeiten zählen: das Restaurant Alain Ducasse, Plaza Athénée (Paris, 2000), das Restaurant 59 Poincaré (Paris, 2000), eine Kunststofffabrik (Nantes, 2001), die Bar Plaza Athénée (Paris, 2001), das Restaurant Spoon Byblos (Saint Tropez, 2002), die Restaurants & Club Chlösterli sowie das Restaurant Spoon des Neiges (Gstaad, Schweiz, 2004), die Terrasse Montaigne, Plaza Athénée (Paris, 2005) und Restaurant und Bar Gilt (New York, USA, 2005), alle in Frankreich, sofern nicht anders vermerkt. **SANJIT MANKU** wurde 1971 in Nairobi, Kenia, geboren. Er absolvierte seinen B.Arch an der Carleton University (Ottawa, Kanada, 1995) und arbeitete an Entwürfen im Büro von Yabu Pushelberg (New York, 1996–2001). Sanjit Manku schloss sich 2001 Patrick Jouin an und wurde 2006 Partner. In dieser Zeit arbeitete er an Innenarchitektur- und Architekturprojekten, darunter den Mix Restaurants in New York (2003) und Las Vegas (2004) sowie an privaten Wohnbauten in London und Kuala Lumpur (Malaysia, 2004–08) und Hotels in England und Frankreich. Unlängst fertiggestellt wurde ein Ladenlokal für Van Cleef & Arpels (Paris, 2006, hier vorgestellt), die Restaurants Alain Ducasse im Dorchester (London, 2007) und Le Jules Verne im Eiffelturm (Paris, 2007), die Auberge de l'Ill (Illhaeusern, Frankreich, 2007) und ein Showroom für Silvera (Paris, 2009, ebenfalls hier vorgestellt).

Né à Nantes en 1967, **PATRICK JOUIN** a étudié à l'École nationale supérieure de création industrielle (ENSCI) à Paris dont il est sorti diplômé en 1992. Il a ensuite travaillé pour la Compagnie des Wagons-Lits, puis les deux années suivantes pour Tim Thom, au département de design de Thomson Multimédia, animé par Philippe Starck, alors directeur artistique de la marque. De 1995 à 1999, il a été designer chez celui-ci. Concepteur de nombreux objets et meubles, ses interventions architecturales comprennent : le restaurant du Plaza Athénée pour Alain Ducasse (Paris, 2000) ; le restaurant 59 Poincaré (Paris, 2000) ; une usine de produits en plastique (Nantes, 2001) ; le bar du Plaza Athénée (Paris, 2001) ; le restaurant Spoon Byblos (Saint-Tropez, 2002) ; le restaurant et club Chlösterli et le restaurant Spoon des neiges (Gstaad, Suisse, 2004) ; la Terrasse Montaigne, Plaza Athénée (Paris, 2005) ; le restaurant et bar Gilt (New York, 2005). **SANJIT MANKU**, né en 1971 à Nairobi (Kénya), a obtenu son B. Arch. de la Carleton University (Ottawa, Canada, 1995) et a travaillé pour Yabu Pushelberg à New York (1996–2001). Il a rejoint Patrick Jouin en 2001 dont il est devenu associé en 2006. Pendant cette période, il a travaillé sur des projets d'architecture et d'aménagements intérieurs dont les restaurants Mix de New York (2003) et Las Vegas (2004) ainsi que des résidences privées à Londres, à Kuala Lumpur (Malaisie, 2004–08) et des hôtels en Grande-Bretagne et en France. Plus récemment, l'agence Jouin Manku a achevé Van Cleef & Arpels (Paris, 2006, publié ici) ; le restaurant Alain Ducasse au Dorchester (Londres, 2007) ; le restaurant Jules Verne à la Tour Eiffel (Paris, 2007) ; l'Auberge de l'Ill à Illhaeusern (France, 2007) et le showroom Silvera (Paris, 2009, également publié ici).

VAN CLEEF & ARPELS

Paris, France, 2006

Address: 22 Place Vendôme, 75001 Paris, France, +33 1 53 45 35 50, www.vancleef-arpels.com/en
Area: 158 m². Client: Van Cleef & Arpels. Cost: not disclosed
Collaboration: Laurent Janvier (Project Manager), Jacques Goubin (Architect of Record)

Set on the prestigious Place Vendôme, the boutique of the jewelers **VAN CLEEF & ARPELS** was entirely renovated by Jouin Manku in beige and blond colors. This change is all the more notable since this is the original boutique opened by Alfred van Cleef with Estelle and Charles Arpels in 1906. The ateliers of the jeweler have been located in the same building since 1933. Undulating walls and rounded furniture create an atmosphere of "douceur et intimité" (softness and intimacy) according to Patrick Jouin. Woodwork inspired by the 18th-century décors of Place Vendôme creates the indispensible link with the traditional entrance of the boutique facing the square. Upper-level space is reserved to private visits or the expertise of jewelry. Patrick Jouin created a line of ovoid furniture specifically for Van Cleef & Arpels and worked here with the noted lighting designer Hervé Descottes. Patrick Jouin states: "The Place Vendôme is unique: its original concept—an esplanade that would serve as the setting for a statue of Louis XIV—indisputably links it to glory and history, and its formal architecture, which is almost austere, is a magnificent illustration of 18th-century style. In addition, the Hôtel de Ségur, the mansion in which Van Cleef & Arpels has been based since 1906, has a particularly strategic location, since it is one of the four mansions set on the angles of the square. Finally, the column in the center of the square is an emblem of Van Cleef & Arpels, forming part of the House's logo. All these things led us to conceive an interior design that focuses on essentials and creates a balance between this rich tradition and contemporary innovation."

Bei seiner Grundrenovierung des Ladengeschäfts der Juweliere **VAN CLEEF & ARPELS** an der berühmten Place Vendôme setzte Jouin Manku ganz auf Beigetöne und helle Farben. Die Sanierung ist umso bemerkenswerter, als dies das originale Ladenlokal ist, in dem Alfred van Cleef sein Geschäft 1906 gemeinsam mit Estelle und Charles Arpels eröffnet hatte. Die Ateliers des Juweliers sind seit 1933 in demselben Gebäude untergebracht. Dank geschwungener Wände und Mobiliar mit entsprechend runden Formen entsteht eine Atmosphäre von „douceur et intimité" (Sanftheit und Intimität), so Patrick Jouin. Holzarbeiten, inspiriert von der Ornamentsprache der Place Vendôme aus dem 18. Jahrhundert, bilden eine unverzichtbare Verbindung zum traditionellen Entrée des Geschäfts am Platz. Das obere Stockwerk ist privaten Kundenterminen und der fachlichen Schätzung von Schmuck vorbehalten. Patrick Jouin entwarf eine Möbelkollektion mit geschwungenen Formen eigens für Van Cleef & Arpels und arbeitete darüber hinaus mit dem renommierten Lichtdesigner Hervé Descottes. Patrick Jouin merkt an: „Die Place Vendôme ist einzigartig: Der Originalentwurf sah eine Esplanade mit einem Reiterstandbild Ludwig XIV. vor – zweifellos ein Hinweis auf die Pracht und Geschichtsträchtigkeit dieses Ortes. Die fast strenge, formelle Architektur ist ein prachtvolles Beispiel für den Stil des 18. Jahrhunderts. Zudem liegt das Hôtel de Ségur, in dem Van Cleef & Arpels seit 1906 seinen Sitz hat, an strategischer Stelle, ist es doch eines der vier Eckgebäude des Platzes. Auch die Säule in der Mitte des Platzes ist ein Symbol für den Juwelier und taucht auf dem Firmensiegel von Van Cleef & Arpels auf. All diese Aspekte brachten uns dazu, ein Interieur zu gestalten, das sich auf das Wesentliche konzentriert und ein ausgewogenes Gleichgewicht zwischen facettenreicher Tradition und zeitgenössischer Innovation erreicht."

Ouvrant sur la prestigieuse place Vendôme à Paris, le magasin des joailliers **VAN CLEEF & ARPELS** a été entièrement redécoré dans une gamme de tons beiges et blonds par Jouin Manku. Le changement est d'autant plus remarquable qu'il touchait au magasin d'origine, ouvert en 1906 par Alfred van Cleef et Estelle et Charles Arpels. Les ateliers de joaillerie se trouvent dans le même immeuble depuis 1933. Les ondulations des murs et le mobilier de formes arrondies créent une atmosphère de « douceur et intimité » selon Patrick Jouin. Le travail de menuiserie, inspiré par le décor du début du XVIIIe siècle de la place Vendôme, crée le lien indispensable avec l'entrée qui ouvre sur la place. Les salons en étage sont réservés aux visites privées à l'expertise des bijoux. Pour ce lieu, Patrick Jouin a spécialement créé une ligne de meubles ovoïdes et collaboré avec le concepteur de lumière Hervé Descottes. Il a déclaré : « La place Vendôme est unique : son concept original – une esplanade servant de cadre à une statue de Louis XIV – la relie à l'histoire et à la gloire, et son architecture formaliste, presque austère, est une magnifique illustration du style du XVIIIe siècle. De plus, l'Hôtel de Ségur, l'ancienne demeure dans laquelle Van Cleef & Arpels est installé depuis 1906, occupe une situation particulièrement stratégique puisque c'est un des quatre hôtels formant les quatre angles de la place. Tous ces éléments nous ont conduits à concevoir un décor intérieur qui se concentre sur les fondamentaux et crée un équilibre entre la richesse de la tradition et l'innovation contemporaine. »

Patrick Jouin uses the theme of the jeweler to create an atmosphere that is modern and yet clearly related to tradition. Elaborate carvings emphasize this relationship.

Patrick Jouin interpretiert das Thema „Juwelier" auf eine Weise, die eine moderne und doch klar der Tradition verbundene Atmosphäre entstehen lässt. Aufwändige Schnitzereien betonen dieses Zusammenspiel.

Patrick Jouin a utilisé les thèmes classiques du joailler pour créer une atmosphère moderne mais qui reste cependant en relation avec la tradition. Des moulures en bois raffinées mettent en valeur cette relation.

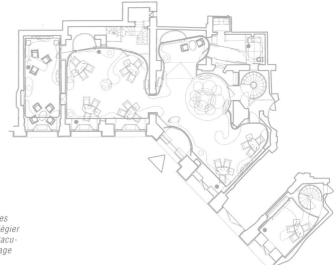

Within spaces that could easily have
been made rectilinear, the designers
decided to privilege curves and such
spectacular gestures as the chandelier seen on the left page.

In Räumen, die man zweifellos
geradlinig hätte interpretieren
können, entschieden sich die
Designer für geschwungene Linien
oder so dramatische Gesten wie
dem Lüster auf der linken Seite.

Dans ce cadre classique qu'ils
auraient pu laisser rectiligne, les
architectes ont décidé de privilégier
les courbes et les gestes spectaculaires, comme le lustre de la page
de gauche.

Furniture and light fixtures were
designed by Jouin Manku with a
marked beige-brown palette whose
neutrality is enlivened by the wall
carvings and ceiling cut-outs.

Jouin Manku entwarf Möbel und
Leuchten in einer beige-braunen
Palette, deren neutrales Spektrum
durch Wandschnitzereien und Ein-
schnitte in den Decken belebt wird.

Les meubles et l'éclairage ont été
dessinés par Jouin Manku dans une
palette beige-brun dont la neutralité
est vivifiée par le décor des murs et
les plafonds découpés.

SILVERA SHOWROOM

Paris, France, 2009

Address: 41 Avenue Wagram, 75017 Paris, France,
+33 1 56 68 76 00, www.silvera.fr
Area: 400 m². Client: Silvera. Cost: not disclosed
Collaboration: Yann Brossier (Project Manager), Jacques Goubin/SLH (Architect of Record)

Working with a difficult narrow entrance (above) and underground space (right), Jouin Manku gave Silvera a showroom that is in keeping with their contemporary image.

Jouin Manku arbeitete hier mit einem schwierigen, schmalen Eingangsbereich (oben) und Räumen im Kellergeschoss (rechts), um Silvera zu einem Showroom zu verhelfen, der dem zeitgenössischen Profil der Firma entspricht.

À partir d'une entrée étroite (ci-dessus) et d'un espace en sous-sol ingrat (à droite), Jouin Manku a créé pour Silvera un showroom en accord avec l'image contemporaine de ce distributeur de meubles.

Located on Avenue Wagram in the 17th arrondissement of Paris, the new **SILVERA SHOWROOM** is located in the Renaissance Hotel designed by Christian de Portzamparc. An entrance sequence five meters wide and 20 meters deep leads to the actual showroom space, which is set in cellar space, where ducts lined the ceiling. The architects state: "This unglamorous shell served as the raw material for our project, inspiring our approach." The entrance passage was deformed and redesigned by Jouin Manku, leading to the steps down, where blades of wood and a "bright lava red surface" link the ground level and the showroom. A colorful alcove 15 meters wide, which the architects call a "window of light," displays armchairs. A work area and bookshop are located at the center of the former basement, surrounded by objects highlighted in relative darkness on a red resin floor. A children's area and furniture display space complete the arrangement, which allows glimpses of the hotel's technical underpinnings here and there.

Der neue **SHOWROOM FÜR SILVERA** an der Avenue Wagram im 17. Arrondissement von Paris liegt in einem von Christian de Portzamparc entworfenen Renaissance Hotel. Vom Eingang her führt eine 5 m breite und 20 m tiefe Raumsequenz zum eigentlichen Showroom im Untergeschoss, wo ursprünglich die Versorgungsleitungen an den Decken entlang liefen. Die Architekten erklären: „Die unspektakuläre Raumhülle war das Rohmaterial unseres Projekts und die Inspiration für unseren Ansatz." Jouin Manku gestaltete den Verlauf der Raumflucht im Eingangsbereich neu, sodass sie zur Treppe zum Untergeschoss führt. Lamellen aus Holz sowie eine „Wandfläche in Lavarot" prägen das räumliche Verbindungsstück zwischen Erdgeschoss und Showroom. Ein 15 m breiter Alkoven, den der Architekt „Fenster des Lichts" nennt, wird für die Präsentation von Sitzmöbeln genutzt. Im Herzen des ehemaligen Kellers liegt eine Werkstatt und eine Buchhandlung, umgeben von Objekten, die im eher dunklen Umfeld auf dem roten Kunstharzboden spotbeleuchtet sind. Ergänzt wird das Ganze durch einen Bereich für Kindermöbel. Hier und dort lässt sich ein Blick hinter die Kulissen des Hotels und dessen Haustechnik erhaschen.

Le nouveau **SHOWROOM SILVERA,** avenue de Wagram dans le 17e arrondissement de Paris ouvre en façade de l'hôtel Renaissance conçu par Christian de Portzamparc. Une séquence d'entrée de 5 mètres de large sur 20 de long conduit au showroom lui-même, aménagé dans un sous-sol dont le plafond a partiellement conservé son aspect technique. « Cette coquille peu séduisante nous a servi de matériau brut et a inspiré notre approche », expliquent les architectes. Ils ont modifié la forme et redessiné le passage d'entrée qui conduit à l'escalier fait de lames de bois tandis qu'« un plan de lave rouge vif » fait le lien entre le rez-de-chaussée et le showroom. Une alcôve brillamment colorée de 15 mètres de large, que les architectes qualifient de « fenêtre de lumière » est réservée à la présentation des fauteuils. Une zone d'accueil et une librairie sont positionnées au centre, entourées de meubles disposés sur un sol en résine et mis en valeur par des projecteurs dans une ambiance lumineuse relativement sombre. Une zone pour les enfants et un espace d'exposition de mobilier complètent l'installation, qui laisse entrevoir ici et là les équipements techniques de l'hôtel.

In the confines of the basement-level showroom, the architects have employed an alternation of relatively dark spaces with colored zones that highlight objects on display.

In den begrenzten Räumlichkeiten des Showrooms im Untergeschoss realisierten die Architekten einen Wechsel zwischen relativ dunklen Bereichen und farbigen Zonen, die die ausgestellten Objekte besonders akzentuieren.

Au fond du showroom, en sous-sol, les architectes ont alterné des espaces relativement sombres avec des zones très colorées qui mettent en valeur les meubles présentés.

By cutting away the ceiling form or adapting the lighting, the designers succeed in making otherwise difficult space ideal for the display of furniture and objects.

Durch Ausschnitte in der Deckenverschalung und passende Beleuchtung schnitten die Designer den ansonsten schwierigen Raum ideal auf die Präsentation von Möbeln und Objekten zu.

En découpant le plafond ou en adaptant l'éclairage, les architectes ont réussi à transformer cet espace difficile en un lieu idéal pour la présentation de meubles et d'objets.

Bright colors and contrasted lighting make the showroom into a kind of cavern of wonders, where objects stand out on their own merits.

Leuchtende Farben und kontrastierendes Licht verwandeln den Showroom in eine Art Wunderkammer, in der sich die einzelnen Objekte behaupten.

Des couleurs vives et des éclairages contrastés font de ce showroom une sorte de caverne au trésor dans laquelle les objets se défendent seuls.

KLEIN DYTHAM ARCHITECTURE

Klein Dytham Architecture
AD Building, 2nd floor
1–15–7 Hiroo
Shibuya-ku
Tokyo 150–0012
Japan

E-mail: kda@klein-dytham.com
Web: www.klein-dytham.com

KLEIN DYTHAM ARCHITECTURE was created in Tokyo by Astrid Klein and Mark Dytham in 1991. Astrid Klein was born in Varese, Italy, in 1962. She studied at the École des arts décoratifs in Strasbourg, France (1986), and received a degree in architecture from the Royal Collage of Art, London, in 1988. In 1988, she also worked in the office of Toyo Ito in Tokyo. Mark Dytham was born in Northamptonshire, UK, in 1964 and attended the Newcastle University School of Architecture, graduating in 1985. He then also attended the Royal College of Art, London (1988). He worked in both the office of Skidmore, Owings & Merrill in Chicago, and with Toyo Ito in Tokyo, before creating KDa. Their projects include the Undercover Lab (Shibuya-ku, Tokyo, 2000–01); Leaf Chapel (Kobuchizawa, Yamanashi, 2003–04); Virgin Clubhouse (Narita Airport, Chiba, 2007); Selfridges (Oxford Street, London, UK, 2007); Wilson House (Isumi, Chiba, 2008); Alpha Tomamu Towers (Niseko, Hokkaido, 2008); and Vertu Ginza (Tokyo, 2009, published here), all in Japan unless stated otherwise.

KLEIN DYTHAM ARCHITECTURE wurde 1991 in Tokio von Astrid Klein und Mark Dytham gegründet. Astrid Klein, geboren 1962 in Varese, Italien, studierte an der École des arts décoratifs in Straßburg, Frankreich (1986), und absolvierte ihren Architekturabschluss 1988 am Royal Collage of Art, London. Im selben Jahr war sie im Büro von Toyo Ito in Tokio beschäftigt. Mark Dytham wurde 1964 in Northamptonshire, Großbritannien, geboren und studierte an der Fakultät für Architektur der Universität Newcastle, wo er 1985 seinen Abschluss machte. Anschließend besuchte auch er das Royal College of Art in London (1988). Vor der Gründung von KDa arbeitete für Skidmore, Owings & Merrill in Chicago und für Toyo Ito in Tokio. Projekte des Büros sind u.a. Undercover Lab (Shibuya-ku, Tokio, 2000–01), Leaf Chapel (Kobuchizawa, Yamanashi, 2003–04), Virgin Clubhouse (Flughafen Narita, Chiba, 2007), Selfridges (Oxford Street, London, 2007), Wilson House (Isumi, Chiba, 2008), Alpha Tomamu Towers (Niseko, Hokkaido, 2008) und Vertu Ginza (Tokio, 2009, hier vorgestellt), alle in Japan, sofern nicht anders vermerkt.

L'agence **KLEIN DYTHAM ARCHITECTURE** a été fondée à Tokyo par Astrid Klein et Mark Dytham en 1991. Astrid Klein, née à Varese (Italie) en 1962, a étudié à l'École des arts décoratifs de Strasbourg (1986). Elle est diplômée en architecture du Royal Collage of Art de Londres (1988). En 1988, elle a également travaillé chez Toyo Ito à Tokyo. Mark Dytham, né dans le Northamptonshire (G.-B.) en 1964, a étudié à l'École d'architecture de l'université de Newcastle dont il est sorti diplômé en 1985. Il a ensuite étudié au Royal College of Art de Londres (1988). Il a travaillé dans les agences Skidmore, Owings & Merrill à Chicago et Toyo Ito à Tokyo, avant de fonder KDa. Parmi leurs projets réalisés : le Undercover Lab (Shibuya-ku, Tokyo, 2000–01) ; la chapelle-feuille (Kobuchizawa, Yamanashi, 2003–04) ; le clubhouse Virgin (aéroport de Narita, Chiba, 2007) ; Selfridges (Oxford Street, Londres, 2007) ; la maison Wilson (Isumi, Chiba, 2008) ; les tours Alpha Tomamu (Niseko, Hokkaido, 2008) et le magasin Vertu Ginza (Tokyo, 2009, publié ici).

VERTU GINZA

Tokyo, Japan, 2009

Address: 5–8–2 Ginza, Chuo-ku, Tokyo, Japan,
+81 3 3572 8650, www.vertu.com/in-en/home#in-en_where-to-buy/store-news
Area: 230 m². Client: Vertu. Cost: not disclosed

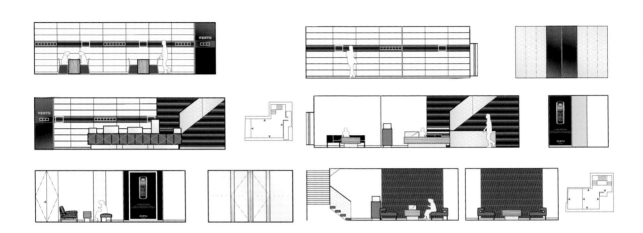

VERTU is a British manufacturer of luxury mobile phones. The black-and-white (the brand colors) ground-floor display area uses materials such as high-gloss UV-hardened urethane lacquer and glass display cases, tinted using techniques normally employed in luxury cars. In the stair to the second floor, set in a four-story void, the custom-designed balustrade is made of stainless-steel mesh embossed with Vertu logos and sandwiched in glass. The apparently simple display tables are in fact quite sophisticated. Triggered by a card sensor, the display units open on invisible rails. The second floor accommodates a VIP area with red leather panels and a hand-tufted red carpet. The architects explain that they have "sought to design elegantly restrained spaces that translate the quality of materials and finishing apparent in Vertu's phones into architecture." The design of the façade was complicated by the fact that the client occupies only half of the building, and that the Vertu entrance is somewhat obstructed by a subway entrance and a tree. Their solution consists in a black aluminum-and-glass façade modulated with Vertu logos in different shades of mattness. The store opened on February 19, 2009.

VERTU ist ein britischer Hersteller von Luxus-Mobiltelefonen. Die Präsentationsflächen im Erdgeschoss sind schwarz-weiß gehalten (den Hausfarben der Marke). Die Materialien sind hochglänzender, UV-gehärteter Urethanlack und Glasvitrinen, die wie die Scheiben von Luxuslimousinen getönt sind. Die Treppe zum Obergeschoss liegt in einem viergeschossigen Schacht, das Geländer ist eine Sonderanfertigung aus Edelstahlgeflecht mit eingeprägten Vertu-Logos, das zwischen doppelte Glasscheiben eingespannt wurde. Die vermeintlich schlichten Vitrinen sind technisch hoch aufwendig. Sie gleiten auf verdeckten Schienen, deren Öffnungsmechanismus per Kartensensor ausgelöst wird. Im Obergeschoss befindet sich ein VIP-Bereich mit rotem Leder und handgetuftetem Teppich. Die Architekten erklären, ihr Ziel sei gewesen, „elegante und dezente Räume zu entwerfen, die ein architektonisches Pendant zur Qualität der Materialien und Verarbeitung der Vertu-Produkte sind". Die Gestaltung der Fassade gestaltete sich kompliziert, da der Auftraggeber nur eine Hälfte des Gebäudes besitzt und der Eingang zum Vertu Store teilweise durch einen U-Bahn-Eingang und einen Baum verdeckt wird. Die Architekten lösten dies, indem sie eine Fassade aus geschwärztem Aluminium und Glas entwarfen, die durch unterschiedlich matte Vertu-Logos aufgelockert wird. Der Store wurde am 19. Februar 2009 eröffnet.

VERTU est un fabricant britannique de téléphones mobiles de luxe. Le décor du rez-de-chaussée du magasin en noir et blanc (les couleurs de la marque) fait appel à des solutions originales comme une laque uréthane haute brillance résistante aux ultraviolets et des vitrines de présentation en verre teintées selon des techniques normalement réservées aux voitures de luxe. Dans l'escalier qui conduit à l'étage, pris dans une cage qui se développe sur quatre niveaux, le garde-corps spécialement dessiné est en maille d'acier inoxydable incrustée de logos Vertu et prise en sandwich entre deux panneaux de verre. Les tables de présentation des produits, de construction apparemment simple, sont en réalité très sophistiquées. Grâce à une carte à capteur, le meuble s'ouvre en coulissant sur des rails invisibles. À l'étage se trouve un salon VIP aux murs tendus de cuir rouge et au sol recouvert d'une moquette du même ton nouée à la main. « Nous avons cherché à concevoir des espaces d'une retenue élégante qui sont en fait la traduction de la qualité des matériaux et des finitions des téléphones Vertu en architecture », expliquent les architectes. Le dessin de la façade extérieure était une opération délicate puisque Vertu n'occupe que la moitié de l'immeuble et que l'entrée du magasin est légèrement masquée par une bouche de métro et un arbre. La solution a consisté à créer une façade en aluminium noir et en verre ponctué de logos Vertu traités selon différents degrés de matité. Le magasin a ouvert ses portes le 19 février 2009.

Section drawings (above) show the rectilinear decorative patterns employed by the architects in the relatively narrow, long space.

Querschnitte (oben) zeigen die dekorativen geometrischen Muster, mit denen die Architekten in den relativ langen, schmalen Räumen arbeiteten.

Les coupes (ci-dessus) montrent les motifs décoratifs rectilignes utilisés par les architectes pour animer l'espace en longueur relativement étroit.

The exterior of the store highlights the logo of the brand, while a black band draws visitors in from the equally black façade. Within, the glossy finish and simple displays bring to mind jewelry as much as mobile phones.

Die schwarze Fassade des Stores betont das Firmenlogo, während ein ebenso schwarzes Band die Kunden in den Verkaufsraum hineinzieht. Die hochglänzenden Oberflächen und schlichten Vitrinen erinnern mindestens ebenso sehr an die Präsentation von Schmuck wie an Mobiltelefone.

La façade entièrement noire du magasin met en exergue le logo de la marque. Un axe de couleur noire attire les visiteurs vers l'intérieur, dont les murs brillants et les vitrines épurées évoquent autant une bijouterie qu'une boutique de téléphones mobiles.

The simplicity of the display cases,
also featuring black bands like the
décor of the store, contributes to the
overall unity of the design. A bright
red band of floor and wall covering
contrasts with the overall black-and-
white scheme.

Die schlichten Vitrinen, an denen das
schwarze Band wieder auftaucht,
das sich durch die gesamte Innengestaltung zieht, betonen die Geschlossenheit des Entwurfs. Ein leuchtend
rotes Band, das sich vom Teppich bis
zur Wand hochzieht, kontrastiert mit
dem überwiegend schwarz-weißen
Designkonzept.

La simplicité des vitrines de présentation incluses dans un bandeau noir
participe à l'unité d'ensemble du
projet. L'axe rouge délimité par le
tapis et l'habillage du mur du fond
contrastent avec le reste du magasin
intégralement traité en noir et blanc.

Tiffany Ginza ▶

KENGO KUMA

Kengo Kuma & Associates
2–24–8 BY-CUBE 2F Minami Aoyama / Minato-ku
Tokyo 107–0062 / Japan

Tel: +81 3 3401 7721 / Fax: +81 3 3401 7778
E-mail: kuma@ba2.so-net.ne.jp / Web: www.kkaa.co.jp

Born in 1954 in Kanagawa, Japan, **KENGO KUMA** graduated in 1979 from the University of Tokyo with an M.Arch. In 1985–86, he received an Asian Cultural Council Fellowship Grant and was a Visiting Scholar at Columbia University. In 1987, he established the Spatial Design Studio, and in 1991, he created Kengo Kuma & Associates. His work includes the Gunma Toyota Car Show Room (Maebashi, 1989); Maiton Resort Complex (Phuket, Thailand); Rustic, Office Building (Tokyo); Doric, Office Building (Tokyo); M2, Headquarters of Mazda New Design Team (Tokyo), all in 1991; Kinjo Golf Club, Club House (Okayama, 1992); Kiro-san Observatory (Ehime, 1994); Atami Guesthouse, Guesthouse for Bandai Corp (Atami, 1992–95); Karuizawa Resort Hotel (Karuizawa, 1993); Tomioka Lakewood Golf Club House (Tomioka, 1993–96); Toyoma Noh-Theater (Miyagi, 1995–96); and the Japanese Pavilion for the Venice Biennale (Venice, Italy, 1995). He has also completed the Stone Museum (Nasu, Tochigi, 2000); a Museum of Ando Hiroshige (Batou, Nasu-gun, Tochigi, 2000); the Great (Bamboo) Wall Guesthouse (Beijing, China, 2002); One Omotesando (Tokyo, 2003); LVMH Osaka (2004); the Nagasaki Prefecture Art Museum (2005); the Fukusaki Hanging Garden (2005); and the Zhongtai Box, Z58 building (Shanghai, China, 2003–06). Recent work includes the Tobata C Block Project (Kitakyushu, Fukuoka, 2005–07); Steel House (Bunkyo-ku, Tokyo, 2005–07); Sakenohana (London, 2007); Tiffany Ginza (Tokyo, 2008, published here); the Nezu Museum (Tokyo, 2007–09); and the Museum of Kanayama (Ota City, Gunma, 2009), all in Japan unless stated otherwise.

KENGO KUMA wurde 1954 in Kanagawa, Japan, geboren und schloss sein Studium an der Universität Tokio 1979 mit einem M.Arch ab. 1985–86 erhielt er ein Stipendium des Asian Cultural Council und war Gastdozent an der Columbia University. 1987 gründete er das Büro Spatial Design Studio, 1991 folgte die Gründung von Kengo Kuma & Associates. Sein Werk umfasst den Showroom für Toyota in der Präfektur Gunma (Maebashi, 1989), die Hotelanlage Maiton (Phuket, Thailand), ein Bürogebäude für Rustic (Tokio), ein Bürogebäude für Doric (Tokio), M2, die Zentrale für das neue Mazda-Designteam (Tokio), alle 1991, ein Clubhaus für den Kinjo Golf Club (Okayama, 1992), das Planetarium Kiro-san (Ehime, 1994), das Gästehaus für Bandai (Atami, 1992–95), das Hotel Karuizawa (Karuizawa, 1993), das Tomioka Lakewood Golfclubhaus (Tomioka, 1993–96), das No-Theater in Toyoma (Miyagi, 1995–96) sowie den japanischen Pavillon für die Biennale in Venedig (1995). Darüber hinaus realisierte er das Steinmuseum (Nasu, Tochigi, 2000), ein Ando-Hiroshige-Museum (Batou, Nasu-gun, Tochigi, 2000), das Gästehaus Great (Bamboo) Wall (Peking, China, 2002), One Omotesando (Tokio, 2003), LVMH Osaka (2004), das Kunstmuseum der Präfektur Nagasaki (2005), die hängenden Gärten von Fukusaki (2005), sowie die Zhongtai Box, Z58 (Shanghai, China, 2003–06). Jüngere Projekte sind u.a. der Tobata C Block (Kitakyushu, Fukuoka, 2005–07), das Steel House (Bunkyo-ku, Tokio, 2005–07), Sakenohana (London, 2007), Tiffany Ginza (Tokio, 2008, hier vorgestellt), das Nezu Museum (Tokio, 2007–09) und das Museum of Kanayama (Ota City, Gunma, 2009), alle in Japan, sofern nicht anders vermerkt.

Né en 1954 à Kanagawa au Japon, **KENGO KUMA** est diplômé en architecture de l'université de Tokyo (1979). En 1984–86, il bénéficie d'une bourse de l'Asian Cultural Council et devient chercheur invité à l'université de Columbia. En 1987, il crée le Spatial Design Studio et, en 1991, Kengo Kuma & Associates. Parmi ses réalisations : le Show Room Toyota de Gunma (Maebashi, 1989) ; le Maiton Resort Complex (Phuket, Thaïlande, 1991) ; l'immeuble de bureaux Rustic (Tokyo, 1991) ; l'immeuble de bureaux Doric (Tokyo, 1991) ; M2, siège du département de design de Mazda (Tokyo, 1991) ; le Kinjo Golf Club Club House (Okayama, 1992) ; l'Observatoire Kiro-San (Ehime, Japon, 1994) ; l'Atami Guest House pour Bandaï Corp (Atami, 1992–95) ; l'hôtel de vacances Karuizawa (Karuizawa, 1993) ; le club house du Tomioka Lakewood Golf (Tomioka, 1993–96) ; le théâtre Nô Toyoma (Miyagi, 1995–96) et le pavillon japonais pour la Biennale de Venise (1995). Il a également réalisé le Musée de la pierre (Nasu, Tochigi, 2000) ; un musée consacré à Ando Hiroshige (Batou, Nasugun, Tochigi, 2000) ; la maison d'hôtes du Great (Bamboo) Wall (Pékin, 2002) ; l'immeuble One Omotesando (Tokyo, 2003) ; l'immeuble LVMH Osaka (2004) ; le Musée d'art de la préfecture de Nagasaki (2005) ; le jardin suspendu de Fukusaki (Osaka, 2005) et la Zhongtai Box, immeuble Z58 (Shanghaï, 2003–06). Plus récemment se sont ajoutés le projet Tobata C Block (Kitakyushu, Fukuoka, 2005–07) ; la maison d'acier (Bunkyo-ku, Tokyo, 2005–07) ; le restaurant Sakenohana (Londres, 2007) ; Tiffany Ginza (Tokyo, 2008, publié ici) ; le musée Nezu (Tokyo, 2007–09) et le Musée de Kanayama (Ota City, Gunma, 2009), toutes au Japon, sauf mention contraire.

TIFFANY GINZA

Tokyo, Japan, 2008

Address: 2–7–17 Ginza, Chuo-ku, Tokyo, Japan, +81 3 3572 1111
Area: 5870 m². Client: Tiffany & Co. Cost: not disclosed

The architect has given a shimmering appearance to the store by using glass and aluminum honeycomb panels. The floor plans below show three of the nearly square levels.

Mit Glas und Honeycomb-Paneelen aus Aluminium verleiht der Architekt dem Geschäft ein schimmerndes Gewand. Die Etagengrundrisse unten zeigen drei der annähernd quadratischen Ebenen.

L'architecte a donné un aspect scintillant à l'intérieur du magasin grâce à des panneaux de verre plaqués sur une structure d'aluminium en nid d'abeille. Les plans ci-dessous représentent les trois niveaux de forme pratiquement carrée.

This project concerned the renovation of a nine-story building with leased commercial space. Kengo Kuma states: "Our approach was to treat the project as architecturally as possible, rather than a mere cosmetic renovation of the exterior." Making use of an 80-centimeter gap between the existing building and the site boundary, the architect fitted 292 special facet panels made of laminated safety glass and double-layered aluminum honeycomb (normally used in airplane wings) at varied angles "in order to penetrate and diffuse the light like a carefully cut diamond, which would enhance the elegant atmosphere in Ginza." Materials such as a transparent security shutter made of reinforced safety glass, a light wall of stone from the Adriatic that was sliced as thin as 4 millimeters, a well-polished floor of mica-like stone from Szechuan, a cloth wall in which aluminum leaves are hand-covered with silk, and showcases made with platane, a precious natural wood, are a number of the design elements that influence the interior. A large atrium in the entrance and a wall of stone and glass facing it (linking the street and the shop), a wide wall of wood drape near the escalator (linking the 1st and 2nd floors), and a chandelier that connects the 2nd floor with the lounge on the 3rd floor are other elements conceived by Kengo Kuma.

Bei diesem Projekt ging es um die Sanierung eines neunstöckigen, gepachteten Geschäftsgebäudes. Kengo Kuma erklärt: „Unser Ansatz war es, das Projekt so architektonisch wie möglich anzugehen, statt es bei einer rein kosmetischen Sanierung der Fassade zu belassen." Der Architekt nutzte den Umstand, dass zwischen dem bestehenden Gebäude und der Grundstücksgrenze 80 cm Spiel waren, und montierte 292 speziell angefertigte, facettierte Paneele aus Verbundsicherheitsglas und doppelschichtigem Aluminium-Honeycomb (normalerweise im Flugzeugbau verwendet). Die Paneele wurden in unterschiedlichen Winkeln angebracht, um „das Licht wie ein mit Sorgfalt geschliffener Diamant brechen und streuen zu können und damit die Eleganz des Ginza-Viertels noch zu steigern." Das Interieur wird geprägt von Materialien wie den transparenten Sicherheitsläden aus Sicherheitsglas, einer Lichtwand aus 4 mm dünn geschnittenem adriatischen Stein, hochglanzpolierte Böden aus glimmerartigem Stein aus Sichuan, eine Textilwand aus Seide, in die von Hand Aluminiumblätter eingearbeitet wurde und Vitrinen aus Platanenholz. Weitere von Kengo Kuma gestaltete Elemente sind ein großes Atrium in der Nähe des Eingangs und eine Wand aus Stein und Glas im Atrium (das Straße und Laden verbindet). Außerdem ein Vorhang aus Holz, der sich großflächig über eine Wand an den Rolltreppen zieht (die Erdgeschoss und ersten Stock verbinden) und schließlich ein Kronleuchter als optisches Bindeglied zwischen erstem Stock und der Lounge im zweiten Stock.

Ce projet portait sur la rénovation d'un immeuble de huit étages réservé aux activités commerciales. «Notre approche a été de traiter le projet sous un angle aussi architectural que possible, plutôt que de se contenter d'une rénovation cosmétique de l'extérieur», a expliqué Kengo Kuma. Mettant à profit un intervalle de 80 centimètres entre l'immeuble et la limite du terrain, l'architecte a inséré 292 panneaux facettés en verre de sécurité laminé et à structure en double strate de nid d'abeille en aluminium, d'un type habituellement utilisé dans les ailes d'avion, disposés selon des angles variés «pour laisser pénétrer et diffuser la lumière naturelle comme un diamant soigneusement taillé qui sublimerait l'atmosphère élégante du quartier de Ginza». Parmi les éléments marquants de l'intérieur figurent un volet de sécurité transparent en verre de sécurité renforcé, un mur paré de pierre de l'Adriatique taillée à l'étonnante épaisseur de 4 mm, un sol poli en pierre du Sichuan à l'apparence de mica, un mur tendu de tissu orné de feuilles d'aluminium recouvertes de soie à la main ou des vitrines en bois de platane. Kengo Kuma a également imaginé à l'entrée, un vaste atrium, un mur de pierre et de verre (faisant le lien entre la rue et le magasin), un grand mur paré de bois près de l'escalator (entre le rez-de-chaussée et l'étage) et un lustre qui crée une liaison entre le premier étage et le salon du second.

Kengo Kuma's elegant simplicity blends well with the image that Tiffany projects as part of its brand. On the right, a showroom seen through the aluminum honeycomb screens created by the architect.

Kengo Kumas schlichte Eleganz verbindet sich kongenial mit dem Image von Tiffany. Rechts ein Blick durch die vom Architekten entworfenen Aluminium-Honeycomb-Wandschirme in einem der Showrooms.

L'élégante simplicité mise en place ici par Kengo Kuma correspond à l'image de la marque Tiffany. À droite, une des salles vue à travers un écran d'aluminium en nid d'abeille dessiné par l'architecte.

OLIVIER LEMPEREUR

Olivier Lempereur
36 Rue de Longchamp
75116 Paris
France

Tel: + 33 1 56 58 62 62
Fax: + 33 1 56 58 62 63
E-mail: info@olivierlempereur.com
Web: www.olivierlempereur.com

OLIVIER LEMPEREUR was born in Ixelles, Belgium, in 1969. He studied cabinetmaking at the Institut Saint-Luc (Tournai, 1983–88), and interior design at the CAD (Brussels, 1988–92), and then worked in the office of Andrée Putman (Ecart International, Paris, 1992–96). He also worked as Artistic Director with AXV (Brussels, 1996–98), before creating his own interior-design and decoration firm in Paris (1998). In 2006, he opened an office in Brussels and, in 2008, a new office in Paris. His clients include Diptyque, Pierre Marcolini, Pierre Hermé, Frédéric Malle, Zimmer + Rhode, Notify, Oberweis, and private individuals. After the Pierre Hermé Macarons & Chocolats store (Paris, France, 2008, published here), he completed boutiques for Pierre Hermé on Avenue Paul Doumer and in the Galeries Lafayette department store in Paris (2009); and for Pierre Marcolini stores on Rue Scribe in Paris and in Antwerp (both in 2009). Galleries for Diptyque in Paris, Doha, London, and Dubai were also completed in 2009.

OLIVIER LEMPEREUR wurde 1969 in Ixelles, Belgien, geboren. Er absolvierte eine Ausbildung als Kunsttischler am Institut Saint-Luc (Tournai, 1983–88), studierte Innenarchitektur am CAD (Brüssel, 1988–92) und arbeitete im Büro von Andrée Putman (Ecart International, Paris, 1992–96). Außerdem war er Künstlerischer Leiter bei AXV (Brüssel, 1996–98), ehe er sein eigenes Büro für Innenarchitektur und -ausstattung in Paris gründete (1998). 2006 eröffnete er ein Büro in Brüssel, 2008 ein weiteres in Paris. Zu seinen Auftraggebern zählen Diptyque, Pierre Marcolini, Pierre Hermé, Frédéric Malle, Zimmer + Rhode, Notify, Oberweis und private Bauherren. Nach dem Ladenlokal für Pierre Hermé Macarons & Chocolats (Paris, 2008, hier vorgestellt) realisierte er Boutiquen für Pierre Hermé auf der Avenue Paul Doumer sowie in den Galeries Lafayette in Paris (2009) und Läden für Pierre Marcolini auf der Rue Scribe in Paris und in Antwerpen (beide 2009). 2009 konnten außerdem Galerien für Diptyque in Paris, Doha, London und Dubai fertiggestellt werden.

OLIVIER LEMPEREUR, né à Ixelles (Belgique) en 1969, a étudié l'ébénisterie à l'Institut Saint-Luc (Tournai, 1983–88) et l'architecture intérieure au CAD (Bruxelles, 1988–92) avant de travailler pour l'agence d'Andrée Putman (Ecart International, Paris, 1992–96). Il a également été directeur artistique d'AXV (Bruxelles, 1996–98), avant de créer sa propre agence d'architecture intérieure et de décoration à Paris en 1998. En 2006, il a ouvert un bureau à Bruxelles et un autre à Paris en 2008. Parmi ses clients figurent Diptyque, Pierre Marcolini, Pierre Hermé, Frédéric Malle, Zimmer + Rhode, Notify, Oberweis, et divers propriétaires d'appartements et maisons. Après la boutique Pierre Hermé Macarons & Chocolats (Paris, 2008, publiée ici), il a réalisé des boutiques pour Pierre Hermé avenue Paul Doumer et aux Galeries Lafayette à Paris (2009) ainsi que les magasins Pierre Marcolini rue Scribe à Paris et à Anvers (tous deux en 2009) et les boutiques Diptyque à Paris, Doha, Londres et Dubaï, achevées en 2009.

PIERRE HERMÉ MACARONS & CHOCOLATS

Paris, France, 2008

Address: 4 Rue Cambon, 75001 Paris, France, +33 1 58 62 43 17, www.pierreherme.com
Area: 25 m². Client: Pierre Hermé. Cost: not disclosed

Despite its limited floor area, the Pierre Hermé store exudes an air of luxurious merchandising, with hints of colored macaroons and chocolate brown dominating the color scheme.

Trotz der kleinen Ladenfläche strahlt das Ladenlokal von Pierre Hermé luxuriöse Exklusivität aus. Farbige Bezüge auf den Makronen und Schokoladenbraun prägen das Farbschema.

Malgré ses faibles dimensions, la boutique Pierre Hermé exprime une image de produits de luxe. La gamme chromatique est dominée par les couleurs du chocolat et des macarons.

Located on Rue Cambon, this elegant boutique was designed for one of the most prestigious new figures in the world of French chocolates and macaroons. **PIERRE HERMÉ** opened his first boutique in Tokyo in 1998, returning to Paris in 1998 with his celebrated store at 72 Rue Bonaparte, known for the long lines of customers who wait in the street to be served. The Rue Cambon boutique retains the intimate atmosphere of the original, with an emphasis on dark colors and colored lights above that recall both the colors of the macaroons themselves and of their packaging. Even the ceiling was painted in a chocolate color, while the lacquered bronze finishing of the furnishings also brings to mind the products of Pierre Hermé. Olivier Lempereur states: "The lighting was very important to emphasize the products—mixing warm and cool lights to create a 'gourmande' atmosphere." The horizontal surfaces of the boutique were made in vanilla-toned Corian. The task of the designer was delicate in that the brand already had an established identity. The point is to carry this new tradition forward with a boutique that confirms what customers had already felt both in terms of the quality of the merchandise and the intimacy of the atmosphere of the store.

Das elegante Ladenlokal auf der Rue Cambon wurde für einen der renommiertesten jüngeren Chocolatiers und Makronenbäcker Frankreichs realisiert. **PIERRE HERMÉ** hatte sein erstes Geschäft 1998 in Tokio eröffnet und kehrte im gleichen Jahr nach Paris zurück. In seinem berühmten Laden an der Rue Bonaparte 72 stehen die Kunden bekanntermaßen bis auf die Straße hinaus an, um dort einzukaufen. Das Ladenlokal auf der Rue Cambon bleibt der intimen Atmosphäre des Originals treu – die Betonung liegt auf dunklen Farben und farbigen Leuchten im oberen Bereich, die die Farbpalette der Makronen und ihrer Verpackung aufgreifen. Selbst die Decke wurde in einem Schokoladenton gestrichen und auch der glänzende Bronzeton der Einbauten erinnert an Produkte von Pierre Hermé. Olivier Lempereur führt aus: „Die Beleuchtung war sehr wichtig, um die Produkte hervorzuheben – es galt, warme und kühlere Leuchtkörper zu kombinieren, um eine ‚Gourmet'-Stimmung zu schaffen." Die horizontalen Präsentationsflächen im Laden wurden aus vanillefarbenem Corian gefertigt. Die Aufgabe des Architekten verlangte Fingerspitzengefühl, da das Unternehmen bereits ein etabliertes Markenimage hatte. Aufgabe war es also, die junge Tradition hinüberzunehmen in ein Ladenlokal, das die Vorstellungen der Kunden hinsichtlich der Qualität der Waren und der Intimität der Räumlichkeiten bestätigt.

Cette élégante boutique de la rue Cambon a été conçue pour l'une des personnalités les plus médiatiques des nouvelles stars françaises du chocolat et du macaron. **PIERRE HERMÉ** a ouvert son premier point de vente à Tokyo en 1998 puis est revenu à Paris la même année pour ouvrir son célèbre magasin de la rue Bonaparte connu pour la longue file de clients qui déborde sur le trottoir. Les installations de la rue Cambon ont conservé l'atmosphère intimiste de la boutique originale tout en mettant l'accent sur des couleurs sombres et des éclairages colorés qui rappellent à la fois les couleurs des macarons et leur conditionnement. Le plafond est de teinte chocolat et les finitions en bronze du mobilier évoquent également la production de Pierre Hermé. Pour Olivier Lempereur : « L'éclairage était très important pour mettre en valeur les produits – mélange de lumière chaude et froide pour créer une atmosphère gourmande. » Les plans horizontaux sont en Corian vanille. La tâche de Lempereur était délicate car la marque Hermé possède déjà une identité bien établie. L'objectif était de traduire une nouvelle tradition dans une boutique confirmant ce que le client ressent, aussi bien en termes de qualité des produits que d'intimité du lieu de vente.

Brown dominates the design, allowing the products to stand out in the store, attracting the gaze of shoppers.

Braun dominiert das Interieur und erlaubt den Produkten, im Laden aufzufallen und die Blicke der Käufer auf sich zu ziehen.

Le brun domine, ce qui met en valeur les produits et attire le regard des passants.

Although it is very close to the street, as can be seen in the image below, the Pierre Hermé outlet immediately establishes its own aesthetic presence with neatly aligned rows of products.

Obwohl sehr dicht an der Straße gelegen, wie unten zu sehen, behauptet die Pierre-Hermé-Filiale mit ihren akkurat aufgereihten Produkten sofort ihre eigene ästhetische Präsenz.

Ouvrant sur la rue, comme le montre l'image ci-dessous, la boutique Pierre Hermé impose sa présence esthétique par ses couleurs et ses alignements impeccables de produits.

LEONG LEONG

Leong Leong
56 Ludlow Street, No. 5E
New York, NY 10002
USA

Tel: + 1 917 262 0027
Fax: +1 917 677 8520
E-mail: info@leong-leong.com
Web: www.leong-leong.com

LEONG LEONG (LLA) is a New York-based design office practicing in "architecture, culture, and urbanism." LLA was founded by brothers Christopher and Dominic Leong in 2008. Christopher Leong was born in 1977 in Saint Helena, California. He received his B.Arch degree from the University of California, Berkeley, and his M.Arch degree from Princeton University. He worked at Gluckman Mayner Architects and SHoP Architects (both in New York), before creating Leong Leong. Dominic Leong was born in 1978, also in Saint Helena, California. He received an M.Sc. in Advanced Architectural Design degree from Columbia University, and a B.Arch degree from California Polytechnic State University (San Luis Obispo). Prior to the founding of LLA, he was a Project Director at Bernard Tschumi Architects. Their recent work includes the 3.1 Phillip Lim Flagship Store (Seoul, South Korea, 2009, published here); a Chelsea Townhouse (New York, under construction); and the Villa Bar, a private residence (Napa Valley, California, under construction), all in the USA unless stated otherwise.

LEONG LEONG (LLA) ist ein Büro mit Sitz in New York, das sich auf „Architektur, Kultur und Urbanistik" spezialisiert hat. Gegründet wurde LLA von den Brüdern Christopher und Dominic Leong 2008. Christopher Leong, geboren 1977 in Saint Helena, Kalifornien, absolvierte seinen B.Arch an der University of California, Berkeley, und seinen M.Arch an der Universität Princeton. Vor der Gründung von Leong Leong arbeitete er für Gluckman Mayner Architects und SHoP Architects (beide in New York). Dominic Leong wurde 1978 ebenfalls in Saint Helena, Kalifornien, geboren. Er absolvierte einen M.Sc. in Architektur (Aufbaustudiengang Entwerfen) an der Columbia University, sowie einen B.Arch an der California Polytechnic State University (San Luis Obispo). Vor der Gründung von LLA war er Projektleiter bei Bernard Tschumi Architects. Zu ihren jüngsten Projekten zählen der 3.1 Phillip Lim Flagshipstore (Seoul, Südkorea, 2009, hier vorgestellt), ein Townhouse in Chelsea (New York, im Bau) und Villa Bar, ein privater Wohnbau (Napa Valley California, im Bau), alle in den USA, sofern nicht anders angegeben.

LEONG LEONG (LLA) est une agence de design basée à New York fondée par les frères Christopher et Dominic Leong en 2008 qui pratiquent « l'architecture, la culture et l'urbanisme ». Christopher Leong est né en 1977 à Saint Helena (Californie). Il a reçu son B. Arch. de l'université de Californie à Berkeley et son M. Arch. de Princeton. Il a travaillé chez Gluckman Mayner Architects et SHoP Architects à New York avant de créer Leong Leong. Dominic Leong, né en 1978 à Saint Helena (Californie), a obtenu son M. Sc. en conception architecturale avancée de l'université de Columbia et B. Arch. de la California Polytechnic State University (San Luis Obispo). Avant de fonder LLA, il a été directeur de projet chez Bernard Tschumi Architects. Parmi leurs réalisations récentes : le magasin amiral 3.1 Phillip Lim (Séoul, Corée du sud, 2009, publié ici) ; une maison de ville à Chelsea (New York, en construction) et la villa Bar, résidence privée (Napa Valley, Californie, en construction).

3.1 PHILLIP LIM FLAGSHIP STORE

Seoul, South Korea, 2009

Address: 79–16 Cheongdam-dong, Gangnam-gu, Seoul 135–954, South Korea,
+82 2 3443 3500, www.31philliplim.com
Area: 543 m². Client: 3.1 Phillip Lim. Cost: not disclosed

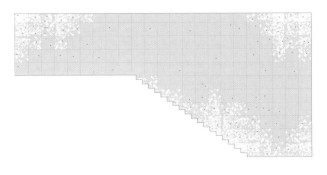

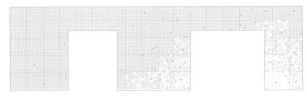

This store is located in the fashion district of Cheongdam-Dong. The architects state: "Elaborating on the concept established in the brand's Los Angeles flagship (2007–08, page 278), the design incorporates a 12-meter façade surfaced in a supple gradient of pillow-like concrete tiles." The store was created within a preexisting retail and office building. Tactile materials have been selected for the interiors to "frame" the clothing. Custom wallpaper inspired by ancient Korean ceramics was designed in collaboration with the Korean artist Wook Kim. The architects further state: "Other wall treatments include a conical wall texture which erodes into a constellation of brass stars, leather herringbone tiles, and an oak floor that slowly transitions through a gradient of gray tones. The perimeter of the interior is lined in mirror creating an 'inkblot' effect by doubling the sequence of spaces." The oak floor provides a light contrast with the essentially white interiors, where the "tactile" effect first seen in the quilted effect of the exterior façades is confirmed at every available occasion. The store opened on October 16, 2009.

Dieser Store liegt im Modeviertel Cheongdam-Dong. Die Architekten erklären: „Als aufwändigere Weiterführung des Konzepts, das wir schon für den Flagshipstore des Labels in Los Angeles eingeführt hatten (2007–08, Seite 278), umfasst der Entwurf eine 12 m breite Fassade aus kissenähnlichen Betonfliesen, die einen weichen Verlauf bilden." Der Laden entstand in einem bestehenden Geschäfts- und Bürogebäude. In den Innenräumen wurden taktile Materialien gewählt, um die Mode zu „rahmen". Gemeinsam mit dem koreanischen Künstler Wook Kim entwarf das Team Tapeten, deren Muster von antiken koreanischen Keramiken inspiriert ist. Die Architekten führen weiter aus: „Die Gestaltung der Wände umfasst auch konische Wände mit Oberflächentexturen, die sich zu kupfernen Sternbildern auflösen, Lederfliesen in Fischgrätmuster und ein Eichenboden mit Farbverlauf in Grautönen. Die umlaufenden Wände des Innenraums sind verspiegelt und erzeugen durch die optische Verdoppelung der räumlichen Sequenz einen ‚Rorschach'-Effekt." Der Eichenboden ist ein dezenter Kontrast zum primär weißen Interieur. Überall wiederholt sich der taktile Eindruck, der sich erstmals in der „Quilt"-Optik der Fassade zeigt. Der Store wurde am 16. Oktober 2009 eröffnet.

Ce magasin est situé dans le quartier de la mode de Cheongdam-Dong. « Élaboré à partir d'un concept établi pour le magasin amiral de la marque à Los Angeles (2007–08, page 278), le projet comprend une façade de 12 mètres de haut habillée de carreaux de ciment en forme de coussins légèrement inclinés, » expliquent les architectes. Le magasin a été créé à l'intérieur d'un immeuble de commerces et de bureaux existant. Des matériaux très tactiles ont été sélectionnés pour l'intérieur afin de « cadrer » les vêtements. Un papier peint spécialement créé, inspiré de céramiques coréennes anciennes, a été conçu en collaboration avec l'artiste coréen Wook Kim. « Le traitement des murs fait également appel à une texture murale à cônes qui s'érode en une constellation d'étoiles de laiton, de carreaux de cuir en chevrons, et à un parquet en chêne qui crée une transition à travers diverses tonalités grises. La périmètre intérieur est doublé d'un miroir qui crée un effet de " test de Rorschach " répétant la séquence des espaces ». Le sol en chêne vient en léger contraste avec la tonalité essentiellement blanche de l'intérieur où, à chaque occasion, sont déclinés des effets tactiles déjà notés sur la façade. Le magasin a ouvert le 16 octobre 2009.

The quilted, even soft appearance of the concrete tiles used in the façade of the store makes an unexpected transition from the architecture to the clothing sold inside.

Die fast weich wirkende Stepp-Optik der Betonfliesen an der Ladenfassade ist ein überraschender Brückenschlag zwischen der Architektur und den im Innern präsentierten Textilien.

L'aspect matelassé, presque doux, des carreaux de béton utilisés pour la façade du magasin crée une transition surprenante entre l'architecture et les vêtements vendus à l'intérieur.

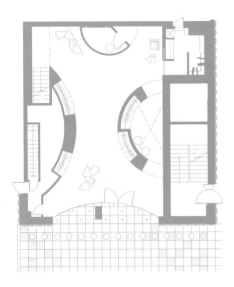
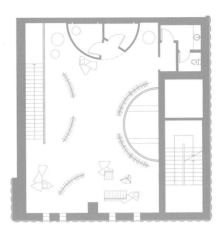

The square floor plan is articulated with a series of arcs that allow the hanging of clothes and the differentiation of spaces.

Der quadratische Grundriss wird durch mehrere Bogenelemente gegliedert, in die Hängemöglichkeiten für die Mode integriert sind und die zugleich den Raum aufteilen.

Le plan au sol de forme carrée s'articule dans une succession de partitions incurvées qui permettent d'accrocher les vêtements et de différencier les espaces.

The clothes are presented in a generously spaced way, while the broad arcs that divide the display areas do not allow a view of the entire floor from any one point.

Die Kleidung ist räumlich großzügig präsentiert. Die ausgreifenden Bögen gliedern die Verkaufsfläche. Die Ladenfläche ist von keinem Standpunkt aus vollständig zu überblicken.

Les vêtements présentés sont largement espacés. Les grandes partitions incurvées qui divisent le volume limitent volontairement toute perception globale de l'espace.

DANIEL LIBESKIND

Studio Daniel Libeskind, Architect LLC
2 Rector Street, 19th floor / New York, NY 10006 / USA
Tel: +1 212 497 9154 / Fax: +1 212 285 2130
E-mail: info@daniel-libeskind.com / Web: www.daniel-libeskind.com

Born in Poland in 1946 and a US citizen since 1965, **DANIEL LIBESKIND** studied music in Israel and in New York before taking up architecture at the Cooper Union in New York (B.Arch, 1970). He received a postgraduate degree in the History and Theory of Architecture (School of Comparative Studies, Essex University, UK, 1972). He has taught at Harvard, Yale, Hanover, Graz, Hamburg, and UCLA. Libeskind has had a considerable influence through his theory and his proposals, and more recently with his built work. His project includes the city museum of Osnabrück, the Felix Nussbaum Haus (Osnabrück, Germany, 1998); the Jewish Museum Berlin, which was an extension of the Berlin Museum (Germany, 1989–2001); the Imperial War Museum North (Manchester, UK, 2001); the Danish Jewish Museum (Copenhagen, Denmark, 2003); an extension of the Denver Art Museum (Colorado, USA, 2006); and that of Toronto's Royal Ontario Museum (Canada, 2007). Libeskind's 2003 victory in the competition to design the former World Trade Center site in New York placed him at the forefront of contemporary architecture, despite changes afterwards that caused him largely to withdraw from the project. Carla Swickerath attended the University of Florida (Gainesville, Florida, B.A., 1995) and the University of Michigan (Ann Arbor, Michigan, M.Arch, 1999). She has worked with Daniel Libeskind since 1999 and is presently CEO and a principal of the firm. Their current work includes Westside Shopping and Leisure Center (Bern, Switzerland, 2005–08, published here); Crystals at CityCenter (Las Vegas, Nevada, USA, 2006–09, also published here); Zlota 44, a residential high-rise in Warsaw (Poland, 2010); the New Center for Arts and Culture (Boston, Massachusetts, 2010); Editoriale Bresciana Tower (Brescia, Italy, 2010); and the Ørestad Downtown Masterplan Site (Ørestad, Denmark, in design).

DANIEL LIBESKIND, 1946 in Polen geboren und seit 1965 amerikanischer Staatsbürger, studierte Musik in Israel und New York, bevor er sein Architekturstudium an der Cooper Union in New York aufnahm (B.Arch, 1970). Darüber hinaus schloss er einen Aufbaustudiengang in Architekturgeschichte und -theorie ab (School of Comparative Studies, Universität Essex, Großbritannien, 1972). Er lehrte in Harvard, Yale, Hannover, Graz, Hamburg und an der UCLA. Besonderen Einfluss hatte Libeskind mit seinen theoretischen Ansätzen und Entwürfen, in jüngerer Vergangenheit auch mit seinen realisierten Bauten. Zu seinen Projekten zählen das Felix-Nussbaum-Haus des Kulturgeschichtlichen Museums Osnabrück (Deutschland, 1998), das Jüdische Museum Berlin, damals eine Erweiterung des „Berlin-Museums" (1989–2001), das Imperial War Museum North (Manchester, Großbritannien, 2001), das Dänische Jüdische Museum (Kopenhagen, 2003) eine Erweiterung des Denver Art Museum (Colorado, 2006) sowie ein Anbau an das Royal Ontario Museum in Toronto (Kanada, 2007). Dass Libeskind sich 2003 beim Wettbewerb für die Gestaltung des ehemaligen Standorts des World Trade Centers in New York durchsetzen konnte, katapultierte ihn an die Spitze zeitgenössischer Architektur – trotz der späteren Änderungen, die ihn letztendlich bewegten, sich größtenteils von diesem Projekt zu distanzieren. Carla Swickerath studierte an der Universität Florida (Gainesville, Florida, B.A., 1995) und der Universität Michigan (Ann Arbor, M.Arch, 1999). Sie arbeitet seit 1999 mit Daniel Libeskind zusammen und ist derzeit Hauptgeschäftsführerin und Partnerin des Büros. Zu den aktuellen Projekten zählen das Westside Einkaufs- und Freizeitzentrum (Bern, Schweiz, 2005–08, hier vorgestellt), das Crystals im CityCenter (Las Vegas, Nevada, USA, 2006–09, ebenfalls hier vorgestellt), Zlota 44, ein Wohnhochhaus in Warschau (Polen, 2010), das New Center for Arts and Culture (Boston, Massachusetts, 2010), der Editoriale Bresciana Tower (Brescia, Italien, 2010) sowie der Masterplan für das Stadtzentrum von Ørestad (Dänemark, in Planung).

Né en Pologne in 1946 et citoyen américain depuis 1965, **DANIEL LIBESKIND** étudie la musique en Israël et à New York avant d'opter pour l'architecture à la Cooper Union à New York (B. Arch., 1970). Il est diplômé d'études supérieures en histoire et théorie de l'architecture (School of Comparative Studies, Essex University, G.-B., 1972) et a enseigné à Harvard, Yale, Hanovre, Graz, Hambourg et à l'UCLA. Il exerce une influence considérable par ses théories et ses propositions et plus récemment par son œuvre construit. Ses réalisations comprennent le musée municipal d'Osnabrück, la maison Felix Nussbaum (Allemagne, 1998) ; le Musée juif de Berlin (1989–2001), l'extension du musée de Berlin ; l'Imperial War Museum North (Manchester, G.-B., 2001) ; le Musée juif danois (Copenhague, Danemark, 2003) ; une extension du Denver Art Museum (Colorado, 2006) et celle du Musée royal de l'Ontario (Toronto, 2007). En 2003, sa victoire dans le très complexe concours pour le site de l'ancien World Trade Center à New York l'a placé au premier rang des grands créateurs contemporains, même si les changements imposés par la suite l'ont amené à se retirer en grande partie du projet. Carla Swickerath a étudié à l'université de Floride (Gainesville, Floride, B. A., 1995) et l'université du Michigan (Ann Arbor, M. Arch., 1999). Elle travaille avec Libeskind depuis 1999 et est actuellement directrice générale associée de l'agence. Parmi leurs réalisations récentes : le centre commercial et de loisirs Westside (Berne, Suisse, 2005–08, publié ici) ; le Crystals at CityCenter (Las Vegas, Nevada, 2006–09, également publié ici) ; Zlota 44, une tour résidentielle à Varsovie (achevée en 2010) ; le New Center for Arts and Culture (Boston, Massachusetts, 2010) ; la tour Editoriale Bresciana (Brescia, Italie, 2010) et le plan directeur du centre d'Ørestad (Ørestad, Danemark, en cours de conception).

WESTSIDE SHOPPING AND LEISURE CENTER

Bern, Switzerland, 2005–08

Address: Riedbachstr. 100, 3027 Bern, Switzerland, + 41 31 556 91 11, www.westside.ch
Area: 23 500 m². Client: Neue Brünnen AG. Cost: $275 million
Collaboration: Joint venture with Burckhardt + Partner AG

The shopping complex bridges across a main freeway, creating its own urban presence within full view of thousands of commuters and visitors to Bern.

Der Einkaufskomplex überspannt eine Autobahn und behauptet sich vor den Augen Tausender Pendler und Besucher von Bern als urbane Präsenz.

Le centre commercial franchit une voie autoroutière et impose sa présence d'objet urbain aux regards de milliers d'automobilistes et de visiteurs de Berne.

This complex houses 55 shops, 10 restaurants and bars, a hotel, a multiplex movie theater, an indoor water park with a wellness center, as well as housing. The architects do not hesitate to declare: "This mixed-use program radically reinvents the concept of shopping, entertainment, and living." Set directly above Bern's A1 freeway and directly connected with the city's train and transport network, Westside was conceived as a "self-enclosed district." The design is intended to integrate itself into the surrounding landscape and to open up from the inside toward the parts of the Bern-Brünnen area, here mainly the freeway, railway tracks, and the landscape to the south. A panoramic window of the food court and spa brings natural light into the complex.

Der Komplex umfasst 55 Geschäfte, 10 Restaurants und Bars, ein Hotel, ein Multiplex-Kino, ein Spaßbad mit Wellnessbereich sowie Wohnungen. Die Architekten erklären ohne jedes Zögern: „Die gemischte Nutzung ist ein Programm, das die Konzepte Einkaufen, Unterhaltung und Wohnen radikal neu erfindet." Der Westside-Komplex verläuft unmittelbar über der Autobahn A1 in Bern, ist direkt an das Bahnnetz und den öffentlichen Nahverkehr angeschlossen und wurde als „in sich geschlossenes Quartier" konzipiert. Der Entwurf wurde daraufhin angelegt, sich in die Umgebung einzufügen und von innen heraus zum Viertel Bern-Brünnen zu öffnen, das hier in erster Linie mit Autobahn und Schienennetz in Erscheinung tritt, nach Süden hin auch als Landschaft. Panoramafenster im Food-Court und Wellnessbereich lassen Tageslicht in den Komplex einfallen.

Ce complexe réunit 55 magasins, 10 restaurants et bars, un hôtel, un cinéma multiplexe, un parc aquatique couvert, un centre de remise en forme et des logements. Les architectes n'hésitent pas à dire que «Ce programme mixte réinvente radicalement le concept de shopping, de divertissement et de vie». Implanté directement au-dessus de l'autoroute A1 à Berne et en lien direct avec le réseau de trains et de transports en commun de la ville, Westside a été conçu comme un «quartier autonome». Le projet devrait s'intégrer dans le paysage environnant et s'ouvrir vers les quartiers de Bern-Brünnen et le sud. Une baie panoramique pour la zone des restaurants en libre service et le spa amène l'éclairage naturel jusqu'au cœur du complexe.

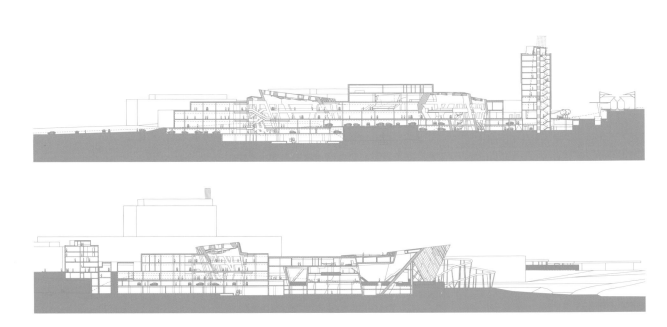

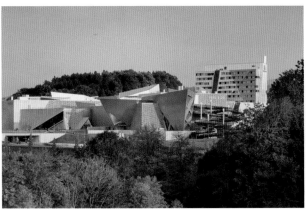

Faithful to the sharply angled, crystalline forms he has often favored, Daniel Libeskind gives this shopping center a feeling of real architectural class.

Daniel Libeskind bleibt den scharf-winkligen, kristallinen Formen treu, die er so häufig bevorzugt, und verleiht dem Shoppingcenter hochka-rätige architektonische Klasse.

Fidèle aux formes anguleuses et cris-tallines qu'il affectionne en général, Daniel Libeskind a su conférer à ce centre commercial une qualité haute-ment architecturale.

The superimposed angular forms
revealed in the sketch to the left are
echoed in these interior views of the
shopping center.

Die einander überlagernden spitzwinkligen Formen auf der Skizze links
tauchen in den Innenansichten des
Shoppingcenters wieder auf.

Les formes anguleuses superposées,
illustrées dans le dessin de gauche,
se retrouvent en écho dans ces vues
intérieures du centre commercial.

Angled supports and escalators combine in this view to create an image of a complex space that allows shoppers to see from level to level without difficulty.

Durch das Zusammenspiel von schrägen Stützen und Rolltreppen entsteht das Bild eines komplexen Raums, der den Besuchern problemlos Blicke von Ebene zu Ebene ermöglicht.

Les colonnes de soutien inclinées et les escaliers mécaniques se combinent ici pour créer une impression d'espace complexe qui permet néanmoins aux visiteurs de voir aisément d'un niveau à l'autre.

CRYSTALS AT CITYCENTER

Las Vegas, Nevada, USA, 2006–09

Address: 3780 Las Vegas Boulevard South, Las Vegas, NV 89109, USA,
+1 702 590 9299, www.crystalsatcitycenter.com
Area: 46 451 m². Client: MGM Mirage. Cost: $11 billion (total cost of CityCenter)
Collaboration: Rockwell Group (Interior Design), Adamson Associates Architects (Architect of Record)

The dramatic, angled shapes of Crystals at CityCenter make it clear immediately, with such brand names as Tiffany or Louis Vuitton in evidence, that this is an unusual, high-end shopping area.

Die dramatischen, spitzwinkligen Formen des Crystals im CityCenter, sowie Markennamen wie Tiffany oder Louis Vuitton, machen unmissverständlich deutlich, dass dies ein ungewöhnliches, exklusives Einkaufszentrum ist.

Hors la présence de marques comme Tiffany ou Vuitton, les formes spectaculaires inclinées du Crystals at City Center signalent au visiteur qu'il s'agit d'un centre commercial de luxe très particulier.

Located on Las Vegas Boulevard, this project is a retail and entertainment space at the center of the much larger MGM Mirage CityCenter that includes 2400 private residences, two boutique hotels, and a 61-story resort casino. The architects state: "The crystalline and metal-clad façade signals to visitors well in advance of arrival that **CRYSTALS** is not a traditional retail environment." Clients include such prestigious brands as Louis Vuitton, Bulgari, and Tiffany & Co. A water feature at the entry, a café, and a grand staircase leading to Casino Square at the end of the shopping arcade are amongst the interior design elements. The crystalline design of the exterior immediately brings to mind other work by Daniel Libeskind, while sketches by the architect and plans confirm that this outside treatment is fully integrated into the floor plans that emphasize angularity. Crystals was granted LEED® Gold Core & Shell certification from the US Green Building Council (USGBC), making it the world's largest retail district to receive this level of recognition for environmental design.

Das Projekt am Las Vegas Boulevard ist ein Einkaufs- und Unterhaltungskomplex im Herzen des wesentlich größeren MGM Mirage CityCenter, das 2400 Wohnungen, zwei kleine Luxushotels und ein 61-stöckiges Hotel und Casino umfasst. Die Architekten führen aus: „Die kristalline Fassade mit ihrer Metallverblendung signalisiert den Besuchern schon von Weitem, dass es sich hier nicht um ein übliches Einkaufszentrum handelt." Zu den Auftraggebern zählen so renommierte Marken wie Louis Vuitton, Bulgari und Tiffany & Co. Gestaltungselemente des Interieurs sind ein Brunnen im Eingangsbereich, ein Café und eine Prachttreppe am Ende der Einkaufspassage, die zum Casino Square hinaufführt. Das Kristalline des Außenbaus weckt unmittelbar Assoziationen zu anderen Entwürfen Daniel Libeskinds. Zugleich belegen Skizzen des Architekten und Grundrisse, dass die Behandlung des Außenbaus umfassend auf die Etagengrundrisse abgestimmt ist, die bewusst Wert auf Winkel und Kanten legen. Das **CRYSTALS** erhielt vom US Green Building Council (USGBC) das LEED® Gold-Zertifikat für Baukern und -Hülle. Damit ist der Bau die größte Einkaufsfläche des Welt, die in diesem Maße für umweltfreundliche Planung ausgezeichnet wurde.

Franchissant le Las Vegas Boulevard, ce centre commercial et de loisirs se trouve au centre du beaucoup plus vaste MGM Mirage CityCenter qui comprend 2400 logements, deux boutiques hôtels et un casino-hôtel de 60 étages. Libeskind fait remarquer que « la façade habillée de verre et de métal signale aux visiteurs dès leur approche que le Crystals ne leur propose pas un environnement de centre commercial classique ». De prestigieuses marques comme Louis Vuitton, Bulgari et Tiffany & Co. sont présentes. Une cascade à l'entrée, un café, un escalier monumental qui conduit au Casino Square à l'extrémité des arcades de boutiques font partie des principaux éléments de la composition intérieure. L'aspect cristallin de l'extérieur rappelle d'autres réalisations de Daniel Libeskind. Les croquis et plans de l'architecte illustrent comment ce traitement extérieur anguleux est déjà pleinement intégré au niveau du plan au sol. **CRYSTALS** a reçu du US Green Building Council (USGBC) la certification LEED® Gold pour l'enveloppe et l'intérieur, ce qui en fait le plus vaste ensemble commercial à bénéficier d'une telle reconnaissance d'efficacité environnementale.

A plunging view of the entrance area, also seen on the previous double page, with large projections on the angled façades.

Eine Ansicht aus großer Höhe zeigt den Eingangsbereich (auch auf der vorigen Doppelseite zu sehen) mit ausgreifenden Lichtprojektionen auf den schrägen Fassadenflächen.

Vue plongeante de la zone d'entrée (aussi à la double page précédente), et des projections sur les façades inclinées.

*Right, interior spaces blend a
sense of luxury with the dynamic
architecture of Libeskind.*

*Innenräume, in denen Luxusflair
und die dynamische Architektur
Libeskinds spürbar sind.*

*Les espaces intérieurs se prêtent
au mélange de luxe et de dynamisme qu'exprime l'architecture
de Libeskind.*

Below, sketches by Daniel Libeskind give an idea of the complexity of the architecture, but also of its dynamic, and decidedly unconventional layout.

Skizzen von Daniel Libeskind (unten) verdeutlichen die Komplexität der Architektur ebenso wie ihre Dynamik und die zweifellos unkonventionelle Gliederung.

Ci-dessous, des croquis de Daniel Libeskind donnent une idée de la complexité de l'architecture, mais aussi de la dynamique de ce projet peu conventionnel.

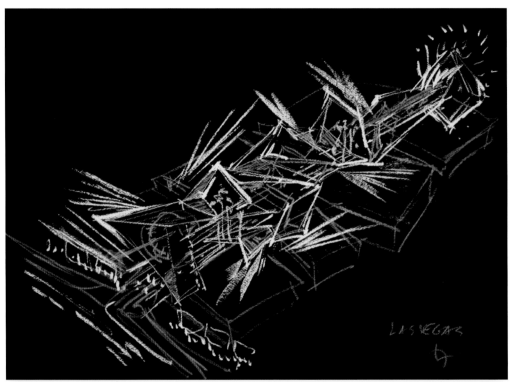

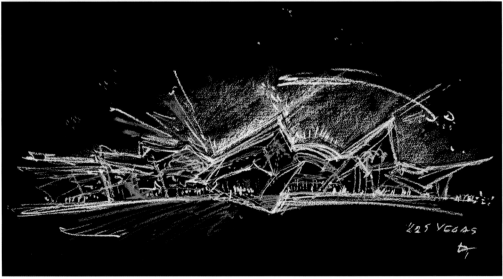

Above, an interior view again combines the feeling of a luxury retail environment desired by the client with
Libeskind's trademark surprising,
angled architecture.

Auch diese Innenansicht (oben) zeigt
die vom Auftraggeber gewünschte
Luxuriösität des Einkaufsumfelds
sowie Libeskinds typische und dennoch überraschende, spitzwinklige
Architektursprache.

Ci-dessus, autre vue intérieure montrant la cohabitation harmonieuse de
l'environnement commercial luxueux
souhaité par le client et de l'étonnante architecture de Libeskind.

LIGANOVA

Liganova—The BrandRetail Company
Herdweg 59
70174 Stuttgart
Germany

Tel: + 49 711 65 22 02 01
Fax: + 49 711 65 22 09 92 01
E-mail: info@liganova.com
Web: www.liganova.com

Liganova is a "brand retail company that mainly works for clients in the fashion and lifestyle sector as well as the automobile and luxury goods industries." Liganova has 105 employees based in Stuttgart and in creative offices in Berlin. The main people involved in this project were **MICHAEL HAISER**, the founder and Managing Director of Liganova, and **THOMAS PAUL KLEIN**, the Account Director responsible for Diesel. Michael Haiser was born in 1972. He created the agency Plan B with Bodo Andrin in 1995, changing the name of the firm to Liganova in 2002. They updated the firm name in 2009, so that it now reads Liganova—The BrandRetail Company. Thomas Paul Klein was born in 1966, and studied architecture and product design at the Universität der Künste in Berlin (1992–97). He joined Liganova as a Creative Director in 2002, and has been Key Account Director of the company since 2005. The firm's recent projects include European window design and production for Tommy Hilfiger since 2004; Cartier European sales events since 2008; visual marketing and POS events for Nespresso since 2009; shop concepts and realization for Esprit since 2009; as well as the Blue Lab Store (Levi Strauss, Cologne, 2008); and the Diesel Interactive Windows (Berlin, 2009, published here), both in Germany.

Liganova „arbeitet als Spezialist für BrandRetail für die Fashion-, Lifestyle-, Auto- und Luxusgüterindustrie". Liganova beschäftigt 105 Mitarbeiter in Stuttgart und unterhält ein Kreativoffice in Berlin. Verantwortlich für das Projekt waren **MICHAEL HAISER**, Gründer und Geschäftsführer von Liganova, und **THOMAS PAUL KLEIN**, Account Director für Diesel. Michael Haiser wurde 1972 geboren und gründete 1995 mit Bodo Andrin die Agentur Plan B, die seit 2002 unter dem Namen Liganova firmiert. Seit einem Update 2009 tritt die Agentur als Liganova – The BrandRetail Company auf. Thomas Paul Klein wurde 1966 geboren und studierte Architektur und Produktdesign an der Universität der Künste in Berlin (1992–97). Er kam 2002 als Creative Director zu Liganova und ist seit 2005 Key Account Director der Agentur. Projekte der letzten Zeit sind u.a. die Schaufenstergestaltung und -produktion für Tommy Hilfiger Europa (seit 2004), Sales Events für Cartier Europa (seit 2008), Visual Marketing und POS Events für Nespresso (seit 2009), Shopkonzepte und -umsetzungen für Esprit (seit 2009) sowie der Blue Lab Store (Levi Strauss, Köln, 2008) und die Diesel Interactive Windows (Berlin, 2009, hier vorgestellt).

Liganova est une « société intervenant sur les marques de grande consommation qui travaille principalement pour des clients dans les secteurs de la mode et du style de vie, ainsi que pour l'automobile et les produits de luxe ». Liganova qui compte 105 collaborateurs est basée à Stuttgart mais son bureau de création est à Berlin. Les principaux protagonistes de ce projet ont été **MICHAEL HAISER**, fondateur et directeur gérant de Liganova et **THOMAS PAUL KLEIN**, responsable du budget Diesel. Michal Haiser, né en 1972, a créé l'agence Plan B avec Bodo Andrin en 1995. Le nom de l'agence est devenu Liganova en 2002, puis Liganova – The BrandRetail Company en 2009. Thomas Paul Klein, né en 1966, a étudié l'architecture et le design produit à l'Université der Künste à Berlin (1992–97). Il est devenu directeur de la création de Liganova en 2002 et est directeur des projets depuis 2005. Les récentes interventions de l'agence comprennent la conception et la réalisation des vitrines de Tommy Hilfiger pour l'Europe depuis 2004 ; les réunions des équipes commerciales de Cartier depuis 2008 ; le marketing visuel et les événements sur le point de vente de Nespresso depuis 2009 ; des concepts de magasins et leur réalisation pour Esprit depuis 2009 ainsi que le Blue Lab Store de Levi Strauss (Cologne, 2008) et les vitrines interactives Diesel (Berlin, 2009, publiées ici).

DIESEL INTERACTIVE WINDOWS

Berlin, Germany, 2009

Address: Neue Schönhauser Str. 21, 10178 Berlin, Germany,
+49 30 24 78 17 90, www.diesel.com/store-locator
Area: store windows. Client: Diesel. Cost: not disclosed

To the right, actual photos of the windows in operation, with passersby activating the movement sensors that drive the changes in the displays.

Rechts Aufnahmen des Schaufensters in Aktion: Passanten aktivieren die Bewegungsmelder, mit deren Hilfe sich die Auslage manipulieren lässt.

À droite, photos de la vitrine en fonctionnement. Des passants activent les capteurs qui provoquent des changements à l'intérieur de la vitrine.

INTERACTIVE WINDOW INSTALLATION
TECHNICAL WINDOW SET-UP

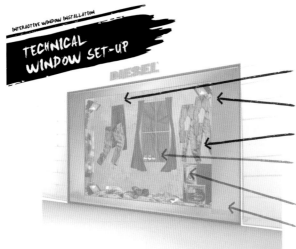

controllable fluid nozzles
for "rain" down backwall
and over specially treated
Denims

controllable flash lights
installed for lightning
flashes

controllable fan units
to inflate Denims in storm
theme

public display screen disguised as window for user-
self-reference and game

optional TV-sets with retro
styling to show old weather
forecasts and product details

thru glass soundsystem
for further attraction of
passing viewers

INTERACTIVE WINDOW INSTALLATION
"STORM"

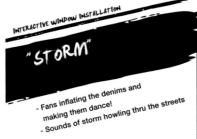

- Fans inflating the denims and making them dance!
- Sounds of storm howling thru the streets

On this page, drawings show how the windows function and detail the mechanisms employed.

Die Zeichnungen auf dieser Seite veranschaulichen, wie das Schaufenster funktioniert und welche Mechanismen zum Einsatz kommen.

Sur cette page, dessin du fonctionnement des vitrines et de leur mécanisme.

ACTIVATE
INSTALLATION

TOUCH THE
HOT SPOTS

STORM!

The **DIESEL INTERACTIVE WINDOW** concept created by Liganova uses motion-tracking technology "whereby live images from a video camera are processed in real time and can activate interaction in the window. This installation was first used in the Berlin Neue Schönhauser flagship store of the Italian fashion brand as part of its 'Destroyed Denim' campaign. The customer in front of the store "is able to move virtual objects on a screen by moving his arms and hands, influencing real objects and actions in the window." The idea is to create the impression that passersby can change the weather inside the window or actually destroy a supplied object. Using new technology that employs sound transducers, the glass of the window itself serves to transmit relevant noises without any visible wiring. The designers state: "The shop window becomes an interactive meeting point; introducing the consumer to the brand, product and shop, and bringing them directly to point of decision via the shop window." Liganova oversaw the overall design, while the Berlin firm Deon conceived the game and interactive elements, and Neumann & Müller the technical solutions. The same principle was later used in Diesel stores in Hamburg, Cologne, Düsseldorf, and Stuttgart, for four-week runs. Additional interactive windows are also planned for Diesel stores in Milan, Tokyo, and New York.

Die **INTERAKTIVEN FENSTER FÜR DIESEL**, entwickelt von Liganova, wurden mit Motion-Tracking-Technologie umgesetzt, „mit deren Hilfe Livebilder von einer Videokamera in Echtzeit verarbeitet werden und Interaktion mit der Fensterdekoration möglich wird". Die Installation wurde erstmals im Diesel Flagshipstore auf der Neuen Schönhauser Straße für die „Destroyed Denim"-Kampagne des italienischen Modelabels realisiert. Potenzielle Kunden vor dem Geschäft konnten „durch Arm- und Handbewegungen virtuelle Objekte auf einem Bildschirm bewegen und damit die realen Objekte und Geschehnisse im Fenster beeinflussen". Den Passanten sollte das Gefühl vermittelt werden, das Wetterszenario im Schaufenster manipulieren oder die im Fenster präsentierten Objekte zerstören zu können. Mithilfe neuester Klangwandlertechnik wurde das Glas des Fensters zum Transmitter eines entsprechenden „Soundtracks", und das ohne sichtbare Verkabelung. Die Designer erklären: „Das Schaufenster wird zum interaktiven Treffpunkt und führt den Konsumenten an die Marke, das Produkt und den Laden heran. So werden sie durch das Fenster direkt zum ‚point of decision' gebracht." Liganova gestaltete das Gesamtdesign, während die Berliner Firma Deon die Spieletechnik und interaktiven Elemente entwickelte; Neumann & Müller sorgte für die technische Umsetzung. Dasselbe Prinzip wurde später in den Stores in Hamburg, Köln, Düsseldorf und Stuttgart – mit einer Laufzeit von je vier Wochen – umgesetzt. Weitere interaktive Schaufenster sind für die Diesel Stores in Mailand, Tokio und New York geplant.

Le concept de **VITRINE INTERACTIVE DIESEL** créé par Liganova fait appel à une technologie de suivi de mouvements « grâce à laquelle des images animées prises par une caméra vidéo sont traitées en temps réel et peuvent déclencher des interactions dans la vitrine. Cette installation a été initialement utilisée dans le magasin amiral de la marque italienne de mode de la Neue Schönhauser Straße à Berlin, dans le cadre de sa campagne « Denim détruit ». Le passant qui se trouve devant la vitrine « peut déplacer des objets virtuels sur un écran en bougeant les bras et les mains et influer des actions et des objets bien réels dans la vitrine ». L'idée est de créer l'impression que les passants peuvent changer le temps à l'intérieur de la vitrine ou même détruire un objet s'y trouvant. Grâce à de nouvelles technologies utilisant des transducteurs de sons, le verre de la vitrine sert à transmettre les sons nécessaires sans câblage apparent. « La vitrine devient un point de rencontre interactif qui rapproche le consommateur de la marque, du produit et du magasin et le met directement en position de décideur via la vitrine », expliquent les designers. Liganova a dirigé le projet. L'entreprise berlinoise Deon a conçu le jeu et les éléments interactifs, et Neumann & Müller les solutions techniques. Le même principe a été repris dans les magasins Diesel de Hambourg, Cologne, Düsseldorf et Stuttgart, par périodes de quatre semaines. D'autres vitrines interactives sont prévues à Milan, Tokyo et New York.

INTERACTIVE WINDOW GRAPHICS

GAMEPLAY

PLAYER TRIES TO HIT BUTTON → ACTIVATED BUTTON GENERATES EFFECT IN WINDOW → BUTTON FADE OUT, GAMEPLAY CONTINUES   WHEN TIME IS UP THE GAME IS OVER

The idea that a bystander can activate a commercial display and make it move is quite revolutionary, and has implications for the ways in which architectural elements might evolve according to their use.

Das Konzept, Passanten ein kommerzielles Schaufenster manipulieren zu lassen, ist revolutionär und dürfte Einfluss darauf haben, wie architektonische Elemente in Zukunft nutzungsspezifisch weiterentwickelt werden können.

L'idée assez révolutionnaire qu'un passant puisse activer le contenu d'une vitrine de magasin ouvre des perspectives sur la façon dont des éléments architecturaux peuvent évoluer en fonction de leur usage.

MAPT

MAPT—Mediating Architecture Process and Technology
Ryesgade 19C 1.tv
2200 Copenhagen
Denmark

Tel: +45 61 28 00 11 / 12
E-mail: lendager@mapt.dk / moller@mapt.dk
Web: www.mapt.dk

Anders Lendager, one of the founding principals of **MAPT—MEDIATING ARCHITECTURE PROCESS AND TECHNOLOGY**, was born in Copenhagen, Denmark, in 1977 and received his degree from the University of Arhus (1999–2005). He also attended the Southern California Institute of Architecture (SCI-Arc, 2004). The other principal, Mods Møller, was born in Holstebro, Denmark, in 1978 and also obtained his degree from the University of Arhus (1999–2005), attending SCI-Arc in 2004. Their work includes the COP 15 Pavilion (Nordhavn, Copenhagen, 2009); Won Hundred Showroom (Copenhagen, 2009, published here); Bølgen Restaurant (Oslo, Norway, under construction); Galleriparken Public Garden (Vanløse, under construction); and the Herlev Shopping Mall (Herlev, also under construction), all in Denmark unless stated otherwise.

Anders Lendager, einer der Gründungspartner von **MAPT – MEDIATING ARCHITECTURE PROCESS AND TECHNOLOGY**, wurde 1977 in Kopenhagen geboren und schloss sein Studium an der Universität Århus ab (1999–2005). Außerdem studierte er am Southern California Institute of Architecture (SCI-Arc, 2004). Mods Møller, zweiter Partner bei MAPT, wurde 1978 in Holstebro, Dänemark, geboren. Auch er schloss sein Studium an der Universität Århus ab (1999–2005) und besuchte das SCI-Arc (2004). Zu ihren Projekten zählen der COP 15 Pavillon (Nordhavn, Kopenhagen, 2009), der Won Hundred Showroom (Kopenhagen, 2009, hier vorgestellt), das Restaurant Bølgen (Oslo, Norwegen, im Bau), der öffentliche Garten Galleriparken (Vanløse, im Bau) und das Einkaufszentrum Herlev (Herlev, ebenfalls im Bau), alle in Dänemark, sofern nicht anders angegeben.

Anders Lendager, l'un des associés fondateurs de **MAPT – MEDIATING ARCHITECTURE PROCESS AND TECHNOLOGY**, né à Copenhague en 1977, est diplômé de l'université d'Arhus (1999–2005). Il a également étudié au Southern California Institute of Architecture (SCI-Arc, 2004). L'autre dirigeant de l'agence, Mods Møller, est né à Holstebro (Danemark) en 1978. Il est également diplômé de l'université d'Arhus (1999–2005) et a étudié à SCI-Arc en 2004. Parmi leurs réalisations, toutes au Danemark sauf mention contraire : le pavillon COP 15 (Nordhavn, Copenhague, 2009) ; le showroom Won Hundred (Copenhague, 2009, publié ici) ; le restaurant Bølgen (Oslo, en construction) ; le jardin public Galleriparken (Vanløse, en construction) et le centre commercial d'Herlev (Herlev, en construction).

WON HUNDRED SHOWROOM

Copenhagen, Denmark, 2009

Address: Illum, Østergade 52, 1001 Copenhagen K, Denmark, +45 33 14 40 02, www.wonhundred.com
Area: 60 m². Client: Won Hundred. Cost: not disclosed

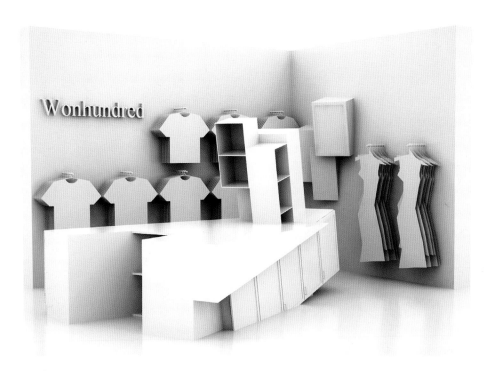

WON HUNDRED is a Danish brand that relies as much on the presentation of its clothes as on its design. MAPT designed a small showroom for Won Hundred in Stockholm, which led them to receiving a commission from the brand for Copenhagen. In this instance, they state: "The idea was to create a store that was more than a showroom for clothes, and rather an exhibition space. We wanted to create a space not constrained by its perimeters. A multidimensional space with twisted boxlike figures emerging from the floor and shelving disappearing through the walls. Everything is covered in white paint to give the illusion that all objects—no matter what form they have—are extruded from the same material. This small installation in Copenhagen is our third investigation of how to produce retail spaces by combining custom pieces with low-cost standard furniture that is cut up and reconfigured."

WON HUNDRED ist ein dänisches Label, das ebensoviel Wert auf die Präsentation seiner Mode wie auf deren Design legt. MAPT hatte bereits einen kleinen Showroom für Won Hundred in Stockholm entworfen, woraufhin sie den Auftrag für den Store in Kopenhagen erhielten. Es ging ihnen dabei um folgendes: „Der Gedanke war, einen Store zu gestalten, der mehr als ein Showroom für Mode ist, sondern vielmehr so etwas wie eine Galerie. Wir wollten einen Raum schaffen, der nicht durch seine Wänden eingeengt wird. Vielmehr ein multidimensionaler Raum, in dem windschiefe Kästen aus dem Boden und Regale aus den Wänden hervorzutreten scheinen. Alles wurde weiß gestrichen, sodass der Eindruck entsteht, alle Objekte – ganz gleich, welcher Form – seien aus demselben Material gefertigt. Diese kleine Rauminstallation in Kopenhagen ist unser dritter Versuch, Ladenräume zu gestalten, indem wir Sonderanfertigungen mit günstigen Standard-Einbaumöbeln kombinieren, die wir auseinanderschneiden und neu konfigurieren."

WON HUNDRED est une marque danoise qui s'intéresse autant à la manière de présenter ses vêtements qu'à leur style. L'agence MAPT a conçu pour elle un petit showroom à Stockholm, ce qui lui a valu cette commande pour Copenhague. « L'idée était de créer un magasin qui soit plus qu'un simple showroom de vêtements, plutôt un espace d'exposition. Nous souhaitions créer un lieu qui ne soit pas contraint par son périmètre. L'espace multidimensionnel est ponctué de meubles-sculptures tordus émergeant du sol tandis que les étagères se fondent dans les murs. Tout est peint en blanc pour donner l'illusion que tous les objets – quelle que soit leur forme – sont extrudés à partir d'un même matériau. Cette petite installation pour Copenhague est notre troisième recherche sur la manière de réaliser des espaces commerciaux en combinant des éléments sur mesure avec un mobilier standard économique découpé et reconfiguré », expliquent les designers.

The drawing provided by the architects corresponds closely to the reality of the Won Hundred Showroom as seen in the pictures on the right-hand page.

Die Zeichnung der Architekten korrespondiert unmittelbar mit dem tatsächlich realisierten Won Hundred Showroom (rechte Seite).

Les dessins de l'architecte correspondent de très près à la réalité du showroom Won Hundred, comme le montrent les photos de la page de droite.

The angling of elements of the display counters gives a dynamism to the small space that it could not have otherwise had.

Die schiefwinklige Anordnung einzelner Einbauelemente verleiht dem kleinen Raum eine Dynamik, die er sonst nicht gehabt hätte.

Les comptoirs de présentation inclinés créent dans ce petit espace une dynamique que seul ce dispositif permettait d'obtenir.

PETER MARINO

Peter Marino Architect, PLLC
150 East 58th Street
New York, NY 10022
USA

Tel: + 1 212 752 5444
Fax: + 1 212 759 3727
E-mail: press@petermarinoarchitect.com
Web: www.petermarinoarchitect.com

PETER MARINO is one of the best-known architects in the world. He received an architecture degree from Cornell University and began his career at Skidmore, Owings & Merrill. Peter Marino created his present firm in 1978 in New York and currently has seven associates and more than 125 employees, with satellite offices in Philadelphia and Southampton. He has designed shops for Fendi, Armani, Valentino, Louis Vuitton, Dior, Ermenegildo Zegna, Chanel, Loewe, Barneys New York, and Donna Karan. He recently completed the Chanel Tower in Ginza, Tokyo, where the Beige Restaurant (2002–04) is located, and has also created boutiques for Chanel in Osaka (2001); Paris (2003); New York (2004); Hong Kong (2005); and Beverly Hills (2007). Along with the flagship Christian Dior (2007) shop in Paris, and Loewe in Valencia (Spain, 2009), three other recent examples of his work, are Fendi Beverly Hills (Beverly Hills, California, USA, 2007, published here); Chanel Robertson Boulevard, Los Angeles (California, USA, 2008); and Ermenegildo Zegna Shinjuku (Tokyo, Japan, 2009, also published here). His current work includes projects for Dior and Chanel in Shanghai (China) and, for Louis Vuitton, two new boutiques in Shanghai as well as the New Bond Street Maison in London.

PETER MARINO ist einer der bekanntesten Architekten der Welt. Er schloss sein Architekturstudium an der Cornell University ab und begann seine Laufbahn bei Skidmore, Owings & Merrill. Sein heutiges Büro gründete Marino 1978 in New York, wo derzeit sieben Partner und über 125 Mitarbeiter tätig sind; weitere Dependancen gibt es in Philadelphia und Southampton. Marino gestaltete Läden für Fendi, Armani, Valentino, Louis Vuitton, Dior, Ermenegildo Zegna, Chanel, Loewe, Barneys New York und Donna Karan. In jüngster Zeit konnte er Projekte fertigstellten wie den Chanel Tower und das Restaurant Beige in Ginza, Tokio (2002–04). Darüber hinaus realisierte er Boutiquen für Chanel in Osaka (2001), Paris (2003), New York (2004), Hongkong (2005) und Beverly Hills (2007). Neben den Flagshipstores für Christian Dior in Paris (2007) und Loewe in Valencia (Spanien, 2009) sind drei weitere aktuelle Beispiele Fendi in Beverly Hills (Kalifornien, 2007, hier vorgestellt), Chanel am Robertson Boulevard (Los Angeles, Kalifornien, 2008) und Ermenegildo Zegna in Shinjuku (Tokio, 2009, ebenfalls hier vorgestellt). Zu seinen laufenden Projekten zählen Projekte für Dior und Chanel in Shanghai (China) sowie, für Louis Vuitton, zwei neue Boutiquen in Shanghai und das New Bond Street Maison in London.

PETER MARINO est l'un des architectes d'intérieur les plus connus au monde. Diplômé en architecture de l'université Cornell, il a débuté sa carrière chez Skidmore, Owings & Merrill. Il a créé son agence actuelle en 1978 à New York, qui compte actuellement sept associés, 125 collaborateurs et possède également des bureaux à Philadelphie et Southampton. Il a conçu des magasins pour Fendi, Armani, Valentino, Louis Vuitton, Dior, Ermenegildo Zegna, Chanel, Loewe, Barneys New York et Donna Karan et a récemment achevé la tour Chanel à Ginza, Tokyo, où se trouve le restaurant Beige (2002–04). Il a également créé des magasins pour Chanel à Osaka (2001), à Paris (2003), New York (2004), Hong Kong (2005). Il a réaménagé le magasin principal de Dior à Paris (2007) et celui de Loewe à Valence (Espagne, 2009), ainsi que Fendi Beverly Hills (Californie, 2007, publié ici) ; Chanel Robertson Boulevard à Los Angeles (2008) et Ermenegildo Zegna Shinjuku (Tokyo, 2009, également publié ici). Il achève actuellement des projets pour Dior et Chanel à Shanghai (Chine) et deux nouveaux magasins Louis Vuitton à Shanghai et à Londres, New Bond Street.

FENDI BEVERLY HILLS

Beverly Hills, California, USA, 2007

Address: 355 North Rodeo Drive, Beverley Hills, CA 90210, USA,
+1 310 276 8888, www.fendi.com/#/en/boutiques/flagshipstores/beverlyhills
Area: 372 m². Client: Fendi. Cost: not disclosed

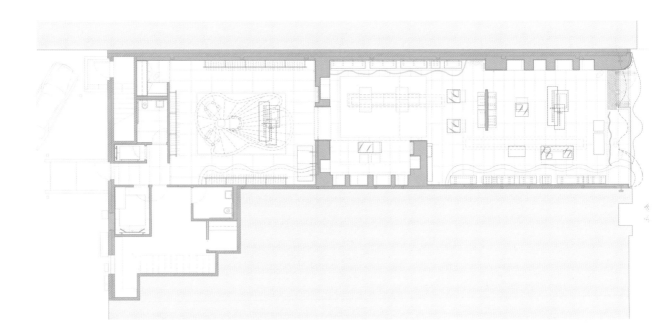

The billowing Cor-ten steel exterior façade of this store, flanked by two larger structures, is conceived as "a natural extension of the interior which specifically identifies **FENDI** with the architectural qualities of Rome, from the ancient to the Baroque to the modern." A column-like shape also in Cor-ten and a truncated cone in striated white aluminium, together with the seamless glass storefront, complete the design of the façade. The deep, narrow interior uses materials that refer clearly to Rome, including striated travertine, basalt floor stones, and rusted metal. The architects conclude: "The design exploits the high ceilings culminating in the back room of the store which features a vortex-like undulating skylight where a curvilinear tower rises to allow for natural light."

Die wellenförmige Fassade aus Cor-ten-Stahl, flankiert von zwei höheren Baukörpern, wurde als „natürliche Erweiterung des Interieurs" entwickelt, „das **FENDI** gezielt in Bezug zur Architektur Roms setzt – von der Antike über das Barock bis hin zur Moderne." Ergänzt wird die Fassade durch einen säulenförmigen Baukörper, ebenfalls aus Cor-ten-Stahl, und einen gekappten Kegel aus gebürstetem weißen Aluminium sowie eine nahtlose Glasfront. Im tiefen, schmalen Innenraum kommen Materialien zum Einsatz, die klar auf Rom Bezug nehmen, etwa gebänderter Travertin, ein Basaltboden und korrodiertes Metall. Die Architekten fassen zusammen: „Der Entwurf nutzt die Deckenhöhe maximal aus und kuliminiert im hinteren Bereich des Stores mit einem strudelartigen Oberlicht, aus dem ein geschwungener Turm aufsteigt, durch den Tageslicht einfällt."

Un important auvent ondulé en acier Corten flanqué de deux éléments métalliques plus volumineux – une sorte de colonne en Corten et un cône tronqué en aluminium strié blanc – encadrent la façade de verre. Celle-ci est « une extension naturelle de l'intérieur qui rapproche spécifiquement **FENDI** du caractère architectural de Rome, que ce soit la cité antique ou la ville baroque et moderne », explique l'architecte. L'intérieur, étroit mais profond, fait appel à des matériaux qui se réfèrent clairement à Rome dont le travertin strié, des sols en basalte et du métal rouillé. « Le projet exploite la hauteur des plafonds qui culminent tout au fond du magasin en une verrière en vortex formant une tour curviligne qui va chercher la lumière naturelle », conclut Peter Marino.

The undulating façade of the Fendi Beverly Hills store offers access to a rigorously rectilinear sales space as seen in the floor plan above.

Hinter der geschwungenen Fassade des Fendi Stores in Beverly Hills verbirgt sich ein streng geradliniger Verkaufsraum, wie der Grundriss oben zeigt.

L'auvent de façade en vague de la boutique Fendi Beverly Hills s'ouvre sur un volume intérieur rigoureusement rectiligne, comme le montre le plan au sol ci-dessus.

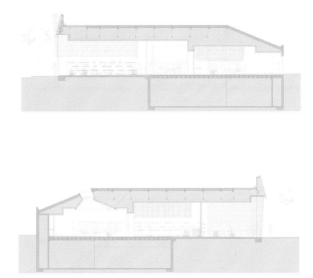

High ceilings and the introduction
of curves and skylights animate the
interior spaces, which are perfectly
suited to the display of Fendi's
merchandise.

Hohe Decken, geschwungene
Elemente und Oberlichter beleben
den Innenraum, der ideal darauf
zugeschnitten ist, Fendis Produkte
zu präsentieren.

La hauteur des plafonds et l'introduction d'éléments incurvés et de verrières animent des volumes intérieurs
parfaitement adaptés à la présentation des collections Fendi.

The curvilinear façade is echoed
here in the travertine elements above
the hanging space of the store, as
well as in the ceiling.

Die geschwungene Fassade wird
mit den Travertinelementen über den
Kleiderstangen im Interieur wieder
aufgegriffen. Auch die Decke spielt
mit demselben Thema.

La façade en partie curviligne revient
en écho dans certains éléments décoratifs muraux ou les plafonds.

ERMENEGILDO ZEGNA SHINJUKU

Tokyo, Japan, 2009

Address: 3–19–7 Shinjuku, Shinjuku-ku, Tokyo, Japan,
+81 3 3355 3311, http://stores.zegna.com
Area: 929 m². Client: Ermenegildo Zegna. Cost: not disclosed

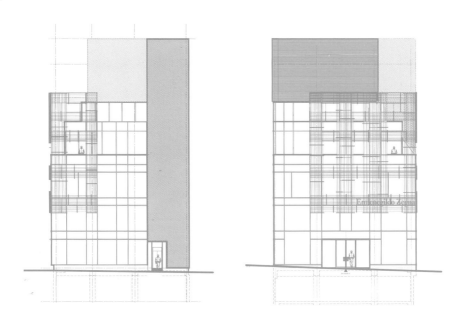

ERMENEGILDO ZEGNA'S SHINJUKU FLAGSHIP BOUTIQUE is laid out on five floors. The architects state: "The architectural details of the boutique were inspired by the company's origins as a producer of textiles, incorporating woven textile imagery throughout the design. The unique essence of the brand is represented in the various materials—marble, stone, different shades of woods, and modern metals—and in the way these are composed and joined. Zegna's spirit and brand story is manifested directly on the building's façade, by a glass curtain wall, overlaid with a woven structure of 2.6 kilometers of crisscrossed, polished, stainless-steel rods resembling woven Zegna fabric." A LED lighting system illuminates the structure at night. A yellow radica marble stripe running from the floor to the wall and three-dimensional custom stucco wall finishes resemble Zegna's signature CashCo fabric. The Couture Room is clad with Zebrano wood and bamboo stucco, as well as alpine-green and sky-blue colored stones.

ERMENEGILDO ZEGNAS FLAGSHIPSTORE in Shinjuku verteilt sich über fünf Etagen. Die Architekten erklären: „Die architektonischen Details des Stores sind inspiriert von den Wurzeln des Unternehmens als Textilhersteller, sodass wir durchgängig textile Webstrukturen als Motiv in den Entwurf einfließen ließen. Das unverwechselbare Profil der Marke wird durch verschiedene Materialien symbolisiert – Marmor, Stein, Holz in verschiedenen Tönen und moderne Metalle – sowie die Art und Weise, wie sie zusammengestellt und kombiniert wurden. Zegnas Philosophie und Firmengeschichte manifestiert sich direkt an der Fassade des Gebäudes: in Form einer Curtain Wall aus Glas, die von einer Webstruktur aus 2,6 km sich kreuzenden, polierten Edelstahlstäben überzogen wird und an einen Zegna-Webstoff erinnert." Nachts wird der Bau mit einem LED-System beleuchtet. Ein gelblicher Streifen aus Radica-Marmor, der über Boden und Wand verläuft, und eine dreidimensionale, speziell gefertigte Gipsputzwand wecken Assoziationen an Zegnas typisches CashCo-Gewebe. Das Atelier für Maßanfertigungen ist mit Zebrano-Holz, Bambusputz und graugrünem und himmelblauem Stein ausgestattet.

Le **MAGASIN AMIRAL D'ERMENEGILDO ZEGNA** à Shinjuku se développe sur cinq niveaux. Comme l'expliquent les architectes : « Les détails architecturaux du magasin s'inspirent de l'histoire de l'entreprise, fabricant de tissu, en incorporant des éléments tirés de l'imagerie du tissage. L'essence de la marque est présente dans divers matériaux – marbre, pierre, bois de différentes teintes, métaux actuels – et dans la façon dont ils se composent et s'assemblent. L'esprit et l'histoire de la marque Zegna se manifestent très directement dès la façade par un mur-rideau de verre recouvert d'une structure "tissée", composée de 2,6 km de barres d'acier inoxydable poli entrecroisées qui évoquent un tissu Zegna. » Un système d'éclairage à base de DELs illumine l'ensemble la nuit. Un bandeau de marbre radica jaune court du sol au mur tandis qu'un mur de stuc travaillé en trois dimensions rappelle le célèbre tissu CashCo de Zegna. Le salon de couture aux sols en pierre verte et bleu ciel est habillé de zebrano et de stuc d'aspect bambou.

The exterior volumes of the building are strict and geometric, but a closer view of the façade (right page) shows the metallic fabric that animates the surface.

Während der Außenbau streng und geometrisch wirkt, offenbart ein genauerer Blick auf die Fassade (rechte Seite) das Metallgeflecht, das die Oberfläche belebt.

La volumétrie extérieure de l'immeuble est strictement orthogonale, mais la façade (page de droite) est néanmoins animée par une sorte de tissage métallique.

The rigor seen in the floor plans is translated in the interior design which is at once elegant and modern, admirably serving the needs of the client.

Die Strenge der Etagengrundrisse spiegelt sich auch in der Innenraumgestaltung, die ebenso elegant wie modern und bewundernswert auf die Bedürfnisse des Auftraggebers zugeschnitten ist.

La rigueur du plan au sol se retrouve dans celle des aménagements intérieurs, à la fois élégants, modernes et admirablement adaptés aux besoins du client.

INGO MAURER

Ingo Maurer GmbH
Kaiserstr. 47
80801 Munich
Germany

Tel: +49 89 381 60 60
Fax: +49 89 38 16 06 30
Email: info@ingo-maurer.com
Web: www.ingo-maurer.com

INGO MAURER was born in 1932 on the Island of Reichenau (Lake Constance, Germany). He trained as a typographer in Germany and in Switzerland before studying graphic design (1954–58). He worked as a freelance designer in New York and San Francisco (1960–63) before settling in Munich. He designed his first lamp (Bulb) in 1966. Since that time, Ingo Maurer has become one of the best-known international light designers, and his work has been exhibited worldwide, for example at the Fondation Cartier ("Ingo Maurer: Lumière Hasard Réflexion," Jouy-en-Josas, France, 1989); the Vitra Design Museum ("Ingo Maurer—Light—Reaching for the Moon," Weil am Rhein, Germany, 2002–03); Cooper-Hewitt, National Design Museum ("Provoking Magic: Lighting of Ingo Maurer," New York, USA, 2007); and the Fondazione Carsipe ("Ingo, Piero e l'uovo," La Spezia, Italy, 2008). Works such as his YaYaHo (1984) and Little Black Nothing (1986), Lucellino Wall (1992), Los Minimalos Dos (1994), Wo bist Du, Edison...? (1997), Zettel'z (1999), and Porca Miseria! (2003) are included in the Design Collection of the Museum of Modern Art, New York. Published here is his new showroom in Munich (Germany, 2008).

INGO MAURER wurde 1932 auf der Insel Reichenau im Bodensee geboren. Er absolvierte eine Ausbildung als Typograph in Deutschland und der Schweiz und studierte schließlich Grafikdesign (1954–58). Bevor er sich in München niederließ, arbeitete er als freier Designer in New York und San Francisco (1960–63). Seine erste Leuchte (Bulb) entwarf er 1966. Seither ist Ingo Maurer zu einem der bekanntesten Leuchtendesigner der Welt geworden. Sein Werk wurde weltweit ausgestellt, u.a. in der Fondation Cartier ("Ingo Maurer: Lumière Hasard Réflexion", Jouy-en-Josas, Frankreich, 1989), dem Vitra Design Museum ("Ingo Maurer – Light – Reaching for the Moon", Weil am Rhein, Deutschland, 2002–03), dem Cooper-Hewitt, National Design Museum ("Provoking Magic: Lighting of Ingo Maurer", New York, 2007) und der Fondazione Carsipe ("Ingo, Piero e l'uovo", La Spezia, Italien, 2008). Entwürfe wie YaYaHo (1984) und Little Black Nothing (1986), Lucellino Wall (1992), Los Minimalos Dos (1994), Wo bist Du, Edison...? (1997), Zettel'z (1999) und Porca Miseria! (2003) befinden sich in der Designsammlung des Museum of Modern Art, New York. Hier vorgestellt ist sein neuer Showroom in München (2008).

INGO MAURER, né en 1932 sur l'île de Reichenau (lac de Constance, Allemagne), s'est formé à la typographie en Allemagne et en Suisse avant d'étudier le design graphique (1954–58). Il a été designer freelance à New York et San Francisco (1960-63), puis s'est installé à Munich. Il a conçu sa première lampe (Bulb) en 1966. Il est aujourd'hui l'un des designers de luminaires les plus célèbres du monde et son œuvre a été exposée dans le monde entier, entre autres à la Fondation Cartier ("Ingo Maurer: Lumière Hasard Réflexion », Jouy-en-Josas, France, 1989) ; au Vitra Design Museum (« Ingo Maurer – Light – Reaching for the Moon », Weil am Rhein, Allemagne, 2002–03) ; au Cooper-Hewitt, National Design Museum (« Provoking Magic: Lighting of Ingo Maurer », New York, 2007) et à la Fondazione Carsipe (« Ingo, Piero e l'uovo », La Spezia, Italie, 2008). Des pièces comme YaYaHo (1984) et Little Black Nothing (1986), Lucellino Wall (1992), Los Minimalos Dos (1994), Wo bist Du, Edison...? (1997), Zettel'z (1999) et Porca Miseria! (2003) figurent dans la collection de design du Musée d'art moderne de New York. Son nouveau showroom munichois (2008) est publié ici.

INGO MAURER
STUDIOSHOWROOMWERKSTATTATELIER

Munich, Germany, 2008

Address: Kaiserstr. 47, 80801 Munich, Germany, + 49 89 38 16 06 91, www.ingo-maurer.com
Area: 700 m². Client: Ingo Maurer. Cost: not disclosed
Collaboration: Brinkmaier + Salz Architekten

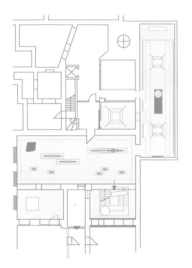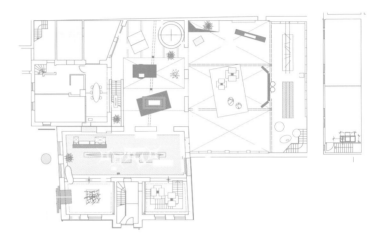

The new **SHOWROOM OF INGO MAURER** is located in an industrial building not far from the center of Munich. It features a series of skylights and is "a remnant of the times when craftsmen had workshops for manufacturing in the cities." The space had been used by Maurer for manufacturing and storage since the 1970s, and it is also the location of his office and design studio. The decision to move production outside the city prompted Maurer to imagine using the space as his showroom. Few modifications were made in the basic space aside from the creation of a 14-square-meter opening, allowing an easier connection between the ground floor and the basement, and the addition of a flight of stairs with three landings. Aside from the lower level, where a distinctive "basement" atmosphere has been maintained, the spaces are simple and clean with the high ceilings that are typical of industrial volumes.

Der neue **SHOWROOM VON INGO MAURER** liegt in einem Industriegebäude unweit des Münchner Stadtzentrums. Der Raum hat mehrere Oberlichter und ist „ein Relikt aus Zeiten, in denen Handwerker noch Produktionsstätten in den Städten hatten". Maurer nutzt die Räume bereits seit den 1970er-Jahren für Fertigung und Lagerung; hier befinden sich auch sein Büro und Atelier. Die Entscheidung, die Fertigung aus der Stadt ins Umland zu verlegen, brachte Maurer auf die Idee, die Räume als Showroom zu nutzen. Abgesehen von einer 14 m² großen Öffnung, um die Anbindung von Erdgeschoss und Untergeschoss zu optimieren, und dem Einbau einer Treppe mit drei Absätzen wurde der schlichte Raum kaum verändert. Während das Untergeschoss deutlich „Kelleratmosphäre" bewahrt, sind die übrigen Räume mit den für Industriebauten typischen hohen Decken schlicht und klar.

Le nouveau **SHOWROOM D'INGO MAURER** est installé dans un bâtiment industriel non loin du centre de Munich. Sous une succession de verrières, « c'est un vestige d'une époque où les artisans possédaient des ateliers de fabrication dans les villes ». Ce lieu utilisé par Maurer pour la fabrication et le stockage de sa production depuis les années 1970 accueille également ses bureaux et son studio de création. La décision de déplacer la production hors de la ville l'a incité à utiliser le bâtiment pour un showroom. Peu de modifications ont été nécessaires en dehors de la création d'une ouverture de 14 m² qui facilite la connexion entre le rez-de-chaussée et le sous-sol, et l'addition d'un escalier à trois paliers. En dehors du niveau inférieur, où l'on a conservé une atmosphère de sous-sol, les volumes simples et nets bénéficient de la hauteur de plafond typique des bâtiments industriels.

The relatively undifferentiated space of the showroom allows lighting and objects to stand out, creating an atmosphere of modernity where illumination is the central element.

Die weitgehend offene Fläche des Showrooms gibt den Leuchten und Objekten Raum zu wirken und schafft eine moderne Atmosphäre, in der das Licht die zentrale Rolle spielt.

L'espace relativement indifférencié du showroom fait ressortir les luminaires de Maurer dans une atmosphère de modernité dont l'éclairage est l'élément principal.

More ample ceiling heights allow
the space (left page) to present a
spectacular Birdie chandelier by Ingo
Maurer. On this page, bright colors
alternate with the basically neutral
and industrial spaces.

Die großzügige Raumhöhe (linke
Seite) schafft Gelegenheit, den beeindruckenden Lüster „Birdie" von Ingo
Maurer zu präsentieren. Diese Seite:
leuchtende Farben im Zusammenspiel
mit den zumeist neutralen, industriellen Räumen.

L'élévation du plafond sous un shed
a permis de mettre en place le spec-
taculaire lustre Birdie d'Ingo Maurer.
Sur cette page, les couleurs vives des
meubles de présentation contrastent
avec l'espace de type industriel traité
de façon neutre.

RICHARD MEIER

Richard Meier & Partners, Architects LLP
475 Tenth Avenue, 6th floor
New York, NY 10018
USA

Tel: +1 212 967 6060
Fax: +1 212 967 3207
E-mail: mail@richardmeier.com
Web: www.richardmeier.com

RICHARD MEIER was born in Newark, New Jersey, in 1934. He received his architectural training at Cornell University, and worked in the office of Marcel Breuer (1960–63), before establishing his own practice in 1963. In 1984, he became the youngest winner of the Pritzker Prize, and he received the 1988 RIBA Gold Medal. His notable buildings include the Atheneum (New Harmony, Indiana, USA, 1975–79); High Museum of Art (Atlanta, Georgia, USA, 1980–83); Museum of Decorative Arts (Frankfurt am Main, Germany, 1979–84); Canal Plus Headquarters (Paris, France, 1988–91); Barcelona Museum of Contemporary Art (Barcelona, Spain, 1988–95); City Hall and Library (The Hague, The Netherlands, 1990–95); and the Getty Center (Los Angeles, California, USA, 1984–97). Recent work includes the US Courthouse and Federal Building (Phoenix, Arizona, USA, 1995–2000); Yale University History of Art and Arts Library (New Haven, Connecticut, USA, 2001); Jubilee Church (Rome, Italy, 1996–2003); Crystal Cathedral International Center for Possibility Thinking (Garden Grove, California, USA, 1998–2003); 66 Restaurant in New York (New York, USA, 2002–03); Ara Pacis Museum (Rome, Italy, 1995–2006); 165 Charles Street (New York, New York, USA, 2003–06); Arp Museum (Rolandseck, Germany, 1997–2007); and the Peek & Cloppenburg Department Store (Mannheim, Germany, 2006–07, published here). More recent work includes the ECM City Tower (Pankrác, Prague, Czech Republic, 2001–08); Rickmers Residence (Hamburg, Germany, 2005–08); and On Prospect Park (Brooklyn, New York, USA, 2003–09).

RICHARD MEIER wurde 1934 in Newark, New Jersey, geboren. Seine Ausbildung zum Architekten erhielt er an der Cornell University. Meier arbeitete anschließend bei Marcel Breuer (1960–63), ehe er 1963 sein eigenes Büro gründete. 1984 wurde er als jüngster Preisträger mit dem Pritzker-Preis ausgezeichnet und erhielt 1988 die RIBA-Goldmedaille. Zu seinen bekanntesten Bauten zählen das Atheneum (New Harmony, Indiana, 1975–79), das High Museum of Art (Atlanta, Georgia, 1980–83), das Museum für Angewandte Kunst (Frankfurt am Main, 1979–84), die Zentrale von Canal Plus (Paris, 1988–91), das Museum für Zeitgenössische Kunst in Barcelona (1988–95), Stadthaus und Bibliothek in Den Haag (1990–95) sowie das Getty Center (Los Angeles, Kalifornien, 1984–97). Zu seinen jüngeren Projekten zählen ein US-Gerichts- und Bundesgebäude (Phoenix, Arizona, 1995–2000), die Bibliothek für Kunst und Kunstgeschichte der Universität Yale (New Haven, Connecticut, 2001), die Jubiläumskirche in Rom (1996–2003), das Crystal Cathedral International Center for Possibility Thinking (Garden Grove, Kalifornien, 1998–2003), das 66 Restaurant in New York (2002–03), das Ara Pacis Museum (Rom, 1995–2006), 165 Charles Street (New York, 2003–06), das Arp-Museum (Rolandseck, Deutschland, 1997–2007) und das Kaufhaus Peek & Cloppenburg (Mannheim, 2006–07, hier vorgestellt). Aktuellere Projekte sind u.a. der ECM City Tower (Pankrác, Prag, 2001–08), das Haus Rickmers (Hamburg, 2005–08) sowie der On Prospect Park (Brooklyn, New York, 2003–09).

RICHARD MEIER, né à Newark (New Jersey) en 1934 a fait ses études d'architecte à l'université Cornell et a travaillé chez Marcel Breuer (1960–63) avant de créer sa propre agence en 1963. En 1984, il a été le plus jeune architecte à avoir été distingué par le prix Pritzker et a reçu la Médaille d'or du RIBA en 1988. Parmi ses réalisations les plus connues : The Atheneum (New Harmony, Indiana, 1975–79) ; le High Museum of Art (Atlanta, Géorgie, 1980–83) ; le Musée des arts décoratifs (Francfort, Allemagne, 1979–84) ; le siège de Canal Plus (Paris, 1988–91) ; le Musée d'art contemporain de Barcelone (Barcelone, 1988–95) ; l'hôtel de ville et bibliothèque (La Haye, Pays-Bas, 1990–95) et le Getty Center (Los Angeles, Californie, 1984–97). Plus récemment, il a construit le tribunal et immeuble de l'administration fédérale (Phoenix, Arizona, 1995–2000) ; la bibliothèque d'histoire de l'art et des arts à l'université Yale (New Haven, Connecticut, 2001) ; l'église du Jubilé (Rome, 2003) ; la cathédrale de cristal, le International Center for Possibility Thinking (Garden Grove, Californie, 2003) ; le restaurant 66 à New York (2002–03) ; le Musée de l'Ara Pacis (Rome, 1995–2006) ; un immeuble au 165 Charles Street (New York, 2003–05) ; le Hans Arp Museum (Rolandseck, Allemagne, 1978–2007) ; le grand magasin Peek & Cloppenburg (Mannheim, Allemagne, 2006–07, publié ici) ; la tour ECM (Pankrac, Prague, République tchèque, 2001–08) ; la résidence Rickmers (Hambourg, Allemagne, 2005–08) et l'immeuble On Prospect Park (Brooklyn, New York, 2003–09).

PEEK & CLOPPENBURG
DEPARTMENT STORE

Mannheim, Germany, 2006–07

Address: 03, 2–8, 68161 Mannheim, Germany,
+49 621 12530, www.peek-cloppenburg.com/en/company/architecture
Area: 13 000 m². Client: Peek & Cloppenburg Dusseldorf. Cost: not disclosed

As is usually the case, Richard Meier's building for the retail chain **PEEK & CLOPPENBURG** is intended to "respond to Mannheim's historic city grid and to provide a state-of-the-art landmark within the cityscape." It is located on Boulevard Planken, a major pedestrian and retail area of the city. Richard Meier makes use here of Roman travertine cladding, which might recall his façades at the Getty Center, for the vertical circulation and mechanical cores. The retail spaces, on the contrary, are marked by a transparent curtain wall that cantilevers out over the street. Bands of transparent glass used as *brise-soleils* are aligned on the top level. The department store makes a number of discreet bows to the alignment of nearby structures rather than seeking to impose itself at the expense of its neighbors. There are five retail floors and an administrative "penthouse" in the building. Despite its undeniable urban presence, this building certainly does not immediately bring to mind the function of a department store, but the transparency of the structure allows its use to become easily apparent. For those who expect Richard Meier always to use white metal in his cladding, this building is also something of a surprise.

Wie zu erwarten plante Richard Meier seinen Neubau für die Kaufhauskette **PEEK & CLOPPENBURG** als „Reaktion auf Mannheims historisches Stadtraster und ein hochmodernes Wahrzeichen in der Stadtlandschaft". Der Bau liegt an der Einkaufsstraße Planken, eine der Hauptfußgänger- und Einkaufszonen der Stadt. Richard Meier nutzt römischen Travertin für seine vertikalen Zirkulationsflächen und Installationskerne, was durchaus an die Fassaden seines Getty Centers erinnert. Die Verkaufsflächen selbst werden von der transparenten Curtain Wall dominiert, die zur Straßenseite hin auskragt. Transparente Glasbänder in der obersten Etage dienen als *brise-soleils*. Das Kaufhaus nimmt in mehrfacher Hinsicht subtil auf die Bauten der Umgebung Bezug statt sich auf deren Kosten zu profilieren. Das Gebäude hat fünf Verkaufsebenen und eine Verwaltungsetage auf der „Penthouse"-Ebene. Trotz seines zweifellos urbanen Charakters tritt es nicht unmittelbar als Kaufhaus in Erscheinung – wenngleich die Transparenz des Baus seine Nutzung leicht erkennbar macht. Für alle, die glauben, Richard Meier arbeite stets mit weißen Metallverkleidungen, könnte dieser Bau eine Überraschung sein.

Comme souvent le cas chez Meier, l'immeuble du grand magasin **PEEK & CLOPPENBURG** à Mannheim se veut « une réponse à la trame historique de la ville qui ajoute un nouvel élément d'avant-garde au paysage urbain ». Le bâtiment est situé Boulevard Planken, une artère piétonnière commerçante majeure. Pour le bloc technique et les circulations verticales, Richard Meier a repris un parement en travertin romain, qui rappelle les façades du Getty Center. Les espaces de vente se trouvent au contraire derrière un mur-rideau en verre transparent qui descend en porte-à-faux au-dessus du trottoir. Des bandeaux de verre transparent forment des brise-soleil au niveau du dernier étage d'une des façades. Le plan de celles-ci rappelle discrètement l'alignement des immeubles voisins au lieu de chercher à s'imposer à leurs dépens. L'immeuble compte cinq niveaux de rayons et le dernier est occupé par une penthouse administrative. Malgré sa présence urbaine indéniable, la structure de l'immeuble n'évoque pas immédiatement un grand magasin, mais sa transparence générale laisse aisément percevoir sa fonction. Pour ceux qui s'attendent toujours à voir Meier utiliser un parement en métal laqué blanc, ce bâtiment constitue presque une surprise.

The strict and rigorous lines of Richard Meier's architecture are evident in the elevation drawings seen above and on the right-hand page.

Die Aufrisse oben und auf der rechten Seite lassen die strenge, rigide Linienführung der Architektur Richard Meiers deutlich werden.

Les lignes strictes et rigoureuses de l'architecture de Richard Meier se révèlent dans les élévations ci-dessus et de la page de droite.

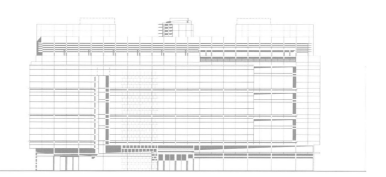

Glass is privileged in the façade of the store, not a typical solution for the architect, but one that is efficient and attractive.

An der Fassade des Kaufhauses spielt Glas die Hauptrolle. Eine eher untypische Lösung für den Architekten, die jedoch ebenso effizient wie attraktiv ist.

La façade du magasin privilégie le verre, solution efficace et séduisante, mais assez rare chez l'architecte.

On the right page, escalator bars criss cross the space, allowing views from floor to floor and also affirming Meier's geometric order.

Die Rolltreppen kreuzen sich im Raum (rechte Seite) – von hier aus sind Durchblicke in die verschiedenen Ebenen möglich. Auch hier zeigt sich Meiers geometrisches Ordnungsprinzip.

Page de droite : les escaliers mécaniques qui s'entrecroisent dans l'espace en permettant des perspectives entre les niveaux affirment avec puissance l'ordre architectural voulu par Meier.

Interior spaces show the geometric style of the architect, but leave room for the somewhat less ordered display of merchandise for sale.

Das Interieur zeugt vom geometrischen Stil des Architekten, ermöglicht jedoch auch eine weniger strenge Anordnung der Warendisplays.

Les volumes intérieurs montrent le style orthogonal strict caractéristique de l'architecte, mais laisse la possibilité d'une présentation un peu moins rigoureuse des articles en vente.

MOATTI ET RIVIÈRE

Agence Moatti et Rivière
11 Cité de l'Ameublement
75011 Paris
France

Tel: +33 1 45 65 44 04
Fax: +33 1 45 65 10 01
E-mail: communication@moatti-riviere.com
Web: www.moatti-riviere.com

ALAIN MOATTI received his DPLG degree in 1986 and worked on theater and exhibition décors (1985–90), décors for the Lyon Opera, Centre de Congrès (Tours), and Centre de conferences internationals de Paris (Agence Babel, 1990–93). From 1993 to 1995, he worked with the architect Jacques Moussafir (Paris), before creating his own office for architecture and décors (1994–2001). **HENRI RIVIÈRE** received a degree in construction and cabinetmaking (Paris, 1985) and his diploma from the École Camondo (Paris, 1990). He worked in the office of Francis Soler (Paris, 1990–95) and Christian Hauvette, Jakob + MacFarlane, Dusapin & Leclercq, Patrick Bouchain, and François Confino for Expo 2000 in Hanover (1995–2000). Moatti and Rivière have worked together since 1990. Their work includes the Champollion Museum (Figeac, 2005–07); Historial Charles de Gaulle (Paris, 2008); and Cité de la dentelle et de la mode (Calais, 2006–09); as well as a number of luxury retail spaces such as the 65 Croisette complex published here (Cannes, 2007–08); a new brand identity for the Yves Saint Laurent boutiques, seen, for example, in the Paris store (2008); and the headquarters of Jean-Paul Gaultier (Paris, 2005–08), all in France.

ALAIN MOATTI absolvierte seinen Architekturabschluss (DPLG) 1986 und gestaltete Bühnenbilder und Ausstellungsarchitekturen (1985–90), darunter Bühnenbilder für die Oper in Lyon, Projekte für das Centre de Congrès (Tours) sowie das Centre de conferences internationals de Paris (Agence Babel, 1990–93). Von 1993 bis 1995 arbeitete er im Architekturbüro von Jacques Moussafir (Paris) und gründete anschließend ein eigenes Büro für Architektur und Bühnenbild (1994–2001). **HENRI RIVIÈRE** absolvierte eine Ausbildung als Bau- und Kunsttischler (Paris, 1985) und ein Architekturdiplom an der École Camondo (Paris, 1990). Er arbeitete in den Büros von Francis Soler (Paris, 1990–95) und Christian Hauvette, Jakob + MacFarlane, Dusapin & Leclercq, Patrick Bouchain und François Confino für die Expo 2000 in Hannover (1995–2000). Seit 1990 praktizieren Moatti und Rivière gemeinsam. Zu ihren Projekten zählen das Champollion Museum (Figeac, 2005–07), das Historial Charles de Gaulle (Paris, 2008) und die Cité de la dentelle et de la mode (Museum für Spitze und Mode, Calais, 2006–09) sowie mehrere Luxusboutiquen, darunter der hier vorgestellte Einkaufskomplex 65 Croisette (Cannes, 2007–08), ein neues Erscheinungsbild für die Boutiquen von Yves Saint Laurent, darunter die Boutique in Paris (2008) sowie die Zentrale von Jean-Paul Gaultier (Paris, 2005–08), alle in Frankreich.

ALAIN MOATTI, architecte DPLG (1986), a travaillé sur des décors de théâtre et d'expositions (1985–90), des décors pour l'opéra de Lyon, le Centre international de congrès (Tours) et le Centre de conférences internationales de Paris (Agence Babel, 1990–93). De 1993 à 1995, il a collaboré avec l'architecte Jacques Moussafir (Paris), avant de créer son agence d'architecture et de décors (1994–2001). **HENRI RIVIÈRE** est diplômé en construction et ébénisterie (Paris, 1985) et de l'École Camondo (Paris, 1990). Il a travaillé dans les agences de Francis Soler (Paris, 1990–95), Christian Hauvette, Jakob + MacFarlane, Dusapin & Leclercq, Patrick Bouchain et François Confino pour Expo 2000 à Hanovre (1995–2000). Moatti et Rivière travaillent ensemble depuis 1990. Parmi leurs réalisations figurent le musée Champollion (Figeac, 2005–07) ; l'Historial Charles de Gaulle (Paris, 2008) ; la Cité de la dentelle et de la mode (Calais, 2006–09), ainsi qu'un certain nombre d'espaces commerciaux de luxe comme le complexe du 65 Croisette publié ici (Cannes, 2007–08) ; une nouvelle identité de marque pour les boutiques Yves Saint Laurent, adopté entre autres par le magasin de Paris (2008) et le siège de Jean-Paul Gaultier (Paris, 2005–08), toutes en France.

65 CROISETTE
Cannes, France, 2007–08

Address: 65 Boulevard de la Croisette, 06400 Cannes, France
Area: 2600 m². Client: Codic. Cost: €4.3 million
Collaboration: Marie-Pierre Guérin (Project Manager), Niccolo Baldassini
(RFR Engineering, façades), Georges Berne (Lighting Designer)

This project involves the creation of eight new luxury boutiques on the prestigious Croisette in Cannes. The address corresponds to that of the Miramar Hotel, between the Hotel Carlton and the Hotel Martinez. Opalescent silkscreen-patterned glass marks the curving façades, shading the store windows from direct sunlight. The billowing line of this glass is set above the glass storefronts, held in place by steel brackets. Six of the boutiques open out onto a partially enclosed 280-square-meter courtyard facing the sea, while two others have entrances directly on the Croisette. The architects praise their own work, stating: "Quality and bold creativity produce a building that has a distinct feminine look, in curve and counter-curve, partly sheltered by an opalescent patterned glass veil that captures sunlight and reflects it: 'praising shadow'. A 'cut diamond' glittering on the seafront."

Für dieses Projekt sollten acht Luxusboutiquen auf der berühmten Croisette in Cannes realisiert werden. Die Adresse entspricht der des Hotel Miramar, unmittelbar neben dem Carlton und dem Martinez gelegen. Glasmarkisen mit opalisierendem Siebdruckmuster ziehen sich entlang der geschwungenen Glasfassade und schützen die Schaufenster vor direktem Sonnenlicht. Das geschwungene Glasband verläuft oberhalb der Glasfassade und wird von Stahlkonsolen gehalten. Sechs der Boutiquen öffnen sich zum teilumbauten, 280 m² großen Innenhof mit Meerblick, weitere zwei haben ihre Eingänge unmittelbar auf der Croisette. Die Architekten sparen nicht mit Lob für ihren eigenen Entwurf: „Dank hoher Qualität und gewagter Kreativität entstand ein Bauwerk, das ausgesprochen weiblich wirkt – mit Schwung und Gegenschwung, teilweise geschützt durch einen Glasschleier aus opalisierendem, gemustertem Glas, der das Sonnenlicht abfängt und reflektiert: ein ,rühmender Schatten'. Ein ,geschliffener Diamant', der an der Küste funkelt."

Ce projet consistait à créer huit boutiques de luxe sur la prestigieuse Croisette cannoise. L'adresse est celle de l'hôtel Miramar, entre le Carlton et le Martinez. Un auvent incurvé en verre opalescent sérigraphié protège les vitrines du soleil direct. Surplombant les vitrines, il repose sur des supports en acier. Six des magasins ouvrent sur une cour de 280 m² dont l'entrée fait face à la mer, tandis que les deux autres sont directement accessibles de la Croisette. Les architectes commentent avec une certaine fierté : « Qualité et audace créative donnent naissance à un bâtiment d'une grande féminité, tout en courbe et contrecourbes, en partie abrité sous une voilette de verre opalescent sérigraphié qui capte le soleil et réfléchit la lumière pour faire " l'éloge de l'ombre ". Un " petit diamant irisé ", face à la mer ... »

The curving, glazed façades of the Moatti & Rivière boutiques contrast with a good deal of the architecture of the Croisette and attract attention to these new spaces.

Die geschwungene Glasfassade der Boutiquen von Moatti & Rivière kontrastieren mit der Architektur an der Croisette und lenken die Aufmerksamkeit auf die neuen Läden.

Les façades en courbe des boutiques créées par Moatti & Rivière contrastent fortement avec l'architecture de la Croisette et attirent l'attention des passants.

Visored to protect store windows from the intense sun, and to tie the boutiques together into a coherent whole, 65 Croisette is also unified by the curving white floor cladding.

Die Schaufenster der Croisette Nr. 65 sind durch „Visiere" vor dem starken Sonnenlicht geschützt. Zudem sorgen sie, ebenso wie der weiße Bodenbelag, für den visuellen Zusammenhalt des Ganzen.

Les boutiques du 65 Croisette sont protégées de l'intensité du soleil par un auvent, ou visière, qui assure l'unité et la cohérence de ce petit ensemble, de même que le calepinage du sol.

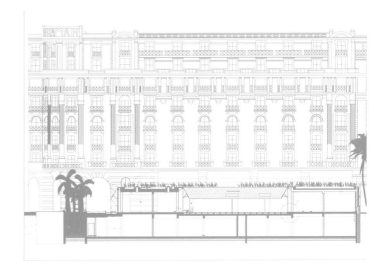

The bulbous form of the central
entrance patio of the complex
is visible at the center of the plan
above. Left, a detail view of the
curving visor.

In der Mitte des Grundrisses (oben)
zeichnet sich die bauchige Form des
zentralen Vorplatzes des Komplexes
ab. Links eine Detailansicht der
geschwungenen „Visiere".

La forme bulbeuse de l'entrée du
patio est visible au centre du plan
ci-dessus. À gauche, vue détaillée
de la visière incurvée et d'un détail
technique.

Evening views show how the boutiques glow from within, making the merchandise on offer all the more appealing on this prestigious street just opposite the beaches of Cannes.

Auf abendlichen Ansichten leuchten die auf der prestigeträchtigen Straße direkt am Strand von Cannes gelegenen Boutiquen von innen und wirken dadurch umso anziehender.

Ces vues nocturnes montrent comment les boutiques semblent briller de l'intérieur, ce qui les rend d'autant plus attirantes dans le cadre du prestigieux front de mer cannois.

PARA-PROJECT

PARA-Project, LLC
82 Pierrepont Street, Suite 3D
Brooklyn, NY 11201
USA

Tel: +1 646 478 6673
E-mail: info@para-project.org
Web: www.para-project.org

Brian Price and Jonathan Lott, partners in **PARA-PROJECT**, both received their B.Arch degrees from California Polytechnic State University (San Luis Obispo). They both obtained their M.Arch degrees at the Harvard Graduate School of Design (GSD). Price worked with SHoP Architects, Preston Scott Cohen, and William Massie, while Jonathan Lott worked with OMA and REX Architects. In 2007, PARA-Project was winner of the Young Architects Forum organized by the Architectural League of New York and in 2009, was a finalist in the Young Architects Program at MoMA/PS1 (New York). Also in 2009, together with Stereo Architects, HWKN, Phu Hoang Office, and WORKac, PARA-Project received first prize in the Open Fort 400 Competition organized by the Ymere Housing Corporation and the NAi (Netherlands Architecture Institute) to commemorate the 400th anniversary of the founding of New York. PARA-Project has completed 3.1 Phillip Lim Flagship Store (Los Angeles, California, 2007–08, published here); and the Crawford Writing Room (Syracuse, New York, 2009); while current work includes the Phillips de Pury Headquarters (New York), all in the USA.

Brian Price und Jonathan Lott, Partner bei **PARA-PROJECT**, absolvierten beide ihren B.Arch an der California Polytechnic State University (San Luis Obispo) und ihren M.Arch an der Harvard Graduate School of Design (GSD). Price arbeitete für SHoP Architects, Preston Scott Cohen und William Massie, während Jonathan Lott für OMA und REX Architects tätig war. 2007 war PARA-Project Gewinner des Young Architects Forum (organisiert von der Architektenkammer New York) und gehörte 2009 zu den Finalisten des Young Architects Program am MoMA/PS1 (New York). Neben Stereo Architects, HWKN, Phu Hoang Office und WORKac wurde PARA-Project 2009 mit dem ersten Preis des Open-Fort-400-Wettbewerbs ausgezeichnet, den die Wohnbaugesellschaft Ymere und das NAi (Netherlands Architecture Institute) zur 400-Jahrfeier der Stadtgründung von New York ausgeschrieben hatte. PARA-Project realisierte den 3.1 Phillip Lim Flagshipstore (Los Angeles, Kalifornien, 2007–08, hier vorgestellt) und den Crawford Writing Room (Syracuse, New York, 2009). Zu den aktuellen Projekten zählt die Zentrale von Phillips de Pury (New York).

Brian Price et Jonathan Lott, partenaires de **PARA-PROJECT**, ont tous deux un B. Arch. de la California Polytechnic State University (San Luis Obispo). Ils ont obtenu leur M. Arch. de la Harvard Graduate School of Design (GSD). Price a travaillé avec SHoP Architects, Preston Scott Cohen et William Massie ; Jonathan Lott avec OMA et REX Architects. En 2007, PARA-Project a remporté le prix du Forum des jeunes architectes organisé par l'Architectural League of New York et, en 2009, a été finaliste du Programme des jeunes architectes au MoMA/PS1 (New York). En 2009 également, ex-aequo avec Stereo Architects, HWKN, Phu Hoang Office et WORKac, PARA-Project a reçu le premier prix du concours Open Fort 400 organisé par la Ymere Housing Corporation et le NAi (Institut néerlandais d'architecture) pour commémorer le 400ᵉ anniversaire de la fondation de New York. PARA-Project a réalisé le magasin amiral 3.1 Phillip Lim (Los Angeles, 2007–08, publié ici) et le Crawford Writing Room (Syracuse, New York, 2009) et travaille actuellement sur le projet du siège de Phillips de Pury (New York), tous aux États-Unis.

3.1 PHILLIP LIM FLAGSHIP STORE

Los Angeles, California, USA, 2007–08

Address: 631 North Robertson Boulevard, West Hollywood, CA 90060, USA,
+1 310 358 1988, www.31philliplim.com/main.cfm#stores?id=1&subid=2
Area: 464 m². Client: 3.1 Phillip Lim. Cost: not disclosed
Collaboration: Dominic Leong (Project Manager), Jonathan Lott, Brian Price, Giancarlo Valle,
Leong Architects, Inc. (Executive Architect)

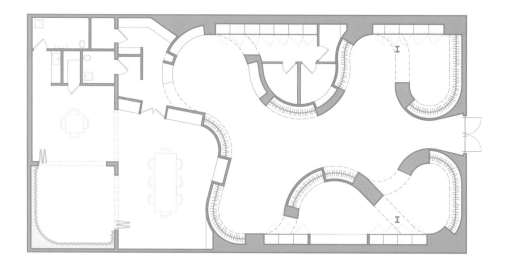

Located at 631 North Robertson Boulevard in West Hollywood, near the Melrose shopping neighborhood, this project involved the transformation of an auto body shop around a main, thick curving wall that "unfolds" into four smaller niches. The wall contains spotlights that obviate the need for track lighting, while a continuous "light diffusing membrane" adds to the intimacy of the space and imparts a "sense of lightness." Like the Seoul store of **PHILLIP LIM** (page 220), this boutique puts considerable emphasis on the tactile nature of the installation. The architects state: "The pyramidal texture on the walls is actually soft to the touch creating a sensation of being both hard and soft. The smaller niche spaces are each lined with different materials: wallpaper, Spanish cork, leather herringbone, and bamboo creating a variety of tactile vignettes for the clothing to be displayed in." Here, too, the exterior, devoid of windows but covered with concrete tiles "shaped like pillows," announces the tactile aspect of the interior design.

Für den am North Robertson Boulevard 631 in West Hollywood gelegenen Store, unweit des Einkaufsviertels an der Melrose Avenue, wurde eine Autowerkstatt umgebaut. Eine massive, geschwungene Mauer „entfaltet" sich zu vier kleineren Nischen. Durch integrierte Spotlights in der Wand wird ein Schienensystem verzichtbar. Eine durchgängige „lichtstreuende Membran" steigert die Intimität des Raums und vermittelt ein „Gefühl von Leichtigkeit". Wie der Phillip-Lim-Store in Seoul (Seite 220) wird auch in diesem Store besonderer Wert auf die Taktilität der Installation gelegt. Die Architekten erklären: „Die pyramidale Textur der Wandflächen fühlt sich bei Berührung weich an und vermittelt dadurch den Eindruck, hart und weich zugleich zu sein. Die kleineren Nischenräume sind mit anderen Materialien ausgekleidet: Tapeten, spanischem Kork, Lederfliesen in Fischgrätoptik oder Bambus, wodurch eine ganze Bandbreite taktiler Vignetten für die Präsentation der Mode geschaffen wird." Auch hier kündigt schon der Außenbau, ohne Fenster und mit „kissenförmigen" Betonfliesen verblendet, die Taktilität des Interieurs an.

Installé au 631 North Robertson Boulevard à West Hollywood, à proximité du quartier de shopping de Melrose, ce magasin résulte de la transformation d'un garage de carrossier autour d'un épais mur principal en courbes « déployé » en quatre niches. Il intègre en partie supérieure des spots qui remplacent l'éclairage sur rail, tandis qu'une « membrane-diffuseur de lumière » assure l'intimité des différents espaces et crée un « sentiment de légèreté ». Comme dans le cas du magasin Phillip Lim à Séoul (page 220), cette boutique met fortement l'accent sur la nature tactile de son décor. Pour l'architecte : « La texture pyramidale appliquée sur les murs est en fait douce au toucher, ce qui crée la sensation d'être confronté à quelque chose de dur et de mou à la fois. Les petits espaces traités en niche sont doublés de matériaux différenciés : papier peint, liège espagnol, chevrons de cuir et bambou pour créer une variété d'effets tactiles devant lesquels viennent se présenter les vêtements. » Comme à Séoul, l'extérieur sans fenêtre est habillé de carreaux de béton « en forme de coussinets », première sensibilisation à l'aspect tactile du décor intérieur.

The basic floor plan is rectangular, but the walls installed by the architects emphasize curving forms. To the right, exterior images show the pillow-like concrete tiles used to unify inside and out.

In den rechteckigen Grundriss zogen die Architekten Innenwände ein, die betont auf geschwungene Formen setzen. Außenansichten (rechts) zeigen die kissenähnlichen Betonfliesen, die Innen- und Außenraum zu einem geschlossenen Ganzen verbinden.

Si le plan est de contour rectangulaire, les architectes n'ont pas hésité à y insérer des partitions curvilignes. À droite, photos des carreaux de béton en forme de coussinets qui viennent en lien avec le traitement intérieur des murs.

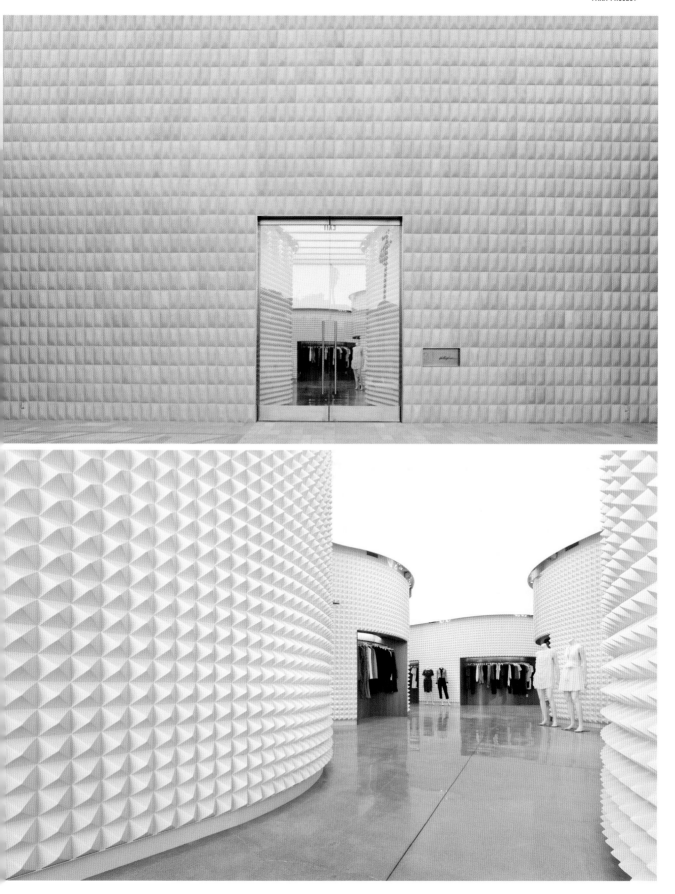

The curving walls with their tactile, three-dimensional aspect make the limited number of mannequins on display stand out, emphasized above by overhead lighting.

Die geschwungenen Wände mit ihrer taktilen, dreidimensionalen Struktur sorgen dafür, dass die wenigen Modepuppen umso stärker zur Geltung kommen. Zusätzlich betont werden sie durch Licht von oben.

Les murs incurvés à motif tridimensionnel d'aspect tactile font ressortir les mannequins en nombre limité que met en valeur le plafond lumineux.

Curving hangars, alcoves, and intriguing wall finishings animate the space and give the sparse presentation its full value. Round overhead openings admit natural light.

Geschwungene Kleiderstangen, Nischen und faszinierende Wandverkleidungen beleben die Räume und lassen die sparsame Präsentation maximal wirken. Durch runde Oberlichter fällt Tageslicht ein.

Les niches incurvées et la finition curieuse des murs animent l'espace et mettent en valeur la présentation peu dense des vêtements. Au plafond, des oculus laissent passer la lumière naturelle.

PURESANG

Puresang
Vleminckveld 68
2000 Antwerp
Belgium

Tel: + 32 3 298 07 70
Fax: + 32 3 298 07 59
E-mail: info@pure-sang.com
Web: www.pure-sang.com

Will Erens was born in Hasselt, Belgium, in 1962. He was self-taught as a designer and created the Creneau design network in 1989. **PURESANG** was created in 2003 by Will Erens in Antwerp. He is also the originator of the "creative platform" All Popstars Welcome (London). The clients of Puresang include Pepe Jeans, Martini, and the Italian fashion firm GURU. Their work includes the Martini Verso Bar (Antwerp, 2006); Pepe Jeans Showroom (London, UK, 2006); the Noxx Club (Antwerp, 2007); the Van Bommel shoe store (Antwerp, 2008); the Spirito Nightclub and Restaurant (Brussels, 2009); and the Hospital store (Antwerp, 2008–09, published here) with the Glorious Restaurant in the same location, all in Belgium unless stated otherwise.

Will Erens wurde 1962 in Hasselt, Belgien, geboren. Als Designer ist er Autodidakt und gründete 1989 das Design-Netzwerk Creneau. 2003 gründete er sein Büro **PURESANG** in Antwerpen. Darüber hinaus ist Erens Initiator der „kreativen Plattform" All Popstars Welcome (London). Zu den Kunden von Puresang zählen Pepe Jeans, Martini und das italienische Modelabel GURU. Projekte des Büros sind u.a. die Martini Verso Bar (Antwerpen, 2006), der Pepe Jeans Showroom (London, 2006), der Noxx Club (Antwerpen, 2007), das Schuhgeschäft Van Bommel (Antwerpen, 2008), Spirito Nachtclub und Restaurant (Brüssel, 2009) und der Hospital Store (Antwerpen, 2008–09, hier vorgestellt) sowie das Glorious Restaurant am gleichen Standort, alle in Belgien, sofern nicht anders angegeben.

Will Erens, né à Hasselt (Belgique) en 1962, designer autodidacte, a créé le réseau de design Creneau en 1989 et l'agence **PURESANG** en 2003 à Anvers. Il est également à l'origine de la « plate-forme créative » All Popstars Welcome (Londres). Parmi les clients de Puresang figurent Pepe Jeans, Martini et la marque de mode italienne GURU. L'agence a réalisé le bar Martini Verso (Anvers, 2006) ; le showroom Pepe Jeans (Londres, 2006) ; le club Noxx (Anvers, 2007) ; le magasin de chaussures Van Bommel (Anvers, 2008) ; le nightcub et restaurant Spirito (Bruxelles, 2009) et le magasin Hospital (Anvers, 2008–09, publié ici), ainsi que le restaurant Glorious à la même adresse.

HOSPITAL

Antwerp, Belgium, 2008–09

*Address: De Burburestraat 4, 2000 Antwerp, Belgium,
+32 3 311 89 80, www.hospital-antwerp.com / www.theglorious.be
Area: 555 m². Client: Jeroen Smeekens. Cost: not disclosed*

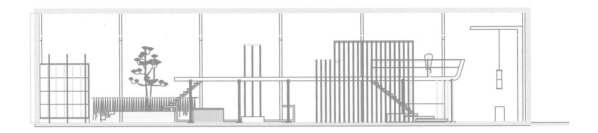

Although the space is called Hospital, the structure served formerly as a stable. The designers have articulated the space with a certain number of sculptural elements, but left it otherwise open.

Seinem Namen zum Trotz ist Hospital in einem ehemaligen Stallgebäude untergebracht. Abgesehen von nur wenigen gliedernden, skulpturalen Elementen beließen die Architekten den Raum offen.

Bien qu'il s'intitule Hospital, ce bâtiment est une ancienne écurie. Les designers ont articulé l'espace grâce au moyen d'éléments sculpturaux qui lui conservent son ouverture.

Jeroen Smeekens and Will Erens transformed the former stables of the Antwerp Hippodrome with their seven-meter-high ceilings and brick walls into a boutique, with an adjoining bar and restaurant. The name **HOSPITAL** was chosen in relation to Smeekens's other boutique, the "denim-and-stuff market" Clinic. Designer brands, such as Viktor & Rolf, Marc Jacobs, Alexander McQueen, Tim Van Steenbergen, and Sonia Rykiel, are displayed with French, Italian and Scandinavian labels, such as Paul & Joe, D&G, and Fifth Avenue Shoe Repair. Jeroen Smeekens states: "With Hospital, we want to create an experience. Think of Corso Como 10 in Milan, or Colette in Paris. Here in Antwerp's south district, we want to deliver a very individual, innovative concept, tailored to a clientele who love to enjoy life. Here, they must be able to find more than just beautiful clothes." A wine bar with a selection made by Jurgen Lijcops, twice named Belgium's best sommelier, is contrasted with a different restored vintage car displayed and offered for sale on the ground floor each month. In addition to the boutique, Hospital incorporates Glorious, a bar and restaurant, and a luxury bed and breakfast with just three rooms. The sales staff are dressed as "style doctors."

Jeroen Smeekens und Will Erens bauten die ehemaligen Pferdeställe des Hippodroms in Antwerpen mit ihren sieben Meter hohen Decken und ihren Ziegelwänden zu einer Boutique mit angrenzender Bar und Restaurant um. Der Name **HOSPITAL** ist eine Anspielung an Smeekens anderen Store Clinic, einen „Jeans-und-Kramladen". Hospital präsentiert Labels wie Viktor & Rolf, Marc Jacobs, Alexander McQueen, Tim Van Steenbergen und Sonia Rykiel ebenso wie französische, italienische und skandinavische Modemarken, darunter Paul & Joe, D&G und Fifth Avenue Shoe Repair. Jeroen Smeekens erklärt: „Mit Hospital wollen wir ein Erlebnis schaffen. Wie der Corso Como 10 in Mailand oder Colette in Paris. Hier im Südviertel von Antwerpen wollen wir ein individuelles, innovatives Konzept umsetzen, das auf ein Klientel zugeschnitten ist, das sein Leben genießt. Hier müssen sie mehr finden können, als nur schöne Mode." Als Kontrast zur Weinbar mit einer Auswahl von Jurgen Lijcops, der bereits zweimal als Belgiens bester Sommelier ausgezeichnet wurde, wird im Erdgeschoss jeden Monat ein restaurierter Oldtimer ausgestellt und zum Verkauf angeboten. Neben der Boutique gehört zu Hospital auch das Restaurant & Bar Glorious und ein Luxus-Bed & Breakfast mit nur drei Zimmern. Die Verkäufer treten als „Style Doctors" auf.

Jeroen Smeekens et Will Erens ont transformé les anciennes écuries de l'Hippodrome d'Anvers – murs de briques et plafonds de sept mètres de haut – en un magasin accompagné d'un bar et d'un restaurant. Le nom d'**HOSPITAL** a été choisi par référence avec l'autre point de vente de Smeekens, le Clinic, « marché de jeans et autres trucs ». Des marques de stylistes comme Viktor & Rolf, Marc Jacobs, Alexander McQueen, Tim Van Steenbergen et Sonia Rykiel sont proposées en même temps que des labels français, italiens et scandinaves comme Paul & Joe, D&G ou Fifth Avenue Shoe Repair. Jeroen Smeekens explique : « À travers Hospital, nous avons voulu créer une nouvelle expérience. Pensez à Corso Como 10 à Milan ou à Colette à Paris. Ici dans ce quartier sud d'Anvers, nous proposons un concept novateur exclusif, adapté à une clientèle qui aime profiter de la vie et qui doit pouvoir trouver chez nous davantage que juste de beaux vêtements. » Un bar à vin dont la carte a été dressée par Jurgen Lijcops, deux fois élu meilleur sommelier de Belgique, contraste avec une voiture ancienne restaurée, un nouveau modèle étant proposé à la vente chaque mois. En dehors de la boutique, Hospital comprend également le Glorious, un bar et restaurant, et trois luxueuses chambres d'hôtes. Le personnel de vente est habillé en « docteurs de style ».

The floor plans show rectilinear, or more precisely rectangular, elements that are pieced together in an unusual manner, offering an unexpected seven-meter-high space to prestigious fashion brands.

Die Etagengrundrisse zeigen geradlinige, genauer gesagt rechteckige, Raumelemente, die auf ungewöhnliche Art und Weise miteinander verknüpft sind. Im überraschenden, sieben Meter hohen Raum werden exklusive Modelabels präsentiert.

Ces plans montrent des éléments rectangulaires assemblés de façon inhabituelle qui dégagent par endroit des hauteurs de plafond de sept mètres.

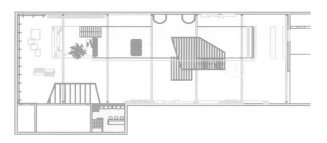

FRANCESC RIFÉ

Francesc Rifé
C/ Escoles Pies 25 bajos
08017 Barcelona
Spain

Tel: + 34 93 414 12 88
Fax: + 34 93 241 28 14
E-mail: f@rife-design.com
Web: www.rife-design.com

FRANCESC RIFÉ was born in Sant Sadurní d'Anoia (Barcelona, Spain) in 1969. He studied architecture at the Universidad Politécnica de Cataluña (Barcelona), and obtained a degree in interior design from the Escuela DIAC-Eiade / La Llotja (Barcelona) and another degree in industrial design from the same institution. He is currently a Professor at the Elisava School of Design, which is part of Pompeu Fabra University (Barcelona). He established his own studio in Barcelona in 1994. His projects range from interior to industrial design, for both commercial and private clients. His work includes the Hotel Blu Almansa (Albacete, 2007); Nino Alvarez (Barcelona, 2007); the Clinica Borrell (Sabadell, Barcelona, 2007); the Gastromium Miguel Díaz (Seville, 2008); Optica XD (Sant Sadurní d'Anoia, Barcelona, 2008); and Pomme Sucre (Oviedo, 2009, published here), all in Spain.

FRANCESC RIFÉ wurde 1969 in Sant Sadurní d'Anoia (Barcelona) geboren. Er studierte Architektur an der Universidad Politécnica de Cataluña (Barcelona), absolvierte einen Abschluss in Innenarchitektur an der Escuela DIAC-Eiade / La Llotja (Barcelona) sowie einen Abschluss in Industriedesign an derselben Hochschule. Derzeit ist er Professor an der Elisava Fakultät für Design an der Universität Pompeu Fabra (Barcelona). Sein Büro gründete er 1994 in Barcelona. Er arbeitet in den Bereichen Innenarchitektur und Industriedesign, für gewerbliche wie für private Auftraggeber. Zu seinen Projekten zählen das Hotel Blu Almansa (Albacete, 2007), Nino Alvarez (Barcelona, 2007), die Clínica Borrell (Sabadell, Barcelona, 2007), das Gastromium Miguel Díaz (Seville, 2008), Optica XD (Sant Sadurní d'Anoia, Barcelona, 2008) und Pomme Sucre (Oviedo, 2009, hier vorgestellt), alle in Spanien.

FRANCESC RIFÉ, né à Sant Sadurní d'Anoia (Barcelone, 1969), a étudié l'architecture à l'Universidad Politécnica de Cataluña (Barcelone) et obtenu son diplôme d'architecture d'intérieur à la Escuela DIAC-Eiade / La Llotja (Barcelone) et un second diplôme en design industriel de la même institution. Il est actuellement professeur à l'École de design Elisava, qui fait partie de l'université Pompeu Fabra (Barcelone). Il a créé sa propre agence à Barcelone en 1994. Ses projets vont de l'architecture intérieure au design industriel pour des clients aussi bien commerciaux que privés. Parmi ses réalisations : l'hôtel Blu Almansa (Albacete, 2007) ; le magasin Nino Alvarez (Barcelone, 2007) ; la clinique Borrell (Sabadell, Barcelone, 2007) ; le Gastromium Miguel Díaz (Séville, 2008) ; le magasin Optica XD (Sant Sadurní d'Anoia, Barcelone, 2008) et Pomme Sucre (Oviedo, 2009, publié ici).

POMME SUCRE

Oviedo, Spain, 2009

Address: Calle de Covadonga 21, 33002 Oviedo, Spain
Area: 70 m². Client: Pomme Sucre. Cost: not disclosed

This is the first of a chain of stores being created in Spain by the master baker Julio Blanco. The shop is divided into two equal floors, with the sales area on the ground floor and the bakery, storeroom, cold room, and bathroom in the basement. The designer explains: "The theme of the project is simply to represent the three key ingredients used at the bakery (flour, eggs, and cocoa) through the materials of white opal, yellow resin, and smoked mirror." These themes are represented in the display cases. White opal is used in the **POMME SUCRE** logo and in the ceiling paneling. A suspended cash desk is also covered in white opal. Smoked mirrors are meant to bring chocolate to mind. Yellow, illuminated niches in the white walls are used to display the store's products. The black façade includes signage, the window, and a night security door. The result, concludes the designer, "is a very smooth, planar shop front juxtaposed with the older, more traditional adjoining buildings."

Dieses Geschäft ist das erste einer spanischen Ladenkette des Meisterbäckers Julio Blanco. Die Bäckerei verteilt sich über zwei gleich große Etagen. Während der Verkaufsraum im Erdgeschoss liegt, befinden sich Backstube, Lager, Kühlraum und Toiletten im Untergeschoss. Der Architekt führt aus: „Thema des Projekts war ganz einfach, die drei wichtigsten in der Bäckerei verwendeten Zutaten (Mehl, Eier und Kakao) zu repräsentieren, und zwar durch die Materialien Opal, gelben Kunstharz und Rauchglas." Diese Themen werden auch in den Vitrinen aufgegriffen. Weißer Opal taucht im Logo von **POMME SUCRE** und der Deckenverschalung auf. Auch der schwebende Kassentresen ist mit weißem Opal ummantelt. Die Rauchglasspiegel sind eine Anspielung auf Schokolade. Gelbe, beleuchtete Wandnischen dienen der Präsentation der Produkte. Auf der schwarzen Ladenfassade ist der Firmenschriftzug zu lesen; hier befinden sich außerdem ein Fenster und eine Nachttür. Das Ergebnis ist, so der Architekt, „eine im Vergleich zu den traditionelleren Nachbargebäuden sehr glatte, plane Ladenfront".

Ce magasin est le premier d'une chaîne créée en Espagne par le maître-pâtissier Julio Blanco. Il est divisé en deux niveaux de mêmes dimensions : la vente au rez-de-chaussée, la préparation, le stockage, une salle réfrigérée et des toilettes au sous-sol. Selon le designer : « Le thème de ce projet est simplement d'illustrer les trois éléments de base de la pâtisserie – la farine, les œufs et le cacao – par des matériaux comme l'opaline blanche, la résine jaune et le miroir fumé. » Ces thèmes sont illustrés dans des vitrines de présentation. Le verre opalin est utilisé pour le logo **POMME SUCRE**, les panneaux du plafond et la caisse suspendue. Des niches jaunes éclairées, creusées dans les murs blancs, mettent en valeur les produits de la maison. La façade entièrement noire regroupe l'enseigne, la vitrine et une porte de nuit sécurisée. Pour le designer, « c'est une façade plane très lisse qui vient se juxtaposer à celles des immeubles adjacents plus traditionnels. »

The designer, Francesc Rifé, has created a bakery that looks more like a jewelry store than a conventional place to buy bread and pastries.

Der Designer Francesc Rifé entwarf eine Bäckerei, die eher wie ein Juwelier wirkt als wie ein Ort, an dem man normalerweise Brot und Gebäck kauft.

Le designer Francesc Rifé a créé ici une pâtisserie qui fait davantage penser à une bijouterie qu'aux points de vente habituels de pains et de gâteaux.

The basically rectangular layout has been animated with alternating volumes, as seen in the floor plan below and the image above.

Der im Kern rechteckige Grundriss wird durch ein Wechselspiel verschiedener Volumina belebt, wie die Zeichnung unten und die Ansicht oben belegen.

Le plan à peu près rectangulaire est animé par une alternance de volumes, comme le montrent le plan au sol ci-dessous et l'image ci-dessus.

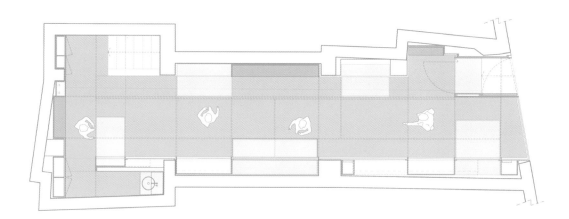

Merchandise is carefully aligned so as to make the best use of the precise rectangular display spaces.

Die Waren sind präzise aufgereiht, um die akkuraten rechteckigen Vitrinen und Podeste optimal zu nutzen.

Les produits sont alignés avec soin pour utiliser au mieux l'effet des niches de présentation rectangulaires.

A lacquered finish and volumes that either protrude or are inserted into the walls make for an unexpected aesthetic experience meant to echo that of the bakery's products.

Die glänzenden Lackoberflächen und Volumina, die aus den Wänden auskragen oder in sie integriert wurden, sorgen für ein ästhetisches Raumerlebnis, das als Pendant zu den Produkten konzipiert wurde.

La laque des murs et la multiplication des volumes en avancée ou en retrait par rapport aux murs suscitent une expérience esthétique inattendue qui fait écho à la qualité des produits.

SANAA/KAZUYO SEJIMA + RYUE NISHIZAWA

SANAA / Kazuyo Sejima + Ryue Nishizawa
1–5–27 Tatsumi / Koto-ku / Tokyo 135–0053 / Japan

Tel: + 81 3 5534 1780 / Fax: + 81 3 5534 1757
E-mail: press@sanaa.co.jp / Web: www.sanaa.co.jp

Born in Ibaraki Prefecture, Japan, in 1956, Kazuyo Sejima received her M.Arch from the Japan Women's University in 1981 and went to work in the office of Toyo Ito the same year. She established Kazuyo Sejima and Associates in Tokyo in 1987. She has been a Visiting Lecturer at Japan Women's University and at Waseda University since 1994. Ryue Nishizawa was born in Tokyo in 1966, and graduated from the National University in Yokohama in 1990. He began working with Sejima the same year, and the pair created the new firm **SANAA/KAZUYO SEJIMA + RYUE NISHIZAWA** in 1995. He has been a Visiting Professor at the Harvard School of Design and at the National University in Yokohama. The built work of Kazuyo Sejima includes the Saishunkan Seiyaku Women's Dormitory (Kumamoto, 1990–91); Villa in the Forest (Tateshina, Nagano, 1993–94); Chofu Station Police Box (Tokyo, 1993–94); Pachinko Parlor III (Hitachi Ibaraki, 1995), all in Japan. The work of SANAA includes the 21st Century Museum of Contemporary Art (Kanazawa, Ishikawa, Japan, 2002–04); Moriyama House (Tokyo, Japan, 2002–05); the Glass Pavilion of the Toledo Museum of Art (Ohio, USA, 2003–06); a theater and cultural center in Almere (The Netherlands, 2004–07); a building for the New Museum of Contemporary Art in New York (New York, USA, 2005–07); the Serpentine Pavilion (London, UK, 2009); the Derek Lam Flagship Store (New York, New York, USA, 2008–09, published here); and an extension of the Valencia Institute of Modern Art-IVAM (Spain, 2002–). Kazuyo Sejima and Ryue Nishizawa won the competitions to design the Rolex Learning Center of the EPFL in Lausanne (Switzerland, 2007–09); and the new building of the Louvre in Lens (France, 2009–12).

Die 1956 in der Präfektur Ibaraki geborene Kazuyo Sejima absolvierte 1981 ihren M.Arch der Japanischen Frauenuniversität und begann noch im selben Jahr für Toyo Ito zu arbeiten. 1987 gründete sie in Tokio ihr Büro Kazuyo Sejima and Associates. Seit 1994 ist sie als Gastprofessorin an der Frauenuniversität und an der Universität Waseda tätig. Ryue Nishizawa wurde 1966 in Tokio geboren und schloss sein Studium 1990 an der Nationaluniversität in Yokohama ab. Noch im gleichen Jahr begann er, für Sejima zu arbeiten. Gemeinsam gründeten sie 1995 das neue Büro **SANAA/KAZUYO SEJIMA + RYUE NISHIZAWA**. Nishizawa hatte eine Gastprofessur an der Harvard School of Design und der Nationaluniversität in Yokohama. Kazuyo Sejima realisierte u.a. das Frauenwohnheim Saishunkan Seiyaku (Kumamoto, 1990–91), die Villa im Wald (Tateshina, Nagano, 1993–94), die Polizeistation Bahnhof Chofu (Tokio, 1993–94), Pachinko Parlor III (Hitachi Ibaraki, 1995), alle in Japan. Zum Werk von SANAA zählen das Museum für Kunst des 21. Jahrhunderts (Kanazawa, Ishikawa, Japan, 2002–04), Haus Moriyama (Tokio, 2002–05), der Glaspavillon am Toledo Museum of Art (Toledo, Ohio, 2003–06), theater und Kulturzentrum in Almere (Niederlande, 2004–07), das New Museum of Contemporary Art in New York (2005–07), der Pavillon für die Serpentine Gallery (London, 2009), der Derek Lam Flagshipstore (New York, 2008–09, hier vorgestellt), sowie eine Erweiterung des Instituts für Moderne Kunst in Valencia (IVAM) in Spanien (2002–). Kazuyo Sejima und Ryue Nishizawa gewannen die Wettbewerbe zum Bau des Rolex Learning Center der EPFL in Lausanne (Schweiz, 2007–09) und das neue Gebäude des Louvre in Lens (Frankreich, 2009–12).

Née dans la préfecture d'Ibaraki en 1956, Kazuyo Sejima obtient son M. Arch. de l'université féminine du Japon en 1981 et est engagée par Toyo Ito la même année. Elle fonde l'agence Kazuyo Sejima and Associates à Tokyo en 1987. Elle est chargée de cours invitée à l'université féminine et à l'université Waseda depuis 1994. Ryue Nishizawa, né à Tokyo en 1966, est diplômé de l'Université nationale de Yokohama (1990). Il a commencé à travailler avec Sejima la même année avant de fonder ensemble **SANAA/KAZUYO SEJIMA + RYUE NISHIZAWA** en 1995. Il a été professeur invité à la Harvard School of Design et à l'université nationale de Yokohama. Les réalisations de Kazuyo Sejima, toutes au Japon, comprennent : le foyer pour jeunes filles Saishunkan Seiyaku (Kumamoto, 1990–91) ; la Villa en forêt (Tateshina, Nagano, 1993–94) ; le poste de police de Chofu (Tokyo, 1993–94) et la salle de jeux Pachinko Parlor III (Hitachi Ibaraki, 1995). Parmi les grandes références de SANAA figurent également le Musée d'art contemporain du XXIᵉ siècle (Kanazawa, Ishikawa, 2002–04) ; la maison Moriyama (Tokyo, 2002–05) ; le pavillon de verre du Toledo Museum of Art (Toledo, Ohio, 2003–06) ; un théâtre et centre culturel à Almere (Pays-Bas, 2004–07) ; le New Museum of Contemporary Art (New York, 2005–07) ; le pavillon Serpentine (Londres, 2009), le magasin amiral Derek Lam (New York, 2008–09, publié ici) et une extension de l'Institut d'art moderne de Valence (IVAM) en Espagne (2002–). Kazuyo Sejima et Ryue Nishizawa ont réalisé après en avoir remporté le concours le Centre d'apprentissage Rolex de l'EPFL à Lausanne (Suisse, 2007–09) et les nouvelles installations du Louvre à Lens (France, 2009–).

DEREK LAM FLAGSHIP STORE

New York, New York, USA, 2008–09

Address: 10–20 Crosby Street, New York, NY 10013, USA, +1 212 966 1616, www.dereklam.com
Area: 251 m². Client: Derek Lam. Cost: not disclosed
Collaboration: Toshihiro Oki (Executive Architect)

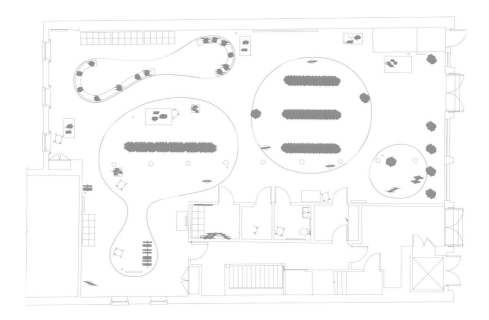

Located on Crosby Street in the Soho area of Manhattan, this flagship store "uses simple but refined materials: white painted brick walls, concrete floors, simple furniture, and gentle partitions, consisting of large free-form transparent acrylic walls." These fairly transparent "bubbles" formed by the acrylic walls are each intended to house a different collection, and are complemented by a series of large mirrors that are placed in a leaning position to accentuate the space. SANAA-designed furniture and simple mannequins provided by Wolf Forms, Inc. underline the architectural simplicity of the project. Ample natural light is admitted through the front façade, and given the use of acrylic walls, it diffuses throughout the space. Though SANAA is best known for their complete buildings, this interior design shows that they are able to give their unique spirit to existing spaces too.

Der auf der Crosby Street in Soho, Manhattan, gelegene Flagshipstore „wurde mit einfachen und dennoch edlen Materialien realisiert: weiß gestrichene Ziegel-wände, Betonböden, schlichte Möbel und dezente Raumteiler aus großformatigen, frei geformten und transparenten Acrylglaswänden." Die transparenten „Blasen" aus Acrylglas dienen der Präsentation der verschiedenen Kollektionen. Sie werden durch großflächige Spiegel ergänzt, die durch ihre leicht schräge Positionierung die Raum-wirkung akzentuieren. Die von SANAA entworfenen Möbel sowie die schlichten Modepuppen von Wolf Forms unterstreichen die Schlichtheit des Stores. Durch die Laden-front fällt großzügig Tageslicht ein, das dank der Acrylwände den gesamten Raum durchdringt. Obwohl SANAA besonders für ihre eigenen Bauten bekannt sind, belegt diese Innenraumgestaltung, dass sie es verstehen, auch bestehenden Räumen einen ganz eigenen Charakter zu verleihen.

Situé Crosby Street dans le quartier de Soho à Manhattan, ce magasin amiral « fait appel à des matériaux simples mais raffinés : murs en brique peinte en blanc, sols en béton, mobilier discret et partitions douces faites de grandes parois de forme libre en acrylique transparent ». Les « bulles » constituées par ces séparations en acrylique accueillent chacune une collection différente et s'accompagnent d'une série de grands miroirs inclinés qui accentuent l'impression d'espace. Le mobilier des-siné par SANAA et les mannequins fournis par Wolf Forms, Inc. participent à l'impression de simplicité architecturale de l'ensemble. La façade laisse généreusement passer la lumière naturelle qui se diffuse à travers le magasin grâce aux parois en acrylique. Si SANAA est surtout connue pour ses réalisations architecturales, ce projet d'aménagement intérieur montre que l'agence sait également appliquer sa démarche particulière à des espaces existants.

As they have already in other retail spaces, SANAA makes use of a certain ambiguity generated by the use of white surfaces, transparent acrylic or mirrors. A plan above shows the curvilinear insertions within the rectangular floor plan.

Wie schon in anderen Shops, arbeitet SANAA auch hier mit einer gewissen Mehrdeutigkeit, die sie durch den Einsatz weißer Oberflächen, Acrylglas und Spiegel erzielen. Ein Grundriss oben zeigt die in den rechteckigen Plan integrierten, gerundeten Einbauten.

Comme elle l'a déjà fait pour d'autres lieux commerciaux, l'agence SANAA joue sur une certaine ambiguïté au moyen de murs blancs, de parois transparentes en acrylique et de miroirs. Le plan ci-dessus montre l'insertion des espaces incurvés dans le périmètre rectangulaire.

Transparent display stands or shining curtains create an impression of ethereal lightness that contrasts with the more "solid" designs usually seen in fashion retailing.

Transparente Einbauten und glänzende Vorhänge erzeugen den Eindruck flüchtiger Leichtigkeit – ein Kontrast zu den sonst im Modebereich eher üblichen, massiveren Entwürfen.

Des présentoirs transparents ou des rideaux brillants donnent une impression de légèreté éthérée qui contraste avec les projets plus « massifs » généralement observés dans les commerces de mode.

SAQ

Studio Arne Quinze (SAQ)
Arenbergstraat 44
1000 Brussels
Belgium

Tel: +32 2 300 59 10
Fax: +32 2 300 59 19
E-mail: info@studioarnequinze.tv
Web: www.studioarnequinze.tv

SAQ is an interdisciplinary design and architecture agency specialized in developing spatial scenography and concepts. **ARNE QUINZE** (born 1971) was the founder of both SAQ and design manufacturer Quinze & Milan. While SAQ has further developed itself as an independent studio, Arne Quinze has broadened and oriented his activity more toward the art scene. Recent examples of this are the installation *Uchronia: Message out of the Future* at the Burning Man Festival (Black Rock City, Black Rock Desert, Nevada, USA, 2006) or the 800-square-meter wood installation *Cityscape* in Brussels (Belgium, 2007–08). As for SAQ, aside from retail projects such as Ferrer (Nieuwpoort-Bad, Belgium, 2008) and L'Eclaireur (Paris, France, 2009, also published here), the information desks for the University Library of Utrecht with Wiel Arets Architects (Utrecht, The Netherlands, 2005), the JAGA Experience Truck (2006), and the KWINT restaurant and SQUARE event-space (Brussels, 2009) are some of the latest high-end realizations of their interior-architecture department. SAQ is currently also involved in the conceptualization of mixed-use developments in both Berlin and Brussels, where its offices are located.

SAQ ist eine interdisziplinäre Design- und Architekturagentur, die sich auf Raumszenografien und -Konzepte spezialisiert hat. **ARNE QUINZE** (geboren 1971) gründete sowohl SAQ als auch die Designfirma Quinze & Milan. Während sich SAQ zum eigenständigen Studio entwickelte, hat Arne Quinze sein Tätigkeitsfeld erweitert und sich zunehmend der Kunstszene zugewandt. Jüngste Beispiele sind etwa *Uchronia: Message out of the Future* für das Burning Man Festival (Black Rock City, Black Rock Desert, Nevada, 2006) oder die 800 m² große Holzinstallation *Cityscape* in Brüssel (2007–08). Zu den aktuellsten und anspruchsvollsten Innenarchitektur-Projekten von SAQ zählen neben den Läden für Ferrer (Nieuwpoort-Bad, Belgien, 2008) und L'Eclaireur (Paris, 2009, hier vorgestellt), auch die Informationstresen der Universitäts-bibliothek Utrecht (Utrecht, 2005) mit Wiel Arets Architects, JAGA Experience Truck (2006) sowie das Restaurant KWINT und die Event-Location SQUARE (Brüssel, 2009). Derzeit arbeitet SAQ u.a. an Konzepten für Projekte mit gemischter Nutzung in Berlin und Brüssel, wo die Agentur Büros unterhält.

SAQ est une agence de design et d'architecture bruxelloise spécialisée en scénographies et concepts spatiaux. **ARNE QUINZE** (né en 1971) a fondé SAQ et l'entreprise de fabrication d'objets de design Quinze & Milan. Alors que SAQ s'est développée de plus en plus indépendamment, Arne Quinze a élargi et orienté ses activités vers le domaine artistique. Par exemple, il a récemment réalisé l'installation *Uchronia: Message out of the Future* au Burning Man Festival (Black Rock City, Black Rock Desert, Nevada, 2006) ou l'installation consistant en une construction en bois de 800 m² intitulée *Cityscape* à Bruxelles (2007–08). SAQ, en dehors de projets de magasins comme ceux de Ferrer (Nieuwpoort-Bad, Belgique, 2008) ou de L'Éclaireur (Paris, 2009, publié ici), a réalisé quelques interventions dans le domaine de l'architecture intérieure sophistiquée comme les bureaux d'information de la bibliothèque universitaire d'Utrecht (avec Wiel Arets Architects, Utrecht, Pays-Bas, 2005), l'aménagement d'un camion « JAGA Experience Truck » (2006), le restaurant KWINT et l'espace événementiel SQUARE (Bruxelles, 2009). SAQ travaille actuellement à la conceptualisation de programmes immobiliers mixtes à Berlin et Bruxelles, ou se trouvent aussi ses locaux.

L'ECLAIREUR

Paris, France, 2009

*Address: 40 Rue de Sévigné, 75003 Paris, France, +33 1 48 87 10 22, www.leclaireur.com.
Area: 435 m². Client: L'Eclaireur. Cost: not disclosed*

The designers have inserted images of eyes into the irregular, sculptural walls seen in the image below.

Der Designer integrierte Bilder von Augen in die unregelmäßigen, skulpturalen Wandflächen (unten).

Le designer a inséré des images d'yeux dans les murs sculpturaux aux formes irrégulières (ci-dessous).

Arne Quinze is known for his impromptu structures usually made from scrap wood (above). Below, a drawing of the floor plan with its irregular display spaces.

Arne Quinze ist bekannt für seine spontan wirkenden Konstruktionen aus Altholz (oben). Unten eine Zeichnung des Grundrisses mit der unregelmäßigen Verkaufsfläche.

Arne Quinze est connu pour ses structures temporaires généralement en bois de récupération (ci-dessus). Ci-dessous, plan au sol et implantation des espaces de présentation de formes irrégulières.

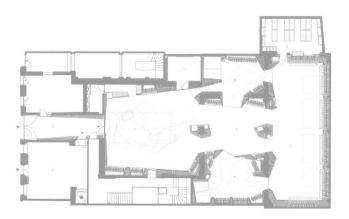

Located on Rue de Sévigné in the fourth arrondissement of Paris, **L'ECLAIREUR** is a haute-couture women's boutique. The designer used more than two tons of recycled wood planks, cardboard, and used aluminum print-plates to create the décor of the store. He states: "The interior is conceived by the perimeter the sculptured walls follow to envelop the space. Though composed of recycled material, the walls have a luxurious finish. The effect is not only visual but also tactile and puts the first-time visitor off guard." As though in an intimate dressing room, the visitor plays a privileged role in the art of discovering and "unveiling" the exposed goods, as though they might well be works of art. This scenography reaches its height in the back area of the store, lit only by sky domes and a video installation.

L'ECLAIREUR, gelegen an der Rue de Sévigné im 4. Arrondissement von Paris, ist eine Boutique für Haute-Couture-Damenmode. Der Designer verarbeitete über zwei Tonnen recycelte Baubretter, Pappe und ausgemusterte Druckplatten aus Aluminium für die Gestaltung des Innenraums. Er erklärt: „Das Interieur wird durch die Kontur der skulptural gestalteten Wände definiert, die den Raum umreißen. Trotz der recycelten Materialien wirkt die Oberfläche der Wände edel. Dieser Effekt ist nicht ausschließlich visuell, sondern ebensosehr taktil und trifft den Besucher beim ersten Mal völlig unvorbereitet." Wie in einem intimen Ankleidezimmer spielt der Besucher die Hauptrolle als Entdecker und „Enthüller" der ausgestellten Mode – gerade so, als handle es sich um Kunstwerke. Ihren Höhepunkt erreicht die Szenografie im hinteren Bereich des Ladens, der nur durch kuppelartige Dachöffnungen und eine Videoinstallation erhellt wird.

Rue de Sévigné dans le 4e arrondissement de Paris, **L'ÉCLAIREUR** est une boutique de prêt-à-porter féminin de créateurs. Le designer a utilisé plus de deux tonnes de planches de bois de récupération, de carton et de plaques d'impression en aluminium pour en créer le décor : « L'intérieur a été conçu à partir de son périmètre, les murs sculptés suivant l'enveloppe de l'espace. Bien qu'en matériaux recyclés, ils donnent une impression d'une finition luxueuse. L'effet n'est pas seulement visuel mais également tactile et surprend le client venu pour la première fois », explique Arne Quinze. Comme dans un dressing-room personnel qui lui serait ouvert, le visiteur détient un rôle privilégié : il peut découvrir et « dévoiler » les articles exposés, comme s'il s'agissait d'œuvres d'art. Cette scénographie atteint son sommet dans le fond de la boutique, uniquement éclairé par des verrières en coupole et une installation vidéo.

Occasional touches of color enliven spaces that are based on richly articulated surfaces and contrasted lighting.

Farbakzente hier und da beleben den Raum, der von den ausdrucks-stark artikulierten Flächen und kontrastreicher Beleuchtung lebt.

Quelques touches de couleur animent les espaces construits à partir de plans richement articulés et d'éclairages contrastés.

Curious objects or books alternate
with images of eyes or the actual
merchandise of the store.

Es entsteht ein Wechselspiel
zwischen ungewöhnliche Objekten,
Büchern, Bildern von Augen und
dem eigentlichen Warenangebot
des Stores.

Des objets curieux ou des livres
alternent avec des images de regards
et les articles en vente.

Shoes or bags are placed in the
completely irregular series of wall
niches seen in the image to the left.

In den konsequent unregelmäßigen
Wandnischen (links) werden Schuhe
und Taschen präsentiert.

Les chaussures et les sacs sont
disposés dans des niches murales
de forme complètement irrégulière
(à gauche).

Patrick Cox ▶

SINATO

Sinato
3-12-5-101 Tsurumaki
Setagaya-ku
Tokyo 154-0016
Japan

Tel: + 81 3 6413 9081
Fax: + 81 3 6413 9082
E-mail: central@sinato.jp
Web: www.sinato.jp

Chikara Ohno was born in Osaka, Japan, in 1976. He graduated from the Department of Civil Engineering at Kanazawa University in 1999, and established his firm **SINATO** in Tokyo in 2004. His work includes VIGORE (Tokyo, 2006); REI (Tokyo, 2006); Kinari (Tokyo, 2007); YURAS (Tokyo, 2007); Clover Clover (Kanagawa, 2007); House of Table (Shiga, 2007); Duras Ambient Funabashi (Funabashi, Chiba, 2008); Salire Hiroshima (Hiroshima, 2008); TTE (Tokyo, 2008); TOYOTA TSUSHO (Aichi, 2008); House O (Mie, 2009); and the Patrick Cox store (Tokyo, 2009, published here), all in Japan. He has also designed numerous objects, such as the Sakazuk bowl (2004); and Punyupunyu light (2003).

Chikara Ohno wurde 1976 in Osaka, Japan, geboren. Er schloss sein Studium 1999 an der Fakultät für Bauingenieurwesen der Universität Kanazawa ab und gründete sein Büro **SINATO** 2004 in Tokio. Zu seinen Projekten zählen VIGORE (Tokio, 2006), REI (Tokio, 2006), Kinari (Tokio, 2007), YURAS (Tokio, 2007), Clover Clover (Kanagawa, 2007), House of Table (Shiga, 2007), Duras Ambient Funabashi (Funabashi, Chiba, 2008), Salire Hiroshima (Hiroshima, 2008), TTE (Tokio, 2008), TOYOTA TSUSHO (Aichi, 2008), House O (Mie, 2009) und der Patrick Cox Store in Tokio (2009, hier vorgestellt), alle in Japan. Darüber hinaus hat er zahlreiche Objekte entworfen, so etwa die Schale „Sakazuk" (2004) oder die Leuchte „Punyupunyu" (2003).

Chikara Ohno, né à Osaka (Japon) en 1976, est diplômé du Département d'ingéniérie civile de l'université de Kanazawa (1999) et a créé son agence, **SINATO**, à Tokyo en 2004. Parmis ses réalisations, toutes au Japon : les restaurants VIGORE (Tokyo, 2006) ; Rei (Tokyo, 2006) ; Kinari (Tokyo, 2007) ; les bureaux YURAS (Tokyo, 2007) ; Clover Clover (Kanagawa, 2007) ; la maison de la Table (Shiga, 2007) ; les boutiques de mode Duras Ambient Funabashi (Funabashi, Chiba, 2008) ; Salire Hiroshima (Hiroshima, 2008) ; les bureaux de TTE (Tokyo, 2008) et de TOYOTA TSUSHO (Aichi, 2008) ; la maison O (Mie, 2009) et le magasin Patrick Cox (Tokyo, 2009, publié ici). Il a également conçu de nombreux objets comme la coupe Sakazuk (2004) et le luminaire Punyupunyu (2003).

PATRICK COX
Tokyo, Japan, 2009

Address: 1F Ao, 3–11–7 Kitaaoyama, Minato-ku, Tokyo, Japan, +81 3 6427 9335, www.patrick-cox.jp
Area: 79 m². Client: BLBG Co. Ltd. Cost: ¥6 million
Collaboration: Ken Kamada (Assistant)

Circular stands are lit from above, creating islands for the display of the merchandise and obliging visitors to take a circuitous path through the shop.

Runde, von oben beleuchtete Podeste werden zu Inseln, auf dem die Waren präsentiert werden. Sie zwingen die Besucher, sich auf verschlungenen Pfaden durch den Store zu bewegen.

Des présentoirs-podiums circulaires sont éclairés par le haut pour créer des îlots de présentation des articles et obligent les visiteurs à suivre un circuit à travers le magasin.

PATRICK COX sells bags, leather goods, and accessories. This shop is located near the main entrance of a 17-story building in the Aoyama area of Tokyo. The designer states: "The important point of this shop seemed to be lighting. The products can shine and look better if the light source is close by, not shining down from the ceiling. So I positioned cylindrical steel pendant fixtures directly over a corresponding display pedestal." Chikara Ohno wanted to create an atmosphere that appeared to be quite dark above and well lit below. Drumlike shades hang over the equally round display stands in the main part of the shop space. Lit from below as well, the display stands appear to hover between the floor and the dark ceiling. "Pathways in the shop seem to meander beneath a canopy formed by the largest of the drum shades," concludes Ohno.

PATRICK COX vertreibt Taschen, Lederwaren und Accessoires. Das Geschäft liegt unweit des Haupteingangs eines 17-stöckigen Gebäudes im Tokioter Stadtviertel Aoyama. Der Designer erklärt: „Der entscheidende Punkt bei diesem Geschäft schien die Beleuchtung zu sein. Die Produkte strahlen stärker und sehen attraktiver aus, wenn die Lichtquelle näher liegt und nicht von der Decke herabstrahlt. Also positionierte ich zylindrische Hängeleuchten aus Stahl unmittelbar über den entsprechenden Präsentationspodesten." Es ging Chikara Ohno darum, eine Atmosphäre zu schaffen, die im oberen Bereich eher dunkel, unten aber heller beleuchtet ist. Trommelartige Lampenschirme hängen über den ebenso runden Podesten, die auch von unten beleuchtet sind und zwischen Boden und dunkler Decke zu schweben scheinen. Ohno fasst zusammen: „Die Verkehrsflächen im Laden mäandern geradezu unter einem Dach der größten Trommelschirme."

PATRICK COX est une boutique spécialisée dans la maroquinerie et les accessoires de mode. Elle se trouve au voisinage de l'entrée principale d'un immeuble de 16 étages du quartier d'Aoyama à Tokyo. Pour le designer : « Le point important paraissait être l'éclairage. Les produits brillent et ont encore meilleur aspect s'ils sont rapprochés de la source lumineuse, et non pas éclairés du plafond. C'est pourquoi j'ai positionné ces lustres cylindriques directement au-dessus de podiums circulaires de dimensions correspondantes. » Chikara Ohno souhaitait créer une atmosphère assez sombre en partie supérieure et très éclairée en partie basse. Ces abat-jour en forme de tambour et les podiums occupent la plus grande partie du magasin. Également éclairés à leur base, ces présentoirs semblent flotter entre le sol et le plafond de couleur foncée. « Le cheminement des clients serpente sous la canopée formée par ces grands abat-jour », conclut Ohno.

The dense accumulation of the stands defines the space, and creates a sculptural impression.

Die dichte Gruppierung der Podeste prägt den Raum und sorgt für einen skulpturalen Gesamteindruck.

La multiplication des podiums définit l'espace tout en donnant une impression de composition sculpturale.

Contrasted lighting is used to
highlight the items on display while
the increasingly complex upper part
of the design is left in relative
obscurity.

Kontrastbeleuchtung akzentuiert die
präsentierten Waren, während der
zunehmend komplexere obere Teil des
Entwurfs vergleichsweise im Dunkeln
bleibt.

L'éclairage contrasté met en valeur
les articles présentés tandis que
l'aménagement complexe du plafond
est laissé dans une obscurité relative.

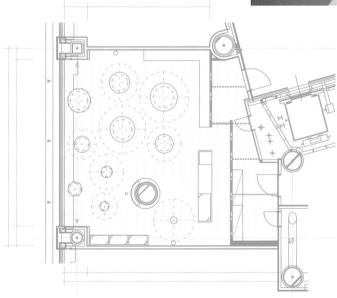

A floor plan shows how circles of
varying diameter are placed within
the rectilinear floor plan.

Ein Grundriss illustriert, wie die
unterschiedlich großen Kreise in den
geradwinkligen Grundriss eingefügt
wurden.

Le plan au sol montre comment les
podiums de diamètres variés se répartissent dans l'espace rectangulaire.

PHILIPPE STARCK

Ubik
18–20 Rue du Faubourg du Temple / 75011 Paris / France
Tel: +33 1 48 07 54 54 / Fax: +33 1 48 07 54 64
E-mail: info@philippe-starck.com / Web: www.philippe-starck.com

PHILIPPE STARCK was born in 1949 and attended the École Nissim de Camondo in Paris. Though he is, of course, best known as a furniture and object designer, his projects as an architect include the Café Costes (Paris, 1984); Laguiole Knife Factory (Laguiole, France, 1987); Royalton Hotel (New York, 1988); Nani Nani Building (Tokyo, 1989); Paramount Hotel (New York, 1990); Asahi Beer Hall (Tokyo, 1990); the Teatriz Restaurant (Madrid, 1990); and the Baron Vert building (Osaka, Japan, 1990). He has also designed a number of private houses and apartment blocks, for example Lemoult in Paris (1987); the Angle in Antwerp (Belgium, 1991); apartment buildings in Los Angeles (California, USA, 1991); and a private house in Madrid (1991). He was responsible for the interior design of the Saint Martin's Lane and Sanderson Hotels in London (1999 and 2000); the Delano in Miami (Florida, USA, 1995); the Mondrian in Los Angeles (1997); the Hudson in New York (2000); and the Clift in San Francisco (California, USA, 2001). He is responsible for the TASCHEN bookstores in Paris (2002), Los Angeles (2004), New York (2007), Brussels (2008), London, Berlin, Copenhagen, Hamburg (all 2009), and more recently Miami (2010, published here). The year 2007 saw the opening of the Faena (Buenos Aires) and Fasano (Rio de Janeiro) hotels, while the Japanese restaurant Katsuya and the S Bar opened in Los Angeles and Le Meurice in Paris. More recent works are the SLS Hotel (Beverly Hills, California, USA, 2008); EastWest Studios (Hollywood, California, USA, 2009); and the hotels Mama Shelter (Paris, 2009); and Palazzina Grassi (Venice, Italy, 2010). The 40 000-square-meter Alhondiga in Bilbao (Spain), a "place of discovery, exchange and living," opened in 2010, and other current work includes Port Adriano (Mallorca, Spain); and the café La Cigale (Paris). Starck's other ventures include his role as Creative Director of Yoo, a property-development company, in which he is associated with the developer John Hitchcox and Jade Jagger.

PHILIPPE STARCK wurde 1949 geboren und besuchte die École Nissim de Camondo in Paris. Obwohl er besonders als Möbel- und Objektdesigner bekannt wurde, realisierte er auch architektonische Projekte, darunter das Café Costes (Paris, 1984), die Messerfabrik in Laguiole (Laguiole, Frankreich, 1987), das Royalton Hotel (New York, 1988), das Nani Nani Building (Tokio, 1989), das Paramount Hotel (New York, 1990), das Hauptgebäude der Asahi Brauerei (Tokio, 1990), das Teatriz Restaurant (Madrid, 1990) oder das Baron Vert-Gebäude in Osaka (Japan, 1990). Außerdem gestaltete Starck einige private Wohnbauten und Apartmenthäuser, etwa das Lemoult in Paris (1987), das Angle in Antwerpen (Belgien, 1991), Apartmenthäuser in Los Angeles (1991) und ein privates Wohnhaus in Madrid (1991). Er zeichnete verantwortlich für die Innengestaltung des Hotels Saint Martin's Lane sowie des Sanderson in London (1999 und 2000), des Delano in Miami (Florida, 1995), des Mondrian in Los Angeles (1997), des Hudson in New York (2000) und des Clift in San Francisco (2001). Darüber hinaus zeichnet er verantwortlich für die TASCHEN Stores in Paris (2002), Los Angeles (2004), New York (2007), Brüssel (2008), London, Berlin, Kopenhagen und Hamburg (alle 2009) sowie kürzlich Miami (2010, hier vorgestellt). 2007 wurden mehrere Hotels eröffnet, darunter das Faena (Buenos Aires, Argentinien) und das Fasano (Rio de Janeiro, Brasilien) sowie das von ihm entworfene japanische Restaurant Katsuya und die S Bar in Los Angeles; zugleich eröffnete das Le Meurice in Paris. Jüngst arbeitete er am SLS Hotel (Beverley Hills, Kalifornien, 2008); den EastWest Studios (Hollywood, Kalifornien, 2009); den Hotels Mama Shelter (Paris, 2009) und dem Palazzina Grassi (Venedig, 2010). Das 40 000 m² große Alhondiga in Bilbao (Spanien), ein „Ort der Entdeckungen, des Austauschs und Wohnens" wurde 2010 eröffnet und er arbeitet derzeit am Port Adriano (Mallorca, Spanien) sowie dem Cafe La Cigale (Paris). Zu Starcks weiteren unternehmerischen Tätigkeiten zählt seine Rolle als Kreativdirektor von Yoo, einer Immobilienfirma mit den Partnern John Hitchcox und Jade Jagger.

Né en 1949, **PHILIPPE STARCK** a suivi les cours de l'École Camondo à Paris. Bien qu'il soit surtout connu comme designer de mobilier et d'objets, il a réalisé des projets architecturaux dont le Café Costes (Paris, 1984) ; l'usine de coutellerie de Laguiole (Laguiole, France, 1987) ; le hôtel Royalton (New York, 1988) ; l'immeuble Nani Nani (Tokyo, 1989) ; le hôtel Paramount (New York, 1990) ; l'Asahi Beer Hall (Tokyo, 1990) ; le restaurant Teatriz (Madrid, 1990) et l'immeuble Baron Vert à Osaka (1990). Il a également conçu un certain nombre de résidences privées et d'immeubles d'appartements, par exemple la maison Lemoult à Paris (1987) ; la maison Angle à Anvers (Belgique, 1991) ; des immeubles de logement à Los Angeles (Californie, 1991) et une résidence privée à Madrid (1991). Il a été responsable des aménagements intérieurs des hôtels Saint Martin's Lane et Sanderson à Londres (1999 et 2000) ; Delano à Miami (Floride, 1995) ; Mondrian à Los Angeles (1997) ; Hudson à New York (2000) ; et Clift à San Francisco (2001). Il a conçu les librairies TASCHEN de Paris (2002), Los Angeles (2004), New York (2007), Bruxelles (2008), Londres, Berlin, Copenhague, Hambourg (toutes en 2009) et Miami (2010, publiée ici). Rien qu'en 2007 ont été inaugurés les hotels Faena (Buenos Aires) et Fasano (Rio de Janeiro), le restaurant japonais Katsuya et le S Bar à Los Angeles, ainsi que les nouvelles salles à manger de l'hôtel Meurice à Paris. Plus récemment, Starck a réalisé le SLS Hotel (Beverly Hills, Californie, 2008), les studios EastWest (Hollywood, Californie, 2009), les hôtels Mama Shelter (Paris, 2009) et Palazzina Grassi (Venise, 2010). Les 40 000 m² de l'Alhondiga à Bilbao (Espagne), « lieu de découverte, d'échange et de vie », ont ouvert leurs portes en 2010. Il travaille actuellement aux projets du Port Adriano (Majorque, Espagne) et du café La Cigale (Paris). Starck est également directeur créatif de Yoo, une société de promotion immobilière, dans laquelle il est associé avec le promoteur John Hitchcox et Jade Jagger.

TASCHEN STORE MIAMI

Miami, Florida, USA, 2010

Address: 1111 Lincoln Road, Miami Beach, FL 33139, USA,
+1 305 538 6185, www.taschen.com/pages/en/stores/27093.store_miami.htm
www.1111lincolnroad.com
Area: 123 m². Client: TASCHEN America. Cost: not disclosed

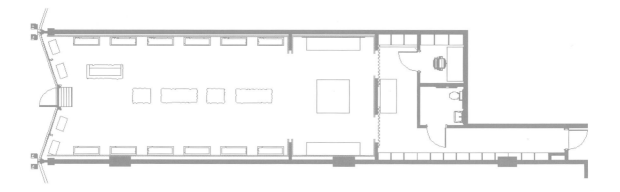

The architects of the building where the new **TASCHEN STORE** is located, Herzog & de Meuron, state: "A garage is a public facility, like a train station or an airport, where people change from one mode of transportation to another. 1111 is to become the place where people leave their cars to go to Lincoln Road Mall, South Beach's main public space leading down to the water." Shops, like the Taschen store published here, and restaurants are spread throughout the building. The structure was designed and built between 2005 and 2010. Raymond Jungles, a Miami-based landscape architect, designed a new public plaza and pedestrian promenade in collaboration with Herzog & de Meuron. The TASCHEN Store located in this building is the tenth one designed by Philippe Starck. The long, rectangular space was designed by the Frenchman using Asian mahogany bookshelves and fiberglass tables oriented on the elaborately patterned hand-poured terrazzo floor made entirely of stones from south Florida and the room-high work by the British artist Toby Ziegler. Limited editions are displayed in the center of the store. The back of the store is used for an office, restroom, and storage space.

Herzog & de Meuron, die Architekten des Gebäudes, in dem sich der neue **TASCHEN STORE** befindet, erklären: „Ein Parkhaus ist ein öffentlicher Bau, wie ein Bahnhof oder Flughafen, wo man von einem Transportmittel in ein anderes umsteigt. 1111 wird ein Ort sein, an dem man sein Auto stehen lässt, um zur Lincoln Road Mall zu laufen, dem größten Boulevard von South Beach, der hinunter zum Wasser führt." Geschäfte, wie der hier vorgestellte Taschen Store, und Restaurants verteilen sich über das Gebäude, das zwischen 2005 und 2010 geplant und gebaut wurde. Raymond Jungles, ein Landschaftsarchitekt aus Miami, entwarf mit Herzog & de Meuron einen neuen Vorplatz und eine Fußgängerpromenade. Der TASCHEN Store in diesem Gebäude ist der zehnte, den Philippe Starck für den Verlag realisierte. Der französische Designer stattete den länglichen, rechteckigen Raum mit Regalen aus asiatischem Mahagoni und Glasfasertischen aus, die nach einem sorgfältig ausgearbeiteten Muster angeordnet wurden. Der handgegossene, gemusterte Terrazzoboden wurde vollständig mit Stein aus Südflorida gefertigt. Das raumhohe Kunstwerk im hinteren Bereich stammt vom britischen Künstler Toby Ziegler. Während im Zentrum des Stores limitierte Auflagen präsentiert werden, befinden sich im hinteren Ladenbereich ein Büro, Toiletten und Lagerräume.

Herzog & de Meuron, architectes de l'immeuble dans lequel s'est installée la nouvelle **BOUTIQUE TASCHEN**, expliquent : « Un garage est un équipement public, comme une gare ou un aéroport, où les gens passent d'un mode de transport à un autre. Le 1111 sera un lieu où les gens laisseront leur voiture pour se rendre au Lincoln Road Mall, le principal espace public de South Beach, qui descend vers l'océan. » Diverses boutiques, dont la librairie TASCHEN, et des restaurants sont répartis dans l'immeuble qui a été conçu et construit entre 2005 et 2010. Raymond Jungles, architecte paysagiste basé à Miami, a conçu pour l'ensemble une nouvelle place et une promenade piétonnière en collaboration avec Herzog & de Meuron. La librairie Taschen est la dixième conçue par Philippe Starck. L'espace rectangulaire allongé est meublé de rayonnages en acajou d'Asie et de tables en fibre de verre disposées sur un sol en terrazzo au motif élaboré entièrement réalisé en pierre du sud de la Floride. Une importante œuvre de l'artiste britannique Toby Ziegler occupe le fond de la salle. Les éditions en tirage limité sont présentées au centre du magasin. À l'arrière ont été aménagés un bureau, des toilettes et un espace de stockage.

The long, narrow floor plan is arranged with a succession of display stands for large-format books and shelves or space for hanging along the walls.

Der lange, schmale Grundriss gliedert sich durch eine Reihe Präsentationstische für großformatige Bücher sowie durch Regale oder Ausstellungsflächen an den Wänden.

L'espace allongé et étroit est meublé d'une succession de tables pour les livres de grand format et d'étagères ou rayonnages muraux.

More colorful than other stores designed by Starck for TASCHEN, the Miami space is also animated by work by the British artist Toby Ziegler.

Der Store in Miami ist bunter als andere von Starck gestaltete Läden für TASCHEN und wird von einer Arbeit des britischen Künstlers Toby Ziegler belebt.

Plus coloré que d'autres librairies TASCHEN conçues par Starck, celle de Miami est également animée par une œuvre de l'artiste britannique Toby Ziegler.

The entrance to the store is seen below, while the overall structure, designed by Herzog & de Meuron, serves in good part as a parking facility (lower right).

Unten der Eingang des Stores. Das Gebäude selbst, ein Entwurf von Herzog & de Meuron, wird überwiegend als Parkhaus genutzt (unten rechts).

Ci-dessous : l'entrée du magasin. À droite, le bâtiment conçu par Herzog & de Meuron, en grande partie occupé par un parking.

STUDIO MAKKINK & BEY

Studio Makkink & Bey
Overshieseweg 52A
3044 EG Rotterdam
The Netherlands

Tel: + 31 10 425 87 92
Fax: + 31 10 425 94 37
E-mail: studio@jurgenbey.nl
Web: www.jurgenbey.nl / www.studiomakkinkbey.nl

Designer Jurgen Bey and the architect Rianne Makkink have operated **STUDIO MAKKINK & BEY** together in Rotterdam since 2002. The studio's projects include public spaces, product design, architecture, exhibition design, and applied arts. Jurgen Bey was born in 1965, studied at the Design Academy in Eindhoven (1984–89), and subsequently taught there for six years. Early in his career he was linked to the Dutch group Droog Design, for whom Makkink & Bey carried out the Blueprint project in New York, published here (New York, USA, 2009). Rianne Makkink was born in 1964 and studied architecture at the Delft University of Technology (1983–90), and had her own office from 1991 until 2001. Their recent work includes the Education Space at the Boymans van Beuningen Museum (Haunting Boymans van Beuningen, Rotterdam, 2007); the Ear Chair designed for Prooff (2009); the Pixelated Chair for the Galerie Pierre Bergé (2009); and the restaurant and shop of the Kunsthal Kade (Amersfoort, 2009).

Jurgen Bey, Designer, und Rianne Makkink, Architektin, führen seit 2002 ihr **STUDIO MAKKINK & BEY** in Rotterdam. Zu den Projekten des Studios zählen öffentliche Räume, Produktdesign, Architektur, Ausstellungsdesign und Kunsthandwerk. Jurgen Bey, geboren 1965, studierte an der Design Academy Eindhoven (1984–89) und lehrte dort anschließend sechs Jahre lang. Zu Beginn seiner Laufbahn war Bey mit der niederländischen Gruppe Droog Design verbunden, für die Makkink & Bey das hier vorgestellte Projekt Blueprint in New York realisierte (2009). Rianne Makkink, geboren 1964, studierte Architektur an der TU Delft (1983–90) und betrieb zwischen 1991 und 2001 ein eigenes Büro. Zu den jüngeren Projekten des Teams zählen Räume für das Bildungsprogramm des Boymans van Beuningen Museum (Haunting Boymans van Beuningen, Rotterdam, 2007), der „Ear Chair" für Prooff (2009), der „Pixelated Chair" für die Galerie Pierre Bergé (2009) und ein Restaurant und Shop für die Kunsthal Kade (Amersfoort, 2009).

Le designer Jurgen Bey et l'architecte Rianne Makkink animent ensemble le **STUDIO MAKKINK & BEY** à Rotterdam depuis 2002. Cette agence se consacre aux espaces publics, au design de produits, à l'architecture, à la conception d'expositions et aux arts appliqués. Jurgen Bey, né en 1965, a étudié à la Design Academy d'Eindhoven (1984–89) où il a ensuite enseigné pendant six ans. Au début de sa carrière, il était lié au groupe néerlandais Droog Design, pour lequel l'agence a réalisé le projet Blueprint publié ici (New York, 2009). Rianne Makkink, née en 1964, a étudié l'architecture à l'Université de technologie de Delft (1983–90) et a dirigé sa propre agence de 1991 à 2001. Parmi leurs travaux récents : l'espace éducatif du musée Boymans van Beuningen (Haunting Boymans van Beuningen, Rotterdam, 2007) ; le *Ear Chair* conçu pour Prooff (2009) ; le *Pixelated Chair* pour la Galerie Pierre Bergé (2009) et le restaurant et boutique du Kunsthal Kade (Amersfoort, 2009).

droog new york

more than a store

BLUEPRINT

New York, New York, USA, 2009

Address: 76 Greene Street, New York, NY 10012, USA, +1 212 941 8350, www.droogusa.com
Area: 467 m². Client: Droog New York. Cost: not disclosed

Located at 76 Greene Street in Manhattan, this store for Droog Design was opened to the public on February 26, 2009. According to the designers, the materials used for the project "were mainly blue foam and furniture made of beech wood." They explain: "Droog's brief to Studio Makkink & Bey was to design an interior that breaks the norms of store design. Droog Design asked for an interior installation to be made of elements that can be purchased. The studio took the brief one step further by blurring architecture, store fittings, and commodities, creating an installation with a multitude of layers—a life of its own." A main element of the design is the first-floor House of Blue, handcrafted out of blue foam. Elements of this house are the basis of the "**BLUEPRINT**" concept of the overall project: "The next step: the materialization of the objects in a 'real' medium such as wood, porcelain or in any material. Each of the 'real' pieces will be made in a small edition. The final step: the customization process, where the blueprint can be interpreted for specific environments." The designers conclude: "This unique blueprint will live on as installation, art, architecture, or design." Decorative elements can be taken out and transformed into usable tables, benches, and stools.

Der Laden für Droog Design liegt an der Greene Street 76 in Manhattan und wurde am 26. Februar 2009 eröffnet. Den Designern zufolge wurden für das Projekt „primär blauer Schaumstoff und Möbel aus Buchenholz" verarbeitet. Die Designer führen aus: „Die Vorgabe von Droog an Makkink & Bey lautete, ein Interieur zu gestalten, dass die Normen für die Gestaltung von Ladenräumen auf den Kopf stellt. Droog Design wollte einen Raum als Installation aus Elementen, die man auch kaufen kann. Unser Studio ging noch einen Schritt weiter und löste die Grenzen von Architektur, Ladeneinrichtung und Waren auf. Wir konzipierten eine Installation aus einer Vielzahl verschiedener Schichten – ein eigenständiges Innenleben." Eines der Hauptelemente des Projekts ist die erste Etage mit dem House of Blue, das aus blauem Schaumstoff handgearbeitet wurde. Grundlage für das „**BLUEPRINT**"-Konzept des gesamtn Projekts sind die einzelnen Bestandteile des blauen Hauses: „Als nächster Schritt folgt die Umsetzung der Objekte in einem ‚realen' Medium wie Holz, Porzellan oder jedem anderen beliebigen Material. Jedes dieser ‚echten' Objekte wird in einer kleinen Auflage hergestellt. Letzter Schritt ist schließlich die Sonderanfertigung nach Wunsch. Der ‚Blueprint' lässt sich dabei an individuelle Raumsituationen anpassen." Die Designer fassen zusammen: „Die einzigartige ‚Blueprint'-Anfertigung wird als Installation, Kunst, Architektur oder Design weiterleben." Elemente der Ladeneinrichtung können gekauft und als Tisch, Bank oder Hocker genutzt werden.

Situé 76 Green Street à Manhattan, ce magasin Droog Design a ouvert ses portes au public le 26 février 2009. Comme l'expliquent les designers, les matériaux utilisés sont « principalement la mousse bleue et le hêtre pour les meubles ». « Le cahier des charges de Droog était de concevoir un intérieur en rupture avec les normes du design traditionnel pour les points de vente. Droog Design a demandé que l'installation soit réalisée à partir d'éléments facilement disponibles sur le marché. Nous sommes allés encore plus loin en mélangeant la perception de ce qui est architecture, équipement du magasin et éléments techniques, pour créer une installation à strates multiples, qui possède sa propre vie ». Un des principaux éléments du projet est le rez-de-chaussée, aux éléments en mousse bleue. Ils sont à la base du concept « **BLUEPRINT** » sur lequel repose le projet : « L'étape suivante est la matérialisation des objets dans un médium « réel » comme le bois, la porcelaine ou n'importe quel autre matériau. Chacune des « vraies » pièces sera exécutée en édition limitée. Étape finale : un processus de personnalisation qui permet d'adapter les plans des objets à des environnements spécifiques … le concept « Blueprint » est applicable à des installations, à l'art, à l'architecture ou au design. » Des éléments décoratifs peuvent être emportés et transformés en tables, bancs ou tabourets utilisables.

The Droog store in New York makes use of a typical Soho space, with its high ceilings and brick walls, to put the varied objects designed by the group on display in an essentially neutral environment.

Der Droog Store in New York ist in für SoHo typischen Räumen mit hohen Decken und Backsteinwänden untergebracht. Hier kommen die verschiedensten Objekte der Designergruppe in einem neutralen Umfeld zur Geltung.

Le magasin new-yorkais de Droog est installé dans un local typique de Soho – hauts plafonds et murs de brique – qui présente les divers objets conçus par le groupe dans un cadre essentiellement neutre.

The blue foam elements on display can be used by clients to order "real" versions made of more durable materials.

Die Elemente aus blauem Schaumstoff dienen den Kunden zur Anschauung, um hier auf Wunsch „echte" Versionen aus haltbareren Materialien zu bestellen.

Les éléments en mousse bleue servent de modèles aux clients pour en commander des versions « réelles », fabriquées dans des matériaux plus durables.

There are also objects made of wood and other materials that give a more solid sense to Droog design while highlighting the adaptability of their system.

Außerdem gibt es Objekte aus Holz und anderen Materialien, die einen handfesteren Eindruck von den Droog-Entwürfen vermitteln und zugleich die Flexibilität des Systems deutlich machen.

On trouve également des objets en bois ou autres matériaux qui donnent un sens plus concret aux projets du groupe Droog et mettent en valeur l'adaptabilité de son système.

SUPPOSE DESIGN OFFICE

Suppose Design Office
13–2–3F Kako-machi
Naka-ku
Hiroshima 730–0812
Japan

Tel: + 81 82 247 1152
Fax: + 81 82 298 5551
E-mail: info@suppose.jp
Web: www.suppose.jp

Makoto Tanijiri was born in Hiroshima, Japan, in 1974. He worked in the Motokane Architects Office (Hiroshima, 1994–99), and the HAL Architects Office (Hiroshima, 1999–2000), before creating his own firm, **SUPPOSE DESIGN OFFICE**, in 2000. It currently employs 15 people in Hiroshima and Tokyo and the work of the office includes the design and supervision of architecture, interiors, landscapes, and exhibitions. It also designs and supervises renovations and design products and furniture. Tanijiri has been a Lecturer at the Anabuki Design College, Department of Architecture Design, since 2003. His work in 2008 included a House in Sakuragawa, a House in Takasu 02, a House in Matsuyama, and a House in Minamimachi 02. In 2009, as well as the installation *Nature Factory* (Tokyo, published here), he worked on houses in Obama, Hiro, Koamichyo, Kamiosuga, Moriyama, Jigozen, Kitakamakura, and Danbara, all in Japan. In all, Tanijiri has designed over 60 houses.

Makoto Tanijiri wurde 1974 in Hiroshima, Japan, geboren. Er arbeitete für Motokane Architects (Hiroshima, 1994–99) und HAL Architects (Hiroshima, 1999–2000), ehe er 2000 sein eigenes Büro, **SUPPOSE DESIGN OFFICE**, gründete. Aktuell beschäftigt die Firma 15 Mitarbeiter in Hiroshima und Tokio. Zu den Arbeitsfeldern zählen Entwerfen und Bauleitung, Innen-, Landschafts- und Ausstellungsarchitektur. Darüber hinaus übernimmt das Büro auch Sanierungen und deren Bauleitung und arbeitet im Bereich Produkt- und Möbeldesign. Seit 2003 ist Tanijiri als Dozent am Anabuki Design College, Fakultät für Architektur, tätig. Zu seinen 2008 realisierten Projekten zählen ein Haus in Sakuragawa, das Haus in Takasu 02, ein Haus in Matsuyama und das Haus in Minamimachi 02. Im Jahr 2009 arbeitete Tanijiri nicht nur an der Installation *Nature Factory* (Tokio, hier vorgestellt), sondern auch an Häusern in Obama, Hiro, Koamichyo, Kamiosuga, Moriyama, Jigozen, Kitakamakura und Danbara, alle in Japan. Insgesamt hat Tanijiri bisher über 60 Häuser entworfen.

Makoto Tanijiri, né à Hiroshima (Japon) en 1974, a travaillé dans les agences Motokane Architects Office (Hiroshima, 1994–99) et HAL Architects Office (Hiroshima, 1999–2000), avant de créer sa propre structure, **SUPPOSE DESIGN OFFICE**, en 2000. Il emploie actuellement 15 personnes à Hiroshima et Tokyo et se consacre à la conception et à la réalisation architecturales, à l'architecture intérieure, à la rénovation, au paysage, aux expositions, au design de produits et de meubles. Tanijiri est maître de conférence pour le Département de conception architecturale du collège de design d'Anabuki depuis 2003. Parmi ses réalisations en 2008, des maisons à Sakuragawa, Takasu (02), Matsuyama et à Minamimachi (02) ; en 2009, en dehors de l'installation *Nature Factory* (Tokyo, publiée ici), il a travaillé sur des projets de maisons à Obama, Hiro, Koamichyo, Kamiosuga, Moriyama, Jigozen, Kitakamakura et Danbara, tous au Japon. En tout, il a déjà conçu plus de 60 maisons.

NATURE FACTORY

Tokyo, Japan, 2009

Address: 6–3–3 Minami Aoyama, Minato-ku, Tokyo 107–0062, Japan,
+81 3 6418 5323, www.diesel.co.jp/denimgallery/index.html
Area: 65 m². Client: Diesel Japan Co., Ltd. Cost: not disclosed
Collaboration: Masaaki Takahashi (Curator)

The Diesel Denim Gallery in the Minami Aoyama shopping district of Tokyo is host to installations twice a year on the first floor of its space, and organizes art exhibitions four times a year. The present installation was held from August 14, 2009, to January 31, 2010. The work of Suppose Design Office consisted in using a complex arrangement of plumbing that seems quite ordered running along the walls, only to take on a more "natural" appearance on the actual floor of the gallery. "It is like a tree that has grown over a long period of time," according to Makoto Tanijiri. "An atmosphere like a natural arbor is created in the space covered with artificial plumbing. This new and somehow attractive scenery is generated with plumbing and fashion items, showing how such primarily functional objects actually are more diverse and can have higher value than one might imagine."

Die Diesel Denim Gallery im Tokioter Einkaufsviertel Minami Aoyama will zweimal im Jahr Installationen im ersten Stock des Ladens zeigen und organisiert viermal im Jahr Kunstausstellungen. Die hier gezeigte Installation war zwischen dem 14. August 2009 und dem 31. Januar 2010 zu sehen. Die Arbeit von Suppose Design Office besteht aus einem komplexen Arrangement aus Rohrleitungen, die zunächst relativ geordnet an den Wänden verlaufen, in der eigentlichen Galerieetage aber eine „natürliche" Dimension annehmen – „wie ein Baum, der über einen langen Zeitraum gewachsen ist", so Makoto Tanijiri. „So entsteht in dem von Rohren durchzogenen Raum eine Atmosphäre wie in einem echten Obstgarten. Diese neuartige, faszinierende Landschaft entsteht ganz einfach aus Rohren und Mode und belegt, dass solche in erster Linie funktionale Objekte weitaus vielschichtiger sind und weit höheren Wert haben, als man vermutet."

La Diesel Denim Gallery située dans le quartier commercial de Minami Aoyama à Tokyo accueille deux fois par an des installations dans son rez-de-chaussée et quatre fois par an des expositions artistiques. L'installation présentée ici a occupé le magasin du 14 août 2009 au 31 janvier 2010. Le travail de Suppose Design Office a consisté à mettre en place un ensemble complexe de tuyaux assez rationnellement ordonné le long des murs mais qui prend un aspect de plus en plus « naturel » en se développant au plafond de la galerie. « C'est comme un arbre qui aurait poussé sur une longue période de temps », explique Makoto Tanijiri. « Cette arborescence " naturelle " est créée dans l'espace par un assemblage de tuyaux de plomberie. Ce décor nouveau et assez séduisant généré à la fois par les tuyaux et les vêtements, montre comment des objets très fonctionnels sont en fait plus riches et peuvent véhiculer des valeurs supérieures à que ce que l'on pouvait imaginer. »

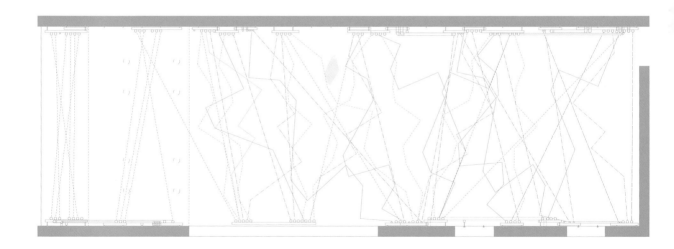

A drawing above demonstrates the idea of using plumbing to approach an organic form. Within the strict form of the space, the designers have imagined a web of pipes.

Die Zeichnung oben veranschaulicht den Ansatz, Rohre als organische Form zu installieren. Innerhalb der strengen Konturen des Raums haben die Architekten ein Netz aus Rohren gesponnen.

Le plan ci-dessus explicite l'idée d'une plomberie de forme organique. Dans le cadre strict du volume du magasin, les designers ont imaginé tout un réseau de tuyaux.

The finished space gives a decidedly organic impression despite the use of standard industrial materials.

Der realisierte Raum wirkt trotz der verwendeten industriellen Standard-materialien eindeutig organisch.

L'espace aménagé donne une impression très organique malgré le recours à des matériaux industriels standard.

From a more logical, industrial arrangement of plumbing on the wall, a web of curving, bending pipes spreads into the space, providing a backdrop for the merchandise.

Aus einer scheinbar logischen, funktionalen Anordnung der Rohre an der Wand entwickelt sich ein Netz aus sich windenden, verschlungenen Rohren, die sich als Kulisse für das Warenangebot im Raum ausbreiten.

À partir d'une implantation logique et technique des tuyaux sur les murs, le réseau s'étend dans l'espace en créant un environnement surprenant pour les articles de la collection.

Clothes hang on suspended bars or are placed on mannequins positioned near the tubes. Right, elevations show the ordered pattern of wall pipes.

Die Kleidung hängt an schwebenden Kleiderstangen oder wird an Mode-puppen präsentiert, die neben den Rohren stehen. Aufrisse (rechts) zei-gen das geordnete Muster der Rohre an den Wänden.

Les vêtements sont suspendus à des barres où placés sur des manne-quins disposés près des tuyaux. À la page droite, des élévations montrent l'agencement ordonné des tuyaux sur les murs.

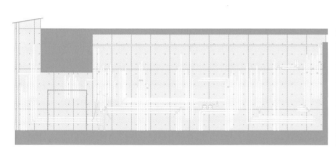
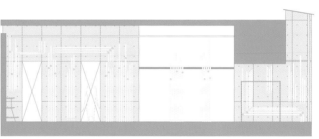

TACKLEBOX

Tacklebox LLC
109 South 5th Street, Suite 201
Brooklyn, NY 11211
USA

Tel: + 1 917 553 1723
E-mail: office@tacklebox-ny.com
Web: www.tacklebox-ny.com

Jeremy Barbour was born in Roanoke, Virginia, in 1976. He obtained his B.Arch degree from Virginia Tech (Blacksburg, Virginia, 2001) and his M.Arch degree from Columbia University GSAPP (New York, 2006). He is an Adjunct Professor at Parson's the New School of Design and an Adjunct Assistant Professor in the Columbia GSAPP Summer Studio program. He is the owner and principal of **TACKLEBOX**, which he founded in 2006. Prior to that date, he worked with Daniel Rowen Architects (New York, 2001–02), and with Andrew Bartle (ABA Studio, New York, 2002–06). His work includes the 3.1 Phillip Lim Boutique (New York, New York, 2007); and Saipua (Brooklyn, New York, 2009, published here), both in the USA.

Jeremy Barbour wurde 1976 in Roanoke, Virginia, geboren. Er absolvierte seinen B.Arch an der Virginia Tech (Blacksburg, Virginia, 2001) und seinen M.Arch an der Columbia University GSAPP (New York, 2006). Er ist Lehrbeauftragter am Parson's, The New School of Design, and Lehrbeauftragter am Summer-Studio-Programm der Columbia GSAPP. Barbour ist Inhaber und Direktor seines Büros **TACKLEBOX**, das er 2006 gründete. Zuvor hatte er für Daniel Rowen Architects (New York, 2001–02) und Andrew Bartle (ABA Studio, New York, 2002–06) gearbeitet. Zu seinen Projekten zählen die 3.1 Phillip Lim Boutique (New York, 2007) und Saipua (Brooklyn, New York, 2009, hier vorgestellt).

Jeremy Barbour, né à Roanoke (Virginie) en 1976 a obtenu son B. Arch. de la Virginia Tech (Blacksburg, Virginie, 2001) et son M. Arch. de l'université de Columbia GSAPP (New York, 2006). Il est professeur adjoint à Parson's The New School of Design et professeur assistant adjoint pour le programme d'ateliers d'été de la Columbia GSAPP. Il a créé **TACKLEBOX** en 2006, qu'il dirige. Auparavant, il avait travaillé chez Daniel Rowen Architects (New York, 2001–02) et Andrew Bartle (ABA Studio, New York, 2002–06). Il a réalisé, entre autres, le magasin 3.1 Phillip Lim (New York, 2007) et la boutique Saipua (Brooklyn, 2009, publiée ici).

SAIPUA

Brooklyn, New York, USA, 2009

*Address: 147 Van Dyke Street, Brooklyn, NY 11231, USA,
+1 718 624 2929, www.saipua.com
Area: 65 m². Client: Saipua. Cost: not disclosed*

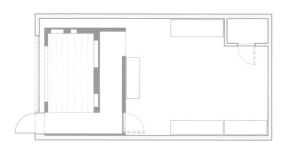

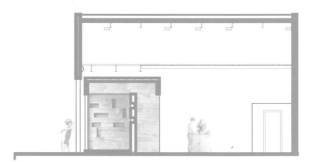

The designers made Saipua look as rugged and rural as possible. In such items as the alcoves destined to contain merchandise, the sophistication of their efforts becomes apparent.

Die Architekten gestalteten die Räume von Saipua so rustikal und ländlich wie möglich. Dennoch zeigt sich an Elementen wie den Wandnischen für die Waren, wie durchdacht das Konzept ist.

Les designers ont donné à la boutique Saipua un style aussi rustique que possible, même si dans les niches destinées à certains articles, la sophistication du projet s'exprime clairement.

The main material used in this project was 167 square meters of reclaimed barn siding from a Shaker barn built in the 1890s in Michigan. **SAIPUA** is a family-run business that sells handmade soaps and floral arrangements. The shop is located in the industrial Red Hook area of Brooklyn. The architect states that the goal was to "create a new timeless space that simultaneously serves as a quiet backdrop and as an active participant in the ongoing act of making that defines Saipua." Located in an existing warehouse, Saipua was imagined as a "freestanding inhabitable box" made with the weathered wood brought from Michigan. The interior is made up of two small rooms, one nested within the other. The outer space dialogues with the street much like the front porch of a house, "serving as a place of gathering and performance: a stage where visitors take on the interchanging roles of performer and audience set against an ever-changing backdrop provided by both the interior life of the shop and the life of the street."

Bei diesem Projekt wurde als Material in erster Linie 167 m² altes Bauholz verwendet, das von der Seitenverkleidung einer alten Shaker-Scheune stammte, die in den 1890er-Jahren in Michigan erbaut worden war. **SAIPUA** ist ein Familienunternehmen, das handgemachte Seife und Blumen verkauft. Das Ladenlokal liegt im industriell geprägten Stadtviertel Red Hook in Brooklyn. Der Architekt betont, Ziel sei gewesen, „einen neuen, zeitlosen Raum zu schaffen, der stille Kulisse und zugleich aktiver Darsteller in der Entstehungsgeschichte von Saipua ist". Der in einem alten Lagerhaus gelegene Laden wurde als „freistehende, bewohnbare Box" konzipiert und aus dem verwittertem Holz aus Michigan gebaut. Das Interieur besteht aus zwei ineinandergeschachtelten Räumen. Der äußere Raum kommuniziert mit der Straße wie die Veranda eines Hauses und „dient als Treffpunkt und Bühne: eine Bühne, auf der die Besucher wechselseitig die Rollen von Darsteller und Publikum übernehmen, vor einer sich ständig wandelnden Kulisse – einerseits dem Interieur des Ladens, andererseits dem Treiben auf der Straße."

Le principal matériau utilisé dans ce projet est un bardage de bois de 167 m², récupéré d'une grange Shaker du Michigan datant des années 1890. **SAIPUA** est une entreprise familiale qui vend des savons artisanaux et des compositions florales. La boutique se trouve dans la zone industrielle de Red Hook à Brooklyn. Pour l'architecte, l'objectif était de « créer un nouvel espace intemporel qui soit en même temps un cadre tranquille et un participant actif à ce qui fait la spécificité de Saipua ». Installé dans un entrepôt existant, le magasin a été pensé comme « une boîte habitable autonome » faite du bois patiné rapporté du Michigan. L'intérieur se compose de deux petites pièces nichées l'une dans l'autre. L'espace extérieur dialogue avec la rue un peu comme le porche d'une maison « servant de lieu de rencontre et de performance à la manière d'une scène sur laquelle les visiteurs peuvent emprunter le rôle à la fois de l'acteur et du public devant le décor en changement permanent de l'activité intérieure de la boutique et du spectacle de la rue ».

Weathered wood, and objects casually placed, as though in an inhabited environment, give Saipua a distinctive flavor that is not obviously modern.

Durch verwittertes Holz und die scheinbar spontan, wie in einem Wohnumfeld platzierten Objekte, gewinnt Saipua ein ganz eigenes Flair, das auf den ersten Blick alles andere als modern wirkt.

Le bois patiné et des objets disposés de manière très libre, un peu comme dans une pièce inhabitée, confèrent à Saipua une personnalité très spécifique qui, à l'évidence, ne se veut pas moderne.

THREEFOLD ARCHITECTS

Threefold Architects
Unit 1, 269 Kensal Road
London W10 5DB
UK

Tel: + 44 20 89 69 23 23
Fax: + 44 20 75 04 87 04
E-mail: info@threefoldarchitects.com
Web: www.threefoldarchitects.com

Jack Hosea was born in 1975 in Norwich, UK. He received his RIBA Part 1 B.Sc. in architecture from the Bartlett School of Architecture, University College London (1995–98), and his Part 2 diploma (2000–01) and Part 3 (2004) from the same institution. He has taught as a Visiting Critic and Visiting Lecturer at Bartlett (2007–08). Jack Hosea worked in the office of Michael Hopkins (London, 1999–2001), DMWR Architects (London, 2001–02), Big Brown Dog Architects (London, 2002–04), and was a founding partner of **THREEFOLD ARCHITECTS** (2004). Matthew Driscoll was born in 1976 in London. He also received the RIBA Part 1, Part 2, and Part 3 qualifications from the Bartlett School of Architecture, University College London (1994–2004). He worked for Michael Hopkins and Partners (London, 1997–99), Sanei Hopkins Architects (London, 2000–01), and Niall McLaughlin Architects (London, 2001–04), before creating Threefold Architects with Jack Hosea. Their recent work includes the refurbishment and extension of a Victorian terraced house (Oakford Road, London, 2008); Pure Groove (London, 2008, published here); the Apprentice Store (conversion of Grade 2 listed structures into a family home, Bath, 2009); the Ladderstile House (sustainable family home, Richmond, London, 2009); and the ongoing Hurst Avenue House (London, 2009–), all in the UK.

Jack Hosea wurde 1975 in Norwich, Großbritannien, geboren. Er absolvierte seinen B.Sc. in Architektur (RIBA Part 1) an der Bartlett School of Architecture am University College London (1995–98) sowie seine weiteren Diplome (Part 2: 2000–01 und Part 3: 2004) an derselben Hochschule. 2007 und 2008 lehrte er als Gastkritiker und Gastdozent an der Bartlett (2007–08). Jack Hosea arbeitete für Michael Hopkins (London, 1999–2001), DMWR Architects (London, 2001–02), Big Brown Dog Architects (London, 2002–04) und war Gründungspartner bei **THREEFOLD ARCHITECTS** (2004). Matthew Driscoll wurde 1976 in London geboren. Auch er absolvierte seine RIBA Part 1-, Part 2- und Part 3-Abschlüsse an der Bartlett School of Architecture am University College London (1994–2004). Er arbeitete für Michael Hopkins and Partners (London, 1997–99), Sanei Hopkins Architects (London, 2000–01) und Niall McLaughlin Architects (London, 2001–04), ehe er mit Jack Hosea das Büro Threefold Architects gründete. Zu ihren jüngeren Projekten zählen die Sanierung und Erweiterung eines viktorianischen Reihenhauses (Oakford Road, London, 2008), Pure Groove (London, 2008, hier vorgestellt), Apprentice Store (Umbau denkmalgeschützter Bauten in ein privates Einfamilienhaus, Bath, 2009), das Ladderstile House (nachhaltiges Einfamilienhaus, Richmond, London, 2009) sowie das in Planung befindliche Hurst Avenue House (London, 2009–), alle in Großbritannien.

Jack Hosea, né en 1975 à Norwich (G.-B.), a obtenu son B.Sc. en architecture (RIBA Part 1) de la Bartlett School of Architecture, University College, Londres (1995–98), et son diplôme RIBA Part 2 (2000–01) et Part 3 (2004) de la même école. Il a été critique invité et maître de conférence invité à Bartlett (2007–08). Il a travaillé dans les agences de Michael Hopkins (Londres, 1999–2001), DMWR Architects (Londres, 2001–02), Big Brown Dog Architects (Londres, 2002–04) et est cofondateur de **THREEFOLD ARCHITECTS** (2004). Matthew Driscoll, né en 1976 à Londres, a passé ses qualifications RIBA Part 1, Part 2 et Part 3 à la Bartlett School of Architecture (1994–2004). Il a travaillé pour Michael Hopkins and Partners (Londres, 1997–99), Sanei Hopkins Architects (Londres, 2000–01) et Niall McLaughlin Architects (Londres, 2001–04), avant de créer Threefold Architects avec Jack Hosea. Parmi leurs réalisations récentes : la rénovation et l'extension d'une maison victorienne mitoyenne (Oakford Road, Londres, 2008) ; le magasin Pure Groove (Londres, 2008, publié ici) ; le magasin Apprentice (reconversion de bâtiments historiques classés en maison familiale, Bath, 2009) ; la maison Ladderstile (maison familiale écologique, Richmond, Londres, 2009) et une maison sur Hurst Avenue (Londres, 2009–), toutes au Royaume-Uni.

PURE GROOVE

London, UK, 2008

Address: 6–7 West Smithfield, London EC1A 9JX, UK,
+44 20 77 78 92 70, www.puregroove.co.uk
Area: 95 m² (plus 90 m² basement offices). Client: Pure Groove
Cost: € 200 000 (including basement offices). Collaboration: Michael Garnett

This is a retail, exhibition, and performance space for the independent record label, music retailer, and publisher **PURE GROOVE**. The architects "stripped and exposed" the existing space in order to insert their intervention. Five steel rails that evoke lines of music wrap around the shop. Music releases called the "Pure Groove Top 100" are displayed on these racks. Each title has a hanging storage bag beneath its number. The space in the middle of the shop is left free for performances, although the architects have provided for movable hanging screens to be hung from the steel ceiling grid. The result, state the architects, is a "dynamic and exciting space that is flexible enough to be transformed from a store to a gallery, to a cinema to a music venue capable of accommodating live bands and hundreds of fans."

Die Räume für das unabhängige Plattenlabel **PURE GROOVE** mit eigenem Plattenladen und Verlag werden als Verkaufs- und Ausstellungsraum und für Konzerte genutzt. Die Architekten legten zunächst die Wände der alten Räume frei um ihre Intervention zu realisieren. Fünf Stahlstangen ziehen sich wie Notenlinien rings um die Wände. An diesen Stangen präsentiert das Label die „Pure Groove Top 100". Unter jedem Musiktitel befindet sich ein Hängeordner zur Aufbewahrung der Platten. Der Bereich im Zentrum des Ladens bleibt frei für Auftritte. Zusätzlich haben die Architekten eine Konstruktion vorgesehen, mit deren Hilfe mobile Leinwände von einem Stahlstangenraster an der Decke abgehängt werden können. Das Ergebnis ist den Architekten zufolge ein „dynamischer und spannender Raum, der flexibel genug ist, um sich vom Laden in eine Galerie, ein Kino oder einen Raum für Gigs zu verwandeln, in dem Livebands und hunderte von Fans Platz finden".

Cet espace de vente, d'exposition et de performances a été conçu pour le label, disquaire et éditeur **PURE GROOVE**. Les architectes ont « dégagé et rendu à son apparence » l'espace existant pour y insérer leur intervention. Cinq rails d'acier évoquant une portée musicale encerclent le magasin. La production maison, le « Pure Groove Top 100 », est accrochée sur ce présentoir. En dessous de chaque couverture se trouve le sac du stock de cet album. L'espace du milieu est dégagé pour accueillir des performances, mais les architectes ont aussi prévu des écrans mobiles suspendus à la trame en acier du plafond. Le résultat est « un espace dynamique et stimulant assez souple pour se transformer de magasin en galerie, en cinéma ou salle de musique capable de recevoir des groupes musicaux et des centaines de fans », précisent les architectes.

It seems quite daring to open a record store at a moment when CDs are being replaced by online purchases, but the designers have taken this into account by creating an event space.

Es mag gewagt scheinen, einen Plattenladen zu eröffnen, während CDs durch Onlineangebote verdrängt werden, doch die Architekten haben dies berücksichtigt und zusätzlich eine Event-Location geplant.

Il semble osé d'ouvrir une boutique de disques quand les CD sont remplacés par les téléchargements, mais les designers ont pris en compte cette évolution en créant un espace pour concerts.

Albums are hung on numbered display racks, creating a constantly changing aesthetic mosaic linked to the most recent music.

Die Alben hängen an nummerierten Stangenplätzen und bilden so ein sich ständig wandelndes, kunstvolles Mosaik, das aus den neuesten Releases entsteht.

Les albums numérotés sont suspendus à des tringles et dessinent une sorte de mosaïque qui évolue constamment en fonction de la sortie des titres.

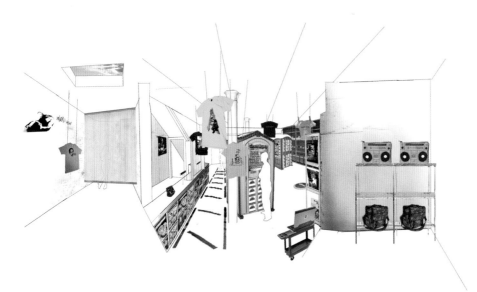

The factory-like atmosphere
inside the store is heightened by the
movable rack system and the simple
neon light arrangements.

Die fabrikartige Atmosphäre im Store
wird durch das flexible Regalsystem
und die einfachen Neonröhren
verstärkt.

L'atmosphère d'atelier de l'intérieur
du magasin est renforcée par le
système d'accrochage et la simplicité
de l'éclairage au néon.

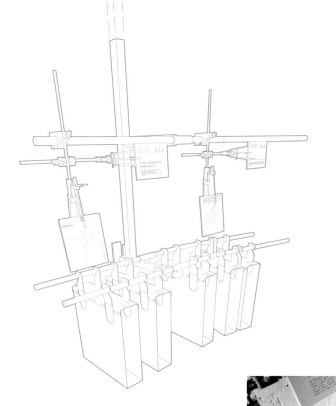

A drawing of the rack system that is used in the Pure Groove store.

Eine Zeichnung des Regalssystems, das im Pure Groove im Einsatz ist.

Dessin du système d'accrochage des albums et de leur stockage.

The numbered recordings are visible above storage bins that also carry numbers. Again, the factory atmosphere is emphasized.

Über den offenen nummerierten Hängeordnern mit den Platten hängen die ebenfalls nummerierten Albencover. Auch hier wird die Fabrikatmosphäre betont.

Les albums en stocks sont rangés dans une sorte de classeur suspendu numéroté, pratique que l'on pourrait retrouver dans un atelier.

MATTEO THUN

Matteo Thun & Partners
Via Appiani 9
20121 Milan
Italy

Tel: + 39 02 655 69 11
Fax: + 39 02 657 06 46
E-mail: info@matteothun.com
Web: www.matteothun.com

MATTEO THUN was born in 1952 in Bolzano, Italy. He studied at the Salzburg Academy with the painter Oskar Kokoschka and received his doctorate in architecture in Florence in 1975. He began working with Ettore Sottsass in Milan in 1978 and was a cofounding member of the Memphis group with Sottsass in 1981. He was the Chair for Product Design and Ceramics at the Vienna Academy of Applied Arts (1982–96), and created his own office, Matteo Thun & Partners, in Milan in 1984. He served as Creative Director for Swatch from 1990 to 1993. According to his description, in his studio Matteo Thun attempts "to offer a complete service to his international clients, developing projects covering different fields, such as architecture, design, and communication." Matteo Thun & Partners comprises a team of 40 professionals, including graphic designers, product designers, and architects, who work on an interdisciplinary basis. The work of the studio ranges from hotels to low-energy prefabrication systems, to watches for Bulgari or Swatch, furniture for Kartell, or lighting systems for AEG and Zumtobel. Two recent examples of his work are the Vodafone Italia Stores (various Italian cities, 2006–08, published here); and the Hugo Boss Special Concept Store (New York, New York, USA, 2008, also published here).

MATTEO THUN wurde 1952 in Bozen, Italien, geboren. Er studierte beim Maler Oskar Kokoschka an der Akademie in Salzburg und promovierte 1975 in Florenz in Architektur. In Mailand begann 1978 seine Zusammenarbeit mit Ettore Sottsass; 1981 zählte Thun mit Sottsass zu den Gründungsmitgliedern der Gruppe Memphis. Er war Professor für Produktdesign und Keramik an der Hochschule für angewandte Kunst in Wien (1982–96) und gründete 1984 in Mailand sein eigenes Büro, Matteo Thun & Partners. von 1990 bis 1993 war er Kreativdirektor bei Swatch. In seinen eigenen Worten geht es Matteo Thun in seinem Studio darum, „internationalen Auftraggebern einen Rundumservice zu bieten und Projekte in den verschiedensten Bereichen zu entwickeln, darunter Architektur, Design und Kommunikation". Thun & Partners umfasst ein Team von 40 Fachleuten, Grafikdesignern, Produktdesignern und Architekten, die interdisziplinär zusammenarbeiten. Zu den Projekten den Studios zählen Hotels ebenso wie Niedrigenergie-Fertigbausysteme, Armbanduhren für Bulgari oder Swatch, Möbel für Kartell oder Lichtssysteme für AEG und Zumtobel. Zwei aktuelle Projektbeispiele sind die Vodafone Italia Stores in verschiedenen italienischen Städten (2006–08, hier vorgestellt) und der Hugo Boss Special Concept Store (New York, 2008, ebenfalls hier vorgestellt).

MATTEO THUN, né en 1952 à Bolzano (Italie), a étudié à l'Académie de Salzbourg auprès du peintre Oskar Kokoschka et a passé son doctorat en architecture à Florence en 1975. Il a débuté sa collaboration avec Ettore Sottsass à Milan en 1978 et fut avec lui un des cofondateurs du groupe Memphis en 1981. Il a occupé la chaire de design produit et céramique de l'Académie des arts appliqués de Vienne (1982–96) et créé son agence, Matteo Thun & Partners à Milan en 1984. Il a été directeur de la création des montres Swatch de 1990 à 1993. Selon sa présentation, il veut « offrir un service complet à ses clients internationaux, en développant des projets qui peuvent couvrir différents domaines comme l'architecture, le design et la communication ». Matteo Thun & Partners compte 40 collaborateurs, graphistes, designers produit et architectes qui travaillent sur une base interdisciplinaire. Les interventions de l'agence s'étendent des hôtels à des systèmes préfabriqués durables, en passant par des montres pour Swatch ou Bulgari, des meubles pour Kartell ou des systèmes d'éclairage pour AEG ou Zumtobel. Parmi les exemples récents de ses travaux figurent les magasins Vodafone Italia (plusieurs villes, 2006–08, publiés ici) et le concept store spécial Hugo Boss à New York (2008, également publié ici).

HUGO BOSS SPECIAL CONCEPT STORE

New York, New York, USA, 2008

Address: 401 West 14th Street, New York, NY 10014, USA, +1 646 336 8170, www.hugoboss.com
Area: 375 m². Client: Hugo Boss USA. Cost: not disclosed
Collaboration: Designed in conjunction with A. J. Weissbard

Located in the Meatpacking District on West 14th Street, this unusual **HUGO BOSS STORE** opened in October 2008. A diamond-shaped pattern of wooden planks envelops the inside of the store, echoing the décor of the firm's Swiss headquarters. According to Matteo Thun: "The wooden framework cocoons the interior of the store, symbolizing the interconnectedness of the various Hugo Boss lines and as such comprising an architectonic manifestation of the corporate identity. The interior assimilates the anima of the Meatpacking District, embracing an austere aesthetic that is attuned to the *genius loci*." An exhibition area is fitted with burnished iron and dark-brown lacquer displays, with leather and glass showcases for accessories. The counter of the cash register, in Corian, is reflected in a metal wall that delimits the fitting-room zone. In this part of the store: "The atmosphere is softer and warmer, featuring rugs, red velvet curtains, a golden colored ceiling, and wood."

Der ungewöhnliche **HUGO BOSS STORE** im Meatpacking District liegt auf der West 14th Street und wurde im Oktober 2008 eröffnet. Eine Rautenkonstruktion aus Holz umfängt den Innenraum des Stores und knüpft an die Gestaltung der Schweizer Zentrale des Unternehmens an. Matteo Thun erklärt: „De Holzkonstruktion umhüllt das Interieur des Ladens wie ein Kokon und symbolisiert die Verknüpfungen zwischen den verschiedenen Modelinien von Hugo Boss. Insofern ist sie zugleich die architektonische Manifestation einer Corporate Identity. Das Interieur macht sich die *anima* des Meatpacking District zu eigen und bejaht eine strenge Ästhetik, im Einklang mit dem *genius loci*." Ein Ausstellungsbereich im Laden wurde mit brüniertem Stahl und dunkelbraunen Lackeinbauten ausgestattet sowie mit Vitrinen aus Leder und Glas für Accessoires. Der Kassentresen aus Corian spiegelt sich in einer Metallwand, hinter der die Umkleiden liegen. In diesem Bereich des Stores „ist die Atmosphäre weicher und wärmer, mit Teppichen, roten Samtvorhängen, einer goldenen Decke und Holz ausgestattet".

Situé dans le quartier du Meatpacking à New York, 14ᵉ Rue Ouest, ce surprenant **MAGASIN HUGO BOSS** a ouvert en octobre 2008. Une enveloppe en lattes de bois formant des losanges délimite l'intérieur, ce qui rappelle le siège suisse de la marque. Selon Matteo Thun : «La structure en bois fait de l'intérieur du magasin un cocon qui symbolise l'interconnexion des diverses lignes d'Hugo Boss et, en tant que tel, constitue une manifestation architectonique de l'identité institutionnelle de la marque. L'intérieur intègre l'âme du quartier du Meatpacking dans une esthétique austère en accord avec le génie du lieu.» La zone de présentation des produits est équipée de présentoirs en fer bruni et laque brun sombre ou de vitrines en verre et cuir pour les accessoires. Le comptoir de caisse en Corian se reflète dans un mur métallique qui délimite la zone d'essayage. Dans cette partie du magasin : «L'atmosphère est plus douce et plus chaleureuse grâce aux tapis, aux rideaux de velours rouge, au plafond de couleur dorée et à la présence du bois.»

West 14th Street has become the place to be for fashion designers and the architects who create their spaces. The Hugo Boss store is a large and rather surprising space that plays on contrasts of light.

Die West 14th Street hat sich zur gefragten Adresse für Modedesigner und deren Architekten entwickelt. Der Hugo Boss Store ist ein großzügiger und vergleichsweise überraschender Raum, der mit Lichtkontrasten spielt.

La 14ᵉ Rue Ouest est l'endroit où il faut être pour les stylistes de mode et leurs architectes. Le magasin Hugo Boss est un espace vaste et surprenant qui joue sur les contrastes d'éclairage.

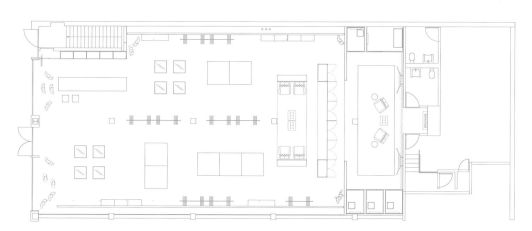

VODAFONE ITALIA STORES

various Italian cities, 2006–08

Address: various. Area: variable
Client: Vodafone Italia. Cost: not disclosed

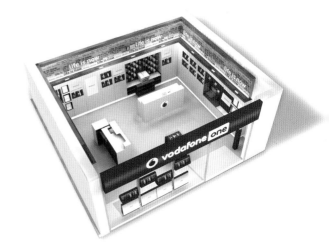

*A 3D model of a typical store
and below an actual interior with
the aligned screens and products.*

*Das 3D-Modell einer typischen
Filiale. Unten ein realisiertes Interieur
mit Reihen von Bildschirmen und
Produkten.*

*Maquette en 3D d'un magasin-type
et, ci-dessous, le magasin réel aux
alignements d'écrans et de produits.*

Red bands with the Vodafone logo are visible on the street side but also within the boutique, where products are either presented in display cases or along the walls.

Rote Bänder mit dem Vodafone-Logo sind ebenso an der Straßenfassade wie in den Läden präsent, wo die Produkte auf Podesten oder an den Wänden präsentiert werden.

Le bandeau rouge qui contient le logo Vodafone est visible en façade mais aussi à l'intérieur du magasin dans lequel les produits sont présentés dans des vitrines ou le long des murs.

The task given to Matteo Thun was to conceive the shop design concept and application for the **VODAFONE** One Retail System, in total more than 800 points of sale. His idea consists in creating a container with white-enamel walls and PVC on the floor. A display runs around the perimeter and a modular layout is used for the furnishings. Four parallel bands intended for product display (eye level) or storage (lowest level) further define the space. A seamless light wall on two levels using LCD screens puts forward the brand identity, while shiny red niches with direct LED lighting, some covered in leather, contain products. Freestanding units focusing on new products and soft furniture on rollers occupy intermediate spaces as required. The entire system is conceived with energy efficiency in mind. The use of the insistent red color and graphics that recall Vodafone's brand identity make these boutiques readily identifiable. The architect has clearly made them both attractive and efficient.

Matteo Thuns Auftrag lautete, ein Design- und Anwendungskonzept für die **VODAFONE**-One-Kette zu entwickeln, mit insgesamt über 800 Niederlassungen. Seine Idee war der Entwurf eines Containers mit weißen Emaillewänden und PVC-Boden. Neben umlaufenden Präsentationsregalen wurde ein Modulsystem für die Einbauten entwickelt. Das Interieur wird darüber hinaus von vier parallel verlaufenden Bändern geprägt, die der Produktpräsentation (auf Augenhöhe) und als Handlager (unterste Ebene) dienen. Eine auf zwei Ebenen verlaufende Lichtwand aus LED-Bildschirmen vermittelt die Brand Identity. In glänzenden, roten Nischen mit direkter LED-Beleuchtung – manche mit Leder ausgekleidet – werden Produkte ausgestellt. Der übrige Raum wird je nach Bedarf von freistehenden Podesten für Produktneuheiten und gepolsterte Möbel auf Rollen eingenommen. Das gesamte System ist so energieeffizient wie möglich konzipiert. Dank des auffälligen Rottons und der typischen Vodafone-Schriftzüge haben die Läden hohen Wiedererkennungswert. Ganz offensichtlich hat der Architekt sie ebenso attraktiv wie effizient gestaltet.

La tâche assignée à Matteo Thun était de concevoir un concept de boutique pour le «Système de distribution **VODAFONE** One» à adapter à plus de 800 points de vente. L'idée a consisté à créer un conteneur à murs émaillés blanc et sol en PVC. Un bandeau support de communication communication fait le tour du point de vente à la hauteur du plafond. La présentation des produits et leur stockage se font dans des meubles modulaires. Quatre éléments parallèles en forme de bandes présentent les produits à hauteur d'œil, le stockage étant cantonné en partie basse. Un mur lumineux en continu à écrans LCD met en valeur l'identité de la marque, tandis que des niches rouges à éclairage à DEL direct – certaines recouvertes de cuir – exhibent des produits. Des petits meubles-vitrines rouges indépendants capitonnés et sur roulettes servant à montrer les nouvelles productions se répartissent dans l'espace en fonction des besoins. Le système a été conçu dans le souci de l'efficacité énergétique. Le recours au rouge omniprésent et à des éléments graphiques qui rappellent l'identité de la marque rendent très identifiables ces boutiques que l'architecte a su rendre à la fois efficaces et séduisantes.

The "Life is now" theme chosen by the client is underlined by generously using the corporate red. Customers are encouraged to use interactive display screens (above).

Das vom Auftraggeber vorgegebene Motto „Life is now" wird durch den umfassenden Gebrauch der Firmenfarbe Rot unterstrichen. Die Kunden werden animiert, interaktive Bildschirme zu nutzen (oben).

Le thème du client, « Life is now » (La vie c'est maintenant), est mis en valeur dans un bandeau rouge, la couleur de la marque. Les clients sont encouragés à utiliser des écrans interactifs (ci-dessus).

UNSTUDIO

UNStudio
Stadhouderskade 113
1073 AX Amsterdam
The Netherlands

Tel: +31 20 570 20 40
Fax: +31 20 570 20 41
E-mail: info@unstudio.com
Web: www.unstudio.com

Ben van Berkel was born in Utrecht, the Netherlands, in 1957 and studied at the Rietveld Academy in Amsterdam and at the Architectural Association (AA) in London, receiving the AA Diploma with honors in 1987. After working briefly in the office of Santiago Calatrava in 1988, he set up his practice in Amsterdam with Caroline Bos. As well as the Erasmus Bridge in Rotterdam (inaugurated in 1996), **UNSTUDIO** has built the Karbouw and ACOM office buildings (1989–93), and the REMU Electricity Station (1989–93), all in Amersfoort; and housing projects and the Aedes East Gallery for Kristin Feireiss in Berlin, Germany. Projects include an extension for the Rijksmuseum Twente (Enschede, 1992–96); the Möbius House (Naarden, 1993–98); Het Valkhof Museum (Nijmegen, 1998); and NMR Laboratory (Utrecht, 2000), all in the Netherlands; a Switching Station (Innsbruck, Austria, 1998–2001); an Electricity Station (Innsbruck, Austria, 2002); VilLA NM (Upstate New York, USA, 2000–06); the Mercedes-Benz Museum (Stuttgart, Germany, 2003–06); and the Arnhem Station (The Netherlands, 1986–ongoing). Recent work includes a Tea House (Groot Kantwijk, Vreeland, The Netherlands, 2005–07); a Music Theater (Graz, Austria, 1998–2008); a Research Laboratory at Groningen University (Groningen, The Netherlands, 2003–08); Star Place (Kaohsiung, Taiwan, 2006–08, published here); and Burnham Pavilion (Chicago, Illinois, USA, 2009).

Ben van Berkel wurde 1957 in Utrecht geboren und studierte an der Rietveld-Akademie in Amsterdam sowie der Architectural Association (AA) in London, wo er 1987 das Diplom mit Auszeichnung erhielt. Nach einem kurzen Arbeitseinsatz 1988 bei Santiago Calatrava gründete er mit Caroline Bos sein eigenes Büro in Amsterdam. Neben der 1996 eingeweihten Erasmusbrücke in Rotterdam baute **UNSTUDIO** in Amersfoort die Büros für Karbouw und ACOM (1989–93) sowie das Kraftwerk REMU (1989–93), und realisierte in Berlin Wohnbauprojekte sowie die Galerie Aedes East für Kristin Feireiss. Zu den Projekten des Teams zählen ein Erweiterungsbau für das Rijksmuseum in Twente (Enschede, 1992–96), das Haus Möbius (Naarden, 1993–98), das Museum Het Valkhof (Nijmegen, 1998) und das NMR Labor (Utrecht, 2000), alle in den Niederlanden, eine Umschaltstation (Innsbruck, 1998–2001), ein Elektrizitätswerk (Innsbruck, 2002), die VilLA NM (bei New York, 2000–06), das Mercedes-Benz Museum (Stuttgart, 2003–06) sowie der Bahnhof Arnhem (Arnhem, 1986–andauernd). Jüngere Arbeiten sind u.a. ein Teehaus (Groot Kantwijk, Vreeland, 2005–07), ein Musiktheater in Graz (1998–2008), ein Forschungslabor an der Universität Groningen (2003–08), Star Place (Kaohsiung, Taiwan, 2006–08, hier vorgestellt) sowie der Burnham-Pavillon (Chicago, 2009).

Ben van Berkel, né à Utrecht en 1957, étudie à l'Académie Rietveld d'Amsterdam ainsi qu'à l'Architectural Association de Londres dont il sort diplômé avec mention en 1987. Après avoir brièvement travaillé pour Santiago Calatrava en 1988, il ouvre son agence à Amsterdam, en association avec Caroline Bos. En dehors du pont Érasme à Rotterdam (inauguré en 1996), **UNSTUDIO** a construit à Amersfoort les immeubles de bureaux Karbouw et ACOM (1989–93), la sous-station électrique REMU (1989–93), ainsi que des logements et l'Aedes East Gallery de Kristin Feireiss à Berlin. Parmi leurs projets plus récents : l'extension du Rijksmuseum Twente (Enschede, 1992–96), la maison Moebius (Naarden, 1993-98) ; le musée Het Valkhof (Nimègue, 1998) ; le laboratoire NMR (Utrecht, 2000), tous aux Pays-Bas ; une gare d'échange (Innsbruck, Autriche, 1998–2001) ; une station d'électricité (Innsbruck, 1997–2000) ; la VilLA NM (État de New York, 2000–06) ; le musée Mercedes Benz (Stuttgart, Allemagne, 2003–06) et la gare d'Arnhem (Pays-Bas, 1986–). Plus récemment, l'agence a réalisé une Maison de thé (Groot Kantwijk, Vreeland, Pays-Bas, 2005–07) ; une salle de concert (Graz, Autriche, 1998–2008) ; un laboratoire de recherche pour l'université de Groningue (Pays-Bas, 2003–08) ; le centre commercial Star Place (Kaohsiung, Taiwan, 2006–08, publié ici) et le pavillon Burnham (Chicago, Illinois, 2009).

STAR PLACE
Kaohsiung, Taiwan, 2006–08

Address: No. 57 Wufu 3rd Road, Cianjin District, Kaohsiung City 801, Taiwan
Area: 36 600 m². Client: President Group. Cost: not disclosed

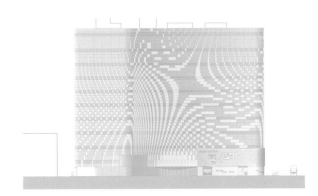

The architects play on the moiré pattern that is generated by the façade and its lighting. An elevation (right) shows the simple outline of Star Place and an appropriately star-like decorative pattern.

Die Architekten spielen mit dem Moiréeffekt, der durch die Fassadenbeleuchtung entsteht. Ein Aufriss (rechts) zeigt die schlichte Grundkontur des Star Place mit dem passend gewählten sternförmigen Muster.

Les architectes jouent du motif moiré généré par l'éclairage de la façade. L'élévation à droite montre celle-ci et un des motifs utilisés.

STAR PLACE is a luxury shopping plaza for Kaohsiung, the second-largest city on the island of Taiwan, with a population of 1.5 million people. Before UNStudio was involved in the project, the architectural firms Dynasty Design Corp and HCF Architects had already made a design for the location, of which the outlines and main structure were preserved, which did not permit UNStudio to create the column-free spaces they favor. The shopping center is located on a roundabout on a triangular lot. A 12-floor void used as a connecting element is located near the main façade. Elevators, twisted in their positioning as they rise through the void, run near circulation spaces around the void, providing access to the stores. Between two and seven shops are located on each floor. The glass façade of the shopping center is marked by "projecting horizontal, aluminum-faced lamellas and vertical glass fins that together form a swirling pattern." The pattern serves as a sunscreen and weather barrier and disguises the actual floor levels. Varied colors light up the building at night, an important factor in a country used to evening shopping. The façade pattern was developed using animation software. A series of images was generated, which the client studied with the aid of a *feng shui* consultant. The final pattern was chosen because it represents a red phoenix. The building includes 10 levels above grade, and has a footprint of 2035 square meters. The façade is 51.3 meters high, excluding the elevator machinery that rises up further seven meters.

Das Luxus-Einkaufszentrum **STAR PLACE** liegt in Kaohsiung, der zweitgrößten Stadt Taiwans mit 1,5 Millionen Einwohnern. Bevor UNStudio in das Projekt mit einbezogen wurde, hatten die Architekturbüros Dynasty Design Corp und HCF Architects bereits einen Entwurf für den Standort vorgelegt, von dem die Konturen und grundlegende Konstruktion beibehalten wurden, weshalb UNStudio nicht die stützenfreien Räume planen konnte, die sie üblicherweise bevorzugen. Das Einkaufszentrum liegt auf einem dreieckigen Grundstück an einem Kreisverkehr. Ein zwölf Stockwerke hoher Hohlraum hinter der Hauptfassade dient als verbindendes Element – hier verlaufen versetzt angeordnete Rolltreppen und erschließen über die angrenzenden Verkehrsflächen die einzelnen Geschäfte. Auf jedem Stockwerk sind zwischen zwei und sieben Stores untergebracht. Dominiert wird die Glasfassade des Shoppingcenters von „horizontal auskragenden, aluminiumbeschichteten Lamellen und vertikalen Glasfinnen, die ein changierendes Musterspiel erzeugen". Diese Struktur dient als Sonnenschutz und Wetterbarriere und kaschiert die Etagengrenzen. Die Fassade leuchtet nachts in verschiedenen Farben – ein entscheidender Faktor in einem Land, in dem man gewöhnt ist, abends und nachts einzukaufen. Das Musterspiel der Fassade wurde mithilfe von Animationssoftware entwickelt. So entstand eine Reihe von Motiven, die der Bauherr gemeinsam mit einem *Fengshui*-Berater begutachtete. Das letztendliche Muster wurde ausgewählt, weil es einen roten Phönix symbolisiert. Der Komplex umfasst zehn oberirdische Etagen und hat eine Grundfläche von 2035 m². Die Fassade hat eine Höhe von 51,3 m – abgesehen von der Aufzugstechnik, die weitere rund sieben Meter aufragt.

STAR PLACE est un centre commercial de luxe situé à Kaohsiung (1,5 millions d'habitants), seconde ville de Taiwan. Il se dresse au milieu d'un rond-point sur une parcelle triangulaire. Avant l'intervention d'UNStudio, l'agence Dynasty Design Corp et HCF Architects avaient déjà établi un projet pour ce lieu, dont la structure principale et le profil ont été conservés, mais qui n'ont pas permis à l'agence néerlandaise de créer les espaces sans colonne qu'elle affectionne. Un atrium circulaire de 12 niveaux de hauteur sert d'axe de liaison interne derrière la façade principale. Les magasins sont accessibles par des escaliers mécaniques dont le positionnement se décale d'étage en étage en tournant autour de l'atrium. Chaque niveau accueille de deux à sept magasins. La façade de verre est animée par « des lamelles d'aluminium se projetant horizontalement et des ailettes de verre verticales qui forment un motif tourbillonnant ». L'ensemble sert d'écran solaire et de barrière thermique tout en masquant les niveaux. La nuit, l'immeuble est illuminé de couleurs variées, élément attractif important dans un pays où l'on aime faire ses courses la nuit. Le motif de la façade a été mis au point à l'aide d'un logiciel d'animation. Les images produites ont été étudiées par le client et un consultant en *feng shui*. Le motif choisi représente un phénix rouge. Ce complexe de dix étages a une surface de 2035 m². La façade mesure 51,3 mètres de haut, sans compter la machinerie des escaliers mécaniques haute d'environ sept mètres.

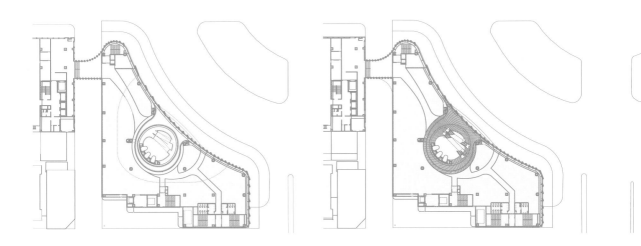

The curved façade of the store is seen in the plans above. To the right, interior escalators continue the impression of fluid, contemporary space already seen in the exteriors.

Die Grundrisse oben zeigen die geschwungene Fassade des Centers. Rechts die Rolltreppen im Innern, in denen sich der fließende, zeitgenössische Raumeindruck fortsetzt, der schon am Außenbau sichtbar wird.

Plans ci-dessus : la façade incurvée du magasin. À droite, les escaliers mécaniques intérieurs confirment l'impression de fluidité de cet espace de style contemporain qui était déjà perceptible à l'extérieur.

A drawing (below) and a photo (left page) resemble a kind of organic spine used for a soaring atrium space and the elevator pods.

Zeichnung (unten) und Foto (links) lassen an eine organische Wirbel-säule denken, aus der sich das hohe Atrium und die Aufzugkapseln entwickeln.

Le dessin ci-dessous et la photo de la page de gauche qui illustrent l'atrium vertical et l'implantation des esca-liers mécaniques évoquent une sorte de colonne vertébrale.

Above, the escalators form an x-pattern as seen from this angle, with views cutting through the interior space of the building.

Aus diesem Blickwinkel (oben) bilden die Rolltreppen ein Zickzackmuster. Die Blickachsen reichen durch den gesamten Innenraum des Gebäudes.

Dans la photo ci-dessus, les escaliers mécaniques se croisent en X en dégageant des perspectives sur le volume intérieur de l'immeuble.

D Jewelry, Pamplona ▶

VAILLO + IRIGARAY ARCHITECTS

Vaillo + Irigaray Architects
C/ Tafalla, 31 bajo
31003 Pamplona, Navarre
Spain

Tel: +34 948 29 00 54
Fax: + 34 948 29 03 03
E-mail: estudio@vailloirigaray.com
Web: www.vailloirigaray.com

ANTONIO VAILLO I DANIEL was born in Barcelona, Spain, in 1960 and studied architecture at the ETSA of Navarre (1979–85). **JUAN LUIS IRIGARAY HUARTE** was born in Navarre, Spain, in 1956 and also studied at the ETSA of Navarre (1974–80). Their most significant recent projects are an Office Silo + Container (Tajonar, Navarre, 2005); B2 House (Pamplona, Navarre, 2005); D Jewelry (Pamplona, 2006–07, published here); Hotel and Office Tower (Vitoria, Álava, 2008); El Mercao Restaurant (Pamplona, 2008); Lounge ms (Cadreita, Navarre, 2009); Audenasa Office Building (Noain, Navarre, 2009); and the CIB Biomedical Research Center, Hospital of Navarre (Pamplona, due to be completed in 2011), all in Spain.

ANTONIO VAILLO I DANIEL wurde 1960 in Barcelona geboren und studierte Architektur an der ETSA in Navarra (1979–85). **JUAN LUIS IRIGARAY HUARTE** wurde 1956 in Navarra, Spanien, geboren und studierte ebenfalls an der ETSA in Navarra (1974–80). Ihre wichtigsten neueren Projekte sind ein Büro-Silo + Container (Tajonar, Navarra, 2005), das B2 House (Pamplona, Navarra, 2005), D Jewelry (Pamplona, 2006–07, hier vorgestellt), ein Hotel- und Bürohochhaus (Vitoria, Álava, 2008), das Restaurant El Mercao (Pamplona, 2008), Lounge ms (Cadreita, Navarra, 2009), das Audenasa Bürohaus (Noain, Navarra, 2009) und das Biomedizinische Forschungszentrum CIB am Krankenhaus von Navarra (Pamplona, geplante Fertigstellung 2011), alle in Spanien.

ANTONIO VAILLO I DANIEL, né à Barcelone en 1960, a étudié l'architecture à l'ETSA de Navarre (1979–85). **JUAN LUIS IRIGARAY HUARTE**, né en Navarre en 1956, a suivi les mêmes études (1974–80). Leurs projets récents les plus significatifs sont un silo-bureaux + conteneurs (Tajonar, Navarre, 2005) ; la Maison B2 (Pampelune, Navarre, 2005) ; la joaillerie D (Pampelune, 2006–07, publiée ici) ; une tour pour un hôtel et des bureaux (Vitoria, Álava, 2008) ; le restaurant El Mercao (Pampelune, 2008) ; le Lounge ms (Cadreita, Navarre, 2009) ; l'immeuble de bureaux Audenasa (Noain, Navarre, 2009) et le Centre de recherches biomédicales CIB de l'Hôpital de Navarre (Pampelune, 2011).

D JEWELRY
Pamplona, Spain, 2006–07

Address: C/ Francisco Bergamin 7, 31003 Pamplona, Spain, +34 948 29 38 76
Area: 50 m². Client: Danieli Joyeros. Cost: €267 000
Collaboration: Daniel Galar (Project Manager)

The architects explain: "The project intends to create an atmosphere—and, therefore, a universe—(not a shop) in these little premises in the city center, whose rectangular, deep and narrow geometry has to contain the elements of jewelry." They further describe the sought-after atmosphere as "mysterious, strange, hollow, and weightless, while Oriental and Baroque." Inspired by a jewelry chest or box holding unique objects, the décor uses theatrical elements inspired by dark curtains and stage lighting. The upper section is dark and matt, while the lower one is "silver, bright, heavy, and rigid." The floor, some wall coverings, and doors to the jewelry boxes are made of thick aluminum plates measuring 100 x 60 centimeters that show the imperfections in their smelting, lending an air of age to recently fabricated elements.

Die Architekten erklären: „In diesem kleinen Ladenlokal im Stadtzentrum, dessen rechteckige, tiefe und schmale Form etwas von einem Schmuckstück hat, will das Projekt eine eigene Atmosphäre schaffen – und damit ein Universum – keinen Laden." Darüber hinaus beschreibt das Team die exklusive Atmosphäre als „geheimnisvoll, fremdartig, hohl und schwerelos, dabei zugleich orientalisch und barock". Das Interieur, inspiriert von einem Schmuckkästchen oder einer Schatulle für wertvolle Objekte, arbeitet mit theaterhaften Elementen wie dunklen Vorhängen und Bühnenscheinwerfern. Der obere Bereich ist dunkel und matt, der untere „silbern, hell, schwer und streng". Der Boden, einige der Deckenpaneele und die Türen zu den „Schmuckkästchen" sind aus massiven, 100 x 60 cm großen Aluminiumplatten gefertigt. Durch Unregelmäßigkeiten im Schmelzprozess gewinnen die erst kürzlich gegossenen Paneele an Patina.

Selon le descriptif des architectes « ce projet veut créer une atmosphère et donc un univers – pas une boutique – dans ce petit espace au centre de la ville dont le plan étroit, profond et rectangulaire doit recevoir des pièces de joaillerie ». Ils parlent également d'une atmosphère « mystérieuse, étrange, en creux, impondérable, orientale et baroque ». Inspiré d'une boîte à bijoux, le décor fait appel à des éléments théâtraux comme des rideaux sombres et un éclairage de scène. L'étage est traité dans des tonalités sombres et mates, tandis que le rez-de-chaussée est « argenté, lumineux, pesant et rigide ». Le sol, certains revêtements des murs et les portes sont en épaisses plaques d'aluminium de 100 x 60 cm qui laissent voir les imperfections de leur fabrication, imposant d'une certaine façon le poids du temps à des éléments qui viennent d'être fabriqués.

The small store is both austere and powerful, seeming to be carved out of solid aluminum, forming what the designers compare to a jewelry box.

Der kleine Laden ist ebenso streng wie eindrucksvoll und wirkt fast, als sei er aus massivem Aluminium geschnitten, um ein – so die Architekten – Schmuckkästchen zu bilden.

Ce petit magasin au style d'une austère puissance semble creusé dans l'aluminium massif pour former ce que ses concepteurs ont appelé une boîte à bijoux.

The arrangement of spaces and displays appears from some angles to be part of an archaic machine.

Die Anordnung der Raumzonen und Vitrinen wirkt aus manchen Blickwinkeln wie das Innere einer archaischen Maschine.

La disposition des vitrines évoque sous certains angles une machinerie archaïque.

To the right, the roughly finished aluminum panels that are used in the lower section of the boutique.

Rechts: Aluminiumpaneele mit rauer Oberfläche, die im unteren Bereich des Ladens zum Einsatz kommen.

À droite, les panneaux d'aluminium brut de fonderie utilisés au rez-de-chaussée de la boutique.

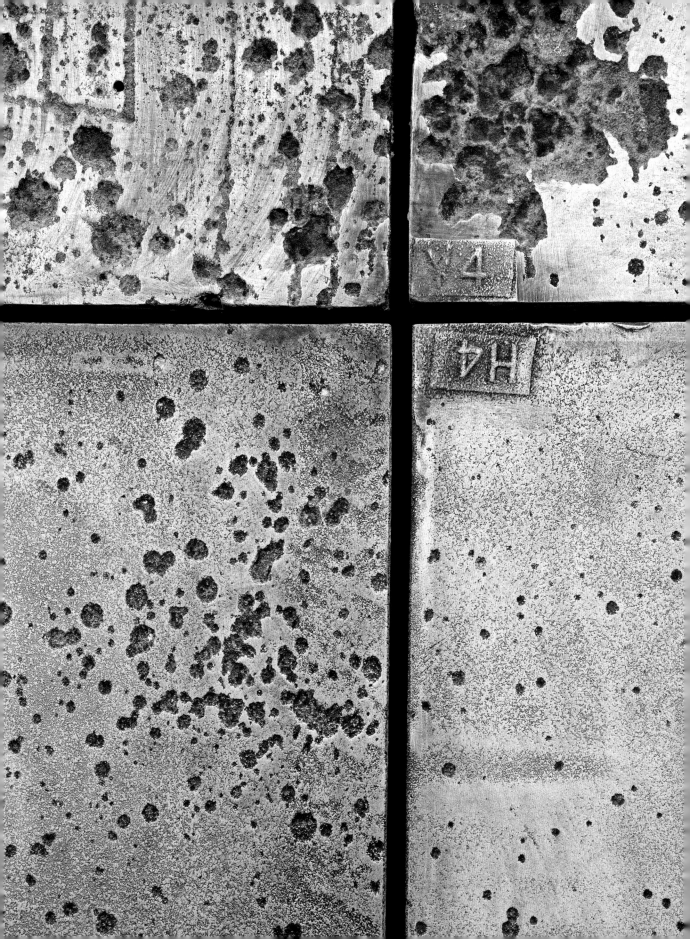

MARCEL WANDERS

Marcel Wanders studio
Westerstraat 187
1015 MA Amsterdam
The Netherlands

Tel: +31 20 422 13 39
Fax: +31 20 681 50 56
E-mail: joy@marcelwanders.com
Web: www.marcelwanders.com

MARCEL WANDERS was born in 1963 in Boxtel, the Netherlands. He graduated from the School of the Arts, Arnhem, in 1988. His reputation was launched by his iconic Knotted Chair, which he produced for Droog Design in 1996. He now works with the biggest European contemporary design manufacturers, such as B&B Italia, Bisazza, Poliform, Moroso, Flos, Boffi, Cappellini, Droog Design, and Moooi, of which he is also Art Director and co-owner. Additionally, he was the editor of the *International Design Yearbook 2005*. In the same year, together with chef Peter Lute, he created the LUTE SUITES hospitality concept. He also designed the interior of the restaurant Thor at the Hotel on Rivington in New York, including bar, lounge, and private club (USA, 2003–04), and the interior of Blits, a restaurant in Rotterdam (The Netherlands, 2005). Works by Marcel Wanders figure in the collections of the Museums of Modern Art in New York and San Francisco, the Victoria and Albert Museum in London, the Stedelijk Museum in Amsterdam, Museum Boijmans van Beuningen in Rotterdam, the Centraal Museum in Utrecht, and the Museum of Decorative Arts in Copenhagen. In 2009, he designed the luxury multi-brand store Villa Moda (Manama, Bahrain, published here).

MARCEL WANDERS wurde 1963 in Boxtel, Niederlande, geboren. Sein Studium schloss er 1988 an der Kunsthochschule Arnhem ab. Bekannt wurde er mit seinem zur Stilikone gewordenen „Knotted Chair", den er 1996 für Droog entwarf. Inzwischen arbeitet er für die größten europäischen Herstellern im Bereich Design: B&B Italia, Bisazza, Poliform, Moroso, Flos, Boffi, Cappellini, Droog Design und Moooi, wo er zugleich Artdirector und Mitinhaber ist. Darüber hinaus war Wanders Herausgeber des *International Design Yearbook 2005*. Im selben Jahr entwarf er mit dem Koch Peter Lute das Hotel- und Restaurantkonzept LUTE SUITES. Außerdem gestaltete er das Interieur des Restaurants Thor im Hotel on Rivington in New York, einschließlich Bar, Lounge und Privatclub (2003–04) sowie das Interieur von Blits, einem Restaurant in Rotterdam (Niederlande, 2005). Entwürfe von Marcel Wanders sind in den Sammlungen des Museum of Modern Art in New York und in San Francisco, dem Victoria and Albert Museum in London, dem Stedelijk Museum in Amsterdam, dem Museum Boijmans van Beuningen in Rotterdam, dem Centraal Museum in Utrecht und dem Kunstgewerbemuseum in Kopenhagen vertreten. 2009 gestaltete er den Luxusmarken-Store Villa Moda (Manama, Bahrain, hier vorgestellt).

MARCEL WANDERS, né en 1963 à Boxtel aux Pays-Bas, est diplômé de l'École des arts d'Arnhem (1988). Sa réputation doit initialement beaucoup à sa fameuse Knotted Chair (chaise de repos en corde), qu'il réalisa pour Droog Design en 1996. Il travaille maintenant pour les plus grandes marques européennes comme B&B Italia, Bisazza, Poliform, Moroso, Flos, Boffi, Cappellini, Droog Design et Moooi, dont il est directeur artistique et copropriétaire. Par ailleurs, il a été rédacteur en chef du *International Design Yearbook 2005*. La même année, avec le chef Peter Lute, il a créé le concept hôtelier des LUTE SUITES. Il a conçu l'aménagement du restaurant Thor pour l'Hotel on Rivington à New York, comprenant un bar, un lounge et un club privé (États-Unis, 2003–04) et du restaurant Blits à Rotterdam (2005). Des œuvres de Marcel Wanders figurent dans les collections des Musées d'art moderne de New York et de San Francisco, du Victoria and Albert Museum à Londres, du Stedelijk Museum à Amsterdam, du Museum Boijmans van Beuningen à Rotterdam, du Centraal Museum à Utrecht et du Musée des arts décoratifs de Copenhague. En 2009, il a conçu le magasin multi-marque de luxe Villa Moda (Manama, Bahreïn, publié ici).

VILLA MODA

Manama, Bahrain, 2009

Address: Moda Mall, WTC Manama, Bahrain,
+973 1332 0505, http://modabwtc.com
Area: 1050 m². Client: Sheikh Majed Al-Sabah. Cost: not disclosed

Located in the Moda Mall in Manama, the **VILLA MODA** is intended as a luxury multi-brand store. "I was looking for someone who'd never designed a real fashion store before," states Sheikh Majed Al-Sabah, Villa Moda's founder, of his decision to commission Wanders, whom he discovered through his furniture designs. The designer explains: "The brief was simple: to be inspired by the chaos of the souk within a luxury fashion context." The store is designed like a "small city" combining regional motifs with elements more typical of the other work of Marcel Wanders. Large pearl-like spheres adorn the façade of the store, while interior space privileges large-scale patterns. A large sculptural flower pattern made in plaster covers the wall behind the cash desk. Other specially designed features include walls with Bisazza mosaics and custom-made carpets created in Germany. Villa Moda Bahrain includes such brands as Anya Hindmarch, Martin Margiela, Ossie Clark, Rue du Mail, Nina Ricci, Christopher Kane, Comme des Garçons, and Junya Watanabe. As well as fashion, objects, such as vases designed by Karim Rashid, are also on offer.

VILLA MODA, ein Luxusmarken-Store, liegt in der Moda Mall in Manama. „Ich habe nach jemandem gesucht, der noch nie ein echtes Modegeschäft entworfen hat", sagt Scheich Majed Al-Sabah, Gründer von Villa Moda, über seine Entscheidung Marcel Wanders zu beauftragen, den er durch seine Möbelentwürfe kannte. Der Designer erklärt: „Der Auftrag war einfach: sich vom Gewirr eines Basars inspirieren zu lassen und dies auf den Kontext luxuriöser Mode zu übertragen." Die Boutique ist wie eine „kleine Stadt" gestaltet; regionale Motive werden mit Elementen kombiniert, die eher typisch für Wanders' übrige Projekte sind. Große perlenähnliche Kugeln schmücken die Fassade des Geschäfts, während im Interieur großmustrige Motive dominieren. Ein großformatiges Blumenrelief ziert die Wand hinter der Kasse. Weitere Sonderanfertigungen sind Wände mit Bisazza-Mosaiken und individuell gefertigte Teppiche aus Deutschland. Villa Moda Bahrain präsentiert Labels wie Anya Hindmarch, Martin Margiela, Ossie Clark, Rue du Mail, Nina Ricci, Christopher Kane, Comme des Garçons und Junya Watanabe. Neben der Mode sind auch Objekte wie Vasen von Karim Rashid im Angebot.

Situé dans le centre commercial Moda Mall à Manama, **VILLA MODA** est un magasin multi marque de luxe. « J'ai cherché quelqu'un qui n'avait jamais conçu de boutique de mode auparavant », explique le sheikh Majed Al-Sabah, propriétaire de la Villa Moda pour justifier le choix de Marcel Wanders qu'il a découvert à travers ses créations de mobilier. Pour le designer, « le brief était simple : s'inspirer du chaos du souk dans un contexte luxueux de mode ». Le magasin a été conçu comme une « petite ville » et combine des motifs régionaux à des éléments plus caractéristiques du style de Wanders. D'importantes sphères faisant penser à des perles ornent la façade tandis que l'intérieur privilégie les motifs grand format. Un grand motif floral en plâtre habille le mur derrière la caisse. Parmi d'autres éléments spécialement conçus figurent des murs ornés de compositions en mosaïque Bisazza et des tapis fabriqués en Allemagne. Villa Moda Bahreïn propose des marques comme Anya Hindmarch, Martin Margiela, Ossie Clark, Rue du Mail, Nina Ricci, Christopher Kane, Comme des Garçons et Junya Watanabe. En dehors de la mode, on y trouve aussi des objets dont des vases de Karim Rashid.

The rather extravagant decorative imagination of Marcel Wanders corresponds well to this geographic location and the specific fashion function of the space.

L'imagination décorative assez extravagante déployée par Marcel Wanders pour ce magasin de mode répond à sa localisation et à son luxe.

Die eher extravagante dekorative Formensprache von Marcel Wanders passt ideal zum Standort der Boutique und ihrer Nutzung als Verkaufsraum für Mode.

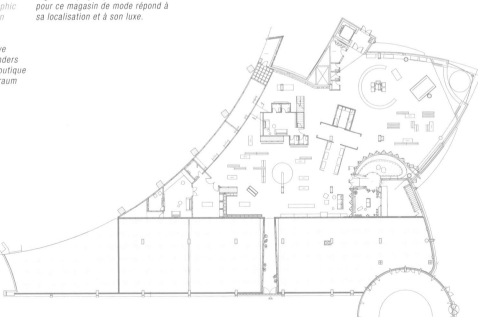

ISAY WEINFELD

Isay Weinfeld
Rua Andre Fernandes 175
Itaim-Bibi
04536–020 São Paulo, SP
Brazil

Tel: +55 11 3079 7581
Fax: +55 11 3079 5656
E-mail: info@isayweinfeld.com
Web: www.isayweinfeld.com

ISAY WEINFELD was born in 1952 in São Paulo, Brazil. He graduated from the School of Architecture at Mackenzie University in São Paulo in 1975. In an unusual mixture of careers, Weinfeld has also worked in cinema since 1974, making 14 short films that have received numerous international awards. In 1988, he wrote and directed his first full-length movie, *Fogo e Paixão*, considered to be one of the 10 best comedies produced that year worldwide. In 1989, the São Paulo Art Critics' Association awarded him the Prize for Best New Director. He has taught theory of architecture courses at the School of Architecture of Mackenzie University and was a Professor of Kinetic Expression at the School of Communications of the Fundação Armando Álvares Penteado. Weinfeld has completed dozens of private homes, commercial projects, banks, advertising agencies, discotheques, a bar, a restaurant, an art gallery, and the Hotel Fasano (São Paulo, 2001–03). He has worked with Marcio Kogan on numerous projects, including the 2001 exhibition "Arquitetura e Humor" at the Casa Brasileira Museum. Recent work includes Livraria da Vila (São Paulo, 2006–07, published here); Sumaré House (São Paulo, 2007); Kesley Caliguere Antique Shop (São Paulo, 2007); Las Piedras Fasano, Hotel Bar (Punta del Este, Uruguay, 2008); Havaianas (São Paulo, 2008–09, also published here); and the 360° Building (São Paulo, under construction), all in Brazil unless stated otherwise.

ISAY WEINFELD wurde 1952 in São Paulo, Brasilien, geboren. 1975 schloss er sein Studium an der Fakultät für Architektur der Mackenzie Universität in São Paulo ab. Weinfeld verbindet zwei Laufbahnen auf ungewöhnliche Weise: Seit 1974 ist er auch Filmemacher – seine 14 Kurzfilme wurden mit zahlreichen internationalen Preisen ausgezeichnet. 1988 schrieb er das Drehbuch für seinen ersten Spielfilm, *Fogo e Paixão*, bei dem er auch Regie führte und der als eine der zehn besten Komödien gilt, die in diesem Jahr produziert wurden. 1989 zeichnete der Kunstkritikerverband São Paulo ihn mit einem Preis als „Bester neuer Regisseur" aus. Weinfeld lehrte Architekturtheorie an der Fakultät für Architektur der Mackenzie Universität und war Professor für Kinetische Ausdrucksformen am Institut für Kommunikation der Fundação Armando Álvares Penteado. Weinfeld realisierte Dutzende von privaten Wohnbauten, gewerbliche Projekte, Banken, Werbeagenturen, Diskotheken, eine Bar, ein Restaurant, eine Galerie sowie das Hotel Fasano (São Paulo, 2001–03). Bei zahlreichen Projekten kooperierte er mit Marcio Kogan, etwa für die Ausstellung „Arquitetura e Humor" am Museum Casa Brasileira (2001). Zu seinen jüngsten Arbeiten zählen die Livraria da Vila (São Paulo, 2006–07, hier vorgestellt), das Haus Sumaré (São Paulo, 2007), der Antiquitätenladen Kesley Caliguere (São Paulo, 2007), Hotel & Bar Las Piedras Fasano (Punta del Este, Uruguay, 2008), der Laden für Havaianas (São Paulo, 2008–09, ebenfalls hier vorgestellt) und das Gebäude 360° (São Paulo, im Bau), alle in Brasilien, sofern nicht anders angegeben.

ISAY WEINFELD, né en 1952 à São Paulo (Brésil), est diplômé de l'École d'architecture de l'université Mackenzie à São Paulo (1975). Sa carrière riche et inhabituellement variée l'a mené à s'intéresser au cinéma depuis 1974. Il a réalisé 14 courts métrages qui ont reçu de nombreux prix internationaux. En 1988, il a écrit et dirigé son premier long métrage *Fogo e Paixão*, considéré comme l'une des 10 meilleures comédies produites dans le monde cette année-là. En 1989, l'Association des critiques d'art de São Paulo lui a remis son prix du Meilleur nouveau metteur en scène. Il a enseigné la théorie de l'architecture à l'École d'architecture de l'université Mackenzie et a été professeur d'expression cinétique à l'École de communication de la Fundação Armando Álvares Penteado. Weinfeld a réalisé des dizaines de résidences privées, de projets commerciaux, de banques, d'agences de publicité, de discothèques, un bar, un restaurant, une galerie d'art et l'Hotel Fasano (São Paulo, 2001–03). Il a collaboré avec Marcio Kogan sur de nombreux projets, dont l'exposition "Arquitetura e Humor" au Casa Brasileira Museum (2001). Parmi ses récentes réalisations, la plupart au Brésil : la Livraria da Vila (São Paulo, 2006–07, publiée ici) ; la maison Sumaré (São Paulo, 2007) ; le magasin d'antiquités Kesley Caliguere (São Paulo, 2007) ; l'hôtel et bar Las Piedras Fasano (Punta del Este, Uruguay, 2008) ; le magasin Havaianas (São Paulo, 2008–09, publié ici) ; et l'immeuble 360° (São Paulo, en construction), toutes au Brésil, sauf mention contraire.

LIVRARIA DA VILA

São Paulo, São Paulo, Brazil, 2006–07

*Address: Alameda Lorena 1731, 01424–002 São Paulo, SP, Brazil,
+55 11 3062 1063, www.livrariadavila.com.br
Area: 790 m². Client: Samuel Seibel. Cost: not disclosed*

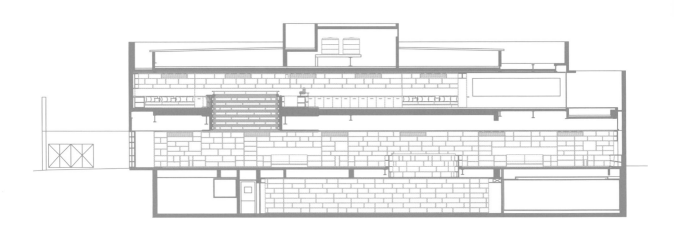

The **LIVRARIA DA VILA** was inserted into a former two-story house set on a very narrow lot. Structural alterations, including reinforcement of the foundations, were undertaken in order to allow the bookshop to benefit from an open space, unencumbered by columns. A children's space and small auditorium were incorporated into the basement level. Relatively low ceiling heights, dark tones on the floors and steps and light ones above, indirect lighting, and a total of 1280 linear meters of bookshelves characterize the completed space. Voids connecting one floor with the next and pivoting window-shelf-doors are amongst the elements that the architect cites as being important in his design. The façade announces the function of the building with its linear display of books and its rather blank upper area.

Die **LIVRARIA DA VILA** wurde in einem ehemals zweistöckigen Haus auf einem schmalen Grundstück eingerichtet. Konstruktive Veränderungen waren unter anderem die Verstärkung des Fundaments, wodurch offene, stützenfreie Räume in der Buchhandlung realisiert werden konnten. Im Untergeschoss wurde ein Bereich für Kinder und ein kleiner Veranstaltungsraum eingerichtet. Geprägt wird der Laden von den vergleichsweise niedrigen Decken, den dunklen Tönen des Bodens und der Treppen und den hellen Farben im oberen Bereich, sowie der indirekten Beleuchtung und den insgesamt 1280 laufenden Metern an Bücherregalen. Als Schlüsselelemente des Entwurfs nennt der Architekt die räumlichen Aussparungen, die die Etagen miteinander verbinden, sowie die Drehschaufenster bzw. -türen mit integrierten Bücherregalen. Die Fassade mit der geradlinigen Buchauslage und dem schmucklosen oberen Bereich kündigt die Nutzung des Gebäudes unmissverständlich an.

La **LIVRARIA DA VILA** a été insérée dans une ancienne maison à étage implantée sur une parcelle très étroite. Des modifications structurelles dont le renforcement des fondations ont été entreprises pour créer un espace ouvert, dégagé de toute colonne. Un espace pour les enfants et un petit auditorium ont été logés dans le sous-sol. L'ensemble se caractérise par des plafonds relativement bas, des tons sombres pour les sols et les escaliers, des escaliers et des plafonds de couleur claire, un éclairage indirect et 1280 mètres linéaires de rayonnages. L'architecte fait remarquer l'importance du vide entre les niveaux et les vitrines-rayonnages pivotantes de la façade. Celle-ci annonce la fonction de l'immeuble par des alignements de livres sous une importante partie supérieure entièrement aveugle.

A section drawing shows the space with its area below grade and ample lengths of display shelves, seen in the images to the right.

Ein Querschnitt zeigt den Laden mit den Räumen im Untergeschoss und großzügigen Regalflächen (rechts im Bild).

Ci-dessus, coupe montrant la librairie, sa partie en sous-sol et la longueur impressionnante des rayonnages (page de droite).

An oval cut-out connects two levels of the store, as seen in the image to the left and the plans below.

Ein ovaler Deckendurchbruch verbindet zwei Ebenen der Buchhandlung, wie links im Bild und auf den Grundrissen (unten) zu sehen.

Un ovale découpé dans le plancher relie deux niveaux de la librairie comme le montrent les photos de gauche et les plans ci-dessous.

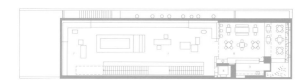

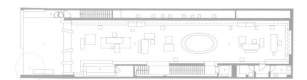

HAVAIANAS

São Paulo, São Paulo, Brazil, 2008–09

Address: Rua Oscar Freire 1116, 01426–000 São Paulo, SP, Brazil,
+55 11 3079 3415, http://br.havaianas.com
Area: 300 m². Client: Alpargatas. Cost: not disclosed

The wide, low opening of the store is highlighted by the large-scale red letters of the name Havaianas.

Die breite, niedrige Front des Stores wird von dem übergroßen roten Haivaianas-Logo dominiert.

L'ouverture du magasin qui occupe toute la largeur du bâtiment est animée par les énormes lettres rouges du logo Havaianas.

Created in 1962, **HAVAIANAS** sandals were inspired by Japanese rice-straw slippers. The idea of selling shoes for prices ranging from €2.30 to €10 on one of the most exclusive streets in São Paulo, the Rua Oscar Freire, was, according to the architect, "the excitement and the joy of the work." In Isay Weinfeld's words: "The shop has a very informal atmosphere and the outcome is nearly a square—a space fully opened onto the street, practically an extension of the sidewalk, without doors or window displays, with lush greenery and intense natural lighting, only covered by a metal grid alternating glass/wooden closures and openings for ventilation and irrigation." Seen from the street, the shop takes the form of an open, inverted "U" with the Havaianas logo visible at ground level. A small lounge on the ground level overlooks the main part of the store, which is located one level below. The shop space has a clear span, and double-height ceilings. The architect achieves the informal atmosphere that he sought for the client, creating an unexpected presence on the chic shopping street.

Die 1962 erfundenen **HAVAIANAS**-Zehensandalen wurden von japanischen Reisstrohsandalen inspiriert. Die Vorstellung, auf einer der exklusivsten Einkaufsstraßen von São Paulo, der Rua Oscar Freire, Schuhe im Preissegment von 2.30 bis 10 € zu verkaufen, war dem Architekten „Anreiz und Freude bei diesem Projekt". Isay Weinfeld führt aus: „Der Laden ist sehr informell, die Grundform ist annähernd quadratisch – ein Raum, der sich vollständig zur Straße hin öffnet, im Grunde eine Erweiterung des Gehwegs, ohne Türen oder Schaufenster, üppig begrünt und voller Tageslicht, nur bedeckt von einem Metallrost und abwechselnden Glas- bzw. Holzsegmenten, die sich öffnen und schließen lassen und Belüftung und Bewässerung ermöglichen." Von der Straße her wirkt das Geschäft wie ein offenes, auf dem Kopf stehendes „U", an dessen unterer Kante das Havaianas-Logo platziert wurde. Eine kleine Lounge im Erdgeschoss bietet Blick auf den Hauptverkaufsraum im Untergeschoss. Der Verkaufsraum ist stützenlos, die Decke hat doppelte Geschosshöhe. Mit diesem überraschenden Auftritt auf der eleganten Einkaufsstraße ist es dem Architekten gelungen, die informelle Atmosphäre zu schaffen, die er für seinen Auftraggeber im Sinn hatte.

Créées en 1962, les sandales **HAVAIANAS** se sont inspirées des chaussons en paille de riz japonais. L'idée de vendre des chaussures valant de 2,30 à 10 € rue Oscar Freire, l'une des artères les plus élégantes de São Paulo, était pour l'architecte « une joie et une source d'excitation ». Selon les termes d'Isay Weinfeld : « La boutique offre une atmosphère très informelle et devient presque une petite place, entièrement ouverte sur la rue. Elle devient pratiquement une extension du trottoir, sans portes ni vitrines, animée de plantes luxuriantes et par un éclairage naturel intense, sous une trame de métal qui alterne ouvertures et panneaux de bois ou de verre pour la ventilation et l'irrigation. » Vu de la rue, signalé par le logo Havaianas posé au sol, le magasin a la forme d'un U inversé. Un petit salon en rez-de-chaussée donne sur la partie principale aménagée en sous-sol. Le magasin lui-même paraît très ouvert et possède des plafonds double hauteur. L'architecte a réussi à créer l'atmosphère informelle recherchée par son client et a apporté une présence insolite dans une rue réservée jusqu'alors au shopping chic.

The inexpensive sandals sold in the store are arranged in regular patterns and ordered by color.

Die im Laden angebotenen preisgünstigen Zehensandalen sind nach Farben zu einem regelmäßigen Raster angeordnet.

Les sandales bon marché vendues dans le magasin sont présentées par couleur et en alignement régulier.

A somewhat tropical atmosphere is generated by the use of palm trees or accumulated bins of products as seen in the image above. A stairway leads down from street level into the main part of the store.

Tropische Atmosphäre entsteht durch Palmen und Körbe mit Waren (oben). Eine Treppe führt von der Straßenebene hinunter in den Hauptverkaufsraum.

Une atmosphère assez tropicale est créée par des palmiers et un stand où les produits sont vendus dans des corbeilles (photo ci-dessus). L'escalier conduit du niveau de la rue à la zone de vente principale.

Nike Flagship Store Harajuku ►

WONDERWALL/MASAMICHI KATAYAMA

Wonderwall Inc.
3–4–10 Sendagaya
Shibuya-ku
Tokyo 151–0051
Japan

Tel: +81 3 5725 9940
Fax: +81 3 5725 9941
E-mail: contact@wonder-wall.com
Web: www.wonder-wall.com

MASAMICHI KATAYAMA was born in Okayama, Japan, in 1966 and set up the firm H. Design Associates (1992–99), before creating **WONDERWALL** in 2000. As his firm description has it: "While respecting conventional and traditional aspects of architecture, he believes in breaking boundaries, and he is on a continual search for new ideas. Hence the name, Wonderwall: a continuous endless journey. Each project is conceived from scratch, rarely repeating details and ideas used in past projects. When designing retail spaces, not only does Katayama address all the elements of the interior, such as lighting, materials, and proportions, he also considers the actual experience of shopping." His work includes Pierre Hermé Paris Aoyama (Tokyo, 2005); BAPE STOREÂ® HONG KONG (Hong Kong, China, 2006); UNIQLO Soho New York (Soho, New York, USA, 2006); A.P.C. Daikanyama Homme (Daikanyama, Tokyo, 2007); UNIQLO 311 Oxford Street (Oxford Street, London, UK, 2007); I.T. Pacific Place (Hong Kong, China, 2007); Tokyo Curry Lab and Kafka (Minato-ku, Tokyo, 2007); BAPE STOREÂ® HARAJUKU (Harajuku, Tokyo, 2008); THE TOKYO TOWERS/Sea Sky Lounge and Sea Sky Guest (Kachidoki, Tokyo, 2008); Colette (Paris, France, 2008); GODIVA Chocoiste Harajuku (Harajuku, Tokyo, 2009, published here); Nike Flagship Store Harajuku (Harajuku, Tokyo, 2009, also published here); and UNIQLO Paris Opéra (Paris, France, 2009, also published here).

MASAMICHI KATAYAMA wurde 1966 in Okayama, Japan, geboren und gründete zunächst H. Design Associates (1992–99), bevor er 2000 sein Büro **WONDERWALL** eröffnete. In seiner Firmenbeschreibung heißt es: „Wenngleich er konventionelle und traditionelle Aspekte der Architektur respektiert, glaubt Katayama an das Überwinden bestehender Grenzen und ist beständig auf der Suche nach neuen Ideen. Darum auch der Name Wonderwall: eine kontinuierliche, nicht enden wollende Reise. Jedes Projekt wird von Grund auf neu entwickelt, Details und Ideen früherer Projekte wiederholen sich nur selten. Wenn Katayama Ladenräume entwirft, befasst er sich nicht nur mit sämtlichen innenarchitektonischen Elementen, wie Beleuchtung, Materialien und Proportionen, er berücksichtigt auch das eigentliche Einkaufserlebnis." Zu seinen Projekten zählen eine Filiale von Pierre Hermé Paris in Aoyama (Tokio, 2005), BAPE STOREÂ® HONG KONG (Hongkong, China, 2006), UNIQLO Soho New York (2006), A.P.C. Homme in Daikanyama (Tokio, 2007), UNIQLO 311 Oxford Street (London, 2007), I.T. Pacific Place (Hongkong, China, 2007), die Restaurants Curry Lab und Kafka (Minato-ku, Tokio, 2007), BAPE STOREÂ® HARAJUKU (Tokio, 2008), THE TOKYO TOWERS/Sea Sky Lounge und Sea Sky Gästesuiten (Kachidoki, Tokio, 2008), Colette (Paris, 2008), GODIVA Chocoiste Harajuku (Tokio, 2009, hier vorgestellt), Nike Flagshipstore Harajuku (Tokio, 2009, ebenfalls hier vorgestellt) und UNIQLO Paris Opéra (Paris, 2009, ebenfalls hier vorgestellt).

MASAMICHI KATAYAMA né à Okayama en 1966 a créé l'agence H. Design Associates (1992–99) avant de fonder **WONDERWALL** en 2000. Selon la présentation de l'agence : « Tout en respectant les aspects conventionnels et traditionnels de l'architecture, il croit en la rupture des limites et reste en quête permanente d'idées nouvelles. D'où le nom de Wonderwall : un voyage continu et sans fin. Chaque projet est conçu à partir de zéro, et il est rare que des détails et des idées utilisés dans des projets antérieurs se voient répétés. Dans sa conception des aménagements d'un espace commercial, non seulement Katayama mobilise tous les éléments intérieurs comme l'éclairage, les matériaux et les proportions, mais il prend en compte également l'expérience même de l'acte d'achat. » Parmi ses réalisations : les magasins Pierre Hermé Paris Aoyama (Tokyo, 2005) ; le BAPE STOREÂ® HONG KONG (Hong Kong, Chine, 2006) ; UNIQLO Soho New York (2006) ; A.P.C. Daikanyama Homme (Daikanyama, Tokyo, 2007) ; UNIQLO 311 Oxford Street (Londres, G.-B., 2007) ; I.T. Pacific Place (Hong Kong, Chine, 2007) ; Tokyo Curry Lab and Kafka (Minato-ku, Tokyo, 2007) ; BAPE STOREÂ® HARAJUKU (Tokio, 2008), THE TOKYO TOWERS/Sea Sky Lounge and Sea Sky Guest (Kachidoki, Tokyo, 2008) ; Colette (Paris, 2008) ; GODIVA Chocoiste Harajuku (Harajuku, Tokyo, 2009, publié ici) ; le magasin amiral de Nike Harajuku (Tokyo, 2009, également publié ici) et UNIQLO Paris Opéra (Paris, 2009, publié ici).

NIKE FLAGSHIP STORE HARAJUKU

Harajuku, Tokyo, Japan, 2009

*Address: 1–13–12 Jingumae, Shibuya-ku, Tokyo, Japan,
+81 3 6438 9203, http://nikeharajuku.jp
Area: 945 m². Client: Nike Japan. Cost: not disclosed*

The deftly patterned exterior of the store does not necessarily immediately bring to mind the products concerned, but it does glow from inside in this night view.

Die auffällig gezeichnete Fassade des Stores wirbt nicht unmittelbar für die angebotenen Produkte, leuchtet jedoch auf dieser nächtlichen Ansicht von innen.

La façade habilement animée qui scintille de l'intérieur la nuit ne fait pas immédiatement penser aux produits Nike.

The idea of the store is to allow clients to create custom shoes, as made clear in the graphics and the cloud of hanging shoes, awaiting customization (above).

Grundkonzept des Stores ist es, Kunden ihre eigenen Schuhe entwerfen zu lassen, wie auch die Grafiken und das Cluster von Schuhrohlingen (oben) signalisieren.

La proposition de personnaliser ses chaussures est annoncée par la signalétique et un nuage de chaussures suspendu au-dessus de l'escalier.

This large facility for **NIKE** opened on November 14, 2009. It contains a NIKEiD Studio that allows clients to customize their shoes with different colors or a personal ID. It also features a "Runner's Studio" where runners get advice on the best shoes for their feet and running style, and a Nike Bootroom for soccer players. Masamichi Katayama of Wonderwall envisioned the store as a playing field that would be accessible to both serious athletes and recreational sports enthusiasts. The main entrance was intentionally placed to the side of the long rectangular floor plan, "to encourage smoother foot traffic and a sense of exploration upon entering the space." The Runner's Studio encased in glass and stainless steel is located down a curved stairway. Stairs up to the second floor feature a chandelier made with white Nike sneakers. The designer states: "The inspiration for the second floor with NIKEiD and Nike Sportswear was a quintessential old American-style gymnasium with wood beams on the ceiling." The "iD Private" room, the NIKEiD by-appointment program, is enclosed in patterned and curved glass. The third floor is dedicated to soccer and the windows are decorated with soccer cleats sandwiched between glass panes. The spiral staircase that connects the second and third floors is hidden behind a circular display case.

Dieser große **NIKE STORE** wurde am 14. November 2009 eröffnet. Integriert ist auch ein NIKEiD Studio, wo Kunden ihre Schuhe in verschiedenen Farben oder mit einer persönlichen „ID" selbst gestalten können. Darüber hinaus gibt es ein „Runner's Studio", wo Läufer Beratung bei der Auswahl ihrer Schuhe unter Berücksichtigung ihres Laufstils bekommen können, sowie einen „Nike Bootroom" für Fußballschuhe. Masamichi Katayama von Wonderwall konzipierte den Store als Spielfeld, das für Leistungssportler ebenso interessant ist wie für Freizeitsportler. Der Haupteingang wurde bewusst an die Seite des rechteckigen Grundrisses versetzt, um „einen zügigeren Verkehrsfluss zu fördern und beim Eintreten das Gefühl einer Entdeckungsreise zu vermitteln". Das „Runner's Studio", ganz in Glas und Stahl, erreicht man unten über eine geschwungene Treppe. Über der Treppe zum ersten Stock schwebt eine Lichtinstallation aus weißen Nike-Schuhen. Der Designer erklärt: „Die Inspiration für den ersten Stock mit den Abteilungen NIKEiD und Nike Sportswear war eine klassische amerikanische Turnhalle mit Holzstreben an der Decke." Der „iD Private"-Bereich für private NIKEiD-Termine befindet sich in einer Box aus bedruckten, geschwungenen Glaswänden. Der zweite Stock steht ganz im Zeichen von Fussball. Hier sind die Fenster mit Stollenschuhen dekoriert, die zwischen Doppelscheiben eingespannt sind. Die Wendeltreppe zwischen der ersten und zweiten Etage verbirgt sich hinter einer zylindrischen Regalwand.

Cet important **MAGASIN NIKE** a ouvert ses portes le 14 novembre 2009. Il comprend un Studio NIKEiD qui permet aux clients de personnaliser leurs chaussures, un « Runners Studio » où les amateurs reçoivent des conseils pour choisir leurs chaussures en fonction de leur style de course, ainsi qu'une « Nike Bootroom » pour les footballeurs. Masamichi Katayama de Wonderwall a conçu le magasin comme un terrain de jeu accessible aussi bien aux athlètes pratiquants qu'aux simples amateurs de sports. L'entrée principale a été volontairement placée sur le côté du plan rectangulaire allongé « pour encourager la marche et donner un sentiment d'exploration en pénétrant dans cet espace ». Le « Runner's Studio » installé dans une cabine en verre et acier inoxydable se trouve à l'extrémité d'un escalier incurvé. L'escalier qui conduit à l'étage est surmonté d'un lustre composé de baskets Nike. « L'inspiration pour l'étage de NIKEiD et Nike Sportswear est tirée du gymnase classique de style américain à plafond à poutres de bois apparentes. Le salon « iD Private » et le programme NIKEiD sur rendez-vous est protégé par une cloison de verre incurvé et sérigraphié. Le second étage est consacré au football et les fenêtres sont décorées de chaussures de football prises en sandwich entre des panneaux de verre. L'escalier en spirale qui relie le premier et le second étage est dissimulé derrière une vitrine circulaire.

A variety of shoes is aligned in the display shelves seen above. To the right, a kind of vortex of runners' numbers hovers above a round computer desk.

Auf den Regalen (oben) ist eine ganze Bandbreite von Schuhmodellen zu sehen. Rechts schwebt eine Art wirbelnder Strudel aus Läufer-Startnummern über einem runden Computertresen.

Toute une gamme de modèles est sagement alignée sur des rayonnages (ci-dessus). À droite, une sorte de vortex composé de dossards de coureurs est suspendu au-dessus d'un point de consultation d'ordinateur.

GODIVA CHOCOISTE HARAJUKU

Harajuku, Tokyo, Japan, 2009

Address: 1F, 2F Cosmo Harajuku Building, 4–31–11 Jingumae, Shibuya-ku, Tokyo, Japan, +81 3 3403 3958, www.godiva.co.jp
Area: 129 m². Client: Godiva Japan, Inc. Cost: not disclosed

The theme of **GODIVA'S NEW CONCEPT FLAGSHIP STORE** was "treat thyself." The designers state: "Wonderwall's intention was to rejuvenate Godiva's traditional image and a very pop-like sensibility merged out of mixing the 'traditional' with the 'new.'" They imagined a "melting-chocolate" ceiling made of lacquered artificial wood molding. Paneling and Ajax marble tile flooring emphasize the traditional aspect of the design, as does a large crystal chandelier. Harajuku is a busy shopping and fashion area near Omotesando in Tokyo, and the designers have taken into account the constant flow of passersby in their design of the entrance and the upper-floor chocolate café, which is also visible from the street. The shop opened on January 23, 2009.

Motto des neuen **KONZEPT-FLAGSHIPSTORE VON GODIVA** lautete „Gönnen Sie sich etwas". Die Designer führen aus: „Absicht von Wonderwall war es, das traditionelle Image von Godiva zu verjüngen – durch eine Pop-Art-ähnliche Optik, die aus einer Mischung von ‚Traditionellem' und ‚Neuem' entstand. So entwarf das Team eine Decke aus „geschmolzener Schokolade", die mit farbig lackierten Wandpaneelen aus Kunstholzfurnier realisiert wurde. Zu den traditionelleren Aspekten des Designs zählen die Wandvertäfelung, der Boden aus Ajax-Marmor und ein großer Kristalllüster. Harajuku ist ein belebtes Einkaufs- und Modeviertel in Tokio, unweit von Omotesando. Entsprechend berücksichtigten die Planer die Laufkundschaft bei der Gestaltung des Eingangsbereichs und des Cafés im Obergeschoss, das von der Straße aus einsehbar ist. Das Geschäft wurde am 23. Januar 2009 eröffnet.

La devise du **NOUVEAU MAGASIN DES CHOCOLATS GODIVA** est « Faites-vous plaisir ! » Selon le designer : « L'intention de Wonderwall a été de rajeunir l'image traditionnelle de Godiva. Une approche d'esprit très pop est dessinée dans la fusion du " traditionnel " et du " nouveau. " » L'agence a imaginé un plafond en « chocolat fondant » traité en moulures de bois artificiel laqué. Des lambris et un sol en marbre Ajax expriment l'aspect traditionnel du projet ainsi qu'un important lustre de cristal. Harajuku est un quartier de shopping et de mode très actif à proximité de celui d'Omotesando à Tokyo et les designers ont pris en compte le flux soutenu des passants pour concevoir l'entrée et le café de l'étage, également visible de la rue. La boutique a ouvert le 23 janvier 2009.

The idea of melting chocolate permeates the Godiva store in Tokyo's fashionable Harajuku district. Chocolate brown covers ceilings and upper walls while lighter colors dominate below.

Das Motiv geschmolzener Schokolade zieht sich durch die gesamte Godiva-Filiale im angesagten Tokioter Stadtteil Harajuku. Decken und obere Wandabschnitte sind Schokoladenbraun gestrichen, während helle Farben in den unteren Bereichen dominieren.

L'image de chocolat fondu a envahi la boutique Godiva de Tokyo dans l'élégant quartier d'Harajuku. La couleur chocolat recouvre certains plafonds et les parties hautes des murs, le reste étant traité dans des tonalités plus claires.

The surfaces of the store, whether chocolate brown or gray-white are formed as a single, almost seamless unit.

Die Oberflächen im Laden, ob nun in Schokoladenbraun oder grau-weiß, verschmelzen geradezu zu einem nahtlosen Ganzen.

Les plans du magasin, qu'ils soient traités en brun chocolat ou gris-blanc, forment un décor unique.

The chocolate looks like it is covering the walls more and more in this stairway image (above).

Fast wirkt es, als wären die Wände im Treppenhaus mit flüssiger Schokolade überzogen (oben).

Le chocolat semble littéralement couler du plafond sur les murs de cet escalier.

UNIQLO PARIS OPÉRA

Paris, France, 2009

Address: 15–17 Rue Scribe, 75009 Paris, France,
+33 1 58 18 30 55, www.uniqlo.com.fr
Area: 2150 m². Client: Uniqlo. Cost: not disclosed

The Uniqlo store located very close to the old Opéra Garnier in Paris is centered around the high, open space seen left and above. Below, the exterior of the building, with the corner entrance of the store.

Die in unmittelbarere Nähe zur alten Opéra Garnier gelegene Uniqlo-Filiale ist um einen hohen offenen Raum organisiert (links und oben). Unten einen Außenansicht des Gebäudes mit dem Eckeingang zum Store.

Le magasin Uniqlo, juste derrière l'Opéra Garnier à Paris, s'organise autour d'un vaste espace ouvert (à gauche et ci-dessus). Ci-dessous, la façade de l'immeuble et l'entrée du magasin à l'angle de la rue.

UNIQLO is a Japanese casual-wear brand. Their Paris global flagship store opened on October 1, 2009, after their facilities in New York (Soho, 2006) and on Oxford Street in London (2007). The Paris store is located near the Opéra Garnier in a Second Empire-style building designed in 1866 as a theater. It is within this shell that Masamichi Katayama imagined an installation on the theme "Beauty Conscious with Ultra Rational Style." The open space has a large skylight and a staircase made of mirror-finish stainless steel and glass connecting the three levels of the store. The designer's intention was to make the mirrored stair "disappear into the environment." LED lights with graphics and large images of models wearing Uniqlo clothes are also part of the design. For the Uniqlo global flagship store projects, Katayama "considered the environment he was creating, including the fixtures, such as spinning mannequins and floor-to-ceiling shelving units, which have become key design elements for all the Uniqlo projects."

UNIQLO ist eine japanische Marke für Freizeitmode. Der Pariser Flagshipstore eröffnete am 1. Oktober 2009, nach weiteren internationalen Niederlassungen in New York (Soho, 2006) und auf der Oxford Street, London (2007). Der Pariser Store befindet sich unweit der Opéra Garnier in einem Altbau aus dem Zweiten Kaiserreich, das 1866 als Theater errichtet worden war. In dieser Gebäudehülle entwarf Masamichi Katayama eine Rauminstallation unter dem Motto „schönheitsbewusst und extrem rational". Der offene Raum hat ein großes Oberlicht und eine Treppe aus spiegelpoliertem Edelstahl und Glas, über die die drei Ebenen des Stores erschlossen werden. Der Designer beabsichtigte, die spiegelnde Treppe „mit ihrem Umfeld verschmelzen" zu lassen. LED-Leuchten mit Textbändern und großformatige Aufnahmen von Models in Uniqlo-Mode sind ebenfalls Teil des Konzepts. Bei allen Flagshipstores für Uniqlo überlegte Katayama, welches Umfeld er schaffen wollte, „einschließlich aller Einbauten, wie etwa die rotierenden Modepuppen oder die deckenhohen Einbauregale, die zum Schlüsselelement bei allen Uniqlo-Projekten geworden sind."

UNIQLO est une marque japonaise de vêtements qui a inauguré ce magasin à Paris le 1er octobre 2009, après avoir ouvert à New York (Soho, 2006) et à Londres (Oxford Street, 2007). Le point de vente parisien est situé sur le côté de l'opéra Garnier dans un immeuble de style haussmannien conçu à l'origine pour être un théâtre. C'est dans cette coquille que Masamichi Katayama a imaginé une installation sur le thème « Conscience de la Beauté, style ultrarationnel ». L'espace ouvert éclairé par une vaste verrière est occupé en son centre par un escalier en verre et acier inoxydable finition miroir qui relie les trois niveaux. L'intention du designer était de faire « disparaître l'escalier dans son environnement ». Le projet s'appuie également sur des éclairage à DEL, des compositions graphiques et de grandes photographies de mannequins portant des articles Uniqlo. Pour les magasins Uniqlo à l'étranger, Katayama « étudie le projet comme un environnement, y compris dans des équipement comme les mannequins tournants ou les rayonnages sol-plafond qui sont devenus des éléments clé de tous les projets des magasins Uniqlo ».

Uniqlo plays on the variety of colors offered for a limited range of products—reasonably priced but of excellent quality. The riot of colors seen in the image to the right is accentuated by crowds of shoppers at most times of the day.

Uniqlo bietet eine begrenzte Anzahl von Produkten in einer breiten Farbpalette an – zu günstigen Preisen und in außergewöhnlicher Qualität. Das Farbenmeer rechts im Bild wird zu fast allen Tageszeiten von zahlreichen Kunden bevölkert.

Uniqlo joue de la variété des couleurs proposées pour sa gamme de produits limitée, mais de prix raisonnable et de bonne qualité. L'explosion de couleurs (photo de droite) est accentuée par la présence d'une foule de consommateurs à n'importe quelle heure de la journée.

TOKUJIN YOSHIOKA

Tokujin Yoshioka Design
9–1 Daikanyama-cho
Shibuya-ku
Tokyo 150–0034
Japan

Tel: +81 3 5428 0830
Fax: +81 3 5428 0835
E-mail: tyd@tokujin.com
Web: www.tokujin.com

TOKUJIN YOSHIOKA was born in 1967 in Saga, Japan. He graduated from the Kuwasawa Design School and worked under the celebrated designer Shiro Kuramata (1987), and subsequently with Issey Miyake from 1988. He established his own studio, Tokujin Yoshioka Design, in 2000 in Tokyo. His work for Issey Miyake over a period of 20 years included extensive shop designs and installations. His work is represented at the Museum of Modern Art in New York, the Centre Pompidou in Paris, the Victoria and Albert Museum in London, the Cooper Hewitt National Design Museum in New York, and the Vitra Design Museum in Germany. He has collaborated with companies such as Hermès, BMW, and Toyota. Among other things, he designed Yamagiwa's lighting ToFU (2000); the paper chair Honey-pop (2000–01); Driade's Tokyo-pop (2002); Water Block made of special glass (2002); Media Skin cell phone (2005); Stardust chandelier for the Swarovski Crystal Palace (2005); the polyester Pane Chair (2003–06); Waterfall (Tokyo, Japan, 2005–06); Venus–Natural crystal chair (2008); and the Swarovski Flagship Store in Ginza (Tokyo, Japan, 2006–08). In 2009, Tokujin Yoshioka worked on an exhibition concerning the archives of Cartier, and completed Pleats Please Issey Miyake Aoyama (Tokyo, Japan, 2009, published here); Camper To&ether (London, UK, 2009, also published here); and Maison Hermès Window Installation (Tokyo, Japan, 2009, also published here).

TOKUJIN YOSHIOKA wurde 1967 in Saga, Japan, geboren. Sein Studium schloss er an der Kuwasawa Design School ab. Er arbeitete für den bekannten Designer Shiro Kuramata (1987) und ab 1988 für Issey Miyake. Sein eigenes Studio, Tokujin Yoshioka Design, gründete er 2000 in Tokio. Zu seinen im Laufe von rund 20 Jahren entstandenen Arbeiten für Issey Miyake zählen zahlreiche Ladengestaltungen und Installationen. Zu sehen ist sein Werk auch im Museum of Modern Art (MoMA) in New York, dem Centre Pompidou in Paris, dem Victoria and Albert Museum in London, dem Cooper Hewitt National Design Museum in New York sowie dem Vitra Design Museum in Deutschland. Tokujin kooperierte mit Firmen wie Hermès, BMW oder Toyota. Er gestaltete unter anderem die Leuchte „ToFU" für Yamagiwa (2000), die Stühle „Honey-pop" aus Papier (2000–01), „Tokyo-pop" für Driade (2002) und „Water Block" aus Spezialglas (2002), das „Media Skin" Mobiltelefon (2005), den Kronleuchter „Stardust" für den Swarovski Crystal Palace (2005), den „Pane Chair" aus Polyester (2003–06), Waterfall (Tokio, 2005–06), den Stuhl „Venus" aus Kristall (2008) sowie den Swarovski-Flagshipstore im Ginza-Viertel (Tokio, 2006–08). 2009 war Tokujin Yoshioka mit einer Ausstellung über die Archive von Cartier beschäftigt und realisierte die Boutique Pleats Please von Issey Miyake in Aoyama (Tokio, 2009, hier vorgestellt), Camper To&ether (London, 2009, ebenfalls hier vorgestellt) sowie eine Schaufenster-Installation für die Maison Hermès (Tokio, 2009, ebenfalls hier vorgestellt).

TOKUJIN YOSHIOKA, né en 1967 à Saga (Japon), est diplômé de l'École de design Kuwasawa et a travaillé auprès du célèbre designer Shiro Kuramata (1987), puis avec Issey Miyake à partir de 1988. Il a fondé son agence, Tokujin Yoshioka Design, en 2000 à Tokyo. Ses réalisations pour Issey Miyake pendant plus de 20 ans comprennent de multiples projets complets de magasins. Son œuvre est représentée au Musée d'art moderne de New York, au Centre Pompidou à Paris, au Victoria and Albert Museum à Londres, au Cooper Hewitt National Design Museum à New York et au Vitra Design Museum en Allemagne. Il a travaillé pour des entreprises comme Hermès, BMW et Toyota. Entre autres projets, il a conçu la lampe ToFU pour Yamagiwa (2000) ; le siège en papier Honey-pop (2000–01) ; le canapé Driade Tokyo-pop (2002) ; le siège Water Block en verre spécial (2002) ; le téléphone cellulaire Media Skin (2005) ; le lustre Stardust pour le Swarovski Crystal Palace (2005) ; le siège en polyester Pane Chair (2003–06) ; le bar Waterfall (Tokyo, 2005–06) ; le siège en cristal Venus–Natural (2008) et le magasin amiral de Swarovski à Ginza (Tokyo, 2006–08). En 2009, Tokujin Yoshioka a travaillé sur un projet d'exposition pour les archives de Cartier et a achevé Pleats Please Issey Miyake Aoyama (Tokyo, 2009, publié ici) ; la boutique Camper To&ether (Londres, 2009, également publiée ici) et une installation de vitrine pour la maison Hermès (Tokyo, 2009, également publiée ici).

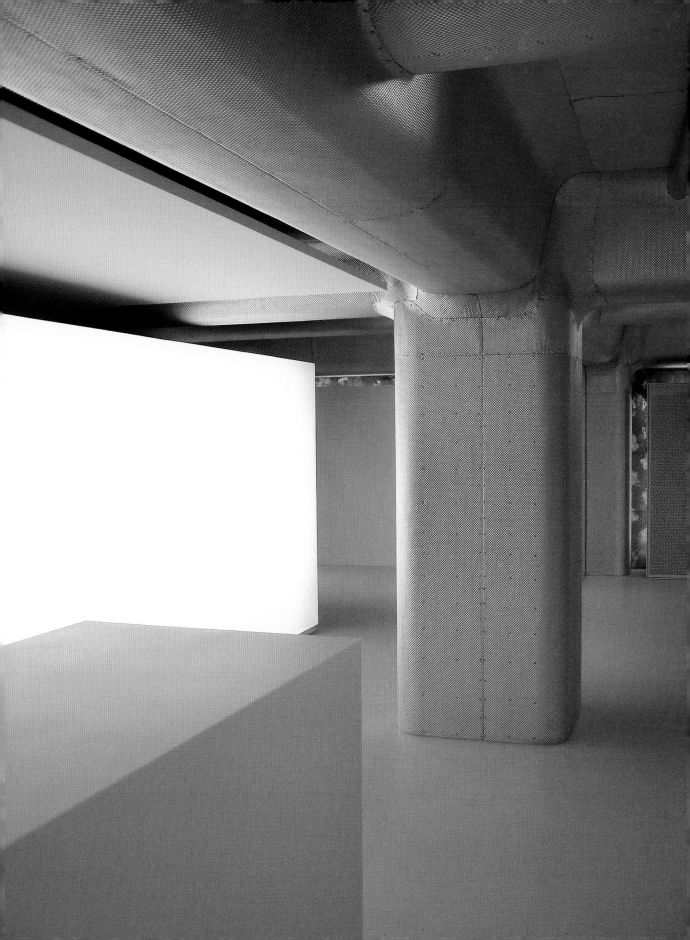

PLEATS PLEASE ISSEY MIYAKE AOYAMA

Tokyo, Japan, 2009

Address: 3–17–14 Minami Aoyama, Minato-ku, Tokyo, Japan, +81 3 5772 7750, www.isseymiyake.co.jp
Area: 220 m². Client: Issey Miyake. Cost: not disclosed

Located on the very fashionable Minami Aoyama Street, this project involved the renovation of an earlier design that Tokujin Yoshioka had realized. Yoshioka states: "This project was carried out based on the conservation of the interior which I had designed before using recycled aluminum material initially developed as automobile parts." The quilted pattern of the aluminum walls serves as an ideal and rather simple backdrop to the brightly colored pleated clothes of **ISSEY MIYAKE**. The designer has added one significant new element aside from simplifying the décor of the boutique—a large back-lit wall. "My proposal is to use a huge lighting wall," says Yoshioka. "The lighting wall serves to accentuate the nature of the material and interfuses modern technology and light."

Für das auf der angesagten Minami Aoyama Street gelegene Projekt sollte eine ältere Ladenraumgestaltung, die ebenfalls ein Entwurf von Tokujin Yoshioka war, renoviert werden. Yoshioka erklärt: „Ausgangspunkt des Projekts war der Wunsch, ein Interieur beizubehalten, das ich zu einem früheren Zeitpunkt entworfen hatte, und es mithilfe von recyceltem Aluminium, das aus Autoteilen stammte, umzugestalten." Das Patchworkmuster der aluminiumverblendeten Wände ist ein idealer und eher schlichter Hintergrund für die leuchtend bunte „Pleats Please"-Kollektion von **ISSEY MIYAKE**. Abgesehen von der Reduzierung des Interieurs fügte der Architekt ein entscheidendes neues Element hinzu – eine großflächige hinterleuchtete Wand. „Mein Vorschlag war eine riesige Lichtwand", erzählt Yoshioka. „Die Lichtwand akzentuiert die Materialien und lässt Technik und Licht miteinander verschmelzen."

Situé dans la très élégante rue Minami Aoyama, ce magasin a déjà une histoire. Comme l'explique Tokujin Yoshioka : « Ce projet a été réalisé à partir d'un aménagement intérieur que j'avais conçu avant d'utiliser un matériau en aluminium recyclé initialement mis au point pour des pièces d'automobile. » Le motif tissé des murs en aluminium sert de fond idéal et discret aux vêtements plissés et très colorés d'**ISSEY MIYAKE**. S'il a simplifié le décor de la boutique, le designer l'a enrichi d'un élément significatif, un grand mur rétro-éclairé. « Le mur d'éclairage sert à accentuer la nature du matériau et fusionne la technologie moderne et la lumière », précise Tokujin Yoshioka.

The designer has opted for extreme simplicity and, in the images on these pages, the number of objects on display is equally reduced. The floor plan confirms this rather austere vision.

Der Designer setzt auf extreme Schlichtheit. Auch die Anzahl präsentierter Waren auf den Abbildungen dieser Seite ist reduziert. Der Grundriss bestätigt den eher strengen Eindruck.

Le designer a opté pour une austérité extrême que confirme le plan du magasin. Le nombre d'articles présentés est lui-même très réduit.

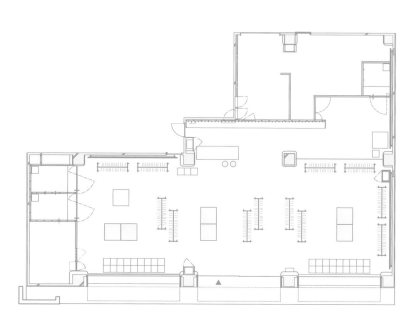

CAMPER TO&ETHER

London, UK, 2009

Address: 207–209 Regent Street, London W1B 4ND, UK, +44 20 74 34 11 44, www.camper.com/together
Area: 32 m². Client: Camper. Cost: not disclosed

In July 2008, Tokujin Yoshioka was asked, along with other designers, to create both a store and a pair of shoes for **CAMPER TO&ETHER**. The designer sought to create "a new value" by embracing Camper's brand identity and bringing the originality of his own design into play. Using a concept that originated in a 2007 New York project, the Japanese designer employed artificial suede and "a natural red color that seems to exist in nature" to cover walls and chairs with a design that resembles a three-dimensional carpet of flowers. This unusual décor certainly does not interfere with the simple and clean display of shoes that it accompanies, and it undoubtedly intrigues passersby, who can see much of the installation from the street. "While the store design incorporates the beautiful and wondrous principles of nature, I think you can see the reflection of my originality in the space," says Yoshioka. "Gathering each flower petal in different appearances has created an ever-changing expression in the scenery of the store. I hope that the scenery will evoke elation in the viewers," he concludes.

Im Juli 2008 erhielt Tokujin Yoshioka, neben mehreren anderen Designern, den Auftrag, ein Ladengeschäft und ein Paar Schuhe für **CAMPER TO&ETHER** zu gestalten. Es ging Yoshioka darum, „Mehrwert" zu schaffen, indem er Campers Markenidentität aufgriff und zugleich seine eigene Originalität in den Entwurf einfließen ließ. Anknüpfend an ein Konzept, das er 2007 für ein Projekt in New York entwickelt hatte, arbeitete der Designer mit einem synthetischen Wildleder und „einem natürlichen Rotton, der so in der Natur vorkommt". Mit diesem Material, das zu einer Art hochflorigem Blumenteppich verarbeitet wurde, überzog er Wand und Stühle. Dennoch erschlägt dieses ungewöhnliche Décor die äußerst schlichte Präsentation der Schuhe nicht und fasziniert ganz offensichtlich die Passanten, die einen Großteil der Installation von der Straße aus einsehen können. „Obwohl der Entwurf mit den wunderschönen und erstaunlichen Prinzipien der Natur spielt, spürt man in diesem Raum wohl auch meine Originalität", sagt Yoshioka. „Die Raffung jedes einzelnen Blütenblatts zu unterschiedlichen Formen verleiht der Kulisse in diesem Laden einen sich ständig wandelnden Ausdruck. Ich hoffe, dass dieses Bühnenbild im Betrachter ein Glücksgefühl auslöst."

En juillet 2008, Tokujin Yoshioka s'est vu demander, ainsi que d'autres designers, de créer une boutique et une chaussure pour **CAMPER TO&THER**. Le designer a cherché à créer une nouvelle « valeur » par la fusion de l'identité de la marque Camper et de son propre style. Reprenant une idée mise au point pour un projet new-yorkais en 2007, il a utilisé une suédine synthétique et « une couleur naturelle rouge qui semble exister dans la nature » pour recouvrir les murs et les sièges d'une sorte de tapis de fleurs. Ce décor surprenant n'interfère pas pour autant avec la présentation simple et nette des produits mais intrigue les passants qui peuvent voir cette installation de la rue. « La conception de ce magasin intègre les merveilleux et étonnants principes de la nature et je crois que vous pouvez y voir le reflet de ma personnalité », commente Yoshioka. « Chaque pétale de fleur présentant un aspect différent crée un changement permanent dans le spectacle offert par le magasin. J'espère que ce décor provoquera un sentiment de plaisir chez les spectateurs », conclut-il.

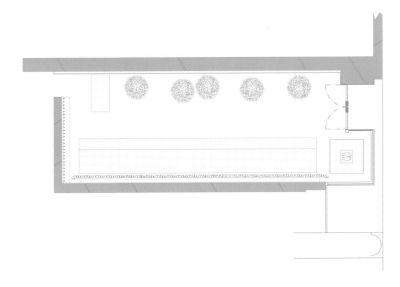

The artificial suede used by the designer is in ample evidence, as can be seen in the image on the right.

Das vom Architekten verwendete synthetische Wildleder ist überall zu sehen, wie die Ansicht rechts zeigt.

La suédine utilisée par le designer occupe entièrement l'espace visuel comme le montre l'image de droite.

The entrance to the store and a floor plan are seen above.

Oben: der Eingang zum Laden und ein Grundriss.

Ci-dessus : l'entrée du magasin et le plan au sol.

MAISON HERMÈS WINDOW INSTALLATION

Tokyo, Japan, 2009

Address: 5–4–1 Ginza, Chuo-ku, Tokyo 104–0061, Japan, +81 3 3289 6811, www.hermes.com
Area: not applicable. Client: Hermès Japan. Cost: not disclosed

Tokujin Yoshioka designed this **WINDOW DISPLAY FOR THE MAISON HERMÈS** in Ginza. It was visible between November 19, 2009, and January 19, 2010. The concept combines a video of a woman lightly blowing on a real Hermès scarf. The designer states: "On designing a window display for the Maison Hermès, I intended to express people's daily 'movements' with a bit of humor. There are moments when I perceive the hidden presence of a person in the movements born naturally in daily life. I created a design where one can perceive someone behind the scarves as if life had been breathed into them. The window is designed with an image of a woman projected on to the monitor. The scarf softly sways in the air in response to the woman's gentle blowing." The juxtaposition of the video image of a woman with the actual scarves, floating in the window, is what gives a "magical" presence to this installation, illustrating the variety of Yoshioka's types of inspiration.

Für das **MAISON HERMÈS** im Ginza-Viertel entwarf Tokujin Yoshioka eine **SCHAUFENSTERINSTALLATION**, die zwischen dem 19. November 2009 und dem 19. Januar 2010 zu sehen war. Sein Konzept basierte auf einem Video, das eine Frau zeigte, die sanft gegen einen – real im Fenster installierten – Hermès-Schal blies. Der Designer erklärt: „Beim Entwurf des Schaufensters für das Maison Hermès wollte ich alltägliche ‚Bewegungen' mit einer Prise Humor interpretieren. Es gibt Augenblicke, da entdecke ich die verborgene Präsenz eines Menschen hinter den ganz selbstverständlichen Bewegungen des alltäglichen Lebens. Und so entwickelte ich einen Entwurf, dem man abspüren kann, dass jemand hinter diesen Schals steht, geradezu als habe ihnen jemand Leben eingehaucht. Gestaltet wurde das Schaufenster mit dem Bild einer Frau, die auf dem Monitor zu sehen ist. Der Schal weht leicht im Luftzug ihres Atems." Der Kontrast des Videobilds einer Frau und des realen, im Fenster wehenden Schals verleiht der Installation eine Magie, die auch ein Beleg dafür ist, wie vielfältig Yoshiokas Inspirationen sind.

Tokujin Yoshioka a conçu cette **VITRINE POUR LA MAISON HERMÈS** à Ginza. Elle a été visible du 19 novembre 2009 au 19 janvier 2010. Son concept combine la vidéo d'une jeune femme soufflant en douceur sur un carré Hermès réel. « ... J'ai voulu exprimer les " mouvements " quotidiens des gens avec un peu d'humour. À certains moments, je perçois, la présence cachée d'une personne dans des mouvements provoqués par la vie quotidienne. J'ai créé ce projet dans lequel on peut percevoir quelqu'un derrière le carré, comme si la vie avait été insufflée en lui. La vitrine est constituée d'une image de femme sur un moniteur vidéo. Le carré réagit doucement au souffle de la jeune femme. » Cette juxtaposition de la vidéo et de la vie qui confère une présence « magique » à cette installation illustre la richesse de la créativité de Yoshioka.

The striking interaction of a video
in black and white and an actual
Hermès scarf makes this window
exceptional—like a work of art in
a shop window.

Was diese Fenster so ungewöhnlich
macht, ist das faszinierende Zusammenspiel von Schwarz-Weiß-Videos
und echten Hermès-Schals – das
Ganze wirkt wie ein Kunstwerk.

L'interaction surprenante d'un
écran vidéo en noir et blanc et d'un
carré Hermès bien réel fait de cette
installation une œuvre exceptionnelle,
presque une œuvre d'art qui serait
accrochée dans une vitrine.

INDEX OF ARCHITECTS, BUILDINGS, AND PLACES

CREDITS